Fraud Hotlines
Design, Performance, and Assessment

Fraud Hotlines
Design, Performance, and Assessment

Chelsea A. Binns

CRC Press
Taylor & Francis Group
Boca Raton London New York

CRC Press is an imprint of the
Taylor & Francis Group, an **informa** business

CRC Press
Taylor & Francis Group
6000 Broken Sound Parkway NW, Suite 300
Boca Raton, FL 33487-2742

© 2018 by Taylor & Francis Group, LLC
CRC Press is an imprint of Taylor & Francis Group, an Informa business

No claim to original U.S. Government works

Printed on acid-free paper

International Standard Book Number-13: 978-1-4987-2743-3 (Hardback)

Library of Congress Cataloging-in-Publication Data

Names: Binns, Chelsea, author.
Title: Fraud hotlines : design, performance, and assessment / Chelsea Binns.
Description: New York : CRC Press, [2017]
Identifiers: LCCN 2017016217| ISBN 9781498727433 (hb : alk. paper) | ISBN 9781315370361 (e)
Subjects: LCSH: Fraud. | Helplines.
Classification: LCC HV6691 .B56 2017 | DDC 658.4/73--dc23
LC record available at https://lccn.loc.gov/2017016217

Visit the Taylor & Francis Web site at
http://www.taylorandfrancis.com

and the CRC Press Web site at
http://www.crcpress.com

Printed and bound in the United States of America by Sheridan

Contents

Author

Chelsea Binns is an assistant professor in the Department of Security, Fire, and Emergency Management at the world-famous John Jay College of Criminal Justice in New York City. She is a licensed private investigator and certified fraud examiner and serves on the board of the New York Chapter of the Association of Certified Fraud Examiners. Her research interests are focused on corporate security matters, including background checks, corporate crime, cybercrime, investigations, and organizational fraud. She has been studying fraud hotlines since 2007. She has extensive corporate security, management, and investigative experience, having worked for prestigious organizations such as Citibank, Morgan Stanley, New York City's Department of Investigation (DOI), and the New York State Office of the Attorney General. At DOI, she received hotline calls from citizens concerning fraud, waste, and abuse matters. Ms. Binns has a doctorate and two master's degrees in criminal justice from the City University of New York (CUNY) Graduate Center/ John Jay College of Criminal Justice.

Chapter 1

Background, Use, and Value

Introduction

Fraud hotlines are confidential reporting mechanisms for employees and third parties to report fraud, waste, and abuse occurring in all organizations.

In basic terms, fraud hotlines aim to detect and prevent organizational fraud. Although not always successful in achieving said goals, the use of hotlines has continued to expand since the 1970s (in the United States and lately in other countries, like China).

The topic of fraud hotlines is more relevant now than ever. Recent American legislation created a fraud hotline operated by the U.S. Securities and Exchange Commission (SEC), which has paid sizable monetary rewards to callers. In 2015, the SEC awarded a $30 million award to a hotline caller—the largest reward ever granted in the history of their hotline (SEC, 2016, p. 1). As of fiscal year 2016, their whistleblower program has awarded more than $100 million to callers in exchange for their valuable fraud tips (SEC, 2016, p. 1).

This book will serve as a reference guide on fraud hotlines, for practitioners and students alike. It will educate readers with respect to the history, purpose, operation, use, and utility of fraud hotlines. It will also provide the readers with the knowledge to create, analyze, and performance assess a fraud hotline.

Chapter 1 discusses the background, use, and value of hotlines. Chapter 2 outlines the major historical developments that pertain to hotlines. Chapter 3 covers hotline design, including management and implementation, cost, name, anonymity, accessibility, advertisement, and the use of rewards in hotline reporting. Chapter 4 covers hotline performance and assessment. Chapter 5 reviews the theoretical perspectives for hotline operation. Chapter 6 contains several case studies of hotlines in the federal, state, and local governments (three studies); private sector (two studies); and nonprofit (one study) organizations. Chapter 7 discusses future trends and developments related to hotlines.

Definitions

A fraud hotline ("hotline") is a confidential reporting method. The general purpose of a fraud hotline is to receive tips about fraud, waste, and abuse. The audience of a hotline includes "employees, customers, contractors, service providers, suppliers and other third parties" whose awareness of the hotline is considered an "important component in ensuring a hotline's effectiveness" (FDIC, 2005).

Employees are the primary callers of fraud hotlines. In their 2016 Report to the Nations, the Association of Certified Fraud Examiners (ACFE) reported over half of their fraud hotline tips came from employees (ACFE, 2016, p. 26). This makes sense because employees are a key source of fraud tips. According to a 2011 National Business Ethics Survey, over half (52%) of Fortune 500 employees polled said they observed misconduct in their workplace (Ethics Resource Center, 2012).

As discussed in this book, there are many ways to refer to a fraud hotline, including whistleblower hotline, ethics line, and tip line. For the purposes of simplicity, this book uses the term *fraud hotline* or *hotline* throughout the text to refer to these hotlines in the collective.

Hotline tipsters have a lot of options today. In many cases, someone who wishes to contact a fraud hotline can submit a tip via web form, e-mail, telephone, regular mail, text, and fax. For simplicity, this book uses the terms *caller* and *tipster* to refer to someone who provides a hotline tip, in general. There is a reason *caller* is used in this context. Although there are several reporting methods, telephone tips are preferred by organizations. Hotline calls lead to the best tips due to the open channel of communication that happens during a telephone conversation.

Hotlines can be managed either internally or externally by a third-party vendor, or both. When this book refers to an internal hotline, it is referring to a hotline operated by the organization by its own employees. When this book talks about an external hotline, it is referring to a hotline service provided by a separate company that is contracted by the organization/employer to provide the hotline services. Those hotline workers are employees of the third party. When an organization uses a third party to manage its hotline, their employees report the findings back to the organization for handling. Either way, the organization is ultimately responsible for investigating the claims.

Background

Federal Government

Fraud hotlines have been used in the government sector since the late 1970s, following the Civil Service Reform Act of 1978 (CSRA). The CSRA was the first piece of legislation to increase the legal protections of federal employees who reported misconduct in the workplace (Shimabukuro, Whitaker, & Roberts, 2013). The widespread use of hotlines began in 1989, following President George Bush's signing of the Whistleblower Protection Act (WPA). The WPA is a federal law that protects government whistleblowers from retaliation by their employer for reporting wrongdoing in the workplace.

One of the first federal fraud hotlines was the U.S. General Accounting Office (GAO) whistleblowing hotline, established in 1979. It was a success, generating 11,000 calls per year. Most callers elected to remain anonymous, and a large number of the tips were accurate (Flesher, 1999). Today, nearly all federal agencies operate hotlines to receive reports pertaining to fraud, waste, and abuse on the part of their respective organizations (Flesher, 1999).

The federal government highly values its fraud hotlines and encourages tipsters to come forward. On the U.S. Office of Personnel Management (OPM) website, they tell the public that "Whistleblower disclosures save lives as well as billions of taxpayer dollars. They play a critical role in keeping our Government honest, efficient and accountable. Recognizing that whistleblowers root out fraud, waste and abuse, and protect public health and safety, Federal laws strongly encourage Federal employees, as well as employees of Federal contractors, to disclose wrongdoing" (OPM, 2017).

Federally operated hotlines may share their data with the public, often through their Office of Inspector General. For some city, state, and federal hotlines, certain hotline data are publicly available for inspection and review on their website.

Private Sector

Hotlines were required in publicly listed companies following the implementation of the Sarbanes–Oxley Act of 2002 (SOX). SOX was named after creators Senator Michael Oxley (R-Ohio) and Representative Paul Sarbanes (D-Maryland). SOX is a federal law created to strengthen the internal controls of publically listed companies following the revelation of internal fraud at several major companies in 2002 (e.g., Enron, Arthur Andersen, Adelphia Communications, Incline, and WorldCom). SOX provisions require that companies have an "anonymous reporting mechanism" for employees to report fraud, and hotlines became the generally accepted way of receiving those tips and satisfying the regulatory requirement.

The Dodd–Frank Wall Street Reform and Consumer Protection Act of 2010 also protects employee whistleblowers against retaliation by their employers for providing a tip, "giving employees who suffer discharge, demotion, suspension, threats, harassment or other forms of discrimination the right to bring a cause of action in federal court" (Government Accountability Project, 2016, p. 3). However, compensation is provided to employees under Dodd–Frank only if they are fired (Government Accountability Project, 2016).

Dodd–Frank reinforced the use of fraud hotlines in the private sector in 2010. Dodd–Frank was instituted in response to major corporate fraud, which contributed to the world financial crisis of 2008 to 2012. In September 2008, there was an unprecedented number of bank closures, and in December 2008, financier Bernard Madoff was arrested after stealing $65 billion from client accounts in a massive Ponzi scheme (McCool & Graybow, 2009). Dodd–Frank is a U.S. federal statute that was signed into law on July 21, 2010. Dodd–Frank is said to represent the most comprehensive change to financial regulation since the Great Depression (Greene, 2011).

Dodd–Frank required regulators to create 243 new rules, designed to enhance accountability and transparency within the financial system (Davis Polk, 2010). Consequently, Dodd–Frank expanded whistleblower provisions in SOX and the Securities and Exchange Act of 1934 (SEA) to provide a whistleblower, who reports violations of certain laws to federal authorities, a payout of between 10% and 30% of recoveries over $1 million (SEC). Under Dodd–Frank, employees may bypass internal hotlines and report known fraud directly to the SEC or the Department of Justice (DOJ). This provision is contrary to SOX, which encouraged employees to report fraud to their company.

The whistleblower rules under Dodd–Frank went into effect in August 2011. The SEC created the Office of the Whistleblower (OWB) within its Division of Enforcement to administer and manage the whistleblower program. The OWB's mission is to "administer a vigorous whistleblower program that will help the [SEC] identify and halt frauds early and quickly to minimize investor losses" (SEC, 2015). In their 2015 report, the SEC reported paying more than $54 million to 22 whistleblowers since 2011 (SEC, 2015, p. 1). The SEC further reports substantial increases in the number of tips received by the OWB, since its inception. In fiscal year 2015, the OWB received 4,000 tips. This represents a 30% increase in the number of tips since 2012 (SEC, 2015, p. 1).

The success of the OWB is laudable. Yet many organizations are unhappy with the OWB insofar as it encouraged employees to report fraud externally, rather than internally as once required by SOX. In their literature, the OWB states their program was "designed to complement rather than replace, existing corporate compliance programs," and it "encourages [tipsters] to work within their company's own compliance structure, if appropriate" (SEC, 2015).

However, there is no mandate for tipsters to report internally—and that was done purposefully. According to one legal expert, "Congress determined that it was important to essentially deputize employees. Congress didn't want to shackle the whistleblower with a potentially ineffective complaint procedure" (LexisNexis, 2013).

Also, there are no reporting requirements for private sector hotlines. In other words, private sector organizations do not have to share their hotline data with the public. Consequently, most hotline data for private sector entities are unavailable to the public, who in turn has no way of knowing whether the mandated hotlines are working to fight fraud. For the investors in these publicly listed companies, some may say this is problematic. Investors cannot determine whether there is internal fraud in the entity in which they seek to invest. This fact seems contrary to the intent and spirit of a fraud hotline. This is unlikely to change unless specifically mandated.

Nonprofit Sector

In the nonprofit sector, fraud hotlines are not required. Following SOX, non-profits were advised to use fraud hotlines as a matter of best practices. But there is no requirement to do so, and those that do employ them are not required to share any data. For that reason, it is unclear exactly which nonprofit entities use fraud hotlines. The only way to determine whether a given entity is employing a hotline is to look on their website and/or call them and ask. However, it is unlikely they will provide their caller data. The nonprofits that do have fraud hotlines basically use them as internal mechanisms and seldom report results to the public.

In this sector, fraud is made aware to the public via the Internal Revenue Service's (IRS) Form 990, which requires a nonprofit organization to publicly disclose fraud. This reporting has more effectively brought nonprofit fraud to the public's attention. Recent public outrage resulting from these disclosures has resulted in meaningful reform.

Chapter 7 of this book discusses the results of an independent examination into the use of fraud hotlines by this sector. The set of organizations examined included the nonprofit organizations listed on the Forbes 2014 list of the 50 largest charities. The author sought to determine whether said organizations operated a fraud hotline, and whether each organization reported fraud on its Form 990.

Overall, it was determined that 10 out of the 50 (20%) nonprofits employed a fraud hotline. Of those hotlines, this book uncovered only one instance of fraud caught via a hotline that was subsequently reported on the subject nonprofit's Form 990.

Based on the information gleaned in this examination, it is clear that today the only source of information for the public about fraud in this sector is Form 990. Hotlines could be a useful source of information for the public. But instead, it is clear that they are being utilized as a source of internal policing only and are not for public consumption.

Value

In studying fraud hotlines, a common question asked is: "are hotlines effective in preventing fraud?" There is no easy answer because it depends on the facts and circumstances of each hotline in question. What we do know today is that hotlines are not functioning exactly as intended to prevent and detect fraud. For that reason major corporate frauds are still occurring, despite the existence of fraud hotlines. In these instances, it is unclear whether whistleblowers are not coming forward out of personal choice, or whether they are being silenced by the company via termination following their complaints. As discussed throughout this book, we have evidence that both situations exist.

One such case is the Volkswagen (VW) Scandal of 2015. Here, witnesses who observed criminal behavior existed and did not come forward. It was recently reported that at least three witnesses are providing information to authorities, and one employee, Oliver Schmidt, the former head of U.S. Environmental Compliance, was arrested (Krisher & McHugh, 2017).

We also have evidence that at least one witness came forward to report criminal activity within VW but was fired after doing so. This former employee, Daniel Donovan, an Electronic Discovery Manager in VW's Office of General Counsel, said he witnessed obstruction of justice on the part of VW. According to Donovan, VW continued to destroy files despite the directive of the U.S. Department of Justice to preserve all files due to a pending U.S. Environmental Protection Agency lawsuit (Golson, 2016). Donovan observed the destruction, notified a supervisor, and was subsequently fired. Donovan is now suing the company for wrongful termination (Golson, 2016).

High-profile cases such as the Bernard Madoff Ponzi Scheme, perpetrated from the early 1990s until 2008, advanced during a time when SOX protections (2002), to include hotlines, were in effect. However, it was Madoff's case that prompted Dodd–Frank (2010) to add the SEC hotline. It was believed that if employees had ways to report fraud outside the company, massive internal crime, such as the Madoff Scheme, could have been thwarted.

Despite the existence of fraud hotlines, organizational fraud is increasing, and studies suggest employees are the most likely perpetrators. According to Kroll's 2013/2014 Global Fraud Report, 72% of those surveyed said their company suffered a fraud involving an employee (Kroll, 2013/2014). This fraud is costing companies a lot of money. Per the same report, the economic cost of crime to businesses increased from an average of 0.9% of revenue to 1.4% due to increases of "every fraud covered in the survey," including "internal financial fraud," which increased by 4% (Kroll 2013/2014).

The research literature supports the use of hotlines as an ideal method of receiving organizational fraud tips. Specifically, research has continually demonstrated that (1) employee tips are the primary way that fraud is discovered within an organization (Association of Certified Fraud Examiners (ACFE), 2002–2012); (2) employees are aware of fraud occurring within their organization (Ernst & Young, 2013b), and (3) employees with knowledge of fraud are willing to report it, and most would prefer to do so anonymously (Malone & Childs, 2005).

Fraud hotlines in some cases are proven to be effective. Overall, hotlines have been known to reduce fraud losses by as much as 50% (Buckhoff, 2003). According to the Association of Certified Fraud Examiners, up to two-thirds of hotline reports have justified additional investigation, and over half of those investigations have led to corrective actions (2002–2012).

Fraud hotlines are also expected to prevent fraud. In an American Institute of Certified Public Accountants (AICPA) 2011 Forensic and Valuation Services Trend Survey, over half of respondents said "internal whistleblower hotlines [will] lead to improvements in preventing fraud in the next two to five years" (Andrews & LeBlanc, 2013).

Hotline performance is difficult to analyze today using the data available. Currently, there are no reporting standards for hotline data. Organizations, including publicly listed companies, which are required to have fraud hotlines, do not have to provide their hotline metrics to anyone. They do not have to be reported in company reports, such as the 10-K, or otherwise shared inside or outside the organization. As a result, it is very challenging today to determine fraud hotline utility and performance.

Hotlines are also not required to monitor their performance. Organizations that have fraud hotlines are encouraged to benchmark their metrics. However, the available benchmarking data are incomplete and may not be a sufficient method for analysis. For instance, benchmarking data available for the financial industry are not provided in disaggregated fashion. Rather, the data are combined with another industry. As a result, this industry is unable to isolate their data for a true performance measure.

Benchmarking is also not a very robust method of performance analysis. The use of benchmarking data as a performance measure ignores all other factors, such as functionality, best practice adherence, employee sentiment, organizational climate, external or historical factors, and so on.

Recent media reports have said agency bureaucracy may be adversely affecting fraud hotlines, specifically, the U.S. Securities and Exchange Commission's Whistleblower Hotline, established by Congress in 2010. Thus, this book endeavored to determine whether organizational bureaucracy affects the fraud hotline process. The bureaucracy literature suggests that agency bureaucracy may adversely affect a hotline in several ways. It may prevent employees from reporting, it may cause employees to conceal fraud, and it may also hinder the hotline's ability to properly handle calls. However, the studies in this book demonstrated there is actually no consistent relationship between dysfunctional agency bureaucracy and hotline performance. In fact, at times, the hotlines in dysfunctional organizations, tended to perform better.

Yet, fraud hotlines in certain circumstances appear to be ineffective at revealing major frauds. This is because bureaucratic processes that exist within organizations can be contrary to the mission of a successful hotline reporting process and can explain the reason why employees may not report fraud via hotlines, why a hotline can be insufficiently communicated to employees, and why the complaints may not be triaged in a manner consistent with the information they intend to collect (major fraud reporting). It is possible, based on the literature, that fraud hotlines have succumbed to institutionalization of the surrounding organization (O'Hara, 2005, p. 149).

Despite the existence of some hotlines, employee crime has persisted and has become increasingly more severe. First, major internal frauds destroyed companies and caused legislators to require public companies to institute fraud hotlines. Then, yet more major internal frauds have occurred, which are believed to have contributed to the financial crisis (2008–2012), which damaged the world economy. In response, legislation further requiring companies to use fraud hotlines was established. However, internal crime has persisted (Kashton, 2011). Some critics believe bureaucracy might limit the efficacy of the hotline process (Kelly, 2012; Kocieniewski, 2012; Singer, 2013; Tobe, 2013).

Employee crime has been one of the biggest threats facing organizations for nearly 40 years. In 1977, the American Management Association (AMA) reported employee theft represented "the single biggest source of loss due to crimes against business." Today, industry surveys indicate this problem persists. In 2011, a PricewaterhouseCoopers (PWC) survey determined internal crime was the most serious crime problem facing organizations (Global Economic Crime Survey). In a 2014 survey, PWC found that one in three organizations is affected by economic crime (Kroll, 2013/2014; PWC, 2014). According to Kroll's recent Global Fraud Report, 72% of those surveyed said their company suffered a fraud involving an employee (2013/2014).

Recent employee thefts have been severe enough to threaten the world economy. According to the Federal Bureau of Investigation (FBI), the global financial crisis of 2008–2012, when hundreds of banks failed, financial assets worldwide declined by $50 trillion, and 51 million jobs were lost, was caused by employee crime (FBI, 2011).

It is difficult to determine the value of calls received to hotlines, from the data that are available today. Specifically, it is unclear how many hotline calls are resulting in criminal prosecutions. Available statistics show tips received by hotlines are not leading to criminal prosecutions. According to the 2013 Corporate Governance and Compliance Hotline Benchmarking Report from The Network, one of the leading third-party hotline providers, none of the tips they handled between 2005 and 2011 led to a single criminal prosecution. In 2012, it was reported that less than 1% lead to a criminal prosecution (2013, p. 20).

Studies, such as a 2002 study conducted by big four accounting firm Ernst & Young, showed that as many as one in five workers are aware of fraud occurring in their place of employment. Furthermore, research has continually demonstrated that employee tips are the primary way that fraud is discovered within an organization (ACFE Report to the Nations, 2002–2012).

Timely notification is critical. According to a 2011 KPMG Report, in the United States alone, the average internal fraud was perpetuated for over 4 years before the time it was discovered, costing victimized firms 1.2 million on average.

Overall, the reason fraud hotlines are critically important to a given organization is that they serve as the predominant mechanism for receiving whistleblower complaints, which are the primary way that fraud is discovered in a given organization. Legislative reform has reinforced the importance of whistleblower complaints by requiring companies to have anonymous reporting mechanisms (Sarbanes–Oxley, 2002) and allowing complainants to bypass internal processes and go straight to the SEC (Davis Polk, 2010).

The SEC program has had tremendous success using this model. They have received tips that were "exceedingly rare" outside of Dodd–Frank, to include tips that have "significantly contributed to an ongoing SEC investigation," many of which came from "outsiders to the company on which they reported" (Thomas, 2016).

Nevertheless, whether the complainant is reporting internally or externally, employee crime persists despite various iterations of the internal complaint process and despite employee knowledge of fraud. This leaves one to believe that, in general, fraud hotlines have room for improvement. Yet it leaves us wondering whether the mere existence of the hotline, in itself, is a fraud deterrent. We may never know, as the paucity of available data doesn't allow for the analysis of potential crimes averted.

Overall, hotlines have enjoyed a fruitful history. Although the primary purpose of hotlines has not changed, the usage has evolved over time to reflect changing societal goals. Fraud hotlines will always exist to prevent and detect fraud. But they can also serve many other purposes, which are compatible with fraud reporting.

Historically, hotlines were viewed almost solely as mechanisms of fraud reporting in the public sector. Today, they are used in all sectors and are viewed a bit more holistically. In fact, in some sectors, more often in the private sector, hotlines are seen as dynamic mechanisms of employee feedback. The new hotline nomenclature "Speak-Up Line" reflects this shift.

Organizations have an interest in opening the lines of communication with their employees. If employees use that opportunity to report known fraud, that is great for the employer. But if they use the opportunity to report something else—such as a policy recommendation—that is good, too. The hope is that employees generally feel comfortable talking to their employer and "speaking up." This way, when there is something critical to report, such as a known corporate embezzler, or cybercriminal, the employee will call again.

When discussing the value of hotlines, it is important to note that some people are skeptical regarding the value in hotlines. One expert from the Society of Corporate Compliance and Ethics, Jim Brennan, says he has heard many complaints about fraud hotlines. Specifically, people have told him the following about hotlines: they undermine a culture of trust; they are a forum for poor performers seeking a lifeline, they are abused by vindictive employees looking for revenge against particular employees by filing complaints, they invalidate leadership, they create confusion, and they lead to employee paranoia (Brennan, 2015).

False complaints to hotlines are a common concern among hotline skeptics. One such skeptic, Rob Jenkins, a university professor, said he was the subject of anonymous complaints submitted to his school's hotline. Citing his experience in academia, he said for some complainants in that industry, the hotline "is little more than a convenient way to harass people, they don't like, discredit political opponents, and settle old scores" (Jenkins, 2014). According to Jenkins, many ethics policies require all tips to be investigated, and the investigative expense is wasted when the allegation is false. To rectify this issue, he recommended "severe penalties" for those who make "repeated false complaints" (Jenkins, 2014).

Should hotline administrators be worried about false complaints? According to Brennan, false complaints to hotlines are "exceedingly rare" (2015). Ultimately, he finds that having a hotline saves companies money, a benefit that is likely to outweigh any concerns about false reporting. Brennan finds that some hotline callers, in the absence of a forum, such as a hotline, to air certain concerns, may have otherwise sued their employer. Therefore, companies save money in lawsuit avoidance. While he recognizes the amount saved is impossible to quantify, he said "experience shows that it is not insignificant" (Brennan, 2015).

Employers can also save money in fee reductions. Under the U.S. Sentencing Guidelines, "convicted companies which are found to have an effective compliance program may have their fines reduced up to 90%." Employers operating a fraud hotline are viewed as having such a program (Brennan, 2015).

Chapter 2

History

In studying fraud hotlines, it is important to understand critical events that led to the establishment of current fraud hotline legislation and its current state of affairs.

Pre-2002 (Before and After Sarbanes–Oxley)

Prior to the Sarbanes–Oxley Act of 2002 (SOX), there was lack of transparency in the financial documents filed by publically listed companies in America; a condition that many of those companies exploited to commit fraud. The most notable of these frauds was by Enron, which collapsed on November 28, 2001. Enron was the biggest American company to go bankrupt, to date ($62 billion in assets as of September 30, 2001) (Oppel & Ross Sorkin, 2001) Overall, in the pre-SOX era, an absence of internal controls was attributed to fraud in many well-known and respected entities, including "Big Four" accounting firm Arthur Andersen (AA). AA was Enron's auditor, who lost their accounting license and no longer exists today.

In summary, fraudulent corporate practices in the pre-SOX period included (1) improper internal loans to company executives, (2) company misrepresentation of their value to investors, and (3) auditing practices failing to detect fraud. This resulted in investor loss of capital; employee loss of jobs, possessions, and retirement funds; company reputational loss; and an overall weakening of the American stock market.

A sample of well-publicized frauds that occurred in the pre-SOX period includes Adelphia Communications, Arthur Andersen, Enron, HealthSouth, ImClone, Tyco, WorldCom Inc., and Xerox, as further described below.

Adelphia Communications

Adelphia Communications was the nation's sixth largest cable television company. The Securities and Exchange Commission (SEC) called Adelphia's fraud "one of the most extensive financial frauds ever to take place at a public company." Adelphia's top executives funneled money out of the company for years and used it to support a lavish lifestyle that included extravagant purchases such as private airplanes and a golf course (Bloomberg News, 2004). Overall, the executives hid $2.3 billion in liabilities from their investors (Barrett, 2002). It was later determined that the company's founder, John Rigas, had given himself $3.1 billion in "off balance sheet loans" (Frank & Solomon, 2002). Rigas was indicted in September 2002 and charged with bank, wire, and securities fraud. Rigas' two sons and two additional executives were also charged. Adelphia filed for bankruptcy protection in June, and Rigas stepped down as chief executive officer (CEO) of the company in May 2002 (BBC News, 2002; Makar et al., 2004). Deloitte was their auditor.

Arthur Andersen

Arthur Andersen was a respected member of the Big Four until their criminal involvement in the Enron scandal. Their relationship with Enron began in the early 1990s, when Enron outsourced its internal accounting function to Arthur Andersen. Ultimately, the firm was convicted of obstructing justice (in connection with the Enron investigation) and their public accounting license was revoked in 2002 (Makar et al., 2004).

Enron

Enron was the first of several major corporate fraud scandals to become public in 2002. It was also one of the more egregious. Enron grossly misled the public by not properly reporting its true financial status. Specifically, Enron overstated their profits by $600 million (Oppel & Ross Sorkin, 2001). In fact, Enron ultimately went bankrupt having never reported having a bad quarter with respect to earnings (Thomas, 2002). The repercussion of Enron's fraud was massive. Overall, investors lost over $60 billion in fewer than 2 years (Associated Press, 2006). Employees lost their jobs and their retirement plans were now worthless, as they were largely invested in Enron stock, which dropped to 26 cents per share (Thomas, 2002). Former Enron workers were thus unable to sell the shares of Enron stock that comprised their 401K/retirement plans. Workers also reported losing their cars and houses and had trouble getting new jobs after being associated with Enron. Employees would later say that Enron management, who didn't lose money in this scandal, had encouraged them to invest with the company, calling it a "sound" investment (Senate Commerce Science and Transportation Committee, 2002). In fact, workers were forbidden from selling their Enron stocks when the price fell

(Oppel & Ross Sorkin, 2001). Employee action groups filed numerous lawsuits against Enron executives, trying to win back some of their lost savings. Workers were victorious in gaining a 10K increase in the severance cap (previously $4,650) but will likely never fully recover their losses due to Enron's fraud (Biegelman, 2004; Makar et al., 2004; Schepp, 2002; Young, 2002).

HealthSouth

In 2003, top executives at HealthSouth were found to have engaged in an accounting scheme that overstated their earnings by an estimated $4 billion. Overall, 15 HealthSouth accounting and finance executives pleaded guilty by the end of 2003. Former HealthSouth CEO Richard Scrushy was indicted in 2004 on 85 criminal charges. After the fraud went public, shares of HealthSouth fell from $4 per share to just 10 cents. Big Four accounting firm Ernst & Young (E&Y) was the auditor for HealthSouth. E&Y later claimed to have no knowledge of the fraud (Freudenheim, 2004; Makar et al., 2004). Scrushy was ultimately acquitted of his criminal charges in relation to HealthSouth, but he later resolved civil charges with them, which included an officer and director ban (Stempel & Gates, 2013). Scrushy was found civilly liable to HealthSouth for $2.88 billion (Stempel & Gates, 2013).

ImClone

In 2002, ImClone Systems, a biotechnology firm, was the subject of a congressional investigation as a result of their failure to tell investors that one of their drugs failed to receive U.S. Food and Drug Administration (FDA) approval. Ex-ImClone CEO Dr. Samuel Waksal ultimately admitted to fraud and pleaded guilty to two counts of securities fraud, one count of bank fraud, one count of perjury, one count of obstruction of justice, and one count of conspiracy. On June 10, 2003, Waksal was sentenced to 87 months in prison, fined $3 million, and ordered to pay restitution (SEC, 2003).

Waksal committed insider trading by telling family members and close friends to sell ImClone shares the day before federal regulators refused to review ImClone's new cancer drug (SEC, 2003). Martha Stewart was one of the people who was given the tip to sell her ImClone stock. Stewart was known to be a personal friend of the Waksal family (BBC News, 2002; Makar et al., 2004).

Tyco

Former Tyco CEO Dennis Kozlowski and Chief Financial Officer (CFO) Marc Swartz were indicted in 2002 for stealing over $600 million from Tyco. To commit their fraud, the executives fraudulently manipulated employee loan programs. They never informed investors of their personal loans and never repaid the money. Kozlowski's and Swartz's fraud outraged the public when the media reported they used the stolen money to purchase opulent luxury items to outfit their multi-million-dollar apartments on Park Avenue in Manhattan (also purchased with stolen funds). Such items included a $15,000 umbrella stand; a $17,000 toiletry case; a $6,300 sewing basket; $5,900 for two sets of sheets; $2,900 in coat hangers; a $2,200 wastebasket; a $1,650 appointment notebook; and a $445 pincushion (Sorkin, 2002). Further purchases by the executives included vacation homes in Nantucket, yachts, Renoir and Monet paintings, and jewelry from Tiffany's (CNN, 2002). They also gave themselves bonuses totaling nearly $100 million that were never disclosed to the board of directors (Makar et al., 2004). PricewaterhouseCoopers audited Tyco.

WorldCom Inc.

WorldCom Inc. perpetrated one of the largest accounting frauds in history. WorldCom's bankruptcy was also the largest in U.S. history (by the size of its assets). However, the crime was relatively basic, involving a reduction in reported line costs and an exaggeration of reported revenues (Beresford et al., 2003). In June 2002, the company disclosed that their accounting improprieties resulted in a loss up to $7 billion and that the former CFO had been charged with fraud. Essentially, their fraud eradicated a stock that was valued at over $180 billion, leaving investors with a stock that was virtually worthless (The Associated Press, 2003). WorldCom simultaneously filed for Chapter 11 bankruptcy with $41 billion in debt and informed 12,800 of its roughly 5,000 workers that they'd be losing their jobs (Young, 2002). And those employees were unable to collect their severance pay due to a recent shift in company policy. Accordingly, WorldCom was not obligated to make a lump sum payment and severance payments to employees were capped at $4,650 under the bankruptcy code (Young, 2002). Overall, employees were left without their jobs, appropriate severance, health insurance, and 401K plans. (WorldCom 401K plans were almost entirely composed of company stock and were now worthless.) In contrast, immediately following the scandal, WorldCom executives were given full pension in excess of $1 million and had received recent bonuses and company loans valued at $10 million and up (Feder, 2002).

Xerox

In 2003, six former Xerox executives, including the CEO, CFO, and company controller, agreed to pay over $22 million in penalties for misleading investors about their earnings in order to boost stock prices (Bandler & Hechinger, 2003). They concealed their fraud by recognizing revenues in the wrong time periods, a practice that is in violation of Generally Accepted Accounting Principles (GAAP). Xerox's fraud reduced shareholders' equity by $137 million and net worth by $76 million (Deutsch, 2001; Makar et al., 2004). KPMG was Xerox's auditor.

In addition to the frauds at Adelphia Communications, Arthur Andersen, Enron, HealthSouth, ImClone, Tyco, Worldcom Inc., and Xerox, similar frauds were reported at AOL Time Warner, Aura Systems, CMSEnergy, Computer Systems International, Global Crossing, Quest Communications, and Safety-Kleen (Hagenbaugh, 2003). The common theme of the above frauds was the misrepresentation by the company of their value, to the public. Despite GAAP accounting requirements, suspected internal controls, and auditing by Big Four accounting firms, said companies were engaging in fraudulent practices. SOX was created to establish internal controls of these and other public companies to prevent similar entities from misleading their employees and investors.

2002

SOX first required hotlines in publicly listed companies. Passed in 2002, SOX was lauded as "the most sweeping law affecting corporations since the 1930s" (USA Today, 2003). SOX was named after Senator Michael Oxley (Republican-Ohio) and Representative Paul Sarbanes (Democrat-Maryland) who each drafted a separate bill in mid-2002 that the House and Senate combined and named after the co-creators. In 2002, the 107th Congress of the U.S. Congress passed SOX. SOX was passed by a vote of 423–3 in the House and 99–0 in the Senate. SOX was signed into law by President George Bush a short time later on July 30, 2002. SOX is enforced by the SEC.

While SOX has several mandates, the primary purpose of SOX is to verify that companies have effective internal controls publicly listed. President Bush said SOX was designed to "deter and punish corporate and accounting fraud and corruption, ensure justice for wrongdoers, and protect the interests of workers and shareholders" (2002). Accordingly, SOX created new penalties for such wrongdoing and a new oversight body, the Public Company Accounting Oversight Board (PCAOB), an independent board created to monitor accounting firms that audit public companies. The PCAOB also has the authority to investigate and discipline accountants (Yormark, 2004).

SOX also enhanced corporate responsibility by requiring CEOs and CFOs to certify the accuracy of their financial reports. SOX enforces corporate accountability by barring corporate executives from using the "lack of knowledge" defense with respect to wrongdoing occurring in their company (Yormark, 2004). SOX also enhanced criminal penalties to enforce accountability. To that end, criminal penalties, including fines and imprisonment, were created and/or enhanced for crimes involving the destruction, falsification, and alteration of records by the company and/or their auditor. Penalties involving these crimes under SOX could result in a prison sentence of up to 20 years and a $5 million fine (Yormark, 2004).

SOX further instituted several reforms relating to auditor independence. SOX required auditors to rotate positions so that no one person is ever in charge of an entire client engagement. SOX also prevented auditors from performing certain functions for a client while also performing their auditing, bookkeeping, financial information system management, appraisal or actuarial services, or other management services (Yormark, 2004).

SOX rules also extended fraud-reporting obligations to lawyers. Under section 307, outside counsel are required to report suspected securities violations to the chief legal counsel of the company in question, and if necessary, escalate their concerns to the company's audit committee or board of directors (Yormark, 2004).

SOX further required companies to create and promulgate a code of ethics for senior financial officers, restrict executive compensation, establish independent audit committees, appoint an in-house "financial expert," and institute a confidential reporting mechanism for fraud (i.e., a fraud hotline) (Hagenbaugh, 2003).

To ensure accurate books and records, SOX required publicly listed companies to establish a financial accounting framework that generates verifiable financial reports with traceable, ineditable, source data. SOX instituted corporate penalties for noncompliance or inaccurate/incomplete certifications, including fines of up to $5 million and a prison term of 20 years (Briggs & Veselka, 2015).

SOX was revolutionary because it created brand-new antifraud legislative safeguards. However, as explained below, the creation of SOX did not totally eliminate corporate fraud in America.

2008 (Global Financial Crisis)

Despite SOX and the existence of fraud hotlines, in 2008, massive corporate frauds were uncovered, which were so egregious they caused a global financial crisis ("crisis"), which lasted from 2008 to 2012. The crisis caused an unprecedented number of bank failures. Banks that didn't close during the crisis suffered other financial loss. During this time, many banks nationalized, recapitalized, merged, were taken over, or received state guarantees (Harkay, 2009).

Overall, this crisis caused the value of financial assets worldwide to decline by as much as $50 trillion and brought the loss of 51 million jobs across the globe (BBC News, 2009; Loser, 2009). From 2007 to 2010, bank closures increased by 4,633%. In September 2008, the collapse of Lehman Brothers, the fourth largest investment bank in the United States, marked the beginning of a massive economic downturn, in what experts called the worst recession in 80 years (*The Economist*, 2013).

During the crisis, 366 U.S. banks failed. The Federal Deposit Insurance Corporation (FDIC), which often serves as a receiver for failed banks, reported most banks closed in Georgia (63) followed by Florida (53) and Illinois (45). By contrast, prior to the crisis, during a 6-year period (2000–2006), 24 banks failed. In 2010 alone, at the peak of the crisis, 142 banks failed. In 2007, three banks failed. As of

January 31, 2011, the FDIC paid out $8.89 billion to banks under loss-share agreements (Sidel 2011). To cover these losses, additional payouts of up to $21.5 billion were expected by 2014 (Sidel, 2011).

Perhaps the most significant of the bank failures was the closure of the traditional investment banks, which were created following the Glass–Steagall Act in 1933. In less than 10 days, between September 14 and September 21, 2008, Lehman Brothers failed, Merrill Lynch was acquired, and Goldman Sachs and Morgan Stanley became bank holding companies (Augar, 2008).

Although banks are FDIC insured, investors can still lose money when banks close. Prior to Dodd–Frank, the FDIC insurable limit for depositors was $100,000. While Dodd–Frank permanently increased the FDIC limit to $250,000, anything above that amount is subject to loss (Chan, 2010).

The FDIC insures bank deposits under the Banking Act of 1933 (Glass–Steagall Act). The FDIC is funded through insurance assessments collected from its member depository institutions and held in a Deposit Insurance Fund (DIF), which is used to pay depositors if member institutions fail (Getter, 2014).

However, FDIC insurance, and other depository insurances, such as the National Credit Union Share Insurance Fund (administered by the National Credit Union Administration [NCUA]), do not cover funds held in investments such as stocks, bonds, mutual funds, life insurance policies, annuities, or municipal securities, even when purchased from an FDIC-or NCUA-insured bank or savings institution (Chan, 2010).

When banks fail, bank employees may suffer sudden and permanent financial loss due to the diminished value of institutional stocks. As a case in point, following the collapse of Bear Stearns in March 2008, an average Bear Stearns employee retirement fund worth $200,000 was now worth $2,000 (Goldman, 2008). It was reported that employees were so devastated by this news that grief counselors were called in to administer immediate therapy (Goldman, 2008). Most of the affected employees were among the support staff (Goldman, 2008).

Similarly, when Lehman Brothers collapsed, it was estimated that 24,000 employees lost an estimated $10 billion in paper wealth (Smith et al., 2008). Half of Lehman's employees also lost their jobs, with most of the losses concentrated among nonmanagement positions. Although key executives were blamed for much of the bank's failures, most of them found similar positions at competitors (Cook, 2009).

Overall, the bank closure policy is geared toward expediency and is often unfriendly to bank employees. The FDIC does not forewarn employees of impending closures. According to FDIC chairwoman Shelia Bair (2006–2011), who was a critic of the policies and practices leading to the crisis (Kolhatkar, 2014), the FDIC closes down most banks on Fridays so they have the 2 extra days over the weekend to complete the transition and make sure customers have immediate access to their money on Monday (Egan, 2009). However, skeptics think this is actually done to prevent customers from panicking and withdrawing funds (Rastogi, 2008).

One example of a bank failure that documents the devastating closure process is that of TeamBank in Paola, Kansas, which was closed Friday, March 20, 2009, by the Office of the Comptroller of the Currency. According to reports, at the end of the workday, 110 TeamBank employees were ushered into the lobby by government agents and told their employer was closing down. According to one employee who had been with the bank for 7 years, the closure was something he would "never want to go through again. There were a lot of tears—many people had spent their entire working lives in that lobby and now it was gone" (Stock, 2010).

One TeamBank employee, Michael McCauley, recounted the experience as follows:

> FDIC agents in conjunction with the Office of Comptroller of the Currency (OCC) swe[pt] in like a Mongol horde, shutting down the institution with ruthless efficiency. FDIC agents pore[d] [sic] over everything in the office, rooting through filing cabinets and rifling through desk drawers. "All of the employees were gathered in one room and kept separate from bank officers," says McCauley, who produced $331,000 in 2008 before all hell broke loose. "Then we were brought to the lobby where an OCC officer announced that TeamBank was no longer operational and that within a few minutes, some people from the FDIC were going to come in, that they would treat TeamBank employees with respect and that they would stay for the whole weekend." A sheriff stood guard by the main door, and the moment the OCC officer started talking, the sheriff taped a closure notice to the door. "I've never seen anything run with such precision," McCauley says. "It was an amazing thing." TeamBank was instantly sold to Great Southern and by seven that night, all signs and advertisements in the bank's hometown of Paola, Kansas had been covered over with Great Southern's logo. On Monday morning, the bank opened under Great Southern's control. (Stock, 2010)

As demonstrated, bank failures were shocking and financially damaging for employees, who suffered some of the greatest losses. While many believe that most employees are innocent victims, many experts believe failed leadership in the financial industry contributed to the crisis (George, 2008; Greene, 2011). Regulators, such as the Office of the Comptroller of the Currency (OCC), have said studies of bank failures show "insider abuse...often contributes to [bank] failures" (OCC, 2013).

Experts believe that employees are aware of frauds occurring in the workplace, and these frauds should be reported to the hotlines established as part of SOX. Research has consistently demonstrated that many employees know about fraud occurring in their workplace. A 2002 study conducted by Ernst & Young showed that as many as one in five workers are aware of fraud occurring in their place of employment. Furthermore, research has continually demonstrated that employee tips are the primary way that fraud is discovered within an organization (Association of Certified Fraud Examiners [ACFE] 2002–2012). In fact, in their 2012 report, the ACFE reported 43% of the frauds in public companies were discovered via a tip, which was up from 40% in 2010.

However, it is difficult to believe that hotlines are functioning well to detect and prevent internal crime, given the magnitude of frauds that have occurred despite the existence of the hotline. In the wake of bank closures, media reports documented employee familiarity with internal crime, which would have been ripe for reporting.

As a case in point, the "largest bank failure in U.S. history" was Washington Mutual bank (WaMu) (Arnall & Herman, 2008; Sidel et al., 2008). WaMu was once one of the largest originators and servicers of residential mortgages in the United States through subprime subsidiary Long Beach Mortgage, holding $307 billion in assets when it failed (Arnall & Herman, 2008). Shortly thereafter, an employee told the media the employees "saw it coming" (Arnall & Herman, 2008). "The executives are the ones who made the decision to take WaMu in this direction. Too many of the middle folks like myself said this is wrong, we're making loans we shouldn't be making, we're qualifying borrowers who we know are going to struggle to pay the loan back" (Arnall & Herman, 2008).

Indeed, WaMu internal documents obtained in connection with the lawsuit demonstrate they approved loans, regardless of borrower risk, in the name of profit (Arnall & Herman, 2008).

The types of schemes perpetuated during the crisis typically involved a large number of employees, and thus would leave many witnesses/tipsters. According to the Department of Treasury (DOT), the biggest financial institution frauds during the crisis involved insiders, and their schemes involved (1) unsound lending practices, such as inadequate collateral and poor loan documentation; (2) excessive concentrations of credit to certain industries or groups of borrowers; (3) unsound or excessive loans to insiders or their related interests or business associates; (4) violations of civil statutes or regulations, such as legal lending limits or loans to one borrower; and (5) criminal violations of law and statute, such as fraud, misapplication of bank funds, or embezzlement (OCC, 2010).

The DOT advises that employees of these firms can be a great source of information, finding the following:

> Insiders often commit crimes using subordinates who do not question their instructions. In some instances, however, the subordinates may be astute enough to know that what the insiders instructed them to do is questionable or wrong and may freely discuss the situation if the regulators simply inquire. (OCC, 2010)

It is believed the internal culture of the companies that failed during the financial crisis didn't support hotline reporting. Experts believe that if more internal crime was reported, then criminal prosecutions might be possible. Once such expert, Robert Gnaizda, who appeared in the "Inside Job," an Academy Award winning documentary about the financial crisis, said the executives of Bear Stearns, Goldman Sachs, Lehman Brothers and Merrill Lynch could be criminally prosecuted if employees came forward. According to Gnaizda, such cases "would be very hard to win...but...they could do it if they got enough underlings to tell the truth." (Furguson et al., 2010).

2010 (Promulgation of Dodd–Frank)

The use of fraud hotlines in the private sector was reinforced under legislation known as Dodd–Frank. Dodd–Frank was designed to regulate Wall Street following the financial crisis. Lawmakers determined additional regulations were required in the wake of the crisis to prevent future instances of employee fraud at financial institutions.

Dodd–Frank was created by Barney Frank (Democrat-Massachusetts) and Senate Banking Committee Chairman Chris Dodd. This U.S. federal statute was proposed on December 2, 2009, and signed into law on July 21, 2010. Dodd–Frank is said to represent the most comprehensive change to financial regulation since the Great Depression (Greene, 2011). Dodd–Frank required regulators to create 243 new federal rule-makings, designed to enhance accountability and transparency within the financial system (Davis Polk, 2010; The Wall Street Journal, 2010).

On November 3, 2010, the SEC issued proposed rules to implement the whistleblower provisions established by Dodd–Frank. Dodd–Frank expanded whistleblower provisions in SOX and the Securities and Exchange Act of 1934 (SEA) to provide tipsters, who report violations of certain laws to federal authorities, a reward based on the amount of money recovered by the SEC.

Section 922 of Dodd–Frank also expanded the whistleblower protection provisions in §806 of SOX to include an increased statute of limitations in which to file complaints and greater compensation for damages. Employees were also provided extra protections against employer retaliation. The amendments include the following protections, which apply to employee complainants who participate in an SEC investigation:

- Protection against retaliation by their employer
- Potential of double back-pay damages awarded to whistleblowers who file a lawsuit claiming retaliation by their employer; statute of limitation for filing such retaliation claims increased to 6 years (The previous statute of limitations was 3 years; the statute of limitation for standard retaliation claims was also increased from 90 to 180 days.)
- Opportunity to file a retaliation complaint directly in federal court, bypassing the Department of Labor administrative process (Exall, n.d.)

- Right to a jury trial for retaliation claims, regardless of whether a mandatory arbitration agreement, often used in the financial services industry, was in place
- Protection of a new independent investigative body, the Bureau of Consumer Financial Protection, created to investigate and commence civil actions against financial industry employers who retaliate against their whistleblower employees

Dodd–Frank further expanded SOX protections to include other related entities named on a given entity's financial statements, including subsidiaries and affiliates, from both public and private industry. SOX is further protected from internal employee agreements that may attempt to supersede or invalidate SOX. Such agreements are now strictly prohibited (Bouchard & Linthorst, 2010; Exall, n.d.; Seyfarth Shaw, 2010).

The amendments to SOX under Dodd–Frank add multiple reporting incentives for potential whistleblowers. They allow whistleblowers to collect substantially more money than they could previously under SOX. Employees can also pursue actions against more entities, in an extended time period, and do so without notifying their employer. The new amendments also allow employees to bypass reporting to their employer. Before Dodd–Frank, employees had to exhaust administrative remedies before filing a claim. Now employees can go directly to the SEC, the Department of Justice (DOJ), and/or the U.S. Commodity Futures Trading Commission (CFTC) and file claims directly in federal court.

This new process is believed to result in larger settlements. According to employment lawyers, "successful employees may obtain substantial remedies, including reinstatement without loss of seniority, double back-pay, reasonable attorneys' fees, costs and expert witness fees" (Seyfarth Shaw, 2010). Employees can also obtain a percentage of the sanctions levied against their employer, in exchange for actionable tips. Sections 922 and 929A of Dodd–Frank added a new section to the Securities and Exchange Act of 1934 (SEA) requiring the SEC to provide a monetary award to whistleblowers up to 30% of the total amount of the sanctions. The statutory language also gives tipsters confidence in their ability to receive an award. The SEC is given the discretion to award the whistleblower anywhere between 10% and 30% of the sanctions. The amount of the award cannot be less than 10% (Exall, n.d.). There are some limitations. The information must be "original" and provided voluntarily to the SEC, rather than in response to inquiry. The sanction in question must also exceed $1 million.

The payout under these terms can be sizable. The SEC has reported settlements since July 2010 in amounts of $75 million, $100 million, and $550 million (Kerschberg, 2011).

Under Dodd–Frank, the whistleblower is also provided an extended reporting timeframe. Section 922 allows the employee to file a claim "up to six years after the violation occurred, or three years after he or she knew or reasonably should have known of facts material to the violation, so long as the complaint is filed within ten years of the violation" (Seyfarth Shaw, 2010). Lawmakers believe the new whistleblower provisions will prevent future corporate fraud by increasing employee reporting to authorities. Congress finds the provisions to be a great way to discover fraud without cost to the taxpayer (funds used for whistleblower bounties are to be paid out from the penalties the company pays to the SEC) (Carton, 2010). Likewise, SEC Chairman Mary L. Schapiro (2009–2012) said the reward may "avoid missing the next Bernard Madoff" (Carton, 2010). Lawyers believe Dodd–Frank "will help restore investor confidence in the financial industry" yet find "Investigating claims of this nature is a real burden on resources" (Reisinger, 2011).

Employers criticized Dodd–Frank's provisions allowing employees to bypass internal reporting processes previously established under SOX. In December 2010, *The Wall Street Journal* reported over 260 companies sent letters to the SEC, complaining about the whistleblower provisions. Specifically, lawyers for Delta, FedEx, Gap, and Pfizer said the new rules were contrary to existing compliance programs in that they "disincentivize employees from looking for ways to improve or correct corporate behaviors, and incent them to find ways to profit from corporate wrongdoing" (Koppel, 2010).

Despite its critics, the Dodd–Frank legislation forever changed the fight against corporate fraud in America, by empowering the whistleblower.

During this time, there was another set of guidelines established to mitigate the instance of fraud and other misconduct by helping organizations strengthen their internal compliance programs. In 2010, the U.S. Sentencing Commission created an updated set of guidelines for organizations to follow, known as the Federal Sentencing Guidelines for Organizations (FSGO). The spirit of the guidelines is to help strengthen the ethics and compliance programs of organizations to lessen their liability when misconduct occurs. These guidelines contain "seven elements of an effective ethics and compliance program," which serve as best practices for hotline programs (The Network, 2012).

As expected, opinions are divided over whether the new whistleblower provisions will function as intended—to reduce corporate fraud by increasing the instance of employee reporting to authorities. While current and past whistleblowers,* certain lawmakers, plaintiff's attorneys, and accounting firms favor the provisions, not surprisingly, employers tend to be critical of them. Congress finds the provisions to be a great way to discover fraud without cost to the taxpayer (the funds used for whistleblower bounties will be paid out from the penalties the company pays to the SEC) (Carton, 2010). Likewise, SEC Chairman Schapiro says the reward may "avoid missing the next Bernard Madoff" (Carton, 2010). It is clear that is the intended spirit of the laws. Whistleblowers will enjoy many benefits, as will the investing public. However, unintended consequences, such as those discussed below, are likely to surface.

---

* As discussed later, whistleblower provisions may be applied retroactively.

The way that Dodd–Frank is written today and tentatively applies to SOX and SEA seems advantageous to the whistleblower. As discussed below, they enjoy job security, the opportunity to bypass internal company policy, sizable reward money, and other benefits. Such benefits have led many to liken the whistleblower to a bounty hunter. Although employers may not like that aspect, theoretically, they should have nothing to fear provided they and their employees are following the rules. But the problem is they may have to spend a lot of money defending frivolous claims in the process.

Also, more importantly, a primary advantage of the new provisions is that the investing public can enjoy increased confidence in the financial system. David Brooks, general counsel of New York-based Fortress Investment Group LLC, said he believes the increased compliance measures "will help restore investor confidence in the financial industry," but he remains concerned that the "bounty... could incent them to report made-up claims. Investigating claims of this nature is a real burden on resources" (Reisinger, 2011).

On the surface, it appears that employers are the most seriously disadvantaged by the Dodd–Frank whistleblower provisions, and lawmakers have assembled to address the issues. At one such debate, which took place on May 12, 2011, before the House Financial Services Subcommittee on Capital Markets and Government Sponsored Enterprises ("debate"), Representative Scott Garrett (Republican-New Jersey), chairman of the subcommittee, said the primary concerns that had been raised to date before the SEC were as follows:

■ Will the incentive structure created by the Dodd–Frank provisions exacerbate violations by encouraging them to fester and become more serious problems?
■ Does the legislation and the proposed rulemaking allow those complicit in violations to not only escape punishment, but potentially receive massive rewards in spite of their malfeasance?
■ If internal compliance programs are bypassed, isn't good corporate citizenship discouraged, and won't there be a greater likelihood that companies will have less accurate financial statements and that companies will need to restate those financials upon which investors had already relied?

In response to those concerns, one representative, Michael Grimm (Republican-New York), proposed legislation designed to preserve the internal reporting structure of SOX (to prevent bogus claims and claims from those involved in crime). With respect to bogus claims, Representative Maxine Waters (Democrat-California) said she didn't think "whistleblowers [would] run to the SEC and put their jobs, 401(k)s and friendships on the line," and Geoffrey Rapp, professor of Law at the University of Toledo College of Law, did not think "that whistleblowers [would] race to the SEC to get a bounty" (Waddell, 2011). That said, it has been reported that the SEC now receives up to two "high quality" whistleblower tips per day, whereas before the Dodd–Frank, they received only 24 per year (Koehler, 2010).

Employers disagree. As discussed, over 260 companies sent letters to the SEC, complaining the whistleblower provisions will turn financial fraud into a veritable "gold mine" for employees. Lawyers for Delta, FedEx, Gap, and Pfizer said the new rules are contrary to existing compliance programs in that they "disincent employees from looking for ways to improve or correct corporate behaviors, and incent them to find ways to profit from corporate wrongdoing" (Koppel, 2010).

Dodd–Frank may certainly cost employers a lot more money, which could in turn overenrich law firms and accounting/consulting firms as they struggle to comply with the new regulations. Employers may now have to defend an increased number of claims and redesign internal programs accordingly. In their advisory documents concerning Dodd–Frank, law firm Morgan, Lewis & Brockius LLP advises their clients to audit their subsidiary compliance (to extend their corporate compliance structures to subsidiaries and other related entities), review their waiver and arbitration agreements (concerning possible existing restrictions on waivers and predispute arbitration), and find new ways to encourage internal reporting (which could mean expanding their existing processes, such as internal hotlines) (Morgan, Lewis & Brockius, 2010). Naturally, a potential expansion in business means that law firms would generally not find fault with the new provisions.

However, accounting/consulting firms may not benefit from the new provisions insofar as they negate internal reporting, as they may advise and support internal hotlines on behalf of major companies. They also have an affiliation and interest in companies that provide these services. As expected, at the debate, the deputy CEO of big four accounting/consulting firm Deloitte LLP, Robert Kueppers, argued to maintain internal reporting by opining that "whistleblowers should be required to report their concerns fully and in good faith through company-sponsored internal compliance systems *before* reporting to the SEC as a *condition of eligibility* to receive a monetary award" (AICPA, 2011).

Plaintiff's attorneys have benefitted from the new rules in the form of increased work. Such firms have reported increased contact from whistleblowers since the provisions were introduced. In fact, one plaintiff's attorney in New York reported getting more calls from whistleblowers in that time than they had received in the previous 3 years (Reisinger, 2011).

In sum, as stated by Schapiro, chairman of the SEC, the most positive outcome of the new whistleblower rules is the potential to uncover major financial fraud, such as the case of Ponzi schemer Bernard Madoff, who somehow eluded all other means of detection. As discussed previously, the possible negative consequences are overwhelming. Are those necessary costs in the effort to fight corporate fraud, or will a careful revision of this policy eliminate some of the potential negative outcomes?

Although well intended, it is clear that the Dodd–Frank whistleblower provisions have some shortcomings that are being attributed to the haste with which it was passed. This phenomenon was acknowledged by Representative

Scott Garrett (Republican-New Jersey), who in 2016, said, "Instead of a coordinated, well-thought out legislative and regulatory approach in the wake of the financial crisis, what we've had instead is a series of ad-hoc initiatives all ostensibly designed to make the financial system safer, but which in reality will only serve to put a lid on our economic potential while sowing the seeds of the next financial crisis. This misguided approach began with the Dodd–Frank Act, which was rushed through Congress on a partisan vote with little regard for what its provisions would mean for Main Street America" (Dodd–Frank Regulations, 2016).

It would seem that the whistleblower protections and increased incentives to report were created because the government believes there are potential whistleblowers who are not coming forward for fear of retaliation and lack of incentive. To that end, the spirit of the provisions is in the right place. However, largely due to the haste with which it was passed, the following potential unintended consequences exist:

- *Perpetuation of crime.* Because the incentives are tied to a percentage of the total value of the monetary penalty (money misappropriated), the would-be whistleblower has the incentive to let the crime continue to increase the value of his or her award (Schuman & Keating, 2011).
- *Payment to crime participants.* Today, a whistleblower who is culpable is eligible to receive an award (Hamiliton, 2012).
- *Excessive complaint filing.* Workers may have a "nothing to lose" mentality and flood the SEC with complaints/information with the hopes that one of their tips leads to a payday.
- *Money wasted on internal compliance programs.* Employees can go complain to the SEC, rather than internally, and this might actually be a positive aspect. Employers are unhappy about this because they will lose the opportunity to rectify any problem internally, especially now they have implemented costly internal reporting mechanisms as a result of SOX. However, perhaps this change will result in increased reporting, as often internal frauds are committed by company executives, who have the power to "ignore" or cover up internal problems reported to them.
- *Increased complaints to the SEC.* There is presently no limitation on employee reporting. With such large potential gains and guaranteed payments, employees have the incentive to report *any* potential violation. Despite having created a new investigative body to handle these claims, they could be overwhelmed and will encounter complicated situations with multiple complainants.
- *Increased legal claims.* Recent legal decisions have demonstrated that Dodd–Frank can be applied retroactively (*Pezza v. Investors Capital Corp.*, 10 CV 10113 D. Mass, Mar. 1, 2011), effectively invalidating preexisting internal arbitration agreements.

As Garrett suggested, perhaps careful revision of these provisions would allow them to better address the financial crisis without a slew of unintended consequences, such as the overenrichment of an employee who may have participated in activities leading to the claim.

Revisions that would address the aforementioned issues have been long under development. Lawyers have suggested improvements and congressmen have actively drafted proposals to address the shortcomings in Dodd–Frank as it is written today pertaining to whistleblowers. Lawyer Jacob Frenkel, a former SEC enforcement attorney, suggested revising Dodd–Frank to require employees to first report possible illegal activity internally, and then to the SEC *only if* their complaint was not appropriately handled by the company. This procedure is similar to Section 10A of the Securities Exchange Act, as it pertains to auditors. However, Frenkel believes this framework would work well for any employee (Carton, 2010).

Over the last 6 years, several bills have been put forward to roll back the provisions of Dodd–Frank (Barr, 2016). Some of those provisions have pertained to whistleblowers.

Former Representative Michael Grimm (Republican-New York) further suggested changing the incentive structure of Dodd–Frank so that it does not guarantee a payout. Such a guarantee of 10%–30% of the penalties paid out by the company incentivize the employee to file *any* claim without reservation and to let criminal activity persist as their potential payout increases accordingly. To rectify this problem, Grimm proposed dropping the guarantee and changing the range from 0% to 30% (Grimm, 2011).

Ultimately, Grimm introduced a proposal, called the Whistleblower Improvement Act, to Congress on July 11, 2011. It proposed amending the Securities and Exchange Act of 1934 and the Commodity Exchange Act to "require a whistleblower employee, as a prerequisite to eligibility for a whistleblower award, to: (1) first report the relevant information to his or her employer before reporting it to the Securities and Exchange Commission (SEC) and (2) report such information to the SEC within 180 days after reporting it to the employer." The proposal further called to "Prohibit a whistleblower award to any whistleblower who fails to report the relevant information to his or her employer first, unless: (1) the employer lacks either a policy prohibiting retaliation for reporting potential misconduct or an internal reporting system allowing for anonymous reporting or (2) the SEC determines that internal reporting was not a viable option" (Summary: H.R. 2011).

Grimm quickly gained support in the financial industry for his bill. These supporters agreed that employees should first report crime internally, so that the employer could remediate the issue (Joseph, 2012). Today, the SEC offers incentives for employees to report internally, but there is no express requirement that they do so. The SEC incentivizes employees to report internally by offering them "extra credit" when the SEC is determining his or her award amount (Bartholomew & Nilson, 2012, p. 11). However, the employee has to report to both the SEC and internally (just internally is not enough). They have 120 days to report to the SEC, after reporting internally, in order to get an award (Bartholomew & Nilson, 2012, p. 11).

SEC data demonstrates that employees tend to report internally first. In their 2016 report, the SEC said most of their whistleblower award recipients, 80%, who were "insiders" or employees of the organizations which were subjects of their tip, reported internally, before going to the SEC (Thomas, 2016). However, the SEC tells whistleblowers they "will not be penalized if they do not avail themselves of the opportunity [to report internally] for fear of retaliation or other legitimate reasons… [but they] will consider higher percentage awards for whistleblowers who first report violations through their compliance programs" (Twardy & Klein, 2011, p. 7).

Yet many financial services companies supported Grimm's proposed changes. They reportedly found their "internal compliance" measures are adequate and do not require supplanting (Wasik, 2012). People who opposed Grimm's Bill argued that employees already report internally, so further legislation is not required. In support of their argument, they cited a study by the Ethics Resource Center that demonstrates only 2%–3% of employees report wrongdoing outside of the company without telling their employer (GAP, 2016, p. 5; Liebelson, 2012).

However, this is contrary to another study, which found that most people, 78%, would indeed go outside their employer to report fraud, "if it could be done anonymously, without retaliation and result in a monetary reward" (Rasor, 2011). Thus, it is possible that by restricting employee access to outside reporting mechanisms, less criminal activity might be reported. Hence, critics have said Grimm's proposal to restrict whistleblower reporting was surprising, given that he was a former Federal Bureau of Investigation white-collar crime investigator (Barnard, 2012).

Despite the opposition, the bill moved through a House subcommittee in December 2010, and supporters such as the U.S. Chamber of Commerce were hoping for its quick passage (Joseph, 2012). However, it ultimately was not enacted.

Ironically, it turned out Grimm himself had been breaking the law. After pushing his bill to restrict whistleblower reporting, Grimm subsequently pleaded guilty in December 2014 to one count of felony tax fraud. According to the indictment, he perpetuated a scheme to hide more than $1 million in earnings and employee wages at a restaurant he owned prior to his election to Congress in 2010 (O'Brien, 2015). Ultimately "he [ ] admitted to paying undocumented workers under the table as the owner of a Manhattan restaurant called Healthalicious, filing false tax returns to profit from it, and then lying about all of it to investigators" (Ratliff, 2014). He resigned from Congress in January 2015, entered prison in September 2015, and was released on house arrest in April 2016.

Incidentally, Grimm was reelected to Congress while under investigation, before he resigned.

Once known for his fierce opposition to Dodd–Frank's whistleblower provisions, now he might be better known as he is portrayed by the *New Yorker*—"a man who betrayed the laws he once made such a show of upholding" (Ratliff, 2014).

With the SEC reporting recent settlements of up to $550 million, it is clear that whistleblowers could benefit greatly to report internal fraud. While some argue this money creates ill incentives, the recent settlements are evidence that illegal practices are indeed occurring. The increased cost of compliance, which includes defending frivolous claims, is proving to be problematic for employers, many of whom have registered in other countries, reduced the number of employees they hire, or closed. Also heavy awards to employees for spotting fraud may have turned them into investigators who concentrate on finding wrongdoing rather than completing their regular job duties.

Clearly these are unintended consequences. However, with losses in the recent financial crisis upwards of $50 trillion, it is easy to see that the incentive moneys provided to whistleblowers are minor when compared to the loss, which the public bears without such provisions in place. Perhaps with enhancements such as those recently proposed, Dodd–Frank could serve as the facilitator for credible tips without obvious drawbacks.

However, the question now is whether Dodd–Frank will endure. Today, the future of Dodd–Frank is quite uncertain. During his 2016 presidential campaign, then-candidate Donald J. Trump and his team remarked he would "get rid of" or "dismantle" Dodd–Frank (Barr, 2016; Geewax, 2016). His nominee for Treasury Secretary, Steven Mnuchin, agreed by saying he would "kill" aspects of it (Barr, 2016).

While some think Dodd–Frank is an asset, others think it is highly flawed. It seems as though there is a partisan divide over the utility of Dodd–Frank. Republicans tend to find the 2,300-page document contains too many regulations. Democrats are inclined to believe the laws represent necessary regulations of a risky industry (Geewax, 2016).

However, there is certainly a measure of bipartisan support for Dodd-Frank. In fact, it is the bipartisan support for Dodd–Frank's whistleblower program, in particular, that experts think may save it from the chopping block (Rubenfeld, 2015).

Regardless of political affiliation, it is clear that people have strong opinions about Dodd–Frank's efficacy. One critic, Dorothy Jetter from Americans for Tax Reform, a nonprofit advocacy group, says Dodd–Frank has "done more harm than good for American consumers by crippling small businesses and stunting job growth" (Jetter, 2015). Meanwhile, a supporter, Michael Barr, a writer for *Fortune*, calls the potential end of Dodd–Frank "deeply misguided and likely to recreate the conditions that led to the 2008 financial crisis" (Barr, 2016).

Although President Trump has indicated his interest in ending Dodd–Frank, experts think he may keep the whistleblower program. One key reason they think he will keep it, is because it's successful. To date, the SEC hotline has received 18,334 tips that have led to $904 million in financial remedies in penalties (SEC, 2016, p. 23). Another reason is that President Trump's allies in congress support the program (Weinberg, 2016). Experts also believe that the program is compatible with President Trump's general interest in "draining the swamp" (Rubenfeld, 2015). Overall, they believe "barring a complete repeal of Dodd–Frank...the whistleblower statute will survive" (Weinberg, 2016).

However, that doesn't mean that it will stay on the books. Recent efforts targeting whistleblower complaint forums suggest the SEC's program might be in trouble. It was recently discovered that Well Fargo's whistleblower site "vanished" from the Internet just days after President Trump took office. It had been removed by the U.S. Department of Labor (DOL) who created the site to hear employee complaints on workplace issues (Post Staff Report, 2017).

As discussed later in this work, in September 2016, Wells Fargo was fined $185 million for fraudulently opened accounts (Corkery, 2016). In the wake of this incident, many employees reported they submitted tips regarding this fraud to the company's internal fraud hotline, and they were fired as a result. These employees responded by filing a federal lawsuit against Wells Fargo (Egan, September 27, 2016).

The DOL created their own website for employees to receive information about employee abuses that may have transpired. On the website's launch under President Obama's administration, the DOL promised to conduct a "top-to-bottom review of Wells Fargo cases, complaints and violations" to include whistleblower complaints against the company. A visit to the former page (https://www.dol.gov/wellsfargo) confirmed that as of this writing, it was no longer operational. When asked, a DOL spokesperson said the site was removed during the Obama administration, on January 9, 2017 (Egan, 2017). As of this writing, the reasons the site is suddenly no longer available haven't yet been revealed. It was reported that Senator Elizabeth Warren is currently looking into the matter (Egan, 2017).

A recent *Forbes* article speculated that Dodd–Frank will also soon "disappear" (Ehrlich & Boggs, 2017). As discussed, it is unclear whether its whistleblower hotline will also be dissolved. But regardless of the SEC hotline's future, its legacy will certainly have lasting value. Successful hotlines such as the SEC hotline, can be evaluated after the fact to learn "what works" in terms of hotline operation. For instance, the SEC hotline reflects the value of offering rewards in exchange for tips—a concept that will be discussed in more detail throughout this work.

The topics of hotline design, performance, and best practices are critical issues in today's corporate culture. Today, more organizations are employing hotlines than ever before. Therefore, it is important to make sure these hotlines are operating optimally to hear important feedback, such as fraud, waste, and abuse. According to recent statistics, 83% of large companies have a fraud hotline (CGMA 2015, p. 4). And the figure is continuing to grow. According to the ACFE's 2016 Report to the Nations on Occupational Fraud and Abuse, the implementation rate of hotlines jumped from 51.2% in 2010 to 60.1% in 2016 (ACFE, 2016, p. 40). This finding was echoed in a study conducted by the Chartered Global Management

Accountants, who determined the number of organizations having hotlines increased from 40% in 2008 to 59% in 2016 (CGMA, 2015, p. 15).

There are many suspected reasons for this increase. While only publicly listed companies are required to have hotlines, other organizations want them too, in an effort to curtail fraudulent practices. These organizations are likely savvy to the research literature, which says that organizations with hotlines tend to have lower overall losses due to fraud (ACFE 2016, p. 43; Anti-Fraud Collaboration, 2014).

Chapter 3

Hotline Design

The design and creation of a hotline is a very important task. The initial design phases are critical to the overall operation of the hotline. A poorly designed and executed hotline can be just as bad as not having a hotline at all. Regardless of the design scheme employed, the critical features of any hotline can be summarized using the following three A's: Anonymity, Accessibility, and Advertisement. Hotlines should be designed with these three A's in mind for optimal performance.

To this end, this chapter will first review hotline management and implementation. It is first important to consider whether a given hotline will be managed internally or externally, by a third party. Next, cost will be addressed, as that is often a major factor when developing a hotline. Then, the three A's will be discussed, and the use of hotline rewards.

Management and Implementation

When determining how a given hotline will be managed, it is important to consider the potential scope and size of the hotline, to include the number and type of anticipated callers, the time they may call, and the potential nature of their calls.

There are estimates that provide an idea of what to expect in terms of call volume. According to experts, organizations can expect 1%–5% of their employees will use the hotline annually (Kusserow, 2012; Walker, 2014, p. 12). A conservative estimate is 1–1.5 calls per month per 1,000 employees (Kusserow, 2012).

A number of factors contribute to the volume of calls received, including corporate culture, promotion and training, confidence in management's commitment, current issues facing the company, and past behaviors and reactions (Walker, 2014, p. 12).

As for the timing of calls, one expert says most calls are received during the day, spiking in the early morning, peaking at lunch and a few hours immediately afterward. However, for 24-hour hotlines, a majority of the calls received are outside of business hours (Deloitte, 2014, p. 9). In fact, as little as 10% or less of the calls are expected to be received during business hours (Kusserow, 2012). In terms of the subject matter, a majority of the calls are said to involve human resources–related issues (Kusserow, 2012). Some of the more common types of reports include observed behavior that "creates a hostile work environment, conflicts of interest, discrimination and violations of health and safety regulations" (Lighthouse, 2016, p. 2).

Hotlines can be managed either internally (in-house) or externally (third-party provider). Experts often recommend using a third-party provider. There are many advantages to having a third-party provider (multilingual capabilities, 24-hour, 7-day-a-week operation) but that option is not always feasible. In some cases, the organization may need to have a third-party provider in order to satisfy SOX requirements. But it is important to note that an internal hotline will also satisfy SOX if it gives callers a way to report anonymously.

When deciding between an in-house and external solution, it is important to consider your potential callers. Will they report potential fraud internally, or will they feel more comfortable contacting a third party? Many experts (who might be the business of operating their own fraud hotlines) will say that employees are more comfortable reporting to external parties. But there is also evidence employees might think the opposite. A majority of respondents to a Deloitte survey favored internal reporting. In fact, 57% of respondents said the most "efficient" hotlines would be run "in-house" with the results reported to the Audit Committee Chairman (35%) or CEO (22%). The remaining 43% thought it was best to outsource the hotline to an independent service provider reporting in to the Audit Committee (Deloitte, 2014, p. 6).

So how do you determine whether you outsource the hotline or operate it internally? There are a number of considerations, including cost, availability, operational requirements, training, etc. (Walker, 2014). Some organizations will need more than others. The best way to determine this is to list out all of the organizations' needs and requirements and determine which service will best meet those objectives.

Operating a hotline in-house might be the most cost-effective measure for many organizations. Third-party hotlines can be expensive, and in-house hotlines can be operated at a very low cost. This aspect will be discussed in more detail later in this chapter.

In-house hotlines have inherent advantages. Hotline employees will be familiar with the organization and its policies and procedures (Kusserow, 2012). Also, keeping the hotline internal limits the transmission of information about the organization to outside parties.

In-house hotlines are often challenged to maintain confidentiality and anonymity (Walker, 2014). In a small organization, it is possible the hotline operator could recognize the voice of the caller, or may otherwise know/recognize the employee(s) involved.

The employee selected for this role will need to be exceptionally mature and independent in his or her reporting and handling of such matters.

With a third-party firm, this is not an issue, as the hotline operator is a third party and is anonymous to the caller. Third-party services also employ personnel who are highly skilled in hotline interviewing, because that is all they do. As a result, they might be more skilled at eliciting information and more adept at handling emergencies (Kusserow, 2012).

Nevertheless, some callers might still be too intimidated to report. These hotlines would be wise to advise their employees on the hotline website of all the ways an employee can remain anonymous. This will be discussed in more detail later in this chapter. But these concerns do not exist with a third-party provider, as their hotline operators are unknown to the caller. The caller also knows he or she does not work for the company, and are just communicating the information to their employer.

While this is a benefit to the organization, this type of communication channel can also have inherent drawbacks. For the best flow of information, ideally, the least amount of people are involved in the chain (remember The Telephone Game?!). In the case of a third-party provider, someone who may not be familiar with a given organization is receiving a call, then typing the details into a report, then handing that report internally (perhaps forwarding to a manager), then that report gets communicated to the division of the employing organization that handles hotline complaints, and then the details get communicated out to the appropriate parties. That is a long chain in terms of information flow. A direct approach might seem more prudent.

Nevertheless, whether the hotline is operated internally or externally, it is considered advantageous to have a very well-trained hotline caller receiving the tips. Trained callers are skilled in "empathetic and investigatory techniques" that can elicit the best information from each caller (Walker, 2014).

It is important to reiterate here that organizations subject to SOX are required to have an "anonymous reporting mechanism." For these organizations, it is critical that they are able to maintain, and demonstrate, if needed, their hotline's ability to provide this feature. Ideally, to best meet these requirements, in terms of placement within the organization, it is recommended that the hotline be operated "by an area independent of finance" such as the compliance, internal audit, or human resources (HR) department (Andrews & Leblanc, 2013). This applies to whether the hotline is operated internally or externally. Organizations with external hotlines will need to report internally on reports received. These reports should also be directed to the aforementioned departments for handling.

There are some additional benefits to hiring a third-party provider. These providers can offer comprehensive case management systems, oversight, reporting, analytical tools, marketing and interpretation services (Walker, 2014, p. 16). Internal hotlines can have the same capabilities, but in many cases, each one will have to be thought out and planned from scratch.

Overall, when launching an in-house hotline program, the following elements should be considered:

- Code of conduct development
- Toll free line set up
- Scripting
- Web portal development
- E-mail method set up
- Responsive workflows
- Anonymous dialogue workflows
- Training in-house personnel
- Marketing and promotion
- Employee engagement
- Language requirements
- Case management
- Reporting

(Walker, 2014; Witt, 2015).

First it is critical to have a code of conduct outlining the standards of behavior expected in the organization, and the steps to take to report behavior or circumstances that may deviate from those standards. The code will also set forth the protections being offered to employees who utilize the hotline. This code will serve to establish a baseline of trust with the employees that is critical to the future success of the hotline. After developing a code of conduct, a training program can be added to enhance employee awareness and understanding of the code. Internal announcements via the company's internal website and via e-mail can also be incorporated. Training can include lunch-and-learns, role-playing, and sanitized case studies (Walker, 2014).

Marketing and promotion can include announcements via e-mail, newsletter, and video. It is also a good idea to offer pens, or business-type cards with the hotline name and phone number to remind employees to call.

Employee engagement is critical to the success of a given hotline. Employees need to feel comfortable coming forward with information. To this end, employee engagement, like marketing and promotion, should focus on assuring employees their tips will remain confidential. One way to do this is to provide an anonymous example of a hotline report that leads to positive corrective action. This way, employees will see that good things can come out of reporting, rather than the loss of their job (Deloitte, 2014, p. 12). Another way to engage employees in the reporting process is in the delivery of the purpose of the hotline. Experts recommend the following approach: "It is important to explain that every employee has a role in preventing and detecting fraud and that the hotline system is a key tool for people to use for that purpose. Armed with this knowledge, employees will be in a better position to act if they experience/witness suspicious behavior" (Deloitte, 2014, p. 12).

Case management of a hotline refers to the way that the organization will handle the information received. Each contact with the hotline, regardless of the medium used to contact it, can be referred to as one "case." Each case will need to be numbered, logged, and managed. Overall, case management systems for fraud hotlines should offer a consistent process, which is defensible and repeatable (Witt, 2015). To achieve this goal, policies and procedures should be developed, and aligned with the hotline system (Witt, 2015). Ideally, each person who contacts the hotline will be acknowledged with a notice of receipt of their "case." Also, ideally, they will receive updates regarding the status of their "case."

It is also possible with a small organization that there would only be one hotline operator. This is not uncommon (see case studies in Chapter 6). This framework is troubling from an information management viewpoint. If only one person is communicating with whistleblowers, it is possible for reporting to be hindered by having a single person talking with the callers, because his or her technique and perspective are limited (whereas a third-party hotline can have hundreds of operators). Also what will the organization do if that person calls out sick? Perhaps it is best to instead have a rotation of employees to receive calls.

For some organizations, it is not possible to offer 24/7, 365 services. These organizations may operate a voicemail system to receive calls after hours. This situation is not ideal, because the message serves as evidence of the caller's voice and can compromise his or her identity (Walker, 2014). But experts say that it is better to have a potentially imperfect system than not have one at all (Walker, 2014).

If the decision is made to use a third-party supplier, there are some key implementation points to consider. One third-party hotline supplier offers the following steps:

- Kickoff meeting
- Detailed project plan
- Configuration training and assistance

First, it is recommended to have a kickoff meeting, to discuss goals and expectations for the hotline rollout. Next, a detailed project plan should be created, which will delineate the goals and timelines for achievement. Finally, the hotline functionality and case management system should be discussed with the vendor. The hotline provider should have a keen understanding of the client's needs, so they can configure the system accordingly (Witt, 2015).

Matters uncovered via hotlines are always handled by the organization—regardless of whether the hotline is managed internally or externally. Therefore, it is important to have a process in place for implementing the reports that are generated from the hotline. The internal process should include distribution protocols to ensure the reports remain confidential (Dunkle, 2015).

There are a few considerations when it comes to report distribution. In one scenario, you could have two people receive each report. This way, it is not possible for a single person to withhold any reporting (Dunkle, 2015). (This is especially important in the event where the person who is subject of the report is one of the receiving parties!) In an alternate scenario, one could have a plan for who is to be notified in each instance, depending on the subject of the tip. For instance, in one case, human resources might be notified, and in another, the accounting or legal department (Dunkle, 2015).

Third Party Hotline Process

To further understand third-party hotline management, an employee of The Network (now NAVEX Global), NE1* was interviewed. By way of background, The Network is a technology company that provides an anonymous, confidential reporting hotline service. In a letter they wrote to the SEC in 2003, they self-reported as being "the nation's first outsourced employee 'hotline.'" At that time, they reported having over 1,000 clients, to include "many" of the Fortune 500. Today, according to available information, they have over 3,400 clients, including nearly half of the Fortune 500.

According to their website, their hotline center never closes and offers toll-free service in over 180 languages, and their call center employees follow a "proprietary interview methodology" that offers "substantial incident reports." They also provide web intake with international web forms.

As for their client list, NE1 advised The Network handles the hotlines of "nearly all the financial industry" including PS2, a case study subject featured in Chapter 6, J.P. Morgan Chase, Bank of America, and Wells Fargo, along with the Federal Reserve, to name a few. According to NE1, the names of these clients were revealed because they have expressly permitted The Network, in advance, to disclose this information. According to HE1, individuals can call hotlines and ask the identity of the administering organization, to learn the third-party provider of a specific hotline.

Other clients of The Network, who have been disclosed in the public domain, include various cities (GS3, a case study subject featured in Chapter 6, California, Tulsa, Oklahoma, Mesa, Arizona, Sacramento, California) colleges and universities (Lafayette College in Pennsylvania, Arizona State University, Vanderbilt University, Purdue University, University of Texas at Dallas and San Antonio, University of Alabama), media organizations (Discovery Communications [the world's largest nonfiction media company]), and travel companies, such as Norwegian Cruise Line.

When asked about the use of third-party hotline providers by the federal government, NE1 advised that the federal government tended to manage their hotlines internally, rather than use a third-party provider.

Regarding their competition, NE1 said their competitors, EthicsPoint and Global Compliance, are now all one company, NAVEX Global. When asked why

---

* The name of the interview subject is being withheld. He will be referred to in this work as NE1.

a company should choose The Network over the competition, NE1 said they offer the most complete, in-depth reports with a more "detailed, technology assisted interview process" with calls lasting 15–20 minutes. While NE1 acknowledged EthicsPoint once said they had the best case management software, "banks didn't care about that" because they "have their own software." With respect to case management, NE1 said The Network offers "standard incident codes" and then banks often supplement these with their own codes.

As for information flow, NE1 advised their hotline tip intake process (via telephone) is as follows: The tipster makes the call to their unique hotline number (each client has their own number in each country). The hotline interviewer, called the "interview specialist" will learn the company and location of a given caller via a "pop up" on their "intake screen." For example, the interview specialist could see on their screen "Bank of America caller from France." The interview specialist also manages the web tip intake process. There is one dedicated URL provided for this purpose, per client.

After the tip is logged, "within 15 minutes" a "triage team feeds [the tip] into the system" and an e-mail is sent to the client. Then, the client sends the tip to another internal designee for handling. The ultimate resolution of the tip is tracked via The Network's software.

When asked about the triage process for immediate matters, NE1 advised they have an "immediate escalation process for cases reported which are time sensitive [handled within 24 hours]." To escalate these matters, The Network is provided with telephone numbers of "key people" to be contacted by The Network in the event of urgent matters, such as "immediate threat of workplace violence, falsification, etc."

If the client wishes to communicate with the anonymous complainant, following the initial tip (i.e., to get further information), they will contact The Network who will make a note in the system to communicate their request for additional detail to the caller, if they call back. According to NE1, most callers do not call a second time.

When asked about their benchmarking report and the complete absence of prosecutions as a result of their services, NE1 said "PS2 and others often don't report back to them on resolution."

As for their employees, The Network's triage team is based in Atlanta, Georgia, where they have over 200 interview specialists. When I asked whether The Network would hire me, I was told I am "overqualified." Rather, according to NE1, they hire "entry level" personnel; some may come straight out of college, yet others are hired without a degree, as it is not required. Interview specialists are paid by the hour and are "incentivized based on quality of report." All candidates are subject to background checks (convicted felons are not hired) and have to sign a nondisclosure agreement.

A review of the The Network's website, on July 22, 2013, under the "careers" section yielded several job advertisements for Interview Specialists, which were described as personnel tasked with "answer[ing] inbound employee assistance-type calls from employees of our Fortune 500 client companies." The Network further said interview specialists "are responsible for accurately documenting these calls using PC and Windows-based applications."

At this time, seven postings for these positions were present on their careers page, where they were seeking speakers in the following languages (in addition to English language fluency): British/English, French, German, Mandarin Chinese, Portuguese, and Spanish. The stated candidate requirements were "A minimum of one year customer service experience; Call center experience preferred; Ability to read, write and speak fluently in English and [in the given language]." The job postings further say the candidate should demonstrate "Ability to conduct a structured interview; Minimum typing speed of 35+ WPM with 90% accuracy required; Excellent grammar, spelling and writing skills; and a pleasant and friendly phone presence."

As for the regional requirements and governing laws, NE1 advised they follow SOX and international laws, and that the laws governing their service are a "Hodgepodge." According to NE1, "in some countries, you cannot ask certain questions." For instance, using France as an example, NE1 advised in this region, certain questions cannot be asked, nor can information be recorded regarding certain matters. They employ a separate data privacy firm, Hunton & Williams, to handle/advise them on regional legal issues.

When asked about the volume of calls received by financial firms, NE1 said that "some financial firms rarely get a call." When asked why, NE1 responded "it is an issue of promotion of the hotline" and that "some say to use the hotline as a last resort. It's a cultural thing. Many want to keep the volume down." Incidentally, NE1 later revealed the cost of service "depends on volume."

As for the actual cost incurred to clients to have The Network manage their hotline, according to NE1, every "report taken [costs] between $40–60 per report" with an "average cost of $400–500 per year" with "additional cost for translation services, etc." and that "all in, companies can expect to pay between $30–100k per year with a minimum cost of $1k allowed [per year]."

When asked how the hotline reporting process changed following Dodd-Frank, NE1 said that Dodd-Frank "didn't change things much" except that "companies want to keep employees from reporting outside, otherwise more money in damages… [companies are] trying to get people to report internally."

Intake

One key functional element in a hotline is intake. It is important to determine the process for how calls will be received and tips logged. This process is especially critical for collecting metrics that will be later utilized to examine the hotline's performance. One way to learn about hotline intake processes is to examine a successful hotline.

One such hotline is the U.S. Securities and Exchange Commission (SEC) hotline. In 2015, the SEC hotline received over 4,000 tips and in 2016 that amount grew to 4,200. To date, they have returned over 15,413 calls to their hotline (SEC, 2016, p. 3). How does the SEC handle all this information? The SEC's Office of the Whistleblower (OWB) utilizes an internal database called the "TCR System," which is short for "Tips, Complaints, and Referrals Intake and Resolution System." The TCR System serves as their central repository for all tips, complaints, and agency referrals (SEC, 2015).

All tipsters are asked to fill out a "Form TCR" electronically (online) or in hard copy (mail, fax). The OWB provides a hard-copy option for those without "ready access" to computers or who prefer to submit in this manner. When hard copies are received by the OWB, they enter it manually into their TCR System (SEC, 2015, p. 7).

The OWB also provides a hotline number (since May 2011) for the public to ask questions about the whistleblower program. Callers are advised to leave messages, and OWB attorneys respond to callers within 24 business hours (SEC, 2015, p. 8). In Fiscal Year 2015, the OWB returned 2,801 calls to this hotline (SEC, 2015, p. 8).

The OWB's process for returning calls demonstrates their attention to confidentiality. According to the OWB, they "do not leave return messages" to callers that do not "clearly and fully" identify themselves on their own voicemail system. This, according to the OWB, is done to "protect the identity of whistleblowers" (SEC, 2015, p. 8). In this instance, OWB will attempt to return their call twice thereafter (making three return calls, in total) to make the best effort to reach the tipster. Overall, via the hotline, callers reportedly ask the OWB questions about submitting their tip, ask about confidentiality concerns, and request status updates on complaints received (SEC, 2015, p. 8).

Although the SEC hotline is considered to be a well-functioning hotline, there were a few shortcomings noted in the Office of Inspector General (OIG) Evaluation of the SEC's Whistleblower Program conducted in 2013. One area of improvement they identified was an absence of performance metrics (p. 18). The OIG noted the SEC hotline "did not have a performance metric for the maximum length of time staff should respond to applications for awards filed by whistleblowers." In one case, a letter of acknowledgement was sent to a tipster 122 days after the application was submitted. There can be consequences for delayed notification. If the application was deemed deficient, the acknowledgment would have been received by the tipster well after their award application deadline, which is 90 days (p. 21). As a result, the OIG recommended sending a letter of acknowledgement within 30 days and developing metrics to track this event.

Cost

Cost is an important consideration when establishing a fraud hotline. Cost can vary and will depend on the unique considerations of each organization. It is important to conduct a cost-benefit analysis and determine the solution that is appropriate for your business.

When calculating costs, it is important to consider the potential savings the hotline may provide. For instance, the Federal Deposit Insurance Corporation (FDIC) advises banks they should "recognize that they may initially incur start-up costs; however, once the hotline has been established, the savings in loss prevention should outweigh the cost" (FDIC, 2005). Organizations need to consider their budget, staffing, and the expected volume of calls to the hotline.

The costs of operating a hotline will include a case management system, experienced interviewers, investigation (of tips received), a secure e-mail system, private space to operate the hotline, staff, a toll-free telephone line, and training costs.

According to one expert, the cost breakdown can look something like this: Hotline Operator: = $50,000, Overhead: +25% = $60,000 + telephone line, training, investigations. So for a company with 1,000 employees, with 12–20 hotline calls per year, the expected cost could be over $3,000 per call. For a company with 10,000 employees, with 120–180 calls per year, the cost per call would be around $300 per call (Kusserow, 2012, pp. 3–4). These estimates will give you a rough idea of what you can expect your hotline to cost.

However, it is possible to establish a hotline rather inexpensively. The city of Palm Desert, California, recently announced their new "ethics hotline" will cost their city under $1,500 per year (Barkas, 2016). This is a bargain considering they are using a third-party provider (The Network). A fiscal analysis included in a May 12, 2016, City of Palm Desert Staff Report, says the "cost is dependent on the volume of reports, based on information provided by other Cities, staff anticipates the cost to be less than $1,500 annually" (Carney, 2016). The city's human resource manager said the decision to use an outside provider was based on industry benchmarking, finding "Most cities I contacted used the third party to collect information and based on what is received, they forward it to the appropriate person, and that is the model we will be using" (Barkas, 2016).

The case of the city of Palm Desert's hotline suggests that there are affordable options for those organizations that may have thought a third-party hotline would otherwise be too expensive.

Another city hotline, established for the city of Santa Fe, New Mexico, comes in at a slightly higher price point. Their 24-hour hotline, established in March 2015, cost $5,950, "including website development" with an "annual renewal fee" of $4,425 (Chacón, 2017). Their hotline is operated by third-party provider EthicsPoint.

While this hotline costs a little more than Palm Desert's hotline, it has been reasonably active, receiving 42 tips since it launched. They have also reported receiving actionable information. One such case involves a city worker, who a tip revealed was selling city-owned scrap metal and keeping the money (Chacón, 2017). However, the efficacy of the hotline has been called into question, because of the time it is taking to investigate the tips received. For instance, the case in question—employee scrap metal sales—has been pending for 18 months. Why? According to the city's internal auditor, the delay is due to competing priorities and a general lack of resources (Chacón, 2017).

As discussed earlier, hotline investigations are the responsibility of the subject company—regardless of whether the hotline is operated internally or externally. As such, in this case, the tips were reported back to the city of Santa Fe, in the form of a report. Once received, it was up to them to take the next steps. Here, that presented several organizational challenges. The agency receiving the tips, audit, with only one employee, lacked the resources to conduct investigations. The investigation also involved partnering with several additional agencies, including human resources and legal, which was a first for their office (Chacón, 2017).

It is unclear whether internal costs, and related logistical factors, were considered before the hotline became operational. But in a news story announcing their hotline, in March 2015, the reporting dynamic is recognized with the statement "you [city employees] are encouraged to report using the EthicsPoint reporting system. The City Auditor will review and investigate all legitimate reports" (Chacón, 2015). Incidentally, it was reported the city auditor requested an additional employee to assist with the workload, but that request was denied (Chacón, 2017).

Their experience serves as an example for any organization considering adopting their own hotline. The take-away here is the investigation of hotline tips should be factored into the overall cost of the hotline.

Nevertheless, in these two examples, the cost for the third-party hotline services for Palm Desert and Santa Fe were different. This is because third-party hotline service pricing varies. There are several different packages of services that can be selected at various price points. Some providers charge by "report" and have a minimum number of "reports" that will be charged per month regardless of the number of actual tipsters. Yet others may have a flat fee arrangement. In 2012, a representative from the Network (since acquired by NAVEX Global) reported their costs were $40–$60 per report, with translation services costing an extra fee. Today, this number is expected to be even higher, due to inflation.

Overall, they advised their clients could expect to pay between $30,000 and $100,000 per year with a minimum cost of $1,000 permitted annually. It sounds like the City of Palm Desert was one lucky city that is able to take advantage of the option at the lower end of the spectrum. However, the internal costs they may have incurred are a separate matter.

Name

The name of the hotline is very important. The hotline name can dictate the overall tone and spirit of the hotline. It can also facilitate or hinder reporting. Today, hotline creators are free to choose any name. There are currently no directives, mandates, or standards for how hotlines are named. Due to the absence of standards, hotline names can vary widely. Thus, there are several schools of thought on how to name a hotline. This section provides some different perspectives on naming hotlines, provides the common names in use today, and discusses how any hotline can be designed to better receive tips, regardless of the name.

There are many hotline names currently in use, and many suggestions regarding the "best" names to use. Today, popular hotline names include Fraud Hotline, Speak-Up Line, Business Ethics Line, Compliance Line, and Integrity Line.

In that sample set, it was noted that of those names, "fraud hotline" tends to be used more often in government/public sector/academic organizations, and softer terms such as "Speak-Up Line" tend to be used in private sector organizations. Other names for fraud hotlines include "Ethics Line," "Team Member Tip Line," and "Whistleblower Hotline."

However, this is not to say that private sector organizations don't use the name "fraud hotline." Peet's Coffee & Tea, a San Francisco coffee roaster and retailer, uses this name for their hotline.

Another popular name is "whistleblower hotline." This name has both positive and negative aspects. While that is a straightforward term for a tip line, which is highly recognizable, some experts say that using names such as this can backfire. For instance, Deloitte says "the word 'whistleblower' tends to have a negative connotation for most people and may evoke the feeling that the action of making a report to the system is an extreme act akin to hosting anti-establishment sentiments" (Deloitte, 2014, p. 9). They also find it may spark fears of retribution (Deloitte 2014, p. 9). Alternatively, they say the names "integrity hotline" or "ethics helpline" will cause an employee to feel like he or she is doing something desirable when calling the hotline (as opposed to being a "whistleblower") (Deloitte, 2014, p. 9).

Another common name for a fraud hotline is, "fraud hotline." Like "whistleblower hotline" it is straightforward, and the name suggests the intended purpose. However, today, some experts believe it is prudent to omit the word "fraud" from the hotline name, fearing it is too alarmist. However, others feel the name "fraud hotline" provides more clarity as to the intended purpose. Which is best? It is up to the organization to decide.

Some experts advise giving the hotline a name that is broad, to suggest the comprehensive nature of tips it endeavors to solicit. One reason for this is to remove potential psychological barriers to reporting. It is believed that if hotlines are given broad capabilities—for instance, to receive process improvement suggestions—that tipsters will be more likely to come forward (Libit et al., 2014). One example of this is the name "Speak-Up Line" (CGMA, 2015, p. 14). Several major organizations, including Pepsico and Toyota, use this name for their hotline today.

Table 3.1 depicts a sample of some popular hotline names and the organizations using these names today.

Selecting a name for a hotline can be very tricky, leaving one expert to say hotline "terminology is a problem" (Flesher, 1999). And this is why—the names

Table 3.1   Popular Hotline Names, and a Sample of Corresponding Organizations Using these Names Today

Hotline Name	Organization	Organization Type
Fraud Hotline	California Department of Social Services	State government agency
	City of Milwaukee	City government
	Government of the District of Columbia's Office of Tax and Revenue	Federal city office
	Hillsborough Community College (Tampa, FL)	Community college
	Maryland Governor's Office of Minority Affairs	State government agency
	New York City (NYC) Human Resources Administration	City government agency
	North Dakota State University	Public research university
	Peet's Coffee & Tea	Specialty coffee roaster and retailer
	South Carolina Department of Motor Vehicles	State government agency
	State University of New York (SUNY)	System of public institutions of higher education
	U.S. Social Security Administration	Federal government agency
	The U.S. Senate Special Committee on Aging	Senate committee
	U.S. General Services Administration OIG	Federal government agency
	University of Arkansas	Public land grant university

(Continued)

Table 3.1 *(Continued)* **Popular Hotline Names, and a Sample of Corresponding Organizations Using these Names Today**

Hotline Name	Organization	Organization Type
Speak-Up Line	Clarks	Shoe manufacturer and retailer
	Deloitte	UK incorporated professional services firm
	Lloyds Banking Group	British financial institution
	Merck & Co	American pharmaceutical company
	PepsiCo	Food, snack, beverage
	Roche Holding AG	Swiss multinational healthcare company
	Toyota	Japanese auto manufacturer
Business Ethics Line	Accenture	Global professional services company
	Colt	Firearms manufacturer
Compliance Line	Tenaris	Manufacturing company
	Genesis Healthcare Inc.	Healthcare company
	Johns Hopkins University	Private university
	Level 3 Communications	Telecommunications company
	Vizient	Health consultant
	SUNY Downstate Medical Center	Academic medical center
	Ericsson	Telecommunications equipment company
	Tecpetrol	Oil and gas company
	Elwyn Pharmacy Group	Specialty pharmacy
	Techint	Manufacturing company
	Mylan	Pharmaceuticals company
	Fujitsu	Information technology equipment and services company

(Continued)

Table 3.1 *(Continued)* **Popular Hotline Names, and a Sample of Corresponding Organizations Using these Names Today**

Hotline Name	Organization	Organization Type
Integrity Line	The Linde Group	German multinational chemical company
	T-Mobile	Mobile operator company
	Providence Health & Services	Healthcare company
	University of Notre Dame	Private research university
	Lululemon	Apparel company
	University of South Carolina	Public university
	Alcoa	Manufacturing company
	Securitas	Security company
	Morgan Stanley	Financial services company
	International Monetary Fund	International organization
	City of Scottsdale Arizona	City government
	Trinity Health	Healthcare company
Business Integrity Line	Marriott	Hospitality company
	McDonald's	Restaurant company
Whistleblower Hotline	NASDAQ	Stock exchange
	Federal Aviation Administration	Federal government agency
	University of South Alabama	Public research university
Other		
Compliance and Fraud Hotline	Duke University	Private research university
Team Member Tipline	Whole Foods Market	Supermarket chain
Enterprise-Wide Hotline	Purdue University	Public research university

that are the best for a hotline in terms of communicating its purpose (fraud hotline, whistleblower line) can also be the most problematic due to their perceived negative connotations (Flesher, 1999). It is believed that employees may not provide tips if negative feelings are invoked in the process. Thus it has been suggested that employees might be more apt to provide tips if the hotline name invokes a positive response, such as "suggestion line" (Flesher, 1999). Certainly, if an employee perceives that calling to give a "suggestion" to the "suggestion line" is a positive act that he or she will consider doing for that reason alone, then the hotline purpose, which is to receive as many viable tips as possible, is satisfied. Whereas, if the same caller with the same information will decline to call a "whistleblower line" because that caller effectively perceives that calling that line brands him or her as a "whistleblower" and would be a negative thing, then this will result in fewer calls to a given hotline.

There are a few problems with this assumption. For one, it is unknown whether that is actually true. A study would have to be conducted to verify that fact. Another problem is that names such as "suggestion line" can instead confuse callers about the purpose of the hotline.

When naming a hotline, it is important for organizations to consider the potential ways that employees and other tipsters will "find" their hotline. Internet search terms are critical.

For instance, say you are an employee who witnesses fraud. What is your first thought? Are you thinking that you need to call the company to "give a suggestion?" Maybe. Perhaps more likely, you are thinking about reporting fraud. But how do you do that? Chances are, you will research internally, while at work, looking for the fraud, or whistleblower hotline—because those are terms that are more often associated with reporting fraud, waste, and abuse. If you "search" for that and instead "find" the "suggestion line" that instructs the employee to call if he or she knows about fraud, then that could result in a phone call. But if the organization's search engine was not designed to "return" a result for the alternate "searches," then this can result in the employee not "finding" the hotline and can result in that tip not being provided. That is exactly what hotlines do not want to happen. Hotlines should be designed to receive as many actionable tips as possible.

However, in the spirit of receiving as much employee "feedback" as possible, which is a current goal of many hotlines, a "suggestion line" might be a good choice. But employees who select names such as these should know that it will take more effort on their part to communicate the purpose to employees. Ultimately, it would take a lot of training on the part of the organization to make sure employees know that the "suggestion line" is intended to hear fraud tips, in addition to other information. Employers who select these names are also relying on the assumption that all employees diligently listen to that training and will retain the information when they witness key events. That could be a dangerous assumption.

Also, other key tipsters, such as vendors and customers, may not know the name of the hotline, because the name is not self-evident and they have not attended the organization's training. In this case, vendors, customers, and so on, may search your external-facing website looking for a way to report fraud. Will they search for the term "suggestion line?" Likely not. In this case, it is important to make sure external-facing websites also return the "suggestion line" when other, more straightforward terms such as "whistleblower line" and "fraud hotline" are searched on the Internet, along with the company name.

Overall, when thinking about hotline names, it is wise to consider the target audience. What might they expect the hotline to be named? If they did an Internet search, would they be able to find your hotline? This is a pivotal issue, as many people who contact hotlines are doing so from home/outside the organization. A customer may not be familiar with the nomenclature used by a given organization because they do not have access to their internal website or literature. What might they search to find it? It may not be "Speak-Up Line." If that is the case, will a search for terms such as "fraud hotline" also yield the same result? A test of some major hotlines demonstrated it didn't. (This issue will be discussed in more detail in the case studies in Chapter 6.)

It was noted that many organizations, including financial firms, were not using the term "hotline" in their hotline name and do not use it in their hotline literature. That was an interesting finding, because anecdotally, it is said that regulators may prefer a name with the word "hotline" in it, as it denotes a sense of urgency (Hotlines, 2012). However, it is believed these organizations might prefer the "positive" connotation of names such as "Integrity Line." But are those names the best in terms of receiving the greatest number of actionable tips? Perhaps, but it is up to the company to analyze and benchmark their own hotline, to determine whether the call volume suggests its hotline is well utilized.

It was also noted that other organizations didn't use the word "hotline" their policy documents. In a review of several business materials available on the Internet, it was noted the word "hotline" was never used. Examples include McDonald's "Standards of Business Conduct"; Colt's "Code of Business Conduct," and Whole Foods Market's "Code of Business Conduct." When searching these documents, the word "hotline" didn't yield any results. This means a potential caller would have to search the page for the word "Line" instead. This seems like an unlikely search term for many potential callers to use.

Again, while positive connotations might be important for some organizations, overall, the intended purpose of a given hotline is to receive anonymous tips. If tipsters cannot "find" the hotline, the hotline will receive less tips, period.

The best way to prevent this issue from happening is to proactively research the hotline name to assess its utility as a conduit to receiving tips. One way to do this is to pretend you are a potential caller and actively "search" for the hotline. When conducting these searches, one will have to assume the name is unknown to the potential caller. Under these conditions, if a search for your hotline doesn't come up with a Google and website search, then that is a problematic issue. It doesn't mean that you have to change the name of your hotline. But it means that additional information technology fixes will be necessary to make your hotline better located via the web using various terminology.

To this end, when considering hotline keywords, it is best to allow for multiple ways of typing the same word for the best results. People do not always use search terms in the same way. As a case in point, at Whole Foods, their hotline is called the "Team Member *Tipline*." A Google search for "Team Member *Tip Line*" as well as "Whole Foods *Hotline*" would ideally yield the same result. However, the later search did not. Yet for Purdue University, a search for the terms "Whistleblower Hotline" returned their hotline page, even though that is not the name of their hotline (it's "Enterprise-Wide Hotline"), which is ideal.

Despite good intentions, sometimes a chosen hotline name can be unwise from a marketing perspective. For instance, the San Jose hotline launched July 2005. It was initially named the "Fraud and Audit Hotline" but was later changed due to user confusion (Barkas, 2016). Today, it is called the "Whistleblower Hotline" (San Jose California, n.d.).

Anonymity

For a hotline caller, the ability to remain anonymous is critical. Research demonstrates employees are more likely to report wrongdoing when they are given the option to remain anonymous, and have their report kept confidential (Libit et al., 2014). To facilitate open communication, hotlines should allow for tipsters to remain completely anonymous, whenever possible. Organizations are advised to contact legal counsel regarding privacy and whistleblower provisions (FDIC, 2005).

There are many ways that hotlines can be fully confidential. They can offer technology that will mask the identity of the caller/e-mailer. Otherwise, the organization can instruct a user on how to remain anonymous. One company that does this is Peet's Coffee & Tea. On its Fraud Hotline website, it offers ways to remain anonymous:

> The above internet address will access an Internet-based message interface that will deliver a message directly to the Chairperson of the Audit Committee. Be advised that to use this system with complete anonymity, you should send this message from an unidentifiable location such as a public library terminal.

Another organization, Prince George's County (Maryland) Crime Solvers, does something similar, telling tipsters:

> When you call the toll-free tip hotline, you will not be asked for your name, where you live, or how you got the tip. The call center does not have caller ID or electronic recording devices. You will be given a

confidential "tip number" that corresponds to the crime being reported. Your confidential "tip number" is what you will use when checking on the status of your tip or picking up your reward.

Some organizations are unable to guarantee anonymity. In this case, they will often communicate that to potential tipsters, who can decide whether or not to report, based on that information. The U.S. Pacific Fleet (U.S. Navy) Inspector General, for instance, tells potential tipsters, "You may request confidentiality, and the IG will make every effort to prevent disclosure of your identity, but we cannot guarantee confidentially."

While organizations welcome all tips, it is common to remind callers their anonymity might impede the investigation. On the U.S. Social Security Administration hotline website, callers are instructed: "You may remain anonymous, but please keep in mind that your decision for anonymity may limit our ability to conduct a complete investigation." This is because anonymous tips do not have the same clearance rate as when the caller is identified.

Overall, most callers to hotlines remain anonymous. However, in the last several years, there was a trend toward hotline callers identifying themselves, rather than remaining anonymous. This trend is likely attributed to the SEC Whistleblower program. In the financial industry, hotline callers may leave their name to ensure they receive a potential SEC whistleblower payout. It is also speculated that tipsters may want to identify themselves to protect against potential retaliation (NAVEX Global, 2015, p. 13; Penman & O'Mara 2015, p. 13).

The potential for retaliation is a serious concern for hotlines. Employees are protected against retaliation under SOX and Dodd–Frank, and those protections have been extended to apply to private citizens Nevertheless, employees have reported being subject to retaliation. Also, the mere perception that retaliation may occur can significantly deter hotline reporting (Walker, 2014, p. 23). As a result, it is important employees trust their organization and its hotline. That's because experts say when "trust is high and perceptions of management and peers are more positive, retaliation is far less prevalent" (Walker, 2014, p. 23).

Fear of retaliation is one of the reasons employees may choose to remain anonymous. And their fear is valid. According to one study of 380 cases of state-level whistleblowers who filed lawsuits against their employers, 74% of them were terminated after submitting a hotline tip. And most of these whistleblowers lost their subsequent lawsuits against their employers (Patrick, 2010).

It is difficult to know the true number of employees who experience retaliation, because many of them may not report it. But from those who do report, we can get an idea of what may happen. One such case was Bill Bado, a former Wells Fargo employee, who said he was fired after calling his whistleblower hotline (Egan, September 21, 2016).

Bado's report came in the wake of an ethics scandal that rocked Wells Fargo in 2016. The financial services company was fined $100 million in penalties by the

Consumer Financial Protection Bureau (CFPB) for the "widespread, illegal practice of secretly opening unauthorized deposit and credit card accounts. Spurred by sales targets and compensation incentives, employees boosted sales figures by covertly opening accounts and funding them by transferring funds from consumers' authorized accounts without their knowledge or consent, often racking up fees or other charges. According to the bank's own analysis, employees opened more than two million deposit and credit card accounts that may not have been authorized by consumers" (CFPB, 2016).

Following the scandal, Wells Fargo fired thousands of employees who they said were responsible for the illegal acts (Egan, September 9, 2016).

Bado, however, didn't participate in the fraud. Instead, he refused to open the fake accounts, and he reported the practice to Wells Fargo's Ethics Hotline. He also sent an e-mail to Well Fargo's Human Resources Department (HR), in September 2013, documenting the fraud (which was obtained by CNN). Eight days after sending the e-mail, he was terminated due to "tardiness" (Egan, September 21, 2016).

Perhaps this was a coincidence? Not according to one human resources employee at Wells Fargo. This employee told CNN that hotline callers were fired "in retaliation for shining light" on sales issues (Egan, September 21, 2016). The employee described situations where "targeted" employees were monitored "to find a fault" and then terminated the hotline-calling employee (Egan, September 21, 2016). This is the situation that Bado believed happened to him.

It should be noted that under SOX and Dodd–Frank, organizations are prohibited from retaliating against whistleblowers. Organizations will typically state their commitment against retaliation of hotline callers in their hotline literature to reassure employees. Hotline callers who believe they have been retaliated against following their call, such as Bado, can pursue legal action against the organization.

In response to Bado's claims, Wells Fargo said "We do not tolerate retaliation against team members who report their concerns in good faith." Their spokeswoman also said that "employees are encouraged to immediately report unethical behavior to their manager, HR representative or 24-hour ethics line" (Egan, September 21, 2016).

This statement, insofar as it urges employees to contact the manager and HR before considering the hotline is standard practice for many organizations. The story of Bill Bado illustrates why employees may not want to report known fraud first to their manager, before contacting the hotline, as organizations often urge them to do. (This issue is addressed in more detail later in this chapter.) Bado sent an e-mail to HR and was fired 8 days later. As such, he found these events to be related. Perhaps if he had not contacted HR, and only reported anonymously to the hotline, he would have been less suspicious of his firing as being related to his complaint.

Wells Fargo's statement also mentioned "good faith." Many organizations will advise users they should be reporting in "good faith." This is done in an attempt to dissuade any potential false complaints. Another example of this is found on

T-Mobile's "Integrity Hotline" page, wherein they say, "There will be no retaliation against anyone who in good faith reports a concern." This language reserves the right of the organization to take action against an employee who might intentionally provide a false report.

Why would someone submit a false report? Typically, this would be done to get someone in trouble. One industry that is reportedly experiencing this issue is academia. Rob Jenkins, an Associate Professor at Georgia State University Perimeter College who spent 30 years in higher education as a faculty member and administrator, finds "at some institutions, the mere existence of such a resource [fraud hotline] creates a kind of third-grade-on-steroids mentality, in which certain faculty members repeatedly report their colleagues—anonymously, of course—for alleged and generally unsubstantiated allegations violations. For them, the hotline is little more than a convenient way to harass people they don't like, discredit political opponents, and settle old scores" (Jenkins, 2014). It is important to note that Jenkins himself was the subject of what he says are "anonymous accusations" and has also contacted a fraud hotline in the past (with a favorable result) although he gave his name (Jenkins, 2014).

Under certain conditions, people who fail to report can also be sanctioned. The Department of Children and Families (DCF) advises the public that under certain conditions, a "failure to report could result in fines, which range from $500 to $2,500 and the individual will be required to participate in an educational and training program."

So what can be done about false reporting? In his article "The Problem with Ethics Hotlines" Jenkins says that one way is to impose "severe penalties for those found to be abusing the ethics hotline by making repeated false complaints" (2014).

There are no concrete data available on the phenomenon of false hotline reporting. However, it is believed to be more problematic in certain organizations, over others. This can sometimes be reflected in their false reporting penalties, for instance, government organizations that receive hotline reports about child abuse. One such organization is the Connecticut Department of Children and Families (DCF). They advise potential callers of their "Careline" that "Anyone who knowingly makes a false report of child abuse or neglect shall be fined up to $2000 or imprisoned for not more than one year, or both. The identity of any such person shall be disclosed to the appropriate law enforcement agency and to the perpetrator of the alleged abuse." Similarly, according to the Missouri Department of Social Services, the "Intentional false reporting of child abuse or neglect to the hotline is a class A misdemeanor and if a person has a previous conviction for false reporting… it is a class D felony" (Child Welfare Manual, 2012).

Evidence suggests officials have indeed imposed these penalties against false complainants. In one such case, in August, a Brevard County, Florida, woman was arrested for filing a false report of child abuse and stalking. She was held on $10,500 bond (Space Coast Daily). In yet another case, a Lake Luzerne, New York, man was arrested in September 2016 after making a false hotline report of child abuse. Reportedly, he made this complaint against an acquaintance in retaliation for comments she made on her Facebook page (The Post Star).

Although some organizations may not prefer anonymous tipsters, recent data show the number of people electing to remain anonymous is decreasing. In 2014, NAVEX Global found their percentage of anonymous callers decreased from 64% in 2010 (the year Dodd–Frank was enacted) to 61% in 2014.

Despite knowing most tipsters chose to remain anonymous, hotlines may still pressure callers to provide names. One reason is because callers who identify themselves have a higher rate of substantiated complaints (Penman & O'Mara, 2015 NAVEXGlobal. 2015, p. 17). Callers who remain completely anonymous cannot be contacted for follow-up questions. The inability to communicate with tipsters can lead to less successful outcomes. In 2014, NAVEX Global reported that callers who identify themselves have a 45% substantiation rate, as opposed to 36% for anonymous callers.

Nevertheless, this data suggests us that over one third of anonymous complaints are valid. This tells us that business leaders are wise to encourage all complaints—anonymous or not.

As a case in point, this author recently called a fraud hotline at FedEx to make an anonymous report about an employee. As discussed in this work, hotlines today are welcoming a wide breadth of feedback, to include process improvement suggestions. For this reason, and in the interest of research, I thought this would be a good opportunity to inform the company of a customer service issue while also testing the effectiveness of a major fraud hotline.

The employee in question worked at a small FedEx location in New York City. She was observed by the author randomly closing the store during busy hours. She was also observed taking "smoke breaks" immediately outside the store, and "yelling" at customers who entered the store and "interrupted" her while she was taking one of these breaks. I personally was unable to ship many packages due to random closures and employee intimidation, and I knew they were losing business. Thus I determined this behavior merited a call to their hotline.

I was confident to call the hotline, based on what I observed. Yet I didn't want to give my name. I was a "regular" at this location and feared retaliation by this employee, if she knew I reported her behavior. She had "yelled" at me more than once in the past, so I knew she was confrontational. And I didn't want to risk getting hurt while trying to do the right thing by the company. This is the same dilemma experienced by many hotline callers.

But before I talk about the hotline call, I will provide some examples of the behavior I observed. During one trip to this FedEx location, I observed a fairly long line of potential customers, waiting at the store's entrance. The line was suspicious, because the store was large enough to accommodate many customers. Upon arriving at the store entrance, I immediately realized the reason for the line. Affixed to the front door was a "back in 5 mins" sign. The customers were literally waiting outside for the opportunity to mail their packages. This seemed very inappropriate for a FedEx store, whose customers have urgent shipping needs—including this author, who had several packages in hand.

During yet another trip to this location, a customer holding several boxes was seen walking up to the store. He was noticeable, because he was struggling to balance the packages during his approach to FedEx's front door. He had finally made it, when I noticed the FedEx employee post the infamous "back in 5 min" sign and walk away! As she stepped away, she passed this potential customer. I thought for certain she would return back to the store to help this gentleman, who was clearly struggling. To my surprise, instead she said "hey, were you going to send those packages with me?" He replied "Yes." Her: "OK, well you are going to have to wait. I'm on break and will be back in 5." Him: "OH, ok." This exchange proved to me that this situation was worse than I originally thought. I thought for sure she would at least take pity on this man who really needed help, although it was her job to help him, regardless.

Meanwhile, during each of these exchanges observed, this author had her own packages in hand, and had to inconveniently send them using another service. Based on these personal experiences alone, I knew FedEx was losing money due to this employee. Naturally, I was curious to know if these "breaks" were authorized by the company. Perhaps some of the breaks were necessary, and she was not provided with someone to assist in her absence.

In the interest of research, and general curiosity, this author called the FedEx fraud hotline. Giving this employee the benefit of the doubt, I first asked the hotline operator if smoke breaks and random store closures were permitted at the location in question, to which the operator replied "absolutely not." Thus in this instance, the store closures were a form of fraud, waste and abuse. The hotline operator seemed very eager to take the complaint, which was constructive and focused on the potential business loss by FedEx at the hands of this employee, due to random closures, poor treatment of customers, and so on.

Despite their interest in this matter, it was a challenge to log this complaint. The woman who took my call didn't seem well trained or experienced in hotline operations. I could tell due to the absence of key questions. For instance, I was not asked when any of these events took place. Also, throughout the conversation, I was placed on very long holds. This is not optimal, because these "holds" inhibit the free sharing of information. They also give the caller an opportunity to "rethink" their call and hang up. I know, because I wanted to end the call several times, during these unnecessary waiting periods.

Finally, the operator returned to the call and thanked me for my report. Next, she asked me for my name. Now, this is perfectly acceptable, and in fact, an advisable practice. Ideally, hotline callers will give their names and telephone numbers, to allow for follow-up questions. As discussed earlier, identified callers result in a greater instance of substantiated reports. A question such as "would you like to give your name" is recommended and appropriate.

However, in this case, I knew I was not going to give my name. I had sent several packages from this FedEx (when I was lucky enough to find the store open!) and my name, address, and phone number were in their system. I was afraid that she would find out that I complained, and retaliate against me—a very realistic fear for any whistleblower.

Yet this hotline operator would not allow me to remain anonymous! When I refused to give my name, and expressed my strong interest in remaining anonymous, she argued with me for quite some time. She told me the report "needed a name" and I was simply unable to remain anonymous. Well, you can probably guess what happened next. Yes, I gave a name—but it was certainly not my "real" name.

There are some important lessons to be learned from this hotline exchange. First, ideally, callers would not be put on hold under most circumstances. The caller could lose their train of thought, or lose their nerve, and simply hang up. Next, callers should be asked, but not "forced" to provide a name. The outcome is a withdrawn complaint or a fake name.

It is important to note there are ways to maintain anonymity for callers who don't want to provide their name. One method is to provide a tracking, or "complaint" number for callers. Callers are provided with a unique ID number that they can use to identify themselves during repeat calls. Callers can also use this number to track the status of their complaint—similar to a FedEx tracking number.

Some organizations also instruct hotline users on how to remain anonymous. On their Whistleblower Hotline website, the University of South Alabama gives potential complainants a couple of ideas: "You can call from a number other than your own or use an anonymous e-mail account to hide your identity. You may also mail your concerns anonymously."

Despite the shortcomings in this case, there may have been a positive outcome. During this author's last (and final) visit to this FedEx location, the subject employee said she was "getting a helper." As it turns out, the company was suddenly providing a second employee—perhaps to relieve this one so that she could take breaks. Alternatively, they may have been hiring her replacement. Either way, this new addition suggested to me that perhaps the hotline call was not made in vain.

Finally, when talking about anonymity in hotlines, it is important to note that full anonymity may at times be impossible. Another related issue for all hotlines is the inability to remain anonymous due to the nature of the corporate reporting structure. For instance, a department experiencing fraud may only have a handful of employees. Similarly, a particular functional area of an organization may only have a small number of workers who handle that particular area that is subject of the fraud report. Should a complaint come through the hotline, although it's anonymous, it may be obvious as to who made it.

It should be noted that companies will often have policies in place to prevent retaliation against employees who call their hotlines. Wells Fargo had such a policy. The employees who claimed they were retaliated against for calling the hotline can seek legal remedies, based on that policy.

To maintain anonymity and confidentiality, it is important for any information about an internal investigation to be shared on a very limited "need to know" basis (Singh, 2015).

Accessibility

Hotlines have to be accessible to all potential tipsters in order to receive the most information. Ideally, hotlines will offer several reporting options to their potential audience. Some tipsters might prefer calling, while others may prefer to submit a tip via the web. Callers may also have "evidence' to share, and would prefer to fax that information. A tipster may also prefer to fax a handwritten tip, or send it by regular mail.

For this reason, many hotlines, especially those operated by third parties, tend to allow multiple avenues of reporting. The public is usually provided with a toll-free telephone number, fax number, e-mail address, and webform. Of all these methods, for hotline providers, phone calls are the preferred avenue of reporting. Why? Telephone reporting provides the opportunity to have a dialogue with the caller. Ultimately, more overall information is gleaned via this method. It is also the most often used method (ACFE, 2016, p. 28). The use of online reporting methods is growing in popularity. Today, more than half of all tipsters reported their tips via an electronic method (Email, 34.1%; Webform, 23.5%; ACFE 2016).

It is recommended that hotlines be available 24 hours a day, 365 days a year (Libit et al., 2014). If the organization is global, then this is a necessity (Andrews & Leblanc, 2013). Also, ideally, hotlines should provide multilingual capabilities to allow for all possible callers to communicate their tips (Andrews & Leblanc, 2013). It is advised for hotlines to include English and Spanish language capabilities, as these are the most common first languages for U.S. residents (Andrews & Leblanc, 2013). For a global company, additional languages will likely be required. Third-party hotline providers offer such expanded options. For instance, hotline provider NAVEX Global offers interpretation support for over 200 languages.

It is critical for hotline reporting information to be available both internally (accessible to employees/contractors) and externally (accessible to anyone, including employees). Employees often contact hotlines outside of business hours. Employees often feel more comfortable to submit a tip outside of the office/after normal business hours, to further ensure anonymity (Libit et al., 2014). As a result, they should be able to access their employer's hotline from their external (public) website.

Information about a given hotline (telephone number, webform, etc.) should be easily accessed/located by any potential tipster. If an organization is unsure whether their hotline is readily known/available, it is recommended to conduct an internal (internal website) and external (corporate website) search.

So how do you ensure you are reaching your target audience? One sure way is to "test" the success of the advertisement by pretending to be a potential tipster and trying to "find" the hotline. Searches for relevant terms (i.e., fraud hotline, ethics hotline, report fraud) on both the internal and external websites should return information about the hotline and the telephone number and links to additional reporting methods.

Several hotlines examined in this work were found to be deficient in this regard. Multiple searches both internally and externally failed to yield important hotline information. The information should be very easily accessible, as tipsters are likely to change their mind about reporting fraud, if the search for the reporting mechanism itself requires too much effort.

For some organizations, the audience for the hotline is vast. In this case, wide accessibility is key. This is especially important for federal organizations, where many citizens may know about fraud, waste, and abuse in federal programs. External advertisement will increase the visibility of the hotline to all members of the public. This is an area that is often overlooked. In 1989, the General Accounting Office (now the Government Accountability Office) conducted an evaluation of 25 federal hotlines and found that the telephone numbers were not always accessible. They also found that during "test calls" to the general agency telephone number, the operator was unable to provide the caller with the hotline number when asked.

Advertisement

Hotline advertisement is critical to its success. All potential tipsters, to include internal (employees, contractors) and external parties (vendors, customers, consultants), have to be aware and informed of the hotline's existence, in order for it to receive tips. Thus the awareness of the hotline by these parties is considered an important component in ensuring its effectiveness (FDIC, 2005). A hotline that doesn't receive tips is not indicative of an absence of fraud. Instead, a hotline with few calls/reports should be examined to determine whether it is being properly advertised.

Savvy hotline administrators are keenly aware of the importance of hotline advertisement. As a case in point, one major financial institution's hotline examined as part of this work was found to receive very few tips. When asked, the hotline administrator immediately blamed the lack of advertisement, and announced plans to increase it.

The SEC knows the value of hotline advertisement. Their Office of the Whistleblower (OWB) conducts outreach to increase awareness of their program. In their 2015 Report, the OWB discussed participating in "over 20 public engagements aimed at promoting and educating the public concerning [their] program" (SEC, p. 8).

Why is it so important to advertise your hotline? Employees have been known to keep fraud to themselves, because they didn't know how to report it. According to the ACFE, employees who have failed to report fraud did so because they were unaware of the existence of a confidential reporting mechanism (2004–2008). That trend has continued to present day. In their 2016 report, the ACFE said "organizations that effectively promote reporting mechanisms actively cultivate [employee] tips" (p. 25).

Advertisement efforts should also extend to nonemployees. The ACFE reported that 40% of tips received in their study came from this group, most notably customers (17.8%) and vendors (9.9%) (2016, p. 26).

Thus, it is imperative to consider the hotline's intended audience and make sure each member is informed. Each organization will have specific audiences and methods of communication, and external parties should also be considered. For example, the Federal Deposit Insurance Corporation (FDIC) offers guidelines that suggest "advertis[ing] and market[ing] the hotline's existence to employers, suppliers, third-party service providers and customers. Suggested channels are bank newsletters, memoranda, written policy, and internal and external bank Web sites" (2005).

But successful hotline advertisement goes beyond website reporting. Additional methods should be employed to ensure potential user awareness. Third-party hotline provider Ethical Advocate provides the following tips for hotline promotion:

- Create a hotline message and a logo, consistent with the organization culture.
- Discuss the hotline's history, purpose, and effectiveness during employee onboarding and ongoing training, and include mention in training materials.
- Include the hotline logo, phone number, and URL on the back of business cards.
- Forward hotline information to company personnel.
- Schedule the CEO and other leaders to promote the hotline.
- Give employees items bearing the hotline contact information such as pens and refrigerator magnets.
- Offer interactive games, puzzles, and contests throughout the year regarding the hotline.
- Broaden the scope of the hotline and include the ability to report process improvement and cost savings suggestions.

Some compliance experts say that hotline advertisement/communications should have a positive message to "help alleviate psychological barriers that prevent or discourage tipsters from using the hotline" (Libit et al., 2014). To this end, it is recommended to use the words "accountability, transparency and responsibility" as opposed to "fraud, corruption, embezzlement, bribery and crime" (Libit et al., 2014).

While hotline functionality is critical, tipsters need to come forward in order for the hotline to be effective. It's imperative that tipsters feel confident in their decision to contact the hotline. To this end, trust is critical. Tipsters need to trust both the employer and the hotline in order to call. There are several ways this trust can be achieved.

Scandinavian Telecommunications Company TeliaSonera fosters trust in their Speak-Up Line with organizational transparency. Their Chief Ethics and Compliance Officer Michaela Ahlberg addressed this issue in the following statement: "We realize that providing the Speak-Up Line is not enough on its own, employees and stakeholders need to trust the system to submit the report. We are continuously raising awareness and are transparent in our communication to maintain the highest level of trust in the organization" (2015). To this end, research demonstrates that advertising hotline results can give employees confidence in the value of their tips.

Effective advertisement of the hotline may persuade employees to report known misconduct. Today, many employees aware of wrongdoing in their organizations are not reporting it. The Institute of Business Ethics (IBE) recently asked 3,000 employees in Continental Europe about their awareness of misconduct in their respective workplaces and whether they reported it. Their responses are illustrated in Table 3.2 from their 2015 Ethics at Work Survey (Johnson, 2015, p. 16).

As seen below, a majority of respondents didn't believe their tip would result in meaningful action and thus decided not to report. Perhaps that is due to the low overall satisfaction rate with how tips are handled. According to the IBE, 39% of tipsters were satisfied with the outcome of their report to their employer's hotline (Johnson, 2015, p. 15). This figure is down from 2012, when 70% of tipsters reported being satisfied.

Table 3.2 The Institute of Business Ethics, 2015 Ethics at Work Survey

Location	Level of Awareness of Misconduct	Percentage Who Didn't Report	Most Common Reason Provided for Not Raising Concerns
Continental Europe	33%	54%	**I did not believe corrective action would be taken.**
France	30%	53%	I felt it was none of my business.
Germany	23%	49%	**I did not believe corrective action would be taken.**
Italy	32%	58%	**I did not believe corrective action would be taken.**
Spain	45%	54%	I felt I might jeopardize my job/I felt it was none of my business.

There are a number of reasons employees are dissatisfied. One major reason stems from a lack of communication. According to a 2016 survey by the Government Accountability Project (GAP) 23% of employees said they never heard from the organization following their tip (p. 17). An additional 27% reported being dissatisfied with their organization in some way, after contacting the hotline (p. 17). One respondent said "they eventually never acknowledged wrongdoing, instead, they did an investigation on me and eventually fired me" (p. 17).

Overall, the results of their survey clearly demonstrated employees are dissatisfied with the way their company handles their tips. In all, 95% of whistleblowers who reported internally said they were dissatisfied with the outcome of their tip, in that they didn't witness any good faith corrective action (GAP, 2016, p. 17). Perhaps if employees had more confidence in their organizations, they would not seek to report externally. The SEC program also offers cash incentives, and internal programs rarely offer such incentives.

This study suggests that employers can make changes to provide satisfaction to hotline callers. There are many ways to provide follow-up reports while maintaining confidentiality and preserving the employee's right to remain anonymous. One way would be to publicly advertise the hotline's corrective actions, using anonymous, general terms. The organizations can also notify tipsters individually, as to the status of their report. This can also be done with complete anonymity by using case numbers as identifiers and by using anonymized webforms and e-mail addresses.

Hotline advertisement methods can be informed by contemporary corporate culture. Today, many organizations are viewing their hotlines as a mechanism of employee engagement, rather than reactive, investigative tools. The recent convention of naming hotlines "Speak-Up Lines" is one example of this cultural shift. Hotlines, once viewed as a reactive means of receiving crime information, are now being viewed by some as an interactive, employee communication tool.

Experts say hotlines can serve as mechanisms to provide "clarification" regarding "standing instructions, policies, procedures, and the company standards of conduct" (Kusserow, 2012). This information is useful to the organization's interest in safeguarding against "discrimination, Occupational Safety and Health Administration (OSHA) matters, and wrongful discharge" (Kusserow, 2012).

As such, today, many organizations are inviting workers to "speak up and raise any concerns they may have" as part of a new "consultative and preventative approach" to hotline operation (Johnson, 2015, p. 20). The overall goal is to get tipsters comfortable with the idea of contacting the organization, and to report any concerns as part of "business as usual" (Johnson, 2015, p. 20).

While this is a valiant goal, many organizations, when advertising their hotlines, seem to send the opposite message and hinder reporting. One example of this can be seen in Lloyds Banking Group's "Code of Personal Responsibility" (2015). In this document, their "Speak-Up Line" is advertised. However, the means for contacting the hotline are not provided in the document. Instead it says to look on "Interchange" for the contact information (which is presumably their internal website). This is an unnecessary extra step, which can inhibit contact.

The hotline advertisement also contains a lot of reporting instructions, which actually seem to hinder reporting. In the case of Lloyds Banking Group, potential callers of the Speak-Up Line are first urged to contact their manager. And if that is not a viable option, they are urged to contact their manager's manager. And if that option is not feasible, then they are told—almost reluctantly—to contact the hotline.

The following statements in their Code of Personal Responsibility illustrate this dynamic:

1. Your first port of call should be your line manager (who is the person you report to on a day-to-day basis).
2. If you are unable or unwilling to speak to your line manager, you should speak to another senior leader in your business area, such as your line manager's manager.
3. We encourage you to raise concerns directly with your line management. However, if this isn't possible, please do not keep it to yourself—contact the Speak Up Line, or raise your concerns through HR Advice and Guidance. (Lloyds Banking Group, 2015.)

While this approach is not uncommon (see Case Studies in Chapter 6) from an employee's perspective, it could be considered a deterrent—especially if the tipster wants to report fraud. As seen in the case of Bill Bado, employees who report fraud to their manager risk potential retaliation. There are many reasons for this. One reason is that statistically speaking, they might be reporting fraud to someone committing the fraud who has an interest in keeping it quiet. Employees also fear retaliation, and speaking directly to a manager is not anonymous.

Organizational fraud is often perpetuated by managers. In fact, as much as 60% misconduct witnessed by employees involved individuals with some management authority and 24% involved senior management (Lighthouse, 2016, p. 2). Urging employees to tell management about concerns may dissuade them from reporting fraud being committed by these individuals.

For an employee who wishes to report a fraud or other serious issue involving a manager, there is little advantage for them to "see a manager" about their concerns. There is also an increased risk of retaliation against these individuals, insofar as they are reporting directly to a manager. They would have been anonymous if they had called the hotline.

Reporting can also be hindered by providing excessive instructions to employees. Using the same document as an example, employees are told the following:

Colleagues should read the guidance on when to call the Speak Up Line before making contact to ensure the report is made correctly.

Mandatory training is available to help colleagues understand what support is available. (Lloyds Banking Group, 2015)

Here, employees are urged to attend training, before the hotline. While that might be ideal, it is not very inviting.

In terms of hotline advertisement mechanisms, one effective vehicle is a poster. A hotline poster displayed in a prominent area is said to be a very effective means of advertisement. In fact, it has been reported that a majority of hotline callers became aware of their employer's hotline via a poster (Security Executive Council, 2007). Experts find the hotline poster "displayed in a high visibility locations through-out the facility...will serve as [a] constant reminder of its availability and help to reinforce the organization's ongoing commitment to creating an ethical culture" (Lighthouse, 2016, p. 10). This suggests that employees could benefit from a visual cue as a precursor to reporting fraud via a hotline. In Chapter 5, this work applies criminological theory to fraud hotlines to explain the apparent success of hotline posters as advertisement.

Hotline Rewards

The legislation enacted between 2002 and 2010 was based on the assumption that callers will use hotlines (2002), and that they are more likely to use them when offered reward money (2010). It is clear that lawmakers believed this legislation would prevent and detect future internal fraud. In fact, in their 2013 Annual Report to Congress, Sean X. McKessy, Chief of the SEC's Office of the Whistleblower (OWB), said the OWB "hope[ed] that award payments...will encourage individuals to come forward..." (SEC).

The question is, do hotline tipsters need incentives to report? Many experts promote the use of rewards to incentivize hotline callers. Some suggest offering cash rewards, or employment-related incentives, such as extra vacation days (Libit et al., 2014).

One expert, Erika Kelton, finds that awards are essential to getting high-quality information from tipsters, and should thus be mandatory. Her reasoning is as follows: "Twenty-five years of experience with whistleblower programs in the United States has shown that most whistleblowers with significant evidence of wrongdoing need the certainty of a reward commensurate with both the value of the information they provide and the amounts that are recovered by law enforcement as a result" (2012). Yet other experts say financial rewards are unnecessary, citing studies that have shown that a majority of whistleblowers have reported "for the genuine well being of the company" (Singh, 2015).

Despite recommendations, promoting incentives, the number of companies providing them is estimated to be quite low, approximately 10% (Libit et al., 2014). However, that figure appears to be steadily increasing. For instance, in 2010, the

ACFE found 7.4% of organizations they surveyed offered rewards to whistleblowers. In 2016, that number increased to 12% representing a 62% increase in 5 years.

The U.S. OWB offers financial rewards of 10%–30% of recoveries to tipsters. Other countries, such as Korea and Indonesia, also offer financial incentives to callers. In Korea, their law provides for awards to whistleblowers whose tips expose corruption and save them money or serve the public interest. For this, they can earn up to USD$2 million. Indonesia also provides "tokens of appreciation" for whistleblowers' corruption tips (OECD, 2012, p. 10).

The use of rewards as an incentive for prospective hotline callers is discussed in more detail in Chapter 7. There, the author discusses the feasibility of incentivizing potential tipsters in the financial industry with monetary rewards.

On a related note, when discussing rewards, it is also important to consider the possibility of imposing sanctions, for those employees with knowledge of criminal activity in their company which they *fail* to report. This issue was discussed within the context of the Volkswagen Emissions Scandal of 2015. One expert, Robert Merkel, speculated employees, specifically engineers, were likely aware of the fraud being perpetuated by Volkswagen and decided not to come forward due to potential job loss and an overall lack of incentives.

To support his position, Merkel cited the case of medical electronics engineer Salvador Castro, who was fired after alerting his employer, Air-Shields Inc., in Pennsylvania, about a design flaw in an infant incubator made by his company. In response to his "tip," Castro reports he was fired.

He had originally thought whistleblower protections would apply in his case, but he quickly learned they did not. While federal legislation exists to protect environmental whistleblowers, the U.S. Food and Drug Administration (FDA) does not offer the same protections to whistleblowers under its purview. Further, the "at-will" employment laws in Pennsylvania meant that Castro could be fired without cause (Kumagai, 2004). All of this happened despite the fact Castro's complaint was validated. The FDA eventually issued a recall of the incubator 4 years later and ordered them to fix the issue Castro identified. Castro has not really worked since this incident. Nevertheless, Castro says he does not regret reporting the issue to the company. He later won a public service award for blowing the whistle (Kumagai, 2004).

His case is indicative of a larger problem of whistleblowers suffering negative consequences for their actions. Experts have said it is "rare" for whistleblowers to expose wrongdoing and remain employed. Whistleblowers are also rarely successful in getting the exposed situation to change. As a result, these experts strongly advise potential whistleblowers to remain completely anonymous when submitting tips (Kumagai, 2004).

It is clear that certain employees lack appropriate incentives to report. Contrary, they are faced with job loss and risk being shunned by their community. While potential tipsters are instilled with fear, and cautioned to remain anonymous, it has also been suggested they should be sanctioned if they decide *not* to come forward. Per Merkel,

> It is time to look at the incentives for all engineers to disclose flawed systems that put the public at severe risk to the appropriate authorities (or to the media). Firstly, we need to find better ways to protect those whistleblowers who do come forward. But we should go further. We should seriously consider those who could, but do not, disclose dangerously flawed systems should, in some circumstances, face some kind of sanction. (2015)

It is clear that reform to protect those who come forward will be required, before potential tipsters can be sanctioned for not doing so.

Chapter 4

Performance, Assessment, and Best Practices

Hotlines need to perform optimally in order to receive quality tips. But how do you know whether it is performing, as it should? The best way is to conduct a performance assessment. A performance assessment will determine whether a given hotline is following best practices. It will also help determine whether a given hotline is catching known organizational fraud.

There are anecdotes that demonstrate hotlines are working to catch fraud. On March 27, 2015, Scandinavian telecommunications provider TeliaSonera reported tipsters to their "Speak-Up Line" disclosed 92 cases of suspected incidents involving "conflicts of interest, corruption, embezzlement, procurement fraud and HR matters." Hotlines must perform at their best in order to catch this fraud. As evinced below, performance issues can be easy to fix, once identified.

If you think your hotline may suffer from performance issues, you are not alone. There have been several reported incidents in recent years of malfunctioning hotlines. In one such case, the hotline wasn't answering its calls or e-mails. In January 2017, the *Irish Independent* reported the Central Bank's hotline was not operating properly. The hotline was established for financial services workers to report any suspicious activity. A worker e-mailed the hotline with a tip and didn't receive a response. A reporter for the *Irish Independent* later contacted the hotline repeatedly to verify its operation, and still no one answered the phone (Weston, 2017). When asked, a Central Bank spokesperson blamed the incidents on an "IT problem" and upon notification; they provided an alternate contact number (Weston, 2017).

In yet another case, in August 2016, Price George's Maryland County Government hotline made headlines saying it was "designed to protect tax dollars [yet] wastes tax dollars." Upon further examination, it was learned this hotline, operated by their Office of Ethics and Accountability (OEA) was not operating properly for at least 6 months. News team ABC 7, was contacted by a tipster, who then contacted the hotline directly, and received a message that said, "Thank you for calling the County of Prince George's MD. Are you calling to file a report? Unfortunately, we no longer take reports at this number." Upon review by ABC 7, the last report to the hotline had been received 6 months earlier. When ABC 7 contacted OEA to report the nonworking hotline number, OEA said it was unaware the hotline, operated by third-party provider NAVEX Global, was not working, nor did it notice the absence of reports received. OEA said it was paying $5,300 per year for the hotline. Now, the county's law office is investigating the "need for the hotline" and is seeking repayment for the time it was not operational (Papst, 2016). Needless to say, this negative press did not inspire confidence in the OEA or the hotline, and could have been avoided with simple, regular testing.

These cases provide useful "lessons learned" concerning hotline performance. At a very fundamental level, the hotline must be operational in order to receive tips. And that functionality cannot be assumed because one uses a third-party provider. The client/originating organization is always the responsible party in terms of making sure the hotline is operating properly.

Some performance issues, such as a nonworking telephone number, can be avoided with preemptive testing. Other performance indicators, such as a low volume of calls, might be harder to assess. How do I know if I am not receiving enough calls? How many calls should a hotline receive? How many calls are other hotlines receiving relative to mine?

Today, hotline performance can be difficult to evaluate, because there are no rules to follow and there is little data available for comparison. There are no universal regulations or reporting requirements for fraud hotlines. Although an anonymous reporting mechanism is required by law (SOX, Dodd–Frank), the fraud hotline process itself is not subject to any particular set of rules, regulations, or provisions.

This chapter provides a holistic assessment methodology, which is an innovative departure from current hotline benchmarking methods. Overall, this assessment methodology provides the framework through which hotline performance can be measured, in terms of its specifications, metrics, functionality, and extent of best practices implementation.

This chapter first provides some background on the issues of hotline performance, assessment, and best practices.

Benchmarking

One way to determine hotline performance is benchmarking. Most hotline assessment guidance today tends to focus on benchmarking metrics as a key performance indicator. Benchmarking involves both internal and external components. Most hotline assessment materials instruct organizations to look at their volume of calls over time (internal benchmarking) and to review volumes of calls against that of peer organizations (external benchmarking) (Penman, 2013).

Yet the factors that influence important hotline characteristics, such as call volume and type, cannot be easily determined via benchmarking. These factors include company and industry risk areas, workforce breakdown and staffing, how the reporting system is promoted, having multiple and alternate reporting channels available, geographic location, organizational culture, and economic climate (ACFE EthicsLine, 2013). A most robust internal benchmarking would be required to determine whether these factors are influencing call volume and quality. But are hotline administrators actually conducting these assessments?

It is likely that administrators are focusing on the statistics they are required to report. Survey respondents have said the most common item they report to boards and executive leadership is report volume (91%) (ACFE EthicsLine, 2013). Thus, unless call volume is low, it is unlikely that further analysis is conducted. The problem is that a healthy call volume, while a good sign, doesn't mean that the calls received are providing quality information to the company.

There are many categories of tips that are received by hotlines. Table 4.1 provides some common hotline tip categories. Sometimes, hotline administrators without fraud training are unaware that certain tips are indicative of fraud. As a result, these tips can be miscategorized as "human resources" or other matters.

For example, when asked by this author, one hotline administrator said she categorized employee complaints about coworkers seen at the office during "odd" hours as a "Workplace Issue/General HR" matter that didn't require any additional investigation. However, fraud experts know this behavior can

Table 4.1 Common Hotline Tip Categories

Accounting, Auditing, and Finance	*Financial Misconduct, Internal Controls, Expense Reporting*
Business integrity	Bribery, falsification of documents, fraud, conflict of interest
Workplace issues	Discrimination, harassment, compensation, general human resources
Health, safety, and environmental	U.S. Environmental Protection Agency (EPA) compliance, assault, safety, Occupational Safety and Health Administration (OSHA) reporting
Misuse/Misappropriation	Computer usage, employee theft, time clock abuse

Source: ACFE EthicsLine, Utilizing hotline benchmarking data to improve ethics and compliance program effectiveness, compiled by Nick Ciancio, 2013.

be exhibited by corporate fraudsters, who may enter the office outside normal business hours to perpetuate corporate crime. While this fact alone doesn't always indicate crime, it should be viewed as a potential indicator, and be appropriately investigated. The hotline administrator admitted she had never considered that to be a possibility.

Internal benchmarking entails reviewing internal company hotline data, and comparing that data over time. This review, combined with an external benchmarking, comparing company hotline data to that of other companies, is viewed today as a complete hotline performance assessment (Table 4.2). In order to conduct this type of hotline benchmarking, appropriate statistics must be tracked. If a hotline is managed internally, the performance will need to be tracked via a series of developed metrics, which will come from the case management system. If a hotline is managed externally, this information will have to be requested from the third-party hotline account manager (if not already provided).

Table 4.2   Potential Areas for Review for Trends and Red Flags

Types of Reports—Call Categories	Discipline/Remediation Actions
Allegations versus inquiries	Case cycle time
Anonymous versus named reporters	Online versus telephone reports
Sources and allegation types: by groups, locations, businesses, or services	Source of awareness
Substantiation percentage: for both named and anonymous groups	Follow-up contacts from anonymous calls
Geographic locations calling (and not calling)	Retaliation cases and outcomes
Levels of employees calling (and not calling)	Case closure time by investigating department/investigator
Characteristics of anonymous calls	Disciplinary actions taken—by business, by location, and by level of employee
Comparisons against prior years or quarters	Any anomalies
High volume of, or spikes in, human resources–related calls	

Source: ACFE EthicsLine, Utilizing hotline benchmarking data to improve ethics and compliance program effectiveness, compiled by Nick Ciancio, 2013.

For the most complete assessment, external hotline benchmarking should also be conducted. By reviewing another hotline's data, hotline administrators can determine whether their organization's hotline is performing similarly to its peers. Any deviations from industry "norms" can provide helpful feedback to improve the performance of one's own hotline. Unfortunately, today, studies suggest that a small number of organizations perform external benchmarking—less than 25%, according to one study (ACFE EthicsLine, 2013). This makes internal benchmarking even more important.

Why aren't more hotline administrators conducting external benchmarking? It is likely due to a conscious lack of appreciation for its importance, or an absence of available data. Why isn't the data available? Because organizations don't have to provide it.

While it is a "best practice" to publicize hotline metrics and findings within the organization (which could be available externally), it is not a requirement. Organizations are also generally not required to disseminate hotline data outside the organization/to the public. Individual government organizations may provide this data in its agency reports, in response to individual mandate, but these reports can be difficult to locate/obtain. Thus, organizations that want to benchmark their hotline data may have to ask other organizations to provide it, or they will have to rely on readily available data, such as data from a third-party provider.

One source of this benchmarking data is NAVEX Global, a leading third-party hotline provider. It creates an annual hotline benchmarking report. In that report, they provide readers with various methods to assess their own hotlines. In their 2016 report, they provide a way for organizations to evaluate the number of "unique contacts" (telephone calls, etc.) received to individual hotlines. This calculation will allow organizations to compare their number of unique contacts against peer organizations to assess hotline performance.

While this data can be useful, there are limitations. One such limitation is the inability to make industry comparisons. For instance, a financial firm would ideally benchmark its data against other financial firms. That comparison cannot be conducted with the third-party data available today, because it is aggregated.

For instance, the Network, now known as NAVEX Global, conducted annual benchmarking reports from 2006 to 2013, where they reported the number of tips received per 1,000 employees in the Finance, Insurance and Real Estate Industries, collectively, in aggregate. This number was 9.41 tips per 1,000 employees. This number has limited value, because the average number of calls actually received in any one of these industries cannot be determined. And they are unwilling to provide these data for research purposes. (This author made a request from this company for disaggregated data, and was told that it is not available.) Another source of benchmarking data is the Security Executive Council. But their benchmarking is also aggregated. While there are presumably good reasons for this (maintain client confidentiality, etc.) it is nevertheless a research limitation.

Organizations have the right to withhold the data, as there isn't a requirement to provide it. But it is important for anyone who wishes to conduct a hotline assessment to know the way that the data are provided impedes research efforts.

Internal and external benchmarking are important, and both should be conducted as part of a robust hotline performance assessment. Research suggests external benchmarking is not often conducted and has limitations. Ideally, most organizations are conducting internal benchmarking, but it is clear that internal benchmarking alone overlooks a few critical performance areas. Internal benchmarking, insomuch as it focuses on whether a given organization is receiving the number of calls it "should" be getting, tells organizations whether its hotlines are getting the same volume and types of calls as last year, in previous quarters, or during the same period, in prior years, and so on.

Although this information is worthwhile, it doesn't reveal whether a given hotline is performing optimally. Hotline managers need to know whether the volume and quality of hotline calls received are appropriate for that particular organization. So how is that determined? Media research, including social media analysis, is used.

What should hotline administrators look for, and where should they look? Social media sites, particularly the ones providing employee reviews of the companies where they work, will provide informative clues, such as the current organizational culture, known organizational fraud/waste/abuse, attitudes toward the fraud hotline, and the number and type of employees reporting this information (which is often provided anonymously). Employees have also been known to provide the real names of people engaging in fraud, waste, and abuse. This information is especially useful. The utility of this analysis will be demonstrated in the case studies in Chapter 6 of this book.

As with other forms of hotline benchmarking data, this data also has limitations. One obvious limitation is that the data is anonymous, and is provided on a third-party site. As a result, it is always possible the information can be false. This is an important limitation. However, this limitation doesn't outweigh the potential usefulness of the data. Also, internal hotline administrators reviewing the data are in a position to assess the viability of the data. As company employees, they can substantiate certain details. And they can also research all comments for validity before acting on any "tip" received from this data.

Another limitation of social media assessments is they can be time consuming. Time is money in the corporate world. Hotline administrators are busy, and time is limited. However, it is believed that a review of this data can provide information that will serve as a benefit outweighing the cost of review.

In 2014, this author completed a case study analysis of six hotlines, including two private sector hotlines, and one of each federal, state, city, and nonprofit hotlines.

In that study, I employed a unique case study analytical method, where I incorporated a social media review (employee reviews of their company) to determine organizational culture and whether employees knew about organizational fraud. I also considered whether best practices were being followed. Detailed steps for duplicating this research can be found in Chapter 6. Any organization can follow this process to assess its own hotline.

As a result of this assessment, I learned critical details about organizational culture and known fraud. In several instances (more than I was expecting!) employees gave specific names of people engaging in crime. Overall, the presence of known organizational fraud suggested in many cases that call volume should have been higher (especially if said fraud was not reported).

Hotline administrators may wonder why employees who know about fraud are reporting it via social media and not to their respective companies. According to hotline experts, there are three primary reasons why employees do not report known fraud to hotlines. As discussed previously, one reason is they are unaware a hotline exists. The other reason is that potential tipsters think the "risk" of reporting outweighs any potential "benefit," because nothing will happen. They may also fear retaliation (which is a conclusion drawn from the employee's cost-benefit calculation) (Penman, 2016).

One indicator known fraud isn't being reported, is low call volume. It is a common misconception that low call volume equals no issues to report. Experts say that low call volume can mean that people are afraid to report, they lack faith in the hotline, or the hotline is not properly marketed (Singh, 2015).

Employee fears of retaliation are confirmed with the recent high-profile issues involving Wells Fargo's hotline. In November 2016, their chief executive officer (CEO) said the bank "found 'some instances' where reports by employees of bad behavior to its ethics line weren't handled correctly" (Glazer, 2016). At first, this seemed like it could have been a simple performance issue. It was later learned that this "incorrect handling" may have been intentional. In January 2017, the new CEO, Tim Sloan, admitted there was "evidence to suggest that some employees may have faced retaliation for calling the company's ethics hotline and reporting objectionable behavior" (Bukhari, 2017). Investigations are underway to examine cases where employees were fired within a year of contacting the hotline.

Best Practices

Another important area to assess is adherence to best practices. A best practices assessment is a critical part of the overall hotline performance assessment process. There are many sources of best practices, and they can be particular to public or private sector organizations. Yet some apply to all sectors, like the Federal Sentencing Guidelines for Organizations (FSGO). Nevertheless, a sample of best practices guidance will be provided here as an essential starting point for anyone operating a fraud hotline.

The FSGO was created by the U.S. Sentencing Commission in 1991 and revised following SOX in 2004. The FSGO is widely used as a source of best practices for hotlines in all sectors (NAVEX Global, 2007; The Network, n.d.). The guidelines "cover all organizations whether publically or privately held and of whatever nature, such as corporations, partnerships, labor unions, pension funds, trusts, nonprofit entities and governmental units" (NAVEX Global, 2007). The Justice Department uses these guidelines to evaluate whether "a company should be given leniency or even avoid prosecution for corporate crimes, the most common of which are fraud, environmental waste discharge, tax offenses, antitrust offenses and food and drug violations" (NAVEX Global, 2007).

The guidelines by design are very broad, and thus the outcome for a given organization can vary based on their culture. But this was intentional. According to the U.S. Sentencing Commission, the guidelines are purposefully broad, and "do not offer precise details for implementation…deliberately…to encourage flexibility and independence by organizations in designing programs that are best suited to their particular circumstances" (Desio, n.d.).

The broad categories of best practices elements extrapolated from the FSGO are as follows:

1. Oversight (by high-level personnel)
2. Due care (in delegating substantial discretionary authority)
3. Effective communication (to all levels of employees)
4. Reasonable steps to achieve compliance (which include systems for monitoring, auditing, and reporting suspected wrongdoing without fear of reprisal)
5. Consistent enforcement (of compliance standards including disciplinary mechanisms)
6. Reasonable steps (to respond to and prevent further similar offenses upon detection of a violation)

While the flexibility offered by the FSGO is a positive feature, it can sometimes leave organizations wondering whether they are "doing it the right way." Organizations can review the process used by other successful hotlines to inform its own practices. Then, it can check its work by reviewing internal documents and conducting employee surveys and interviews. It can also analyze media reports, to include social media, to see what members of the media and employees are saying about the organization's best practice adherence as it relates to hotlines. This process will be discussed in more detail in the case studies in Chapter 6.

There are also recommendations available which highlight the way that organizations can operationalize the FSGO. The Network (now NAVEX Global) offers the following guidance for implementing the FSGO:

- Implement compliance standards, codes of conduct, and policies and procedures.
- Specify certain executive-level individual(s) with the responsibility to oversee compliance.
- Apply due diligence toward not delegating substantial discretionary authority to individuals who have had a propensity to engage in illegal activities.
- Establish communication, awareness, and employee training programs to specific compliance standards.
- Implement compliance monitoring and auditing systems, including a reporting system so that employees can report misconduct without fear of retribution.
- Apply consistent and adequate processes and procedures for enforcement and discipline.
- Respond appropriately to incidents and take steps to prevent further similar offenses, including any necessary modifications to compliance programs intended to prevent and detect violations of law.

(The Network, 2012, p. 2).

Other sources of best practices guidance can be found in publications offered by major organizations such as accounting and consulting firms, federal government organizations, and third-party hotline providers. These sources can provide additional, useful guidance in developing a hotline. Each of these sources should be evaluated against the FSGO before implementation.

One source that provides useful information on hotline development is KPMG. Proper hotline development is integral for ensuring adherence to best practices. According to KPMG, a well-designed hotline contains the following features:

- Anonymity
- Confidentiality
- Follow-up on nonretaliation
- Organization-wide availability
- Real-time assistance
- Data management procedures
- Classification of financial reporting concerns
- Audit committee notification
- Prominent communications

Table 4.3 Best Practice Guidance For Hotlines

Best Practice Element	Implementation
Effective communication of ethics policies and programs	• The reporting system reflects an organization's commitment to ethical behavior through web pages and printed materials made available to employees, customers, and vendors. • The reporting system reflects closely an organization's potential risks and violations associated with its operation to help guide reporters and enable analysis of reporting activity. • In large organizations, the reporting system should reflect the potential risks and violations associated with individual business units.
Confidential, anonymous stakeholder report intake	The reporting system ensures reporters' confidentiality and anonymity, and is available to employees, customers, and vendors. • The reporting system is universally accessible 24 × 7 × 365 and offers secure reporting via the web, telephone, fax, or mail. • The reporting system makes available highly trained interviewers to help reporters feel comfortable with the reporting process and provide complete information. • The reporting system is accessible in any language and reflects sensitivity to linguistic and cultural differences. • The reporting system facilitates follow-up by the reporter, enabling ongoing two-way communication while maintaining confidentiality and anonymity.
Targeted report distribution and oversight	• The reporting system facilitates targeted distribution of reports to predefined individuals based on violation type, materiality level, business unit, and geography. • The reporting system precludes from the distribution list anyone named in the report as well as his or her subordinates. • The reporting system immediately alerts appropriate individuals to new reports and follow-up feedback from reporters. • The system generates summary and trend reports for the audit committee and Board of Directors or Trustees for effective oversight.

(Continued)

Table 4.3 *(Continued)*   **Best Practice Guidance For Hotlines**

Assessment and classification of reports	The system facilitates review of reports to determine next steps, such as following up with the reporter for more details, closing a nonactionable report, or starting an investigation. • The system minimizes the impact of frivolous reports and delivers actionable data.
Review, management, and resolution of reported issues	The system facilitates the collection, management, and retention of information concerning reported matters. • The system helps organize follow-up investigative activity and associated details through case management tools.
Secure retention of all information	The system maintains data security at all times and provides a repository for all report information that is retained in accordance with an organization's policies. • The managing organization has strong policies for storing and handling sensitive data and the information technology expertise to fully secure servers from internal and external attacks. • The system generates an audit trail for all activities associated with each report.
Ethics program review and refinement	• The system enables sensitive analysis of reporting activity and violations across the organization, with data broken down by business unit, divisions, and locations for targeted remedial activities. • The system enables reporting of resolution status and action taken for each report, as well as for subsets of reports, based on violation type, materiality level, location, etc.

Source: EthicsPoint, Beyond compliance: implementing effective whistleblower hotline reporting systems, EthicsPoint Inc. 2007.

Major hotline providers such as EthicsPoint (now NAVEX Global) provide best practice guidance as presented in Table 4.3.

For federal hotlines, there are many helpful resources. One such resource is the Department of Homeland Security Office of the Inspector General (DHS OIG) "Recommended Practices for Office of Inspector General Hotlines" created in October 2010. The DHS OIG recommends the following:

Recommendation #1: OIGs should consider ensuring that their hotline intake staff are adequately trained with respect to interview skills and program and mission-specific information.

Recommendation #2: OIGs should consider ensuring that hotline intake staff handle complaints consistently, providing training sufficient to ensure that all complainants receive the same information and that all complaints are handled similarly, without regard to the skill and experience level of a particular staff member.

Recommendation #3: OIGs should consider evaluating the technology available to assist in the complaint intake process in order to determine what, if any, technology might aid their hotlines in processing incoming complaints faster, more efficiently, and more cost effectively.

Recommendation #4: OIG hotline managers should consider collecting and analyzing data relating to incoming complaints in order to (1) evaluate and improve the efficiency of their intake process and their hotline operations and (2) identify trends in the nature of the allegations received, particularly as they relate to systemic weaknesses in an agency's programs and operations.

Recommendation #5: OIG hotline managers should consider meeting regularly with appropriate senior OIG managers and staff to discuss hotline performance, trends in incoming complaints, and prioritizing complaints in a manner that best furthers the OIG's mission- and program-related initiatives.

Recommendation #6: During its initial contact with a complainant, an OIG hotline should consider managing the complainant's expectations with respect to further contact with the OIG, including providing information as to whether the complainant should expect status updates from the OIG.

Recommendation #7: OIGs should provide a mechanism for reporting information relating to fraud, waste, and abuse via their websites.

Recommendation #8: OIGs should consider providing educational information on their websites, such as (1) information about the whistleblower's protections against retaliation, including a link to the Office of Special Counsel; (2) an explanation of how the OIG responds to complaints; and (3) general information on the OIG's mission and how the hotline relates to that mission.

Recommendation #9: OIG hotlines should consider engaging in education and outreach efforts to raise the profile of their hotline and its purpose to the parent organization's employees and contractors, thereby increasing the number of relevant and actionable complaints the hotline receives.

Recommendation #10: The OIG community should consider creating an ongoing forum through which hotline operators can share information and best practices, such as a CIGIE Subcommittee, training conference, hotline community website, or electronic mailing list.

As demonstrated, proper assessment will help to ensure a given hotline is performing as expected. In Chapter 6, the assessment methodology will be demonstrated in case studies that will (1) identify the known organizational conditions in six case study organizations, to include known internal frauds (determined via media analysis); (2) examine the fraud hotline data in each of these organizations; (3) identify organizational conditions via social media analysis; and (4) provide a clear and articulable framework for organizational hotline assessment.

Chapter 5

Theoretical Perspectives

Symbolic Interaction Theory

Criminological theories can be applied to fraud hotlines to inform hotline performance. For instance, a review of the literature suggests that symbolic interactionism could be successfully applied to the phenomenon of crime reporting in the workplace. Specifically, symbolic interactionism explains how a hotline poster displayed in a workplace could trigger fraud reporting. The model of "hotline poster display" can also be accomplished virtually, for those employees who work remotely.

This chapter examines the role of symbolic interaction theory in explaining this phenomenon and applies this theory to the organizational culture of the four major types of organizations—public, private, government, and not-for-profit/religious—in an attempt to explain why employees are more apt to use the fraud hotline when posters are present in the workplace.

In conducting this examination, several sources of literature were consulted. To determine fraud hotline reporting habits, I reviewed leading publications and studies conducted in the field of fraud examination. Due to an employer's reluctance to report fraud occurring in their workplace, surveys conducted by major fraud-fighting organizations that provide forensic accounting/internal investigation services to major employers are one of the best sources of data concerning fraud occurring in private companies. The second major source of data concerning employment fraud is the semi-annual report conducted by the Association of Certified Fraud Examiners (ACFE), a major global fraud-fighting organization that is the credential-granting organization for Certified Fraud Examiners (CFE), a premiere credential in the field of fraud examination.

The ACFE generates a semi-annual report, which provides recent insight and allows for comparison data from previous years. I further reviewed recent fraud reports generated by major accounting firms (KPMG, Ernst & Young,

PricewaterhouseCoopers [PWC] and Deloitte & Touche). These firms conduct regular fraud studies using information gleaned from data obtained as part of their forensic accounting practices. Their budget allows for rich studies and their contacts built from their practices allow for a rich insight not typically obtained from independent research. I further consulted recent (2003 forward; post SOX period) reputable academic books and publications (2003 forward) that discussed the possible reasons/theories concerning employees' reluctance to report fraud via their internal hotlines. Noteworthy publications included the Security Executive Council's 2007 Corporate Governance and Compliance Hotline Benchmarking Report.

I also reviewed the literature concerning the theory of symbolic interactionism. Over the course of my research, I reviewed the work of the man who is distinguished with having coined the term "symbolic interactionism," Herbert Blumer. I also looked at the work of other influential theorists on the theory, including George Herbert Mead. To support my position on the theory's ability to explain a specific fraud reporting trigger (poster) for a human being, I also reviewed the literature for additional research on the application of the theory to people and how they relate to inanimate objects. In this research, I indeed found support for my position.

In addition, as part of my review on symbolic interactionism, I searched for available research concerning the theory, from its inception (1700s) to present to see if it had ever been applied to the phenomenon of fraud reporting and hotline posters. Nothing was located. As a result, this is the first known work concerning this unique topic.

Overall, I learned the following:

> Employees know about fraud, but they do not report fraud because they are unaware of the existence of a confidential reporting mechanism.

The literature suggests that employees are indeed aware of fraud occurring in their workplace, yet they do not report it because they do not know their employer has a confidential hotline for them to call. One key source of literature concerning this subject is the fraud studies routinely conducted by big four accounting firm Ernst & Young (E&Y).

E&Y routinely conducts studies concerning occupational fraud, including a semi-annual global fraud study wherein they interview the executives of major companies across multiple industries to learn about the fraud occurring therein.

In 2002, E&Y conducted a study concerning employee attitudes regarding fraud. Their results confirmed that employees know about the fraud occurring around them. In this study, E&Y interviewed 617 American workers. Overall, they discovered that 21%, which translates into roughly one in five employees, had *personal knowledge* of fraud occurring in their workplace. What's more, 80% of those employees aware of fraud said they would indeed report it to their employer.

Of those employees, all of them preferred an anonymous reporting method, and nearly 60% said they would prefer to report anonymously via telephone/hotline.

Other important studies in this area have been conducted by KPMG. In 2009, KMPG published an "Integrity Survey" where over 5,000 employees nationally contributed information. Their responses suggested the number of employees who know about fraud might be increasing over time. In the survey, KPMG asked employees whether they had "personally seen" or had "firsthand knowledge" of specific frauds in their organizations over the previous year. In 2008, approximately three quarters of respondents (74%) reported they did.

In 2013, KPMG's reported the results of another survey, based on responses received from over 3,500 U.S. employees in 16 job functions, 13 industry sectors, and 5 thresholds of organization size. This survey had similar findings, with 73% of employees reporting they observed misconduct in the last year. More than half of them said the conduct they observed was serious, and would cause "a significant loss of public trust if discovered" (2008–2009; 2013).

Other studies have confirmed that employees remain unaware of their employer's fraud hotlines. In their 2008 study, E&Y interviewed key executives from 1,200 major companies in 33 countries. Overall, E&Y reported that more than half of their study respondents were unaware of the existence of their employer's fraud hotline.

Another major source of employment fraud information is the ACFE's semi-annual Report to the Nations on Occupational Fraud and Abuse ("Report"). Established in 1996, the ACFE has conducted their report on a semi-annual basis since 2002. The 1996 ACFE Report was recognized as the first privately funded study concerning occupational fraud. Recently releasing their 9th Edition, the report is considered an leading resource on occupational fraud.

The ACFE Report consists of a survey of fraud examiners nationwide concerning their subject caseload over the past reporting period. In addition to their report, the ACFE conducts independent research on many aspects of fraud available on their website. Many of their articles are accessible only through private subscription to their website.

While each ACFE Report pertains to unique cases of fraud over distinct time periods, one essential fact has been consistent in their reports since the generally accepted existence of fraud hotlines in 2002. In all their reports (2002–2016), employee tips were the primary way that fraud was detected in a subject organization.

Fraud investigators echo those findings. One such investigator, Tracy Coenen, an experienced white-collar crime investigator and author of "Essentials of Corporate Fraud," a fraud manual that has been promoted by Joseph T. Wells, the chairman and founder of the ACFE, finds that employees are more likely to report fraud if they have a confidential way to report such information (2006). What employees don't seem to know is that a confidential reporting mechanism likely exists in their organization—but studies suggest they are not calling at expected rates.

It is important to note this assumption is based on a small amount of available data and anecdotal evidence. Very little individual-level data exists concerning calls to fraud hotlines. Therefore, I conducted a case study into the fraud hotline reporting in a major global company of over 55,000 employees "Company X" to learn about such hotline reporting habits. I learned that in 2007, this organization received only 35 tips. Based on figures contained in a major benchmarking report concerning fraud hotlines, this figure is shockingly low. According to this report, conducted by the Security Executives Council, in 2006, companies on average received an average of 8.3 complaints per 1,000 employees. Using this figure as a benchmark, the subject company should have received 456.5 complaints.

One must ask why fraud is not being reported to Company X's hotline. Research has demonstrated that fraud is rampant in any given organization and employees know about it. Benchmarking shows that Company X's hotline should receive over 400 more calls annually than they presently receive. A subsequent examination into fraud hotline awareness has provided a likely explanation—Company X, at the time, did not actively promote their hotline to employees. Multiple studies suggest that fraud hotline callers learned of their hotline from a poster displayed at the workplace The Network and BDO Consulting conducted an annual Corporate Governance and Compliance Hotline Benchmarking Report from 2006–2015. Each year, they consistently found that the poster was "the most popular [hotline] awareness and communication method named by incident reporters" (2015). However, Company X did not consciously display such posters nor did they otherwise display/promote their hotline number. In fact, despite being located in their internal and external websites, independent research proved that the fraud hotline number at Company X was challenging to locate.

Hotline benchmarking has confirmed that hotline underutilization can be directly attributed to a failure to communicate the hotline (Bishop et al., 2007; SEC, 2007). Consequently, as noted by Company X, the hotline was not presently advertised via a poster. Although Company X expressed a general interest creating and displaying such a poster, still, 1 year later, they have not yet done so.

Most Hotline Callers Became Aware of Their Employer's Hotline via a Poster

Research demonstrates that posters are the primary way employees become aware of their employer's fraud hotline. The literature suggests that employers need to actively promote their hotlines. Research indicates that employees will *indeed* use hotlines to report irregularities (Biegelman, 2004), but they require encouragement to do so (Coenen, 2008). Further research suggests a poster effectively provides such encouragement (Buckhoff, 2003).

In fact, studies concerning corporate fraud reporting hotlines indicate that posters are the most effective mechanism through which employees learn about their fraud hotline. In 2006, The Network,* the CSO Executive Council, and the ACFE joined efforts to conduct the first ever benchmarking report concerning organizational fraud hotline activity. Their unique report gives organizations the rare opportunity to compare their fraud hotline usage to that of other industries and companies worldwide.

In 2006, The Network et al. looked at 200,000 reports from more than 500 organizations over 4 years. In 2007, they analyzed over 277,000 hotline incident reports from 650+ organizations from major industries over a 5-year period. Overall, year over year, they found that most hotline callers (39% in 2006, 34% in 2007) became aware of the existence of their organization's fraud hotline via a poster. That trend has continued to the present day.

Despite research that has demonstrated the effectiveness of a hotline poster in prompting employees to report internal fraud, Company X does not currently display such posters (nor is the fraud hotline number otherwise displayed). But it should be noted that private employers are not required to display a hotline poster. Public sector agencies who conduct business with the federal government must display a fraud hotline poster *only if* they have not satisfied other ethics requirements. Specifically, amendments to the Federal Acquisition Regulations (FAR) require most organizations that are doing business with the federal government to adopt a code of business ethics and educate employees on the provisions. If a given organization is in compliance with the aforementioned, they need not display a poster.

Similarly, the private sector was required to implement ethics training and establish fraud reporting mechanisms following the Sarbanes–Oxley Act in 2002, and amendments to the Federal Sentencing Guidelines in 2004. Although they require that such provisions be made known to employees, they do not require that such awareness be established via a poster (Gusdorf, 2008). In fact, independent research proved that the fraud hotline number at Company X, despite being located on both the internal and external websites, was challenging to locate.

Given that multiple studies by leading fraud organizations and benchmarking prove increased hotline calls results in increased fraud detection (ACFE, 2002–2008; The Network et al., 2006, 2007), reduced calls do not mean less fraud is occurring in an organization. Therefore, it is likely that Company X employees searching for a means through which to report fraud are simply unable to locate the number, and thus conclude that an anonymous reporting mechanism does not exist in Company X (as research suggests).

---

* On August 31, 2015, The Network was acquired by NAVEX Global and is now known as NAVEX Global.

Theoretical Analysis

Although benchmarking and fraud research have proven the effectiveness of fraud hotlines and their successful use when promulgated via a poster, Company X has chosen not to display such a poster. But why? Perhaps criminological theory can further convince Company X, and other companies, to use such posters to prompt employee fraud reporting. Symbolic interactionism, a micro-level criminological theory, can explain why a visual cue, such as a fraud poster, is an effective tool in an organization's fraud-fighting regime insofar as it prompts employees to use the fraud hotline to report known fraud.

First, I discuss the overarching themes found upon examining fraud hotline posters in leading government industries and the relevance of this theme. Then I discuss how symbolic interactionism prompts an employee to report fraud generally and specifically with respect to the elements reflected in common poster design.

Analysis of Fraud Hotline Posters: Most Fraud Hotline Posters are Simple in Design

A review of available fraud hotline posters uncovered common themes among fraud hotline posters. Fraud hotline posters were located via general Internet searches. The posters located were all from government agencies, who incidentally, due to the nature of their role (service for the citizens) widely disseminate their fraud hotline posters via the Internet. Meanwhile, private employers, who also welcome complaints to their fraud hotline from outside their organization, might make their fraud hotline available via the Internet, independent research suggests that they do not make this information available via a poster. It should be noted that while Company X makes their fraud hotline available on their public website, many competitor organizations did not.

Most fraud hotline posters reviewed displayed the word "hotline" in bright attention-getting red and do not otherwise plead with the employee to report the fraud in question. For instance, the U.S. Department of Energy Fraud Hotline poster, which was a bright primary color blue, read "HOTLINE" in all caps in a fire-engine red colored font. Very little information besides the corresponding telephone number was displayed. In addition, the U.S. Department of Defense hotline poster, which had more subdued background shade (white), still contained the word "hotline" in bright red letters and contained little additional information. However, such information included positive additions—additional ways for an employee to report fraud, including an e-mail address and designated fraud-reporting website. The Naval Office of the Inspector General and the Special Inspector General for Iraq reconstruction, among others, all had similar posters.

The simplicity of the posters suggests that the poster is, in itself, considered sufficient to prompt the employee to report fraud. Although it cannot be definitively concluded that guidelines do not exist, it can be said, based on the available fraud posters, that any guidelines likely did not require elements that were absent from available posters from leading government agencies. After all, if the poster needed to make a plea to the potential reporter, or contain a similar detail, it would have likely been located in the posters of leading government agencies. Thus the simplicity of the posters was prevalent enough that it could not be attributed to chance.

Also, if guidelines exist that assist the employer in creating such posters, they are not widely available. Independent research was conducted in an attempt to locate suggested elements of a fraud hotline poster, and none could be located.

How Fraud Hotline Posters Can Be Analyzed Under the Theory of Symbolic Interactionism

Brief History of Symbolic Interactionism

There is a lively debate that surrounds the development of this theory that is worth mentioning. Herbert Blumer (1900–1987), a member of the Second Chicago School of sociologists, who was credited with coining the term "Symbolic Interactionism" (1937), studied under and was influenced by the First Chicago School's George Herbert Mead (1863–1931). While Mead is said to be the originator of this theory, and Blumer as the "sponsor," Blumer was the first person to set forth the basic tenets of this theory in his book by the same name in 1969. Authors McPhail and Rexroat in 1979, along with Lewis and Smith in 1981, argue that Blumer's theory is not compatible with Mead's work. Yet, the same authors note that Mead's "intellectual prestige" was suffering during the time that Blumer wrote *Symbolic Interactionism* and that Blumer's text resulted in a renewed interest in Mead. That said, overall, it would seem that Blumer's text served to advance Mead and not undermine him, as the authors indicate.

To complicate the issue, yet other texts indicate that the theory of symbolic interactionism actually predated both Blumer and Mead. These texts find that they were both influenced by earlier scholars who discussed this type of theory, including John Dewey, and that the basic ideas of symbolic interactionism were originally set forth in the 1700s. It has been written that symbolic interactionism can be traced back to the 1700s where sociologists such as Adam Smith (1759) wrote that people look to society to learn how to behave (Rosenberg & Turner, 1990).

Given that Blumer is credited with defining the proper framework in which to analyze and apply this theory, in this work, I focus on Blumer and his work on symbolic interactionism.

Basic Tenets of Symbolic Interaction Theory

Despite its rich history, the theory of symbolic interactionism is ultimately credited to Blumer who set forth the major tenets of the theory beginning with three premises, which are as follows:

1. Humans act toward things on the basis of the meaning that the things have for them. According to Blumer, the meaning of "things" is quite broad and can be "everything that the human being may note in his world" including physical objects, other people, and/or ideals, such as independence.
2. The meaning of such things is derived from, or arises out of, the social interaction that one has with one's fellows.
3. These meanings are handled in, and modified through, an interpretive process used by the person in dealing with the things he encounters.

Blumer finds that the above premises must be considered in tandem to completely understand the theory. In fact, it is the consideration of all the principles together that Blumer believes serve to distinguish this theory from all others (4–5). As a result, we consider all three premises when analyzing their application to the fraud hotline poster.

Overall, in its most simple form, symbolic interactionism is a process where the individual determines how to behave through society. For Blumer, the three premises above reflect the process by which an individual attaches meaning to objects through interpretation. This interpretative process is an internal one that includes an active self-process where the actor determines his or her behavior based on the individual situation (Blumer, p. 6). In other words, meanings, language, and thought come together, are internalized, and eventually become socialized behavior (Griffin, 1997). It is important to note that as a micro-level theory that explains individual behavior, this theory finds that reactions to objects are unique to the person based on the process of self-analysis that is central to the meaning that is attached to the object.

Application of Symbolic Interactionism to Employees and Their Reaction to Fraud Hotline Posters

Blumer's broad definition of "things" (Premise #1) allows for the fraud hotline poster to be considered an object for further analysis under the theory of symbolic interactionism ("the Theory"). Thus per the Theory, the individual employee has viewed the poster and has understood the action to take in response to viewing the poster (call the hotline). The employee performs this action because he or she has determined the meaning of the poster through his or her individual experience in society (his or her workplace).

Rosenberg and Turner discuss this process wherein they say that symbols, such as a poster, invoke a socially dictated response. In *Social Psychology*, they discuss this phenomenon as follows:

> Objects become stimuli and function in the context of acts and become to be defined as relevant in completing the act; they acquire meaning in the course of activity. The same principle holds for acts implicating other humans in their completion. Such social acts are the source of personality and of organized social behavior, outgrowths of the social process made possible by communication through language. (Rosenberg & Turner, 1981, p. 7)

A key component in the analysis of this response involves considering the workplace as the "society" to which the individual refers. Rosenberg and Turner discuss Blumer's interpretation of the society based on Mead's analysis as follows:

> Society must be conceived in a manner consistent with these "easily verified" premises, he believes, and he conceives society as consisting of people's actions taking place in and with regard to a situation and constructed by interpreting the situation, identifying and assessing things that must be taken into account, and acting on the basis of the assessment. (Rosenberg & Turner, 1981, p. 9)

While Blumer is quick to say that his definition of society is contrary to the conventional sociologist, who views society as an "organization" (as a workplace could be defined), he goes on to say that the Theory finds that such an organization enters action "to the extent that it shapes situations and provides symbols used in interpreting situations" (Rosenberg & Turner, 1990). In that framework, the workplace, as it applies as the medium through which the poster is viewed, is effectively established as a "society" according to the Theory.

How Symbolic Interactionism Informs an Employee's Motivation to Report Fraud upon Viewing the Fraud Hotline Poster

Symbolic Interactionism Explains Why People within the Same Organization Would Attach a Similar Meaning to an Object

Symbolic interactionism is rooted in the idea of the symbiotic relationship between the individual and society (Rosenberg & Turner, 1981, p. 23). According to Blumer, participants of a society learn the appropriate lines of action through a process of "repetitive joint action," wherein they accept the "norms and values" of that society (p. 18). As a member of the organization, the employee is in an environment that is unique to those members alone. As such, the employee, as an individual who has a shared society with only those members, has a unique perspective from that of other individuals. Specifically, employees know, upon seeing the poster (that research suggests may simply state the word "hotline") that the "hotline" refers to the internal fraud hotline wherein that employee can report acts of known or suspected conduct occurring within the organization.

Furthermore, the employee is prompted to act via a twofold internal process whereby that individual sees that poster and is motivated to act based on the meaning he or she has attached to that poster based on society (the workplace). But why? Some researchers argue that this motivation involves an incentive (MacKinnon, p. 55). For symbolic interactionists, according to Theory analyst Neil Joseph MacKinnon, that incentive can be found in a clear and precise recognition (1994). Below I discuss that incentive and how it manifests in the common fraud hotline poster.

According to the Theory of Symbolic Interactionism, the Poster Need Not Be Elaborate to Serve as a Visual Cue

According to MacKinnon, symbolic interactionists believe that people are motivated by simple phrases, as they find the immediate recognition of same "rewarding" (p. 55). Specifically, in his book entitled *Symbolic Interactionism as Affect Control*, MacKinnon finds as follows:

> At the most general level…Mead and symbolic interactionists (find) that people try to experience an orderly, knowable world as much as possible within the vagaries and vicissitudes of everyday existence. In vernacular terms, people "get off on" confirming meanings…and the confirmation of both "cold" and "hot" cognitions, cognitive problem-solving as well as sentiment-confirming activity, can be motivating and rewarding. (p. 55)

In the above framework, the fraud hotline poster operates as a stimulus that effectively communicates the intended response (fraud reporting) through language (the word "hotline"). In other words, the word "hotline" in red, the color that symbolizes a warning in American society,* when situated on a poster displayed at the workplace naturally invokes a response from the employee to act.

Furthermore, the act of fraud reporting on the part of the employee is mutually beneficial. The employee is "rewarded" by the mere symbolic interaction process and its positive meaning to the employee (the feeling of doing a good deed, fighting crime, supporting their employer, stopping crime against their employer so that

---

* It should be noted that fire engines and stop lights, among other common warnings, are also displayed in the color red.

their employer does not lose money and cease to employ them as a result, etc.). For the employer, the poster represents both a proactive and a reactive approach to crime control. The employer is naturally benefited by having crime occurring within thwarted while in progress, thus saving them precious dollars. In addition, the poster acts as a crime prevention tool in that it implicitly serves as a warning to the employee that his or her fellow employees are "watching" and could easily report criminal behavior.

Symbolic Interactionism Explains Why the Poster in Itself Is Sufficient to Prompt the Employee to Report Internal Crime

We have already learned in earlier sections of this work that employees are keenly aware of crime occurring in their workplace and are not reporting it via their internal fraud hotline unless prompted upon seeing a poster. Thus, symbolic interactionism operates as a self-fulfilling prophecy, convinces a person to behave in such a way, that is pleasing to them, as prompted by their employer, upon the employee's realization that their employer *wants* them to act. The poster thus serves as the trigger that sets the proverbial wheels in motion. But why?

Michael R. Solomon, who researches the relationship of symbolic interaction and product symbolism, can explain this phenomenon. "The Role of Products as Social Stimuli: A Symbolic Interactionism Perspective" Solomon finds consumers ascribe meaning to products, which guides their social behavior. Although Solomon speaks in terms of products, his analysis successfully applies to the fraud hotline poster in the sense that he is describing an immediate reaction based on a visual cue. Accordingly, Solomon finds the following:

> Products with ascribed social meaning, then, may be used in a broad sense to facilitate role performance, in that they increase the probability of portraying the behavior pattern appropriate to that role. (p. 324)

Solomon further illustrates the powerful role of the self in making a decision to act on such cues with the following observation:

> One need only observe someone preening in front of a mirror or hear a child alone in an animated conversation with a menagerie of dolls to understand the often solitary symbolic nature of symbolic consumption. (p. 324)

Solomon's analysis successfully explains why, upon merely viewing a poster, a self-analysis is prompted, that without audience or additional validation, prompts action.

Fraud reporting in the workplace is a sensitive, yet important research topic. With American companies alone losing $600 billion per year to internal fraud, this is a costly problem that simply cannot be ignored. And this problem can be prevented. At present, the number of employees who know about fraud occurring in their workplace vastly outweighs the amount of people reporting such fraud. All we need to do is get them to talk. Research suggests and symbolic interactionism demonstrates that a poster could indeed provide the stimulus necessary to increase fraud reporting.

Theory Relevant to Research Question

The case studies in Chapter 6 consider the possible effects of organizational bureaucracy on fraud hotline performance. The theory relevant to this aim is the Theory of Bureaucracy.

Theory of Bureaucracy

The foundation of the Theory of Bureaucracy was first established in the 1890s, beginning with theorists such as Max Weber, who set forth the characteristics of an ideal organization. In 1940, Weber conducted a "classical analysis of bureaucracy," emphasizing hierarchical structure and a fixed division of labor in the pursuit of "precision, reliability, and efficiency." Bureaucracy was seen as the means to achieve that goal (Tompkins, 2005).

Bureaucracy was not "defined" in the traditional sense but rather was characterized by a set of attributes. Weber said that this criterion was integral to achieving the "ideal state" in an organization (Tompkins, 2005). The "specific list of criteria for the fully developed bureaucratic form" included "technical training of officials, merit appointments, fixed salaries and pensions, assured careers, the separation of organizational rights and duties from the private life of the employee, and a fixed and definite division of work into distinct offices or jobs" (Thompson, 1961, p. 11). Thus, the state of bureaucracy was defined by the presence of the following conditions: (i) hierarchy of authority, (ii) system of rules, (iii) technical expertise, (iv) career service, and (v) insistence on the rights of office (Thompson, 1961).

Bureaupathology

The state of bureaucracy was viewed both positively and negatively by scholars. While most scholars agree that bureaucracies are "rational" and "necessary," problems were noted. For many, problems arose due to an individual's response to the organizational climate created by bureaucracy. Researchers such as Victor A. Thompson found that when the characteristics that defined a bureaucracy were "exaggerated," the situation could turn "bureaupathic" which is a deviation from the organizational ideal (1961, p. 159).

Over time, theorists became critical of the notion of an "ideal organization" when they determined organizations had inherent flaws. Those flaws were due in part to the workers' reaction to the state of bureaucracy, which caused them to become very deliberate in their actions. Specifically, theorists such as Merton said bureaucracies resulted in workers becoming "methodical, prudent and disciplined" (Merton, 1957, pp. 195–206).

In the 1960s researchers determined that inflexible workers made bureaucratic organizations incapable of making necessary changes. In fact, in 1964, in *The Bureaucratic Phenomenon*, Michel Crozier said a bureaucratic organization was akin to "an organization that cannot correct its behaviour by learning from its errors" (p. 187).

Specifically, Thompson said "personal behavior patterns" such as "excessive aloofness, ritualistic attachment to routines and procedures, and resistance to change" and a "petty insistence upon rights of authority and status" could "exaggerate the characteristic qualities of bureaucratic organization" (1961, pp. 152–153). Thompson found these behaviors to be bureaupathic, in that they do not serve to advance the organization's mission and instead "reflect the personal needs of individuals" (1961, p. 153; Caiden 1991, p. 491).

In 1967, Anthony Downs developed a list of "bureaucratic personalities" which further documented bureaupathic behaviors.

Researchers also began to acknowledge that bureaucracy could cause workers to act against the organization. One such scholar was Anthony Downs, who said workers in a bureaucracy have an inherent tendency to conceal information from superiors that is unfavorable (1964, pp. 10–12).

Meanwhile, scholars still advanced the need for bureaucracies in spite of flaws. For instance, in 1964, Downs said hierarchy was necessary in bureaucracies, although hierarchy could cause information flow between workers to be distorted (pp. 9–10).

In the 1970s, researchers detected organizational problems in bureaucracies. Robert Kharasch examined organizational behavior in the federal government, and found organizational "malfunctioning" that was "out of control." (p. 116). In 1974, Christopher Hood looked at British public administration and determined administrative failures, including "over-organization, red-tape" and "ritualized procedures" (Caiden, 1991, pp. 114–15).

In the 1970s and 1980s, scholars further attributed bureaucracy to organizational crime. In a study conducted in the early 1970s, Bowden determined that bureaucracy could prevent innovation, resulting in "anomie, distrust and lawlessness" which give rise to misconduct (Caiden, 1969, p. 114–115). In 1981, William Pierce said bureaucracies could result in "bureaucratic failure," causing theft, corruption and waste (Caiden, 1969, p. 116)

In the 1990s, researchers concluded bureaupathology could result in public harm. In 1999, Diane Vaughn found "formal organizations can deviate from the rationalist expectations of the Weberian model" where worker behaviors, both "conforming" and "deviant," can "adversely affect the public," leading to organizational "failure, crime, and deviance" (pp. 272–273). In 1991, Gerald E. Caiden elaborated the list of worker bureaupathic behaviors, first created by Downs, resulting in 175 bureaucratic pathologies, or bureaupathologies (Bozeman & Rainey, 1998).

Although researchers focused on individual behaviors, bureaupathologies were now viewed as faults of the organization, as a whole. According to Caiden, bureaupathologies were inherent in bureaucracies, were pervasive, and "lived" beyond individual actors. Per Caiden, bureaupathologies are:

> The systematic shortcomings of organizations that cause individuals within them to be guilty of malpractices. They cannot be corrected by separating the guilty from the organization for the malpractices will continue irrespective of the organization's composition. They are not random, isolated incidents, either. While they may not be regular, they are not so rare either. When they occur, little action is taken to prevent their recurrence.... (Caiden, 1991, p. 490)

Additional research during this time suggested the full breadth of organizational problems, including crime, might never be fully known. Caiden said there are latent problems in all organizations, which may never come to light as a result of bureaucracy (Caiden, 1985, 1991). In 1991, Caiden advanced the concept of "Public Maladministration" where he observes that organizations may have problems, which sometimes only come to light via the investigative process or from a whistleblower (Caiden, 1991, p. 491).

Caiden's analysis would explain the reluctance of a bureaucratic employee to report fraud in all sectors. Caiden said, in a bureaucracy, organizational problems, such as crime, could remain hidden forever, because employees are reluctant to come forward. Per Caiden, employees may "agree what is being done is unsatisfactory" but they "[are not] prepared to take the first step" (Caiden, 1991, p. 491). Caiden found "public maladministration" was present in both the public and private sectors (Caiden, 1991, p, 492).

Overall, the Theory of Bureaucracy explains how organizational processes may not always function for the good of the organization as a whole, namely, to advance and foster a fraud hotline.

Current Literature Relevant to the Research Question

The central question of this work is as follows: Does organizational bureaucracy affect fraud hotline performance? The state of organizational bureaupathology can affect a fraud hotline in several ways. For one, it can prevent employees from reporting known fraud. It can cause them to conceal known fraud, and it can also impede the organization's ability to handle hotline calls. Overall, research demonstrates that the presence of excessive bureaucracy can adversely affect a fraud hotline. Because employees are the primary audience for employer-sponsored hotlines, the perception of the employees as to the presence of bureaucracy in their organization is central to this work.

A review of the bureaupathology literature demonstrates an association between high levels of bureaucracy and employees both underreporting, and concealing, fraud. In addition, the state of complexity and hierarchical rigidity, characteristic of bureaucracies, can create an organizational environment that could impede the successful operation of a fraud hotline.

Bureaupathology and Hotlines

First, it is important to review the potential effects bureaupathology can have on a fraud hotline, which include crime concealment, reduced fraud reporting and reduced hotline performance.

Crime Concealment

Employees can react to excessive bureaucracy by concealing crime. In his work "Excessive Bureaucratization: The J-Curve Theory of Bureaucracy and Max Weber through the Looking Glass," Caiden (1985) says the "excessive division of labor" present in an excessive bureaucracy results in a "detachment" on the part of the employee, which causes them to conceal known crime.

Specifically, according to Caiden (1985),

> For most caught in excessive division of labor, there is a detachment that cares not whether the job is spoilt or targets are reached, or property is stolen, or the work is constantly disrupted. While they themselves may not deliberately act wrongly, they do not prevent others from doing so. They keep their minds on their own business, which is staying out of trouble. They do not inform on wrong doing which could be a breach of work etiquette in their position, and, when required by peer pressure and identification, they protect wrongdoers by covering up. They drift through life, or at least their work life, in a dream, doing whatever is necessary to justify their continued employment and membership, but not much more. They do not believe—with reason—that anything they do will change their job situation. It will all be much the same wherever they go and whatever they do." (p. 25)

Excessive bureaucracy can also cause employees to become insecure. As a result, employees may not report potential crime for fear of being wrong. In 1998, Bozeman and Rainey found that bureaucracy creates a work environment that has "an inherent flaw ... providing a work environment highly conducive to the insecurities that flow between specialization and authority" (1998, p. 168).

Researchers say employee insecurity can result in:

> "information asymmetry" where those at the top are responsible for tasks and outputs they neither perform nor fully understand, and in such cases they tend to rely on procedural control mechanisms (e.g., the number of forms filled out, number of clients processed) as substitutes for substantive control. The attempt to control the work of subordinates in this fashion creates a tendency for workers to "go by the book," avoid innovation, reduce the risk of error, and do little more than what they are told." (Scott, 2002, p. 478)

Reduced Fraud Reporting

There are several reasons why an employee may not report fraud in an excessively bureaucratic environment. For one, organizational bureaupathology can cause an employee to have misaligned goals (Thompson, 1961). When this happens, employees place their own goals over the success of the organization, which makes them reluctant to come forward to report fraud (Giblin, 1981, p. 22). Per Giblin (1981), the "dense interpersonal environment of modern bureaucracy ... by its very nature, elicits and rewards a narcissistic response" (p. 22). In other words, instead of focusing on the goals of the organization (preventing and detecting fraud), the employees focus on their personal goals (getting raises, promotions) (Caiden, 1985; Giblin, 1981; Thompson, 1961).

In the extreme, theorists say bureaupathology can cause an employee to focus solely on himself or herself. As a result, employees subject to these conditions would not be concerned with organizational fraud. Giblin says organizational bureaupathology can generate "neurotic organizational behavior" in workers, which causes them to be overly concerned with their own "hierarchical position and power" as opposed to fraud reporting (Giblin, 1981).

In addition, employees subject to bureaupathology with an excessive hierarchical structure, decide their own job tasks. Therefore, if employees decide that fraud reporting will not be a part of their job, it will not occur. Per Giblin (1981), excessive bureaucracy manifesting in excessive hierarchy gives employees "excessive latitude to determine their own roles and activities," and they may tend to select to engage in only those activities that contribute to their own personal power or wealth (p. 23).

Also, where excessive hierarchy exists, bureaupathology theorists say employees spend much of their time navigating the complex work environment, rather than focusing on meaningful activities, such as fraud detection (Giblin, 1981).

Furthermore, bureaupathology causes employees to become routinized in their duties. When this happens, employees may not consider deviating from their regular work routine, to do something such as reporting fraud to a hotline. Bureaucracy theorists have said that organizational bureaucracy breeds an environment where employees become insecure in their responsibilities. As a result, employees can have a "pathological response" where the individual worker will tend to do only "what they are told" (Thompson, 1961, p. 150). Per Thompson (1961),

> Strict control from above encourages employees to "go by the book," to avoid innovations and chances of error which put black marks on the record. It encourages decision by precedent, and unwillingness to exercise initiative or take a chance. It encourages employees to wait for orders, and only do what they are told. (p. 150)

Reduced Hotline Performance

Bureaupathology may also result in an ill-functioning hotline that is unable to properly handle tips. One reason for this is that managers may not be focused on the hotline's success. According to theorists like Giblin, managers in an excessively bureaucratic organization tend to devote a majority of their attention on navigating the organization, as opposed to process improvement. As a result, process and people management become secondary concerns. Giblin says "the importance of the professional's knowledge and ability...become(s) secondary to the social skills required in the job—the ability to move oneself through the dense interpersonal environment" and that "the higher the jobs are in the organization, with corresponding emphasis on social intercourse, the more difficult it becomes to truly evaluate these jobs" (p. 23).

Excessive bureaucracy can also prevent managers from evaluating their programs. As a result, performance issues with hotlines can go unnoticed. Per Giblin (1981), excessive bureaucracy can keep management focus on himself or herself and away from "functional job content" (p. 24).

Hotline management by third-party companies can also add to program bureaucracy. Third-party hotline providers manage many, sometimes thousands, public and private sector hotlines. While using an outside provider may add independence, researchers find that the third-party provider can add an additional layer of bureaucracy that may hinder the investigative process (Anechiarico & Jacobs, 1996, p. 72).

Bureaucracy can also inhibit the collaborative process associated with hotline success. Deloitte (2011), in a report about whistleblowing post-Dodd–Frank, says the bureaucracy in most organizations presents a challenge for information sharing and oversight of fraud hotline programs (p. 2).

Other Relevant Literature

Additional literature that is relevant to this study is recent literature regarding the potential effect of bureaucracy on a major hotline, the Securities and Exchange

Commission's hotline. Also relevant is literature concerning the use and value of Glassdoor data in research.

U.S. Securities and Exchange Commission's Hotline and Bureaucracy

Critics have said that the U.S. Securities and Exchange Commission (SEC) hotline is underperforming due to bureaucracy (Sidel, 2011). Therefore, it is important to briefly review this hotline in light of organizational bureaucracy.

The SEC hotline was established in 2011, and 2012 represented their first full year of operation. In that year, they received 3,001 reports (SEC OIG, 2013). In 2013 they received 3,238 complaints, representing an 8% increase from FY 2012 (p. 8). Overall, since 2011, 6,573 tips have been received by the SEC Office of the Whistleblower (OWB) (SEC, 2013, p. 8).

Despite the number of calls received, statistics suggest that the "success" rate of the hotline, to date, is low. The SEC defines the success of their whistleblower hotline tips as "original information ... that leads to the successful enforcement of a covered action...[which makes the complainant] eligible to apply for a whistleblower award" (SEC OWB, 2014). Of these tips, as of October 2013, six resulted in an award to the tipster (U.S. Securities and Exchange Commission, 2013, p. 14). With 6,573 tips provided to the hotline, the program has a "success rate" of 0.09%.

Meanwhile, program evaluators for the SEC Whistleblower Program identified performance issues—specifically, their absence of metrics. After their first year of operation, the SEC Office of the Inspector General (OIG) conducted a full evaluation of the Whistleblower Program. Upon review, they noted the absence of performance metrics. Per the OIG, "the whistleblower program's internal controls need to be strengthened by adding performance metrics" to "measure process performance." (2013, pp. v, 38) According to the OIG, the absence of performance metrics "may result in the degradation in performance and unnecessary long response times to whistleblower information." (p. 21).

The program's absence of attention to performance is consistent with Giblin's theory, wherein he finds "This phenomenon of complex organizations facilitates, indeed encourages people in managerial and administrative positions to engage in non-organizational goal-directed behavior" (1981, p. 23).

It is possible that potential callers have avoided the hotline due to perceived agency bureaucracy. Recent media reports have said that the SEC could not properly vet whistleblower complaints (Singer, 2013; Tobe, 2013). Experts have said tipsters are "not coming forward with even valid claims because they are intimidated by the length of the bureaucratic process" one that Forbes called "ponderous" (Singer, 2013; Tobe, 2013).

Glassdoor Data in Research

This study analyzed anonymous employee reviews submitted to the website Glassdoor.com for indicators of dysfunctional bureaucracy and bureaupathology. Glassdoor.com is defined by *Bloomberg Businessweek* as follows:

> Glassdoor, Inc. operates as a free online jobs and career community. The company helps employees, job seekers, employers, and recruiters in finding and sharing information about the companies and jobs. It offers company reviews, interview questions and reviews, off ice photos, salary details, and information to make career decisions. Glassdoor, Inc. was founded in 2007 and is based in Sausalito, California. (Bloomberg Businessweek, 2013)

The use of Glassdoor as an information source is becoming an industry trend. At present, according to a recent article in Business Insider, 700 employers are currently partnering with Glassdoor to gather information on job seekers (Giang, 2013). In addition, their data are gaining popularity as a key industry resource. For instance, online Information Technology news provider ZD Net recently published an article where they used Glassdoor data as the determining factor for business outlook projections over the ensuing 6 months (King, 2013). In this article, Glassdoor ratings of leading companies such as Google and Amazon were was included in the analysis.

Glassdoor is also conducting their own reporting on major companies using data entered by their users as a measure of the company's success. For instance, in May 2013, Glassdoor examined Facebook using the measures of how respondent employees "[felt] about their work environment" (King). Quotes from reviews taken directly from the website were included in the analysis. In fact, Glassdoor reports, including one conducted annually called their "Top 25 Companies for Work Life Balance,"' have appeared prominently in recent articles featured in highly respected media outlets, such as Forbes.com ("Glassdoor: Digital Exuberance Hampers Work-Life Balance," Judy Martin, Forbes.com, July 19, 2013), CNET ("Nokia, Yahoo Rank Among Top Companies For Work-life Balance," Rachel King, Tech Culture, July 19, 2013), NBC ("Glassdoor: 5 Companies with Best Work-Life Balance Sit in Bay Area," Scott Budman, July 19, 2013), and North Bay Business Journal ("Glassdoor Breaks Into Global Online Job Search," Loralee Stevens, April 15, 2013).

Chapter 6

Case Studies

The central research question of this study is "Does organizational bureau-cracy affect fraud hotline performance?" This study examines the relationship between organizational bureaucracy and fraud hotline performance by examin-ing the answers to a series of sub-questions to isolate performance indicators. This research employs a case study method and uses organizations as a unit of analysis. Six organizations' hotlines, including two private sector, three government sector, and one nonprofit sector hotline, are analyzed in this study. This study focuses on employee callers of hotlines, as they are the primary audience of fraud hotlines. This study also focuses on internal crime, as it is the type of crime committed by employees.

This study considers the following sub-questions. Does dysfunctional organi-zational bureaucracy exist in the six subject organizations? Do employees perceive bureaupathology in the six subject organizations? Does bureaupathology result in reduced hotline functionality? Does bureaupathology result in low number of hot-line calls? Does bureaupathology result in reduced best practices compliance? Does bureaupathology result in fraud, waste, and abuse?

To measure the above, the following conditions will be established: (i) state of dysfunctional organizational bureaucracy in each of the subject organizations; (ii) perception of employees as to bureaucracy in their organizations; (iii) func-tionality of the hotline, to include the number of hotline calls received by the subject organization; (iv) level of adherence of best practices compliance by the subject organization; and (vi) state of internal fraud, waste, and abuse in the subject organization.

To establish the state of dysfunctional organizational bureaucracy, this study uses relevant literature, to include organizational documents and media reports.

To determine the perception of employees as to the state of bureaucracy in their organizations, this study examines social media data in the form of employee reviews, for statements suggesting organizational bureaucracy indicators. To ascertain the number of calls received to the hotline, this study examines individual-level fraud hotline data for each organization and compares that with established benchmarking levels. To understand the level of adherence of best practice compliance in the subject organization, this study examined organizational documents, media records, and other public documents, and evaluated that information against the U.S. Sentencing Guidelines for Organizations. To determine the level of internal fraud, waste, and abuse, in each of the subject organizations, this study examined media records and other public documents.

Significance of the Problem

Employee crime has persisted despite the existence of fraud hotlines. Fraud hotlines are advanced by legislation as a fraud prevention and detection tool. Hotlines were required by legislation as a measure to protect the public in the wake of massive employee crime. The assumption of the legislation enacted from 2002 to 2010 was that employees would use hotlines to report fraud. Employees are said to know about crime occurring in their organizations. Hotlines are receiving tips, yet these tips are not thwarting major crime.

Hotlines cannot be sufficiently analyzed using the data available, and methods commonly employed, today. Presently, there are no reporting standards for hotline data. Organizations, including publicly listed companies who are required to have fraud hotlines, do not have to provide their hotline metrics to anyone. They do not have to be reported in company reports, such as the 10-K, or otherwise shared inside or outside the organization. As a result, it is very challenging today to determine fraud hotline utility and performance.

Hotlines are not currently subject to robust performance monitoring. Organizations that have fraud hotlines are encouraged to benchmark their metrics. However, the available benchmarking data are incomplete and may not be a sufficient method for analysis. For instance, benchmarking data available for the financial industry are not provided in a disaggregated fashion. Rather, they are combined with the data of another industry. As a result, this industry is unable to isolate their data for a true performance measure.

Benchmarking is also not the only method of performance analysis. The use of benchmarking data as a performance measure ignores certain factors, such as functionality, best practice adherence, employee sentiment, organizational climate, external or historical factors, etc.

Recent media reports have said that agency bureaucracy may be adversely affecting fraud hotlines—specifically, the U.S. Securities and Exchange Commission's Whistleblower Hotline, established by Congress in 2010. Thus, this work seeks to determine whether organizational bureaucracy affects the fraud hotline process.

The bureaucracy literature suggests that agency bureaucracy may adversely affect a hotline in several ways. It may prevent employees from reporting, it may cause employees to conceal fraud, and it may also hinder the hotline's ability to properly handle calls.

Contribution to the Literature

There are several aspects to this research, which make it relevant and provide a significant contribution to the literature. For one, today, the research literature is very light on fraud hotlines, in general. Fraud hotlines have also never been analyzed individually, and comprehensively, for performance. Hotlines have also never been analyzed against any organizational theory. This study is also unique in that it uses social media data to determine organizational climate.

Theoretical Basis

Organizational bureaucracy may affect a fraud hotline in several ways. For one, it may prevent the hotline from receiving necessary tips, by hindering employee reporting and/or causing employees to conceal fraud. It can also result in reduced fraud reporting. It may also prevent the organization from properly handing calls received.

Critics say program bureaucracy can limit the efficacy of hotline programs (Kelly, 2012; Kocieniewski, 2012). While legislation supports the use of hotlines to receive fraud tips, hotlines may not function well in certain organizational environments. For example, the Dodd–Frank Wall Street Reform and Consumer Protection Act of 2010 augmented The Sarbanes–Oxley Act of 2002 (SOX) to add the U.S. Securities and Exchange Commission's (SEC) Whistleblower Program, which provides rewards for tipsters, who may now report directly to the SEC. However, in light of the number of tipsters, the program has not produced many rewards.

A review of the literature demonstrates that there is an association between high levels of bureaucracy and employees both underreporting, and concealing, fraud.

There are several reasons why an employee may not report fraud in an excessively bureaucratic environment. For one, the literature suggests that an employee's tendency to underreport fraud can be a result of misaligned goals (Thompson, 1961, pp. 92–100). According to some researchers, such as Edward Giblin (1981), the state of excessive bureaucracy, or bureaupathology, causes employees to place their own goals over the success of the organization, which makes them reluctant to come forward to report fraud (pp. 22–25).

Overall, fraud hotlines appear to be ineffective at revealing major frauds. A case study of individual fraud hotlines in light of organizational bureaucracy may shed light on this issue. Research regarding the Theory of Bureaucracy suggests that bureaucratic processes that exist within organizations can be contrary to the mission of a successful hotline reporting process, and can explain the reason why employees may not report fraud via hotlines, why a hotline can be insufficiently communicated to employees, and why the complaints may not be triaged in a manner consistent with the information they intend to collect (major fraud reporting). It is possible, based on the literature, that fraud hotlines have succumbed to institutionalization of the surrounding organization (O'Hara, 2005, p. 149).

Relevant Literature

Fraud hotlines, used in government organizations since the 1970s, have been advanced as a method of fraud prevention and detection since the passage of SOX in 2002. As a confidential reporting mechanism where employees can report fraud occurring in their workplace, hotlines are valued for their ability to receive anonymous tips, and their ability to receive such tips from internal sources.

Despite the existence of hotlines, employee crime has persisted and has become increasingly more severe. First, major internal frauds destroyed companies and caused legislators to require public companies to institute fraud hotlines. Then, yet more major internal frauds have occurred, which are believed to have contributed to the recent financial crisis (2008–2012), which damaged the world economy. In response, legislation further requiring companies to use fraud hotlines was established. However, internal crime has persisted (Kashton, 2011). Some critics believe bureaucracy might limit the efficacy of the hotline process (Kelly, 2012; Kocieniewski, 2012; Singer, 2013; Tobe, 2013).

According to the literature, hotlines are the best way to prevent fraud but they may not function well due to organizational bureaucracy, which can impede hotline performance.

While legislation supports the use of hotlines to receive fraud tips, it is believed that hotlines may not function well in certain organizational environments. A review of the literature demonstrates that there is an association between high levels of bureaucracy and employees underreporting, and concealing, fraud.

Problem Statement

Employee crime has been one of the biggest threats facing organizations for nearly 40 years. In 1977, the American Management Association (AMA) reported that employee theft represented "the single biggest source of loss due to crimes against business." Today, industry surveys indicate that this problem persists. In 2011, a PricewaterhouseCoopers (PWC) survey determined that internal crime was the most serious problem facing organizations (Global Economic Crime Survey). In a 2014 survey, PWC found that one in three organizations is affected by economic crime (Kroll, 2013/2014; PWC, 2014). According to Kroll's recent Global Fraud Report, 72% of those surveyed said their company suffered a fraud involving an employee (2013/2014).

Recent employee thefts have been severe enough to threaten the world economy. According to the Federal Bureau of Investigation, the global financial crisis of 2007–2012, when hundreds of banks failed, financial assets worldwide declined by $50 trillion, and 51 million jobs were lost, was caused by employee crime (FBI, 2011).

Evidence demonstrated that employees with knowledge of crime were not reporting it to company hotlines. Hotlines were first established to prevent corporate fraud under The Sarbanes–Oxley Act of 2002. Following the crisis in 2010, The Dodd–Frank Wall Street Reform and Consumer Protection Act ("Dodd–Frank") was created, which incentivized employees with monetary rewards and expanded the scope of their crime reporting audience to include the SEC.

It is difficult to determine the value of calls received to hotlines, from the data available today. Specifically, it is unclear as to how many hotline calls are resulting in criminal prosecutions. Available statistics show tips received by hotlines are not leading to criminal prosecutions. According to the 2013 Corporate Governance and Compliance Hotline Benchmarking Report from The Network, one of the leading third-party hotline providers, none of the tips they handled between 2005 and 2011 led to a single criminal prosecution. In 2012, it was reported that less than 1% lead to a criminal prosecution (2013, p. 20).

Hotlines are believed to prevent corporate crime. Studies, such as a 2002 study conducted by the big four accounting firm Ernst & Young, showed that as many as 1 in 5 workers are aware of fraud occurring in their place of employment. Furthermore, research has continually demonstrated that employee tips are the primary way in which fraud is discovered within an organization. (ACFE Report, 2002–2012)

A likely mechanism to receive such tips would be through the fraud hotline, the reporting mechanism employed by many major public companies since SOX. Yet, in their 2010 Report to the Nation, the ACFE reported that only half of their subject organizations that employed a fraud hotline, and received notification of fraud by employee tip, actually received the tip via the hotline.

Timely notification is critical. According to a 2011 KPMG Report, in the United States alone, the average internal fraud was perpetuated for over 4 years before it was finally discovered, costing victimized firms 1.2 million on average.

Overall, the reason fraud hotlines are critically important to a given organization is because they serve as the predominant mechanism for receiving whistleblower complaints, which are the primary ways in which fraud is discovered in a given organization. Legislative reform has reinforced the importance of whistleblower complaints by requiring companies to have anonymous reporting mechanisms (Sarbanes–Oxley, 2002) and allowing complainants to bypass internal processes and go straight to the SEC (Dodd–Frank Wall Street Reform and Consumer Protection Act, 2010).

Nevertheless, whether the complainant is reporting internally or externally, employee crime persists despite various iterations of the internal complaint process and despite employee knowledge of fraud. This leaves one to question the purpose and utility of the fraud hotline.

Research Question

This work explores the relationship between organizational bureaucracy and fraud hotlines, using six organizations' hotlines as case studies. The central question of this work is as follows: Does organizational bureaucracy affect fraud hotline performance?

The dependent variable in this study is fraud hotline performance. The independent variable in this study is organizational bureaucracy. The unit of analysis in this study is organizations.

This central question will be divided into a series of sub-questions.

In answering those sub-questions, this work will identify and isolate specific indicators, which will be used to measure an organization's fraud hotline performance. This study considers the following sub-questions:

1. Does dysfunctional organizational bureaucracy exist in the six subject organizations?
2. Do employees perceive bureaupathology in the six subject organizations?
3. Does bureaupathology result in reduced hotline functionality?
4. Does bureaupathology result in low number of hotline calls?
5. Does bureaupathology result in reduced best practices compliance?
6. Does bureaupathology result in fraud, waste, and abuse?

The first two questions establish whether the organization has dysfunctional bureaucracy conditions present and whether they are perceptible by employees. To measure the above, the following conditions will be established: (i) state of organizational bureaucracy in each of the subject organizations; (ii) perception of employees as to bureaucracy in their organizations; (iii) number of hotline calls received by the subject organization; (iv) functionality of the hotline; (v) level of adherence of best practices compliance by the subject organization, and (vi) state of internal fraud, waste, and abuse in the subject organization.

Methodology

This chapter discusses the research methodology employed in this work. This discussion includes a detailed description of the study subjects; the research method; and the threats to validity, variables, procedure, and data.

Subjects

This study uses a case study research method. The population of this study consists of six organization's hotlines—two in the private sector, three in the public sector (government entities), and one in the nonprofit sector. The subjects of this study will not be named. The reason their identity is being withheld is because their identity is irrelevant to the overall research purpose. In addition, the hotline administrators and interview subjects were advised that their personally indefinable information would not be provided in writing. This study could service the government entities that do not have an expectation of privacy due to Freedom of Information Laws (FOIL). However, for consistency, their names will also be withheld.

The two private sector companies involved are from the financial industry. They are bank holding companies that are ranked in the top ten by the United States Federal Reserve System, based on consolidated assets as of June 30, 2012. Represented among the government sector hotlines are hotlines in the federal, state, and local government sectors, along with a city agency–level hotline. The subject of this study was named by Forbes as one of the top 200 largest charities (Forbes, 2006).

The names of the subjects of this research will be referenced throughout this study as ("Private Sector," PS) PS1, PS2; ("Government Sector," GS) GS1, GS2, GS3; and ("Nonprofit," NP) NP1.

PS1 is a financial services firm of approximately 61,899 employees (per their most recent Form 10-K, filed February 27, 2012). The hotline data from PS1 are from the years 2006–2007 (3Q 2006 to 4Q, 2007). During that time, PS1 had anywhere from 48,000–55,000 employees.

PS2 is a financial services firm of approximately 266,000 employees (per their most recent Form 10-K, filed February 24, 2012). The fraud hotline data obtained from PS2 are from the years 2004–2010. During that time, PS2 had anywhere from 259,000–387,000 employees.

GS1, a federal organization, can expect to receive tips from anyone in the United States (U.S.). The U.S. population as of July 2011 was 311,591,917, according to the U.S. Census. According to agency documents, GS1 had 17,359 employees as of 2011.

GS2, a state-level government, can expect to receive tips from anyone who resides in the state, which has a population of 5,711,767 as of July 2011, according to the U.S. Census. According to agency documents, GS2 had 283,351 public workers as of 2011.

GS3, a city-level government, can expect to receive tips from anyone who resides in their city, which has a population of 1,326,179 as of July 2011, according to the U.S. Census. According to agency documents, GS3 had 19,500 employees.

NP1 is a large nonprofit organization. According to agency documents, in 2012, NP1 had 28,973 employees.

Design

This study used a case study research method. The unit of analysis in this study is organizations. This case study examined the fraud hotline process in six organizations.

The case study method was appropriate for several reasons. For one, there is a lack of available data. Specifically, individual-level fraud hotline data are difficult to obtain. There are no reporting requirements and information in the public domain is limited. Hotline administrators sometimes make hotline data available upon request for research purposes. But overall, the paucity of available empirical data limits the scope of quantitative analysis.

In addition, the data provided often lacked the granular detail necessary to establish an association based on data alone. Rich qualitative detail, provided in case study format, was necessary to establish a relationship between the independent variable, organizational bureaucracy, and the dependent variable, fraud hotline process.

In addition, case studies are appropriate for this research endeavor, for their unique ability to illuminate specific incidences of deviance. For that reason, researchers often use this method when analyzing organizations. In the "*Dark Side of Organizations: Mistake, Misconduct and Disaster*," researcher Diane Vaughan advances case studies, insofar as they "hold memorable lessons about how organizational processes systematically produce unanticipated outcomes that deviate from formal design goals and normative standards" (1999, p. 277). In his book, *Why Law Enforcement Organizations Fail*, Patrick O'Hara (2005) used a case study method to analyze organizational deviance.

The case study is a collective case study design, in that six organization's fraud hotlines were examined. Per qualitative researcher Robert E. Stake (1995), collective case studies examine individual matters, yet appreciate the relationships found between the subjects. Specifically, Stake finds collective case studies embrace how "each case study is instrumental to learning about the effects of [the independent variable on the dependent variable] but [consider the] important coordination between the individual studies" (p. 4).

This study included both a primary and secondary data collection approach, insofar as the researcher collected original data from interviews, yet used the data of the subject organization to assess their hotline's performance. This case study is also both qualitative and quantitative in nature, although it leans primarily qualitative, due to data limitations.

The case study method was used to examine whether, for a set of fraud hotlines, the hotline was performing according to expectations, by analyzing the individual calls received against the known frauds that occurred in the organization.

Interviews

In order to obtain organizational data, four hotline managers were interviewed. Three of the interview subjects were hotline managers in three of the subject organizations (PS1, PS2, NP1), and one interview subject was a hotline account manager at The Network, a third-party provider of hotline services to several of the subject organizations (PS1, PS2, and GS3) and whose benchmarking data were used in this study. For the most part, in this study, the data and information were obtained from the public domain or was obtained by the author in the normal course of business and/or provided to the author for research purposes and therefore is not considered confidential.

The subjects were interviewed in their capacity as the keepers of organizational data. The conversations took place with the purpose of obtaining their data, and to gain a general understanding of their fraud hotline process. This data and information were a part of their ordinary business records. As such, these data are not considered to be confidential. Nevertheless, the identity of the interview subjects will be kept private, as it is not relevant to the research purpose.

Interviews for this study were primarily conducted using a convenience and snowball sampling method, and the subjects were selected on the basis of availability to the researcher and their willingness to participate in the interview process. Interviews were conducted between 2007 and 2013. The interviews were primarily conducted to obtain organizational data (hotline metrics). For organizations where interviews were not required to obtain metrics, (GS1-3) interviews were not conducted.

For PS1, one person was interviewed in 2007; a current employee of the company (at the time of the interview) served as the hotline administrator for the company. For PS2, two people were interviewed in 2012. The subjects interviewed included a hotline administrator for the company and a representative of The Network, which manages the company's fraud hotline.

The hotline administrator was asked questions that could not be gleaned directly from the data, such as the general number of financial services and government clients they manage; the way that hotline complaints are handled from the point of receipt, to the point of reporting to the client; whether individual-level advice/analysis is provided to clients about their organization's reporting trends; and how their employees are trained to manage calls.

Threats to Validity

The threats to validity in this research effort relate to the number of cases, self-selecting participants, and descriptive and interpretative validity.

Number of Cases

Case study research, although a highly celebrated method for organizational research, has been challenged with respect to validity, reliability, and generalizability (Merriam-Webster Dictionary, 2014). One of the primary reasons as to why validity is challenged is due to the isolated number of items, or cases, researched. Here, to control for that challenge, several organizations' hotlines were chosen as subjects for review (six), and represent a range of business, in both the private and public sectors, including a medium and large financial services firm; a city, state, and federal government entity; and a nonprofit organization. Complete randomization is simply not possible in this instance, due to a limited availability of data.

To assure validity of this study's measurements, triangulation was used. In "The Art of Case Study Research," Robert Stake (1995) advances triangulation as a method to overcome threats to validity. Sharan Merriam (1995) further advances this method, which in this case will entail conversations with the sources of the data, where possible, and peer consultation, which will further help to establish validity.

Here, interviews were conducted with three hotline administrators, including one from each private sector organization, and with a representative from The Network, the third-party hotline provider for several subjects of this study. Employee review data from Glassdoor.com was also used to validate research findings. Extensive company research in the public domain was also conducted on each of these organizations, to validate information gleaned from employees.

Self-Selecting Participants

The employees who submitted reviews on Glassdoor.com can be considered self-selecting participants, which creates a level of bias. Glassdoor is a website that is available to the general public. Employees provide reviews of companies to this website on a completely voluntary and anonymous basis.

Overall, Glassdoor respondents came to the website independently, and chose to supply information on their own and without compensation. In Glassdoor, employees are incentivized to provide their review as a condition of gaining access to the website to conduct their own research (the website also provides salary information, interview experiences, among other information). However, due to the detailed nature of the comments, the respondents believe the company monitors the content, and believe as respondents, they can effect organizational changes.

Descriptive Validity

Per Maxwell, qualitative research can suffer from descriptive validity (Maxwell, 1992). Here, this potential exists, as individual researcher interpretation of the qualitative data (the analysis of employee reviews) is potentially subject to interpretation. However, Maxwell finds this problem can be overcome by having "different observers come to agree on their descriptive accuracy" (Maxwell, 1992, p. 288). Here, the original data and the corresponding interpretation are provided by this study and can therefore be validated by the reader.

Ideally, the comments could be validated via interview, or otherwise. However, in this case, the contributors are anonymous. There is value in anonymous information, as is the spirit of an anonymous reporting mechanism (fraud hotline) that is the very subject of this study. Therefore, it is clear anonymous information has merit.

In addition, many of the comments were quite detailed and included information specific to the organization, which would have been difficult to fabricate. Although there is an expected margin of error with anonymous web-based reviews, the validity of the reviews is supported by the detailed information supplied.

Interpretative Validity

Maxwell acknowledges the possibility of interpretative validity in qualitative research but says that it is essentially impossible to overcome because researchers are constantly interpreting information provided by participants (1992, p. 290). And obtaining additional data would not address this issue. Per Maxwell, "there is no in principle access to data that would unequivocally address threats to validity. Interpretative validity is inherently a matter of inference from the words and actions of participants in the situations studied" (1992, p. 290).

Here, the data entry process in Glassdoor further validated the data. On Glassdoor, participants are not lead toward any particular outcome. The data field is open-ended, consisting of a simple text box for "pros" and "cons." In response, as indicated in this study, employees typed out very detailed responses. This detail served to validate the content, and gave credence to the content insofar as it indicated strong emotion on the part of the employee, whether negative or positive in nature. As a result, the fact that respondents may have indicated an excessive bureaucracy condition is a significant finding, considering the options for comment were unlimited.

Notwithstanding the inherent bias, from a qualitative research perspective, these data are extremely valuable, insofar as they provide a unique insight into a population that is otherwise unavailable to researchers. The subject organizations would not permit such interviews or surveys of their employees for research purposes. Therefore, the use of existing data was critical in establishing employee mindset regarding the presence of the independent variable in this study.

The use of social media data was an ideal method for this research endeavor. The perception of bureaucracy by the employee is essential to this research effort, as the employees are the target audience of company/agency fraud hotlines. Employees could not be interviewed for this study for this purpose (only certain hotline administrators could be interviewed). Here, social media data provided insight to the mindset of an otherwise unreachable population. Second, these data are publically available and accessible to researchers. In addition, Glassdoor contained data from all of the subject organizations, providing consistency. Finally, the anonymous, online interviews provided rich, candid detail from the perspective of the employee that may not have otherwise been gained from a personal interview.

Data interpretation was also required due to the format in which the data were provided. On Glassdoor, the reviews are not provided in a spreadsheet or otherwise in a readily analyzable form. Instead, they are free-form reviews where the respondent freely chooses the language used (not selected from a list, etc.). As a result, while the reviews can be "sorted" by rating level, and other limited criteria, overall research efforts involve reading each individual review for the qualitative informational content.

Inter-Coder Reliability

To establish inter-coder reliability with the social media data analyzed in this study, two external coders were used to verify the data. Coders received 10% of randomized social media comments, which were randomized using the randomization feature in Excel. The operationalized definitions they coded included the "type" which refers to comments relating to either "bureaucracy" or "bureaupathic" (relating to bureaupathology), as defined in this work.

Once the comment type was determined by the coders, it was coded according to the defined attributes of bureaucracy and bureaupathology, which were defined for the coders by a description of the attributes, as set forth in this work: (i) state of bureaucracy: (ii) hierarchy of authority; (iii) system of rules; (iv) technical expertise; (v) career service; and (vi) insistence on the rights of office (Thompson, 1961).

The state of bureaupathology, determined by the presence of bureaupathic conditions, was measured using the following attributes: (i) impersonal treatment; (ii) prolonged role enactment; (iii) resistance to change; (iv) resistance to interrogation and investigation; and (v) strict reliance on organizational rules and procedures (Thompson, 1961, pp. 153–177).

It was found that there was 95% inter-coder reliability with bureaucratic/bureaupathological designations, and 92% inter-coder reliability with the attributes.

Variables

This work explores the relationship between organizational bureaucracy and fraud hotlines, using six organizations' hotlines as case studies. The central question of this work is: Does organizational bureaucracy affect fraud hotline performance? The variables in this study are as follows: The dependent variable is fraud hotline performance, and the independent variable is organizational bureaucracy.

Additional variables are identified in the research sub-questions. The research sub-questions are as follows: (i) Does dysfunctional organizational bureaucracy exist in the six subject organizations? (ii) Do employees perceive bureaupathology in the six subject organizations? (iii) Does bureaupathology result in reduced hotline functionality? (iv) Does bureaupathology result in low number of hotline calls? (v) Does bureaupathology result in reduced best practices compliance? (vi) Does bureaupathology result in fraud, waste and abuse?

The variables in the sub-questions include "low hotline calls"; "reduced hotline functionality"; "reduced best practices compliance"; and "fraud, waste, and abuse."

Primary Research Question

The central question of this work is as follows: Does organizational bureaucracy affect fraud hotline performance? The independent variable is organizational bureaucracy and the dependent variable is fraud hotline performance. There are also six sub-questions in this work.

Independent Variable

The independent variable in this study is organizational bureaucracy. The dependent variable is fraud hotline performance. The variables were operationalized as follows. In this study, organizations are the unit of analysis. Organizations are, by definition, "a company, business club, etc. that is formed for a particular purpose" (Merriam-Webster Dictionary, 2014). In this study, the organizations subject to analysis were two private sector organizations, three public sector/government organizations, and one nonprofit sector organization.

The organizations subject to this study are not identified by name in this work, for a number of reasons. For one, some organizations (private sector and nonprofit sector) provided their data for research purposes, yet others were obtained in the public domain (public sector). While the organizations did not object to being identified, this study determined that their identity was not relevant to the research purpose, which is to determine the effect of organizational bureaucracy on fraud hotline performance.

The independent variable of organizational bureaucracy was operationalized as follows. First, it is of interest to note that bureaucracy is not "defined" per say, but rather is known and determined by the presence of a set of attributes (Tompkins, 2005). The state of bureaucracy can be measured using the following known attributes: (i) hierarchy of authority; (ii) system of rules; (iii) technical expertise; (iv) career service; and (v) insistence on the rights of office (Thompson, 1961).

Bureaupathology is the state of excessive bureaucracy, which is determined by the presence of bureaupathic conditions, which represent the negative effects of bureaucratic leadership (Thompson, 1961). This study establishes the state of bureaupathology in the subject organizations, as it reveals that the organization exhibits an excessive state of organizational bureaucracy. The state of bureaupathology, determined by the presence of bureaupathic conditions, was measured using the following known attributes: (i) impersonal treatment; (ii) prolonged role enactment; (iii) resistance to change; (iv) resistance to interrogation and investigation; and (v) strict reliance on organizational rules and procedures (Thompson, 1961, pp. 153–177).

The presence of the independent variable of organizational bureaucracy in the subject organizations was determined by a literature review and also via a content analysis of employee reviews of their company on the Glassdoor.com.

Employees' comments submitted to this website were analyzed for indicators of bureaucracy and bureaupathology, which were determined by qualitative evaluation. The employee statements were analyzed for specific reference to the established attributes, and itemized in chart form then tabulated.

The analysis also included a review of language for general mention of bureaucracy, such as the words "bureaucracy" and "red tape." In addition, language suggesting fraud, waste, or abuse was also noted, demonstrated in the statements "misuse of funds" and a "waste of donated income."

Dependent Variable

The dependent variable of fraud hotline performance was operationalized as follows. The dependent variable of hotline performance was measured in terms of the subject hotline's metrics, functionality, and extent of best practices implementation. The metrics refers to the number of calls received by the hotline during the time period analyzed. The functionality of the hotline was operationalized using the following elements: marketing, mechanics, intake/process, and incentives.

Hotline best practices were operationalized using the Organizational Sentencing Guidelines ("guidelines") from the U.S. Sentencing Commission (USSC), effective November 1991. The USSC developed key criteria for establishing an "effective compliance program" (Desio). The guidelines were established as a mitigating factor in organizational sentencing. Per Paula J. Desio, Deputy General Counsel (1997–2007) to the USSC,

> Criminal liability can attach to an organization whenever an employee of the organization commits an act within the apparent scope of his or her employment, even if the employee acted directly contrary to company policy and instructions. An entire organization, despite its best efforts to prevent wrongdoing in its ranks, can still be held criminally liable for any of its employee's illegal actions. Consequently, when the Commission promulgated the organizational guidelines, it attempted to alleviate the harshest aspects of this institutional vulnerability by incorporating into the sentencing structure the preventive and deterrent aspects of systematic compliance programs. The Commission did this by mitigating the potential fine range—in some cases up to 95 percent—if an organization can demonstrate that it had put in place an effective compliance program. This mitigating credit under the guidelines is contingent upon prompt reporting to the authorities and the non-involvement of high-level personnel in the actual offense conduct. Compliance standards and procedures reasonably capable of reducing the prospect of criminal activity are (i) oversight (by high-level personnel), (ii) due care (in delegating substantial discretionary authority),

(iii) effective communication (to all levels of employees), (iv) reasonable steps to achieve compliance (which include systems for monitoring, auditing, and reporting suspected wrongdoing without fear of reprisal) (v) consistent enforcement (of compliance standards including disciplinary mechanisms), and (vi) reasonable steps (to respond to and prevent further similar offenses upon detection of a violation. (p. 1)

Per Desio, the organizational guidelines were designed to be flexible for organizations. In other words, the guidelines are not absolute.

The organizational guidelines criteria embody broad principles that, taken together, describe a corporate "good citizenship" model, but do not offer precise details for implementation. This approach was deliberately selected in order to encourage flexibility and independence by organizations in designing programs that are best suited to their particular circumstances. (p. 1)

Sub-question Variables

The additional research variables are defined as follows. Low hotline calls are defined as calls below established benchmarking levels. Reduced hotline functionality will be established by measuring the hotline on the following criteria: (i) marketing, (ii) mechanics, (iii) intake/processing, and (iv) incentives. Reduced best practices compliance will be measured using the standards set forth by the Sentencing Guidelines for Organizations: (i) oversight (by high-level personnel), (ii) due care (in delegating substantial discretionary authority), (iii) effective communication (to all levels of employees), (iv) reasonable steps to achieve compliance (which include systems for monitoring, auditing, and reporting suspected wrongdoing without fear of reprisal) (v) consistent enforcement (of compliance standards including disciplinary mechanisms), and (vi) reasonable steps (to respond to and prevent further similar offenses upon detection of a violation.

In this work, "fraud, waste, and abuse" is limited to corporate crime that was located in the public domain during the relevant time period, corresponding to the hotline metrics analyzed in this study. In this work, corporate crime refers to employee embezzlement. The Federal Bureau of Investigation (FBI) defines embezzlement as the "misappropriation or misapplication of money or property entrusted to one's care, custody, or control" (2001).

The presence of fraud, waste, and abuse will be determined by a review of organizational documents, media reports, and employee statements among other sources.

Procedure

Overall, the methodology of this study was planned to evaluate whether organizational bureaucracy had a consistent relationship with hotline performance.

The procedure evaluates the presence and level of the independent variable of organizational bureaucracy in the organizations and the dependent variable of fraud hotline performance. The presence of crime was also measured to determine the possibility of reduced fraud reporting or crime concealment, per bureaucracy theory.

This methodology was employed using a case study design method. For each organization, the following procedure was followed.

The presence of organizational bureaucracy was determined, generally, from the literature. Then the perception of employees was determined by analyzing company reviews in social media. The individual comments were evaluated for the presence of the defined attributes of bureaucracy and bureaupathology. Each of these comments was evaluated and the presence of each attribute was measured. The presence of bureaupathology was measured, based on the comments, using an established scale. The strongest presence of various attributes was noted.

Fraud hotline performance was determined using the three performance criteria: (i) metrics benchmarking; (ii) functionality assessment; and (iii) best practices implementation. These three performance criteria were measured using defined scales to determine an overall assessment value.

Further, to determine the presence of known internal fraud, each organization was analyzed in the public domain. The time period of this analysis corresponded directly to the time period of the hotline metrics data obtained from the organization. Evidence of internal fraud was determined and tabulated.

The historical context of each organization was also evaluated. Again, this evaluation was conducted to correspond with the time frame of the hotline metrics data obtained from the organization.

The case studies of each of the six organizations were conducted as follows. First, the organization was researched for information relevant to determine the length of operation, number of employees, and other relevant background information. The hotline specifications of each organization were gleaned from their available organizational documents, company website, and interviews with hotline administrators. Organizational documents analyzed include company annual reports and fraud hotline reports. The website for each organization was also analyzed from the perspective of the employee (i.e., was the number externally accessible, as employees often call hotlines after business hours and from locations other than the office). This study evaluated whether the hotline process potentially deterred reporting, with complicated processes or deterrent language.

Using Glassdoor data, the reviews of current and former employees of the subject companies, for all of the case study subjects, PS1 (sample set), PS2 (sample set), GS1 (entire population), the GS2 (entire population), GS3 (entire population), and NP1 (sample set), were examined and measured. The Glassdoor interview data were measured using the indices of bureaucracy and bureaupathology.

The number of reviews analyzed for each organization varied. For the private sector organizations (PS1 and PS2) and the nonprofit entity (NP1), due to the large size of the population (of reviews available for research), the dataset analyzed was limited to a sample set consisting of the reviews that were deemed by Glassdoor measurement criteria to be below average for that organization.

The entire population of reviews for the organizations identified above was limited to a select sample size to make the research effort purposeful. The reason for limiting the sample size to "below-average" reviews is because it was reasoned that the employee reviewers were likely to use the language indicating dysfunctional bureaucracy and bureaupathology in "negative" reviews. The reason for this is because people tend to associate a negative connotation with the word "bureaucracy." It was believed, especially in an online review of their employer, an employee would be more likely to use language indicating bureaucracy in a review that was categorized by Glassdoor as "below average." This sampling method was purposeful, and is a common sampling technique for researchers wherein they "actively seek the most productive sample to answer the research question" (Marshall, 1996).

For the remaining subjects, GS1, GS2, and GS3, the entire population of data was examined and measured using the indices of bureaucracy and bureaupathology.

Upon collection, these data were analyzed as follows. To evaluate the level of bureaucracy and excessive bureaucracy, or bureaupathology, the comments indicating each one of the measurement criteria was counted and tabulated. The percentage of respondents, who indicated each measurement criteria, was viewed in light of the population, or sample size of reviews evaluated.

This study separated its evaluation of respondents and comments, for clarity. This method was necessary to indicate where a single reviewer made comments indicating more than one aspect of measurement criteria. For instance, if one respondent made comments indicating three measurement criteria, they were tabulated as one respondent, three comments. At the end of the analysis, a percentage of respondents versus comments was tabulated so that the distinction between the number of individual respondents and the number of actual comments was clear.

Evidence of negative employee sentiment was reported by this study, and was determined via the analysis of the general consensus of employee interviews posted on Glassdoor.

The performance of the individual hotline was further assessed by benchmarking its fraud hotline metrics using established industry figures produced by The Network, which publishes an annual benchmarking report.

The Network is the hotline administrator for approximately 3,000 clients. Its client base is not publicized, but research demonstrated that certain clients sometimes publicly reveal they are clients of The Network. Hence, this study determined

The Network is the administrator for at least three of the hotlines to be examined as part of this study (PS1, PS2 and GS3). As a result, it can be reasonably inferred that the benchmarking data provided by The Network include the data from the aforementioned organizations.

Next, the functionality and adherence to best practices was assessed. The individual functionality of the hotline was assessed with respect to the following key hotline elements: marketing, mechanics, intake/processing, and incentives.

Best practices implementation was determined by evaluating the presence of the key criteria outlined by the U.S. Sentencing Commission Sentencing Guidelines for Organizations in the subject organizations by reviewing organizational documents, media reports, and other information. These guidelines were used because they were identified by industry personnel (including the hotline administrators interviewed for this study) as their source of best practices for their hotlines.

The level of internal fraud in the organization was determined from a review of organizational documents, media records, and other public sources. The fraud included in this analysis was limited to fraud that involved employees, with a particular focus on fraud involving multiple parties and was reportedly known to many people—in other words, fraud that should have been reported to the hotline. The timeframe of fraud reported as part of this analysis corresponds to the timeframe of the hotline metrics analyzed.

Next, the incidence of employee fraud was established for the organization, during the relevant time period, which is the time frame corresponding to the hotline data. While the entire universe of employee fraud cannot be established with the data available today, the level of employee fraud was evaluated based on data obtained in the public domain (media reports). The presence of employee fraud in the given subject organization established whether employees committed internal fraud, during the relevant time period, which could have been reported via the hotline.

Best practices implementation was determined by evaluating the presence of the key criteria outlined by the U.S. Sentencing Commission in the subject organizations by reviewing organizational documents, media reports, and other information.

To determine a final performance level, each performance criterion was measured using a scale. The scale weighed the result of the three performance criteria: (i) metrics benchmarking; (ii) the functionality assessment; and the (iii) best practices implementation.

Next, the historical context for each time period corresponding to the hotline data collected was analyzed. Here, the "historical context" included any data, which could serve to supplement the understanding of the potential state of hotline reporting at that time corresponding to the metrics. Historical context could include: the state of the subject industry; any known social or environmental conditions giving rise to fraud; and the results of surveys conducted during this time period, among other relevant information. The historical context was determined by a literature review, to include media reports from the pertinent timeframe.

In each case study, the focus of the organizational analysis, to include the waste, fraud, and abuse, was limited to the period corresponding to the hotline data received. The data used to benchmark the case study data corresponded to the year of hotline data.

When benchmarking the data, the two known benchmarking figures were averaged to determine a true benchmark. In the hotline benchmarking data, two different benchmarking numbers are provided—one for size, and another for industry. Here, in each case study, an average of these figures was obtained to determine a true benchmarking figure.

Measurement Scales

The measurement scales in this study were designed to interpret the information in the following ways. The bureaupathology scale was created to assess the degree of comments present (indicating dysfunctional bureaucracy and bureaupathology). The remaining scales were designed to measure the general presence of indicators (functionality and best practices). Overall, the scales were designed where the lower number of points was a "better" score for the organization and the higher number of points was a "worse" score for the organization.

The presence of bureaupathology in each organization was measured using the following scale, corresponding to the percentage of employee comments indicating the presence:

1. 0–10% Present
2. 11–20%
3. 21–30%
4. 31–40%
5. 41–50% Elevated
6. 51–60%
7. 61–70%
8. 71–80%
9. 81–90%
10. 91–100% Extreme

Fraud hotline performance was determined using the three performance criteria: (i) metrics benchmarking; (ii) functionality assessment; and (iii) best practices implementation. These three performance criteria were measured using defined scales to determine an overall assessment value. Overall, the scales were designed where the lowest score determined a more successful hotline.

The hotline metrics were scaled as follows: (1 point) High, Meets or exceeds benchmarking in each year of analysis; (3 points) Low, Does not meet benchmarking estimates in many years of analysis; (5 points) Poor, Does not meet benchmarking estimates in any year of analysis.

The hotline functionality was scaled as follows: The functionality assessment criteria of (i) marketing, (ii) mechanics, (iii) intake/processing, and (iv) incentives were assessed on a scale where failure in each area was assessed with a single point, where scores indicate the following: Failure: 4 of 4; Poor: 3 of 4; Moderate: 2 of 4; Great: 1 of 4; and High: 0 of 4.

The best practices were assessed on a scale where one point was assessed for each of the areas that were not satisfied, including (i) oversight, (ii) due care, (iii) effective communication, (iv) reasonable steps to achieve compliance, (v) consistent enforcement, (vi) reasonable steps to prevent future offenses, where scores indicate the following: Failure: 6 of 6; Poor: 5 of 6; Weak: 4 of 6; Moderate: 3 of 6 ; Good: 2 of 6; Great: 1 of 6; High: 0 of 6.

The points for each of the hotline metrics, functionality, and best practices were added to achieve a final performance scale, as follows: Low: 14–15 points; Below Average: 10–13 points; Average: 7–9 points; Above Average: 5–8 points; and High: 0–4 points.

The historical context was analyzed using the following scale: It was considered conducive to fraud if it is established that conditions indicated there was significant employee fraud at the time of analysis and it is key.

Organization	PS1	PS2	GS1	GS2	GS3	NP1
Size						
Hotline Name						
Management						
Respondents Indicating IV						
Bureaucracy IV						
Bureaupathology IV						
Hotline metrics (DV)						
Hotline functionality (DV)						
Best practices (DV)						
Historical context (DV)						
Evidence of internal fraud						
Evidence of negative employee sentiment						
Result IV						
Result DV						
Notes						

Indices

Bureaucracy: (a) hierarchy of authority; (b) system of rules; (c) technical expertise; (d) career service, and (e) insistence on the rights of office.

Bureaupathology: (f) impersonal treatment, (g) prolonged role enactment, (h) resistance to change, (i) resistance to interrogation and investigation, and (j) strict reliance on organizational rules and procedures.

Functionality: (k) marketing, (l) mechanics, (m) intake/processing, and (n) incentives.

Best practices: (p) oversight (by high level personnel), (q) due care (in delegating substantial discretionary authority), (r) effective communication (to all levels of employees), (s) reasonable steps to achieve compliance (which include systems for monitoring, auditing, and reporting suspected wrongdoing without fear of reprisal) (t) consistent enforcement (of compliance standards including disciplinary mechanisms), and (u) reasonable steps (to respond to and prevent further similar offenses upon detection of a violation).

Scales

Hotline Metrics
    (1 point) High- Meets or exceeds benchmarking in each year of analysis
    (3 points) Low- Does not meet benchmarking estimates in many years of analysis.
    (5 points) Poor- Does not meet benchmarking estimates in any year of analysis.

Functionality Scale
    (points) 4 of 4 Failure; 3 of 4 Poor; 2 of 4 Moderate; 1 of 4 Great; 0 of 4 High.

Best Practices Scale
    (points) 6 of 6 Failure; 5 of 6 Poor; 4 of 6 Weak; 3 of 6 Moderate; 2 of 6 Good;
      1 of 6 Great; 0 of 6 High.

Performance Scale
    Low: 14–15 points
    Below Average: 10–13 points
    Average: 7–9 points
    Above Average: 5–8 points
    High: 0–4 points

Bureaupathology Scale (by percentage of comments)
    1. 0–10% Present
    2. 11–20%
    3. 21–30%
    4. 31–40%
    5. 41–50% Elevated
    6. 51–60%

7. 61–70%
8. 71–80%
9. 81–90%
10. 91–100% Extreme

Historical Context

- Conducive to fraud if it is established that conditions indicate there was significant employee fraud at the time of analysis, and it is believed to have been underreported via the hotline.
- Conducive to increased calls if it is established that conditions indicate the hotline should have been getting a higher volume of calls, or if it is determined employees are underreporting.
- Not conducive to fraud if it is established that conditions indicate there was not significant employee fraud at the time of the analysis, and it is not believed to be underreported via the hotline.
- Not conducive to increased calls if it is established that conditions indicate the hotline was receiving the proper amount of calls, or if it is determined employees have reported crimes via the hotline.

Case Studies

Specifically, this chapter will review six case studies, identified as Case Studies 1–6. Case Study 1 (PS1) is a medium-sized private sector organization in the financial industry. Case Study 2 (PS2) is a large, private sector organization in the financial industry. Case Study 3 (GS1) is a public sector/government organization in the federal government. Case Study 4 (GS2) is a public sector/government organization in the state government. Case Study 5 (GS3) is a public sector/government organization in the city government. Case Study 6 (NP1) is a large, nonprofit organization. Note that said organizations (and their employees) are not specifically named in the case studies, for the sake of anonymity.

The case studies analyze numerous factors including, but not limited to, each organization's hotline experience, call statistics, fraud metrics, and employee feedback.

Case Study 1 (PS1)

Background

Incorporated in 1981 with predecessor companies established as early as 1924, PS1 is a well-known and established financial services firm. PS1 has a global presence, including regional offices and branches throughout the United States, along with principal offices in London, Tokyo, Hong Kong, and other world financial centers; their client base includes corporations, governments, financial institutions, and individuals (Annual Report, 2007). According to their 2007 Annual Report, as of November 2007, PS1 had 48,256 employees worldwide. This figure does not include contract or consultant employees, which, if included, would increase this number. However, the precise number of these employees is unknown, so the figure used for analysis was the confirmed number of employees per their 2007 Annual Report. For PS1, their 2007 corporate documents, including the 2007 Annual Report, were analyzed to correspond to the context of the fraud hotline data sample being analyzed. To this end, the most recent year of data was used for analysis (2006–2007).

Bureaucracy

There are volumes of materials that relate the financial industry, generally, and PS1, specifically, to the concept of bureaucracy. Bureaucracies are often characterized as such due to their complexity. In the case of PS1, their complexity is fully acknowledged by the company. And they hold their employees responsible, to their shareholders, via their Annual Report, for navigating it. They further recognize their employees have the ability to cause great harm to their business, including monetary loss and outright business failure. Specifically, in their 2007 Annual Report, PS1 reports the following:

> Our businesses are highly dependent on our ability to process, on a daily basis, a large number of transactions across numerous and diverse markets in many currencies. In general, the transactions we process are increasingly complex. We perform the functions required to operate our different businesses either by ourselves or through agreements with third parties. *We rely on the ability of our employees* [emphasis added], our internal systems and systems at technology centers operated by third parties to process a high volume of transactions. We also face the risk of operational failure or termination of any of the clearing agents, exchanges, clearing houses or other financial intermediaries we use to facilitate our securities transactions. In the event of a breakdown or improper operation of our or third party's systems *or improper action by third parties or employees, we could suffer financial loss, an impairment to our liquidity, a disruption of our businesses, regulatory sanctions or damage to our reputation.* [Emphasis added] Despite the business contingency plans we have in place, our ability to conduct business may be adversely affected by a disruption in the infrastructure that supports our business and the communities where we are located. This may include a disruption involving physical site access, terrorist activities, disease pandemics, electrical, communications or other services used by PS1, its employees or third parties with whom we conduct business.

The complexity of PS1 is further evinced in their organizational structure (see Appendix for chart), as enumerated in their 2007 Annual Report. Here, the organization is described as a multi-division company with several highly specialized departments:

> PS1 is a global financial services firm that maintains significant market positions in each of its business segments—Institutional Securities, Global Wealth Management Group and Asset Management. A summary of the activities of each of the business segments follows. **Institutional Securities** includes capital raising; financial advisory services, including advice on mergers and acquisitions, restructurings, real estate and project finance; corporate lending; sales, trading, financing and market-making activities in equity and fixed income securities and related products, including foreign exchange and commodities; benchmark indices and risk management analytics; research; and investment activities. **Global Wealth Management Group** provides brokerage and investment advisory services covering various investment alternatives; financial and wealth planning services; annuity and other insurance products; credit and other lending products; cash management services; retirement services; and trust and fiduciary services. **Asset Management** provides global asset management products and services in equity, fixed income, alternative investments, which includes hedge funds and fund of funds, and merchant banking, which includes real estate, private equity and infrastructure, to institutional and retail clients through proprietary and third-party retail distribution channels, intermediaries and PS1's institutional distribution channel. Asset Management also engages in investment activities.

Upon review, it is clear from their organizational records that PS1 has a bureaucratic structure. This study will next consider whether the employees of PS1 perceive the effects of organizational bureaucracy.

To further examine this phenomenon, employee reviews of the company were examined via the website Glassdoor.com (Glassdoor). On Glassdoor, as of July 1, 2013, 1,001 reviews of PS1 were posted by anonymous sources that are identified as current and past PS1 employees. Overall, from these reviewers, PS1 received an average of a 3.4 on a 5-point scale. This average translates into an "average" rating by Glassdoor. The reviews analyzed for this examination were limited to those reviews where the respondents "rated" the company to be "below average," or in this case, rated it under three stars. This limited the number of reviews included for examination to 195, which constituted approximately 19.5% of all reviews.

Of these reviewers, 45, or 23% made reference to specific terminology related to bureaucracy and excessive bureaucracy. The number of respondents and comments are not equivalent, because in certain cases, respondents' comments were counted more than once when their comments spanned multiple categories. The total number of comments was 54. Overall, the "below average" reviews examined referenced a bureaucratic atmosphere, where employees reported having limited professional latitude, in roles that were tedious, boring, and repetitive. Employees further reported, generally speaking, they did not believe anything was to be gained from going above and beyond the job description. In addition, they also had a generally unfavorable view of management, who in their view largely spent their time protecting their own job. The comments examined were posted to the website between and June 12, 2008, and May 9, 2013.

General and specific references to attributes of bureaucracy and bureaupathic or excessive bureaucracy are presented in Tables 6.1 and 6.2.

Table 6.1 PS1 Social Media/Bureaucracy Analysis Summary

Attribute	Data	Analysis
Time frame	6/12/08–5/9/13	5-year time period
Population	1,001	2.1% of all employees (48,256)
Sample set	195	19.5% of the population (1,001) 0.40% of all employees (48,256)
Respondents indicating bureaucracy or bureaupathic behaviors	45	23.1% of the sample set (195) 4.5% of the population (1,001) 0.09% of all employees (48,256)
Total comments indicating bureaucracy and bureaupathology	54	31 Bureaucracy + 23 Bureaupathic
Bureaucracy	31	General (12) Hierarchy of authority (4) System of rules (3) Technical expertise (3) Career service (3) Insistence on the rights of office (6)
Bureaupathic	23	Impersonal treatment (6) Prolonged role enactment (9) Resistance to change (1) Resistance to interrogation and investigation (5) Strict reliance on organizational rules and procedures (2)

Table 6.2 PS1 Social Media/Bureaucracy Dataset

Count	Type	Attribute	Comment	Date
1.	Bureaucracy	General	"Red tape"	6/12/08
2.	Bureaucracy	Hierarchy of authority	"Too many chiefs and not enough Indians"	6/12/08
3.	Bureaucracy	Technical expertise	"You are expected to… accomplish incredibly complex tasks"	6/25/08
4.	Bureaucracy	Hierarchy of authority	"Highly stratified environment"	9/7/08
5.	Bureaupathic	Resistance to interrogation and investigation	"Immoral practices"	1/5/09
6.	Bureaucracy	Systems of rules	"Very complex"	2/6/09
7.	Bureaucracy	Hierarchy of authority	"Middle management too layered"	3/18/09
8.	Bureaucracy	General	"Feels more bureaucratic by the day"	6/12/09
9.	Bureaucracy	General	"Silo[ed]"	8/18/09
10.	Bureaupathic	Impersonal treatment	"Sweatshop"	11/23/09
11.	Bureaucracy	General	"It was like working for government"	1/8/10
12.	Bureaupathic	Prolonged role enactment	"Too compartmentalized; they have people do [sic] the same function over and over with little opportunity to learn outside small role"	10/1/10

(Continued)

Table 6.2 *(Continued)* **PS1 Social Media/Bureaucracy Dataset**

Count	Type	Attribute	Comment	Date
13.	Bureaucracy	Career service	"It is almost impossible to get fired"	2/11/11
14.	Bureaupathic	Prolonged role enactment	"Work is boring and repetitive"	3/11/11
15.	Bureaupathic	Prolonged role enactment	"Everyday is the same thing over and over again"	3/27/11
16.	Bureaucracy	Insistence on the rights of office	"My manager… expected a great amount of respect for her position"	4/26/11
17.	Bureaupathic	Prolonged role enactment	"Can get stuck doing one function for a long time"	5/30/11
18.	Bureaucracy	Insistence on the rights of office	"Egos rule the roost and only those who stroke them get ahead"	8/1/11
19.	Bureaupathic	Prolonged role enactment	"The same exact thing everyday"	11/24/11
20.	Bureaucracy	Career service	"Low attrition"	2/5/12
21.	Bureaucracy	General	"There is a lot of red tape"	2/27/12
22.	Bureaucracy	General	"The environment does not need to become more bureaucratic"	3/8/12
23.	Bureaupathic	Impersonal treatment	"You are often just a number"	3/29/12
24.	Bureaupathic	Prolonged role enactment	"Tedious work"	4/14/12

(Continued)

Table 6.2 *(Continued)*   PS1 Social Media/Bureaucracy Dataset

Count	Type	Attribute	Comment	Date
25.	Bureaupathic	Prolonged role enactment	"Extremely dull, repetitive place to work"	4/17/12
26.	Bureaucracy	General	"Bureaucratic overhead is staggering here"	4/23/12
27.	Bureaupathic	Resistance to interrogation and investigation	"So much corporate waste"	4/26/12
28.	Bureaupathic	Resistance to interrogation and investigation	"Dishonest"	4/30/12
29.	Bureaucracy	General	"Extremely political and bureaucratic"	5/8/12
30.	Bureaupathic	Resistance to change	"You will not be rewarded for innovation, intelligence, or even a job well done if it contradicts the politics that impact the manager's bonus calculation"	5/13/12
31.	Bureaupathic	Strict reliance on organizational rules and procedures	"Way too much politics and not very innovative"	7/13/12
32.	Bureaupathic	Prolonged role enactment	"Repetitive tasks"	9/14/12
33.	Bureaupathic	Impersonal treatment	[To managers] "have a heart; you are not managing robots in a production line"	9/23/12

(Continued)

Table 6.2 *(Continued)* **PS1 Social Media/Bureaucracy Dataset**

Count	Type	Attribute	Comment	Date
34.	Bureaucracy	Insistence on the rights of office	"Senior managers… more often than not use their subordinates to bolster their positions"	9/23/12
35.	Bureaupathic	Resistance to interrogation and investigation	"Self-centered, public deceiving scoundrels at best; crooks and liars and cheats even"	9/25/12
36.	Bureaupathic	Resistance to interrogation and investigation	"Wake up with cold sweats of guilt and shame"	9/25/12
37.	Bureaucracy	General	"Increasing regulatory red tape"	9/30/12
38.	Bureaupathic	Impersonal treatment	"Cold and impersonal…no concern for the individual"	10/4/12
39.	Bureaupathic	Strict reliance on organizational rules and procedures	"The simplest tasks become an almighty chore involving multiple layers of nonvalue adding bureaucracy"	11/14/12
40.	Bureaucracy	General	"At the end of the day, you are fully aware you are a small cog in a giant machine"	12/3/12
41.	Bureaupathic	Impersonal treatment	"You are truly headcount here and nothing more"	12/5/12
42.	Bureaucracy	Insistence on the rights of office	"[Employees] are just peasants there to serve the kings"	12/5/12

(Continued)

Table 6.2 *(Continued)* PS1 Social Media/Bureaucracy Dataset

Count	Type	Attribute	Comment	Date
43.	Bureaupathic	Prolonged role enactment	"You learn your role thoroughly"	12/26/12
44.	Bureaucracy	Insistence on the rights of office	"Top heavy"	2/9/13
45.	Bureaucracy	Hierarchy of authority	"Very hierarchical, almost with military rigidity"	2/9/13
46.	Bureaucracy	Technical expertise	"Good opportunity to learn/specialize in one area"	2/28/13
47.	Bureaupathic	Impersonal treatment	"You feel like a number"	3/7/13
48.	Bureaucracy	Career service	"[In the past 7 years] workers…[career longevity was] probably….10+ years"	3/7/13
49.	Bureaucracy	General	"Approach is segmented"	3/7/13
50.	Bureaucracy	General	"It seems to be more like working in a government organization"	3/25/13
51.	Bureaucracy	Insistence on the rights of office	"Senior management are 'yes men' afraid to disagree"	5/6/13
52.	Bureaucracy	Systems of rules	"Tedious processes to get even the simplest task done"	5/9/13
53.	Bureaucracy	Systems of rules	"New systems are complicated, cumbersome and difficult to navigate"	5/9/13
54.	Bureaucracy	Technical expertise	"Systems are complicated, cumbersome and difficult to navigate"	5/9/13

Overall, 23% of the sample set, which constituted 5% of the population, have confirmed and validated the general existence of bureaucracy, which was demonstrated to have reached a bureaupathic level. Next it is important to understand the specifics regarding PS1's hotline and how it is operated.

Hotline Specification

At PS1, their hotline is called the "integrity hotline." Although PS1's hotline was technically operational as of May 2004, the calls received were so few that formal statistics were not maintained until the third quarter of 2006. The statistics concerning the number of calls made to their hotline is not externally publicized.

In terms of public disclosure regarding their hotline, PS1 invites the public in their Proxy Statement, dated February 23, 2007, to examine their hotline policy via their website or by requesting it in writing (p. 11):

> Our Corporate Governance Policies (including our Director Independence Standards), Code of Ethics and Business Conduct, Board Committee charters, Policy Regarding Communication by Shareholders and Other Interested Parties with the Board of Directors, Policy regarding Director Candidates Recommended by Shareholders, Policy Regarding Corporate Political Contributions, Policy Regarding Shareholder Rights Plan, information regarding the Integrity Hotline and the Management Committee Equity Ownership Commitment are available at our corporate governance webpage and are available to any shareholder who requests them by writing.

Upon visiting the web address supplied, the following information is provided regarding their Integrity Hotline:

Integrity Hotline

> Concerns relating to ethical or business conduct matters, including accounting, internal accounting controls or auditing matters, may be brought to the Company's attention through an independent vendor engaged to receive calls regarding such concerns. The calls may be made anonymously and confidentially. Click here [linked content] to view the vendor's telephone numbers by country.

When the link was visited, a global list of hotline telephone numbers was returned. At the end of the page, they invite the user who may experience any problems with the telephone numbers to contact a PS1 Integrity Hotline contact. However, no specific contacts were linked or named and could not otherwise be located. Specifically, the language on their web page stated, "If you experience difficulty accessing the toll-free hotline, please visit AT&T's International Dialing Guide to confirm that you are using the correct access code for your country. If the problem persists, please advise one of the PS1 Integrity Hotline contacts."

To learn more about their hotline, and to obtain the organizational data, PS1's Hotline Administrator (HA1) was interviewed. The identity of the Hotline Administrator is being withheld for privacy. The interview was conducted on November 6, 2007, and follow-up conversations took place in the ensuing days via e-mail.

According to HA1, most callers chose to remain anonymous. Callers to their hotlines, especially those who elect to remain anonymous, are encouraged to call back to check on the progress of the investigation (the caller is given a reference number). However, according to HA1, most callers, around 99%, do not call back.

Third-party hotline service provider, The Network, manages PS1's hotline. (A Hotline Administrator for The Network, interviewed for this study on September 4, 2012, validated this fact.) However, in 2007, PS1's third party hotline administrator was Global Compliance (which is now known as Navex Global). Internally, the Legal and Compliance department manages their hotline. According to court documents filed in the case of *United States v. Garth Peterson* (EDNY, 12-CR-225, March 26, 2012) between 2002 and 2008, PS1 employed 500 Compliance Officers (Complaint p.12). The Legal and Compliance department receives the data from The Network, compiles the data, and manages the complaint escalation process. At PS1, the keeper of the hotline data, or the hotline administrator, was a single employee, who was in a nonofficer position with the company.

At that time, PS1 had the following employee levels for most employees in the legal and compliance department: analyst, associate, manager, director, vice president, executive director, and managing director. The levels below vice president are nonofficer titles. The subject employee, keeper of the hotline data, was a nonofficer. Despite being a member of the legal and compliance department, this employee was also not a lawyer.

To obtain the hotline data from the third-party provider, HA1 electronically accesses a system maintained by the provider. HA1 advised 10 employees total from PS1 had access to this system "on paper," but HA1 was the only employee who actually used it. As for disclosure, according to HA1, all calls to the hotline are reported to the firm's audit committee and are logged in a quarterly report.

According to HA1, the internal advertisement for the fraud hotline consists of a web posting, a mention in an internal procedural manual, and a monthly e-mail reminder sent to employees. In terms of external advertisement, in their 2007 Annual Report that year, the hotline is mentioned a single time, to say the integrity hotline is posted on the corporate governance page of their website. However, additional information is provided to shareholders (and accessible to the general public) in their proxy statements.

In public documents the hotline number is not provided. The global numbers are provided on their website. However, there is some challenge in finding those numbers in a simple Internet search, unless the researcher specifically types in the terminology used for the fraud hotline in their organization "Integrity Hotline."

According to HA1, PS1's attorney/managers who have knowledge of the hotline's performance are very interested in efforts to make the hotline better known to the general employee population. However, HA1 said these managers are also viewing the hotline as a SOX requirement. Per HA1, "They do not seem to understand why an employee would not report criminal activity to their supervisor." However, per HA1, management had future plans to incorporate an anonymous reporting mechanism via a website.

Hotline Metrics

The sample size of the data is the fraud hotline callers, internal (employees) or external (i.e., vendors) persons, who called the fraud hotline from March 1, 2006, to November 31, 2007, or between 3Q FY 2006 and 4Q FY 2007. No identifying data was provided regarding the callers (i.e., race, sex, age). This time period is significant, in that it represents the first year that statistics were formally maintained for this hotline (which could also be interpreted as the first full year of the hotline's operation).

The data supplied were limited to a breakdown of the overall number of calls received to the hotline, broken down by FY Quarter, from 3Q of FY 2006 to December 6, 2007 (to reflect the total for 4Q FY, 2007). This time frame corresponds to the dataset obtained. At this time, the FY, or fiscal year, for PS1 was from December to November. Their fiscal year quarters were as follows: 1Q: December–February; 2Q: March–May; 3Q: June–August; 4Q: September–November (Table 6.3).

To benchmark this data, this study used the 2009 Corporate Governance and Compliance Benchmarking Report. The Network and BDO Consulting produce this report on an annual basis. As the hotline provider for this organization, it can be assumed their data is included in the benchmarking figures.

In the benchmarking reports, produced by The Network, there are an average number of calls expected per company size and per industry, per year. These figures were averaged to produce the ideal benchmarking figure per year, tailored to the organization's industry and size. It should be noted that the benchmarking report groups the financial industry along with the construction and real estate industry (and they would not provide disaggregated data). Therefore, this figure has inherent limitations, which have been controlled by using the size of the company to adjust the figure. The number was rounded to the nearest decimal.

In summary, according to the data, this organization, a major, global financial services firm, in the latter half of FY 2006, received only 14 complaints when benchmarking figures suggest they should have received 194. This means they only

Table 6.3 PS1 Hotline Metrics

Q/FY	Time Period	Number of Employees	Calls	Average Benchmarking Figure Size, Industry	Calls Expected per Benchmarking	Delta	Percentage of Actual versus Benchmarking
3Q 2006	June–August	55,310 (As per November 30, 2006)	6	7.9, 6.06 = 7	387/2 = 194	194 − 14 = 180	7%
4Q 2006	September–November		8				
1Q 2007	December–February	48,256 (As of November 30, 2007)	8	8.5, 7.93 = 8	386	386 − 35 = 351	9%
2Q 2007	March–May		9				
3Q 2007	June–August		14				
4Q 2007	September–November		4				

received 7% of the calls that they should have received, based on their industry and size.

In 2007, this organization received only 35 complaints when benchmarking figures suggest they should have received 386. Therefore, in 2007, they only received 9% of the calls they should have received, based on their industry and size.

Although we do see an extremely slight improvement from 2006 to 2007, this organization is not receiving the number of calls they should receive, based on the level of internal fraud.

Fraud Metrics

Internal crime metrics for financial firms are difficult if not near impossible to obtain. Many internal crimes are handled internally. These records are generally not provided to the public. Only the crimes/litigation matters that are determined to have a "material adverse effect" against the company are reported in their annual reports. All crimes committed by employees in a financial firm are required to have a corresponding Suspicious Activities Report (SAR) filed by the company. However, these SARs are not made available for public inspection or review.

Litigation records may yield limited results for employee crimes, but to obtain these records for a global financial firm would be an exhaustive task, as the records in each county, city, state, and federal jurisdiction would have to be searched in all 50 states, along with individual commonwealths, just in the United States alone. Global litigation records are equally challenging to obtain, and often require an individual to personally retrieve them. As a result, the indicators of fraud in the subject organizations were obtained via publically available media reports. It should be noted that PS1's 2007 Annual Report does not contain any disclosures regarding employee crime.

It is well known that during the relevant time period, massive employee fraud was occurring in the financial industry. In the case of PS1, specific evidence was located that implicated particular employees in the larger schemes taking place at the time, as well as those who were engaged in separate internal incidents, which resulted in major losses for the company.

For instance, according to an SEC press release dated September 20, 2007, two PS1 employees and three associates/relatives were indicted in a criminal case where it was alleged that these employees engaged in a securities fraud scheme, which was investigated from 2005 to 2007. These employees were believed to have charged erroneous finder's fees and received kickbacks. One such employee, PS1 Vice President Peter Sherlock, pleaded guilty to defrauding PS1 of over $4 million (Chung, 2010). The relatives of both employees were found to have hidden the stolen money in shell companies (SEC, 2007). Sherlock died in an accident before his sentencing, so it is unclear whether PS1 was ever able to fully recoup these losses.

In addition to money, PS1 employees were conspiring to steal sensitive client data. In 2007, it was reported that a PS1 employee, Ronald Peteka, a client service representative, was arrested and charged with conspiracy after stealing proprietary information from his hedge fund clients from 2005 to 2006. It is believed that Peteka conspired with several additional PS1 workers in furtherance of his crimes, including a computer consultant (Bosworth, 2007).

Furthermore, during the relevant time period, another PS1 employee was found to have been stealing client money. Between September 2001 and December 2009, employee Richard Garaventa, former vice president of Institutional Securities Operations, created a fictitious company and wrote checks to himself from an in-house account totaling $2.5 million (Kelly, 2009). He was charged with 43 counts of grand larceny, criminal possession of stolen property, and falsifying business records (Kentouris, 2009). Garaventa apparently used this money to fund vacations to tropical locations such as Aruba and Florida, and to buy jewelry (Kelly, 2009). Ironically, he was on one of these vacations when his fraud was discovered.

An employee was also found to have been engaging in corruption. In March 2012, the U.S. Department of Justice (DOJ) reported that between 2002 and 2008, former PS1 Managing Director Garth Peterson had violated Foreign Corrupt Practices Act (FCPA) requirements and evaded internal controls by conspiring with external parties to have PS1 transfer their property ownership to what he claimed was a third party, which was actually his own company. In all, the conspiracy, led by Peterson, netted a profit on paper of at least $2.5 million. Peterson pleaded guilty and faced a maximum of 5 years in prison and a fine of $250,000, which represented twice his gross gain in the offense (DOJ, 2012). The DOJ reported PS1 would not face charges relating to this matter, because they demonstrated proof their system of internal controls was adequate and sufficient (DOJ, 2012).

As evinced, there are many examples of internal crimes conducted by PS1 employees during the relevant time period. However, the most egregious charges at this time for PS1 employees are related to the global financial crisis ("crisis"). On January 13, 2013, *The New York Times Dealbook* published an article entitled "Financial Crisis Suit Suggests Bad Behavior at PS1," wherein it was reported that e-mails between PS1 employees on March 16, 2007, demonstrated that they had knowledge of the "toxic assets" which "helped blow up" the world economy (Eisinger, 2013). According to the article, e-mails between PS1 investment banker team members discussed how to "name" the "toxic assets" suggesting names such as "Subprime Meltdown," "Hitman," "Nuclear Holocaust," and "Mike Tyson's Punchout" (Eisinger, 2013). Eventually this fund was named and sold to a Chinese bank (Eisinger, 2013). Overall, according to the author, these e-mails, which are rarely obtained due to stringent discovery thresholds, demonstrate that PS1 bankers knew the housing market was in trouble, and exploited that knowledge to dupe buyers (Eisinger, 2013).

Historical Context

The financial crisis that lasted from 2007 to 2010 was considered to have begun in 2007, when PS1 received 35 calls to their hotline. In fact, the Whistleblower provisions of Dodd–Frank were enacted in direct response to this crisis. Why? Because many believed that the crisis of 2007–2010 was a result of rampant employee fraud at financial institutions.

As part of the new financial incentives within Dodd–Frank, which expanded Whistleblower provisions in the Sarbanes–Oxley Act of 2002 (SOX) and the Securities and Exchange Act of 1934, a whistleblower who reports violations of certain laws ("violations of federal securities laws that lead to the successful enforcement of a covered judicial or administrative action, or a related action") to federal authorities (SEC, DOJ, or the U.S. Commodities Trading Commission) stands to earn between 10% and 30% of recoveries over $1 million. With recent awards of up to $550 million, the SEC has reported settlements from July 2010 in the amounts of $75 million, $100 million, and $550 million that can mean a sizable amount of cash for the whistleblower. And the employee also gets to keep his or her job. The whistleblower is further protected by Dodd–Frank from any retaliation by the employer.

During the financial crisis, it is estimated the value of financial assets worldwide declined by as much as $50 trillion, and 51 million jobs were lost worldwide (Asian Development Bank 2009; FDIC n.d.). With that, a historically large number of bank closures and bankruptcy/restructuring occurred, marking the end of several long-standing financial institutions such as Lehman Brothers, the fourth largest investment bank in the United States that had been in existence since 1850. Lehman Brothers filed for bankruptcy in September 2008.

Overall, according to the Federal Deposit Insurance Corporation (FDIC), 366 U.S. banks failed. To put this into perspective, prior to the downturn, from 2000 to 2006, only 24 banks failed. In 2010 alone, which is considered to be the peak of the economic crisis, 142 banks failed (compared to only three failures in 2007—representing a 4,633% increase). To date, U.S. banking regulators have paid almost $9 billion to cover these losses—and additional payouts of up to $21.5 billion are expected by 2014 (Sidel, 2011). As of January 31, 2011, the FDIC paid out $8.89 billion to banks under loss-share agreements (Sidel, 2011).

During this time period, many U.S. investment banks, including PS1, also filed for bankruptcy, or were nationalized, recapitalized, merged, taken over, or received state guarantees (Harkay, 2009). In fact, the traditional investment bank, created by the Glass–Steagall Act in 1933, was effectively obliterated in a matter of days (Table 6.4).

Indeed, from September 14 to 21, 2008, Lehman Brothers failed, Merrill Lynch was acquired, and Goldman Sachs and PS1 became bank holding companies (Sorkin & Bajaj, 2008). Some of the better-known cases include (1) Bear Stearns (sold to J.P. Morgan Chase on May 30, 2008); (2) Lehman Brothers (bankruptcy, September 15, 2008); (3) Merrill Lynch (acquired by Bank of America September 14, 2008, itself bailed out by the U.S. government); (4) PS2 (recapitalization by the U.S. government, November, 2008); (5) Goldman Sachs (recapitalization by the U.S. government; became a bank holding company on September 21, 2008); and

Table 6.4 PS1 Table of Results

Organization Assessment Element	PS1
Size	48,256
Hotline name	Integrity Hotline
Management	Third party and internal
Respondents indicating IV	23% (sample size 195; 45 indicated IV; 54 comments indicated IV)
Bureaucracy IV	Strong, 5 of 5 general (12); **a (4)** b (3) c (3) d (3) **e (6)**
Bureaupathology IV	Strong, 5 of 5 **f (6)** **g (9)** h (1) i (5) j (2)
Hotline metrics (DV)	Poor Calls below benchmarking Historical context (calls were low immediately preceding the financial crisis)
Hotline functionality (DV)	Poor, 3 of 4 **k (Number hard to find internally and externally)** **l (Not enough parties engaged)** m (Third-party managed) **n (Managers didn't understand value of hotline)**
Best practices (DV)	Weak, 4 of 6 **p (One delegate only)** q (Clear process) **r (Not well communicated)** s (Yes, third-party managed) **t (Data unavailable)** **u (Data unavailable)**
Historical context (DV)	Conducive to fraud; conducive to increased calls (Financial Crisis, 2008)

(Continued)

Table 6.4 *(Continued)* PS1 Table of Results

Organization	
Assessment Element	*PS1*
Evidence of internal fraud	Yes
Evidence of negative employee sentiment	Yes
Result IV	**IV Present** **Bureaucracy, strong** Hierarchy of authority Insistence on the rights of office **Bureaupathology, strong** Impersonal treatment Prolonged role enactment
Result DV	**DV metrics, functionality and best practices affected** Metrics, poor Functionality, poor Best practices, weak Evidence of historical context, internal fraud, disgruntled employees
Notes	Despite an "average" rating, comments indicate fraud, massive bureaucracy

(6) PS1 (recapitalization by the U.S. government; became a bank holding company September 21, 2008) (Harkay, 2009).

Summary

According to the evidence, PS1 has excessive bureaucracy and a hotline with performance issues. A review of the literature (organizational documents, 2007 Annual Report) and an analysis of employee reviews found bureaucracy and excessive bureaucracy were present in this organization. Overall, 23% of the sample set (195 reviews), which represented 4.5% of the total reviewers (1,001) and 0.09% of all employees, represented reviews indicating bureaucracy and excessive bureaucracy. In sum, the comments were made by 45 separate respondents. Of their responses, 31 comments indicated bureaucracy and 23 indicated excessive bureaucracy.

Employee statements prove bureaucracy and excessive bureaucracy are recognized on the part of employees. Employee comments indicating all indices evincing bureaucracy and excessive bureaucracy were present at varying degrees. While 12 respondents' comments indicated the general existence of bureaucracy, specifically, employee comments suggest the indices of bureaucracy "insistence on the right of office" (six comments) and "hierarchy of authority" (four comments) were especially problematic for employees. In terms of excessive bureaucracy, comments indicated "prolonged role enactment" (nine comments) and "impersonal treatment" (six comments) were the most notable for those employees who submitted reviews for this organization.

As for PS1's hotline, evidence suggests it has performance issues. For one, benchmarking revealed the hotline receives a low number of calls for the industry and size. Specifically, in 2006, the hotline received only 7% of the calls that it should have received; in 2007, it received only 9% of calls expected per benchmarking estimates.

With respect to the hotline's functionality, the hotline underperformed in four out of five areas. As for marketing, the hotline telephone number was proven difficult to locate, both internally and externally. PS1, at the time of this analysis, also did not have fraud hotline posters displayed. Next, as for mechanics, the hotline is managed by a third-party provider and has an internal process for further call handling. As a result, the hotline is not perceived to have issues with its mechanics.

As for intake/processing, the hotline is managed internally by a single person. Thus, the intake/processing of this hotline is lacking in that representatives from multiple areas of the organization were not engaged in the process (The Network 2008, p. 5). With respect to incentives, the hotline administrator advised PS1 management did not understand the value of the hotline. Thus it is believed that management's attitude toward the hotline negatively affected the potential reporting incentives.

Per the employee reviews, this organization is believed to have a dominating management (insistence on the rights of office, six comments), which keeps employees in the same role for a long period of time (prolonged role enactment, nine comments), providing impersonal treatment (six comments) and with a dominating hierarchy of authority (four comments).

This study further learned via the interview process that management believes workers will report any known internal crimes to their supervisors. This belief on the part of management is shortsighted and contrary to the very spirit of an anonymous hotline.

With respect to best practices, this hotline is believed to be lacking in several areas. For one, the hotline should have oversight by high-level personnel. This fact could not be proven, as this study learned in the interview process that the hotline is accessed by the designated hotline administrator only. As for due care, the hotline appears to be well managed, in that there is a clear escalation process. With respect to communication, the hotline is not well communicated. Hotline data are not provided internally to employees, which is an element of best practices. Although the hotline administrator said the hotline is communicated in a web posting, an internal procedural manual and a monthly e-mail, upon review, this study demonstrated the number was difficult to locate externally. This factor is significant, given most employee hotline callers call after business hours (ACFE, 2002–2012).

As for this hotline's "reasonable steps to achieve compliance," that require-ment is satisfied with their third-party hotline management, the process of having calls reported to the Firm's Audit Committee, and logging the calls in a quarterly report.

With respect to the other two best practices elements, "consistent enforce-ment" and "reasonable steps to respond and prevent similar offenses upon detec-tion," this study was unable to rate this organization on these factors, as the hotline was too new at the time of analysis to fully establish the existence of these elements.

Furthermore, the level of internal fraud, the historical context, and the per-ception of employees of their organization are also factors in gauging the overall performance of this fraud hotline. As for internal fraud, upon review of public records, this study was able to establish the presence of a high amount of internal fraud. A review of the historical context suggests the hotline should have received far more calls than it did, considering the fraud hotline data analyzed in this study represented the time period immediately preceding the financial crisis of 2008, a time where massive internal crime occurred in the financial industry. Employee reviews also made reference to the existence of internal fraud, with employees saying he or she "wake(s) up with cold sweats of guilt and shame" that manage-ment is "self-centered, public deceiving scoundrels at best; crooks liars and cheats." Other comments indicating potential fraud include "dishonest" and "immoral practices."

As for employee sentiment, employee reviews suggest employees are likely dis-gruntled. With an overall rating of "average" on Glassdoor, it is clear employees, in their reviews, appear to not lean positively, or negatively. However, upon review of the negative comments, it is clear employees who are unhappy make specific statements, which should not be ignored by management. Specifically, to recap, employees stated "you will not be awarded for innovation, intelligence…" that the work was "extremely dull" there was "so much corporate waste" and "at the end of the day you are fully aware you are a small cog in a giant machine." These comments are suggestive that the organization's employees are experiencing an excessively bureaucratic state, which is not otherwise discernible via a review of the commentary results as "average."

Case Study 2 (PS2)

Background

Founded in 1812, PS2 is a global financial services firm that has been in existence for over 200 years. In 2010, PS2 had a presence in over 1,000 cities and 160 coun-tries and serviced approximately 200 million customer accounts (Form 10K). As of December 2010, PS2 had 260,000 full-time employees (Form 10K). Data for the year 2010 are being used in this case study to correspond with the time period of fraud hotline data obtained from this organization (2004–2010). As with PS1, the most recent year will be used.

Bureaucracy

PS2, by all accounts, is considered highly bureaucratic. There have been count- less books, articles, Internet postings, and so on, which make reference to the presence of bureaucracy at PS2. To demonstrate the general volume of materi- als, a Google search for "PS2" and bureaucracy yields 12,600,000 results. It can be reasonably inferred not all of these results speak specifically to bureau- cracy at PS2—each reference would have to be read and validated for accuracy. Nevertheless, this statistic is being provided to demonstrate generally the large volume of results.

Its own chief executive officer (CEO) also acknowledged PS2's bureaucracy. For instance, in a 2007 Times-News article, it was reported then CEO Charles O. Prince III (CEO 2003–2007; Chairman 2006–2007) was making great efforts at the time to "unclog [PS2's] vast bureaucracy" (Dash & Timmons, 2007). Specifically, it was reported that Prince called upon PS2 to "eliminate overlap- ping jobs and unclog its vast bureaucracy, not just cutting back on magazine subscriptions and the use of company limousines" and "questioned the logic of having three separate regional headquarters for every main business unit, each with its own staff" (Dash & Timmons, 2007). At this time, Prince was facing extreme pressure from powerful shareholders who were also reeling from the effects of PS2's overwhelming bureaucracy, causing one such investor, Prince Walid bin Talal of Saudi Arabia, to publically call upon PS2 to use "draconian measures" to cut costs (Dash & Timmons, 2007).

PS2's organizational structure is set forth in their 2010 Form 10K (see Appendix for chart) where it was reported "PS2 currently operates, for manage- ment reporting purposes, via two primary business segments: PS2, consisting of PS2's *Regional Consumer Banking* businesses and *Institutional Clients Group*; and PS2 Holdings, consisting of PS2's *Brokerage and Asset Management* and *Local Consumer Lending* businesses, and a *Special Asset Pool*. There is also a third seg- ment, *Corporate/Other*."

PS2 sets forth the role and function of each of these segments and their divi- sions in their 2010 Annual Report as follows:

> PS2 consists of the following businesses: Regional Consumer Banking (which includes retail banking and PS2-branded cards in four regions— North America, EMEA, Latin America and Asia) and Institutional Clients Group (which includes Securities and Banking and Transaction Services). PS2 is the Company's global bank for consumers and busi- nesses and represents PS2's core franchise. PS2 is focused on providing best-in-class products and services to customers and leveraging PS2's

unparalleled global network. PS2 is physically present in approximately 100 countries, many for over 100 years, and offers services in over 160 countries and jurisdictions. PS2 believes this global network provides a strong foundation for servicing the broad financial services needs of large multinational clients and for meeting the needs of retail, private banking, commercial, public sector and institutional customers around the world. PS2's global footprint provides coverage of the world's emerging economies, which PS2 believes represent a strong area of growth. At December 31, 2010, PS2 had approximately $1.3 trillion of assets and $760 billion of deposits, representing approximately 67% of PS2's total assets and approximately 90% of its deposits.

Regional Consumer Banking (RCB) consists of PS2's four RCB businesses that provide traditional banking services to retail customers. RCB also contains PS2's branded cards business and PS2's local commercial banking business. RCB is a globally diversified business with over 4,200 branches in 39 countries around the world. During 2010, 54% of total RCB revenues were from outside North America. Additionally, the majority of international revenues and loans were from emerging economies in Asia, Latin America, Central and Eastern Europe and the Middle East. At December 31, 2010, RCB had $330 billion of assets and $309 billion of deposits.

North America Regional Consumer Banking (NA RCB) provides traditional banking and PS2-branded card services to retail customers and small to mid-size businesses in the U.S. NA RCB's approximate 1,000 retail bank branches and 13.1 million retail customer accounts are largely concentrated in the greater metropolitan areas of New York, Los Angeles, San Francisco, Chicago, Miami, Washington, D.C., Boston, Philadelphia, and certain larger PS2es in Texas. At December 31, 2010, NA RCB had $30.7 billion of retail banking and residential real estate loans and $144.8 billion of average deposits. In addition, NA RCB had 21.2 million PS2-branded credit card accounts, with $77.5 billion in outstanding card loan balances.

EMEA Regional Consumer Banking (EMEA RCB) provides traditional banking and PS2-branded card services to retail customers and small to mid-size businesses, primarily in Central and Eastern Europe, the Middle East and Africa. Remaining activities in respect of Western Europe retail banking are included in PS2 Holdings. EMEA RCB has generally repositioned its business, shifting from a strategy of widespread distribution to a focused strategy concentrating on larger urban markets within the region. An exception is Bank Handlowy, which has a mass-market presence in Poland. The countries in which EMEA RCB has the largest presence are Poland, Turkey, Russia and the United Arab Emirates. At December 31, 2010, EMEA RCB had 298 retail bank branches with 3.7 million customer accounts, $4.4 billion in retail banking loans and $9.2 billion in average deposits. In addition, the business had 2.5 million PS2-branded card accounts with $2.8 billion in outstanding card loan balances.

Latin America Regional Consumer Banking (LATAM RCB) provides traditional banking and PS2-branded card services to retail customers and small to mid-size businesses, with the largest presence in Mexico and Brazil. LATAM RCB includes branch networks throughout Latin America as well as Banco Nacional de Mexico, or Banamex, Mexico's second largest bank, with over 1,700 branches. At December 31, 2010, LATAM RCB had 2,190 retail branches, with 26.6 million customer accounts, $21.3 billion in retail banking loan balances and $42.6 billion in average deposits. In addition, the business had 12.5 million PS2-branded card accounts with $13.4 billion in outstanding loan balances.

Asia Regional Consumer Banking (Asia RCB) provides traditional banking and PS2-branded card services to retail customers and small to mid-size businesses, with the largest PS2 presence in South Korea, Japan, Taiwan, Singapore, Australia, Hong Kong, India and Indonesia. At December 31, 2010, Asia RCB had 711 retail branches, 16.1 million retail-banking accounts, $105.6 billion in average customer deposits, and $61.2 billion in retail banking loans. In addition, the business had 15.1 million PS2-branded card accounts with $20.4 billion in outstanding loan balances.

Institutional Clients Group (ICG) includes Securities and Banking and Transaction Services. ICG provides corporate, institutional, public sector and high-net-worth clients with a full range of products and services, including cash management, trade finance and services, securities services, trading, underwriting, lending and advisory services, around the world. ICG's international presence is supported by trading floors in approximately 75 countries and a proprietary network within Transaction Services in over 95 countries. At December 31, 2010, ICG had $953 billion of assets and $451 billion of deposits.

Securities and Banking (S&B) offers a wide array of investment and commercial banking services and products for corporations, governments, institutional and retail investors, and high-net-worth individuals. S&B includes investment banking and advisory services, lending, debt and equity sales and trading, institutional brokerage, foreign exchange, structured products, cash instruments and related derivatives, and private banking. S&B revenue is generated primarily from fees for investment banking and advisory services, fees and interest on loans, fees and spread on foreign exchange, structured products, cash instruments and related derivatives, income earned on principal transactions, and fees and spreads on private banking services.

Transaction Services is composed of Treasury and Trade Solutions (TTS) and Securities and Fund Services (SFS). TTS provides comprehensive cash management and trade finance and services for corporations, financial institutions and public sector entities worldwide. SFS provides securities services to investors, such as global asset managers, custody and clearing services to intermediaries such as broker-dealers, and depository and agency/trust services to multinational corporations and governments globally. Revenue is generated from net interest revenue on deposits in TTS and SFS, as well as from trade loans and fees for transaction processing and fees on assets under custody and administration in

PS2 Holdings contains businesses and portfolios of assets that PS2 has determined are not central to its core PS2 businesses. Consistent with its strategy, PS2 intends to exit these businesses as quickly as practicable in an economically rational manner through business divestitures, portfolio run-offs and asset sales. During 2009 and 2010, PS2 made substantial progress divesting and exiting businesses from PS2 Holdings, having completed more than 30 divestiture transactions, including Smith Barney, Nikko Cordial Securities, Nikko Asset Management, Primerica Financial Services, various credit card businesses (including Diners Club North America) and The Student Loan Corporation (which is reported as discontinued operations within the Corporate/Other segment for the second half of 2010 only). PS2 Holdings' GAAP assets of $359 billion have been reduced by $128 billion from December 31, 2009, and $468 billion from the peak in the first quarter of 2008. PS2 Holdings' GAAP assets of $359 billion represent approximately 19% of PS2's assets as of December 31, 2010. PS2 Holdings' risk-weighted assets of approximately $330 billion represent approximately 34% of PS2's risk-weighted assets as of December 31, 2010. PS2 Holdings consists of the following: Brokerage and Asset Management, Local Consumer Lending, and Special Asset Pool.

Brokerage and Asset Management (BAM), which constituted approximately 8% of PS2 Holdings by assets as of December 31, 2010, consists of PS2's global retail brokerage and asset management businesses. This segment was substantially reduced in size due to the sale in 2009 of Smith Barney to the PS1 Smith Barney joint venture (MSSB JV) and of Nikko Cordial Securities (reported as discontinued operations within Corporate/Other for all periods presented). At December 31, 2010, BAM had approximately $27 billion of assets, primarily consisting of PS2's investment in, and assets related to, the

MSSB JV. PS1 has options to purchase PS2's remaining stake in the MSSB JV over three years starting in 2012.

Local Consumer Lending (LCL), which constituted approximately 70% of PS2 Holdings by assets as of December 31, 2010, includes a portion of PS2's North American mortgage business, retail partner cards, Western European cards and retail banking, PS2Financial North America and other local Consumer finance businesses globally. The Student Loan Corporation is reported as discontinued operations within the Corporate/Other segment for the second half of 2010 only. At December 31, 2010, LCL had $252 billion of assets ($226 billion in North America). Approximately $129 billion of assets in LCL as of December 31, 2010 consisted of U.S. mortgages in the Company's PS2Mortgage and PS2Financial operations. The North American assets consist of residential mortgage loans (first and second mortgages), retail partner card loans, personal loans, commercial real estate (CRE), and other consumer loans and assets.

Special Asset Pool (SAP), which constituted approximately 22% of PS2 Holdings by assets as of December 31, 2010, is a portfolio of securities, loans and other assets that PS2 intends to actively reduce over time through asset sales and portfolio run-off. At December 31, 2010, SAP had $80 billion of assets. SAP assets have declined by $248 billion, or 76%, from peak levels in 2007 reflecting cumulative write-downs, asset sales and portfolio run-off.

Corporate/Other includes global staff functions (including finance, risk, human resources, legal and compliance) and other corporate expense, global operations and technology, residual Corporate Treasury and Corporate items. At December 31, 2010, this segment had approximately $272 billion of assets, consisting primarily of PS2's liquidity portfolio, including $87 billion of cash and deposits with banks.

As discussed earlier, the organizational complexity is the hallmark of bureaucracy. The organizational structure of PS2, as they have set forth in their Annual Report, is evidently highly complex. Additionally, PS2 specifically acknowledges their complexity, and informs shareholders that it can bring dire consequences. In their 2010 Form 10K, PS2 reports:

> PS2's businesses are highly dependent on their ability to process and monitor, on a daily basis, a very large number of transactions, many of which are *highly complex* [emphasis added] across numerous and diverse markets in many currencies. These transactions, as well as the information technology services PS2 provides to clients, often must adhere to client-specific guidelines, as well as legal and regulatory standards. Due to the breadth of PS2's client base and its geographical reach,

developing and maintaining PS2's operational systems and infrastructure is challenging, particularly as a result of rapidly evolving legal and regulatory requirements and technological shifts. PS2's financial, account, data processing or other operating systems and facilities may fail to operate properly or become disabled as a result of events that are wholly or partially beyond its control, such as a spike in transaction volume, cyberattack or other unforeseen catastrophic events, which may adversely affect PS2's ability to process these transactions or provide services.

PS2 also specifically informs shareholders that the complexity of their systems, which could result in cyberattack, may originate internally, at the hands of their own employees:

In addition, PS2's operations rely on the secure processing, storage and transmission of confidential and other information on its computer systems and networks. Although PS2 takes protective measures to maintain the confidentiality, integrity and availability of PS2's and its clients' information across all geographic and product lines, and endeavors to modify these protective measures as circumstances warrant, the nature of the threats continues to evolve. As a result, PS2's computer systems, software and networks may be vulnerable to unauthorized access, loss or destruction of data (including confidential client information), account takeovers, unavailability of service, computer viruses or other malicious code, cyberattacks and other events that could have an adverse security impact. Despite the defensive measures PS2 has taken, these threats may come from external actors such as governments, organized crime and hackers, third parties such as outsource or infrastructure-support providers and application developers, *or may originate internally from within PS2.* [emphasis added] Given the high volume of transactions at PS2, certain errors may be repeated or compounded before they are discovered and rectified.

In yet another statement in the same report, PS2 acknowledges and discloses the occurrence of employee fraud as follows:

There have also been a number of highly publicized cases involving fraud or other misconduct by employees in the financial services industry in recent years and PS2 runs the risk that employee misconduct could occur.

As discussed, the possibility of PS2 employees committing fraud is fully acknowledged by the company in their 2010 Annual Report. However, they attempt to alleviate shareholder concerns about the prospect of such fraud by informing them that employees can be whistleblowers, but that such protections may come at a price. Specifically, PS2 reported the following:

> while PS2 seeks to prevent and detect employee misconduct, such as fraud, employee misconduct is not always possible to deter or prevent, and the extensive precautions PS2 takes to prevent and detect this activity may not be effective in all cases, which could subject PS2 to additional liability. Moreover, the so-called "whistle-blower" provisions of the Financial Reform Act, which apply to all corporations and other entities and persons, provide substantial financial incentives for persons to report alleged violations of law to the SEC and the Commodity Futures Trading Commission. These provisions could increase the number of claims that PS2 will have to investigate or against which PS2 will have to defend itself, and may otherwise further increase PS2's legal liabilities.

Now that the presence of bureaucracy at PS2 has been established on the part of the company, it is important to consider the impressions of PS2's employees when determining whether this bureaucracy has reached a bureaupathic level.

Ideally, PS2 employees themselves would be interviewed directly for this study. However, PS2 would not permit such interviews of their employees to take place. In addition, despite best research efforts, the number of employee "interviews" (200+) that can be analyzed on this website would be challenging, if not possible, for any researcher to obtain independently.

According to the website Glassdoor, PS2 has been reviewed by 1,314 employees, as of July 8, 2013, whose overall rating of the company averaged at 3 out of 5, which is considered to be "average" by the website.

Of these reviews, research efforts were focused on those employees who rated the company "below average," or in this case, rated it under three stars. This limited the number of reviews included for examination to 403, which constituted approximately 31% of all reviews. These comments were posted between June 13, 2008, and June 20, 2013.

The reviews were limited to this population because it was believed this population would be more likely to have communicated that the company may exhibit signs of excessive bureaucracy. It is important to note the reviews are not provided in a spreadsheet or otherwise readily analyzable form. Instead, they are free-form reviews where the respondent freely chooses the language used (not selected from a list, etc.). As a result, while the reviews can be "sorted" by rating level, and limited other criteria, overall research efforts involve reading each individual review for the qualitative informational content. Note the comments may add up to greater than the total indicated, as the given reviewer sometimes provided comment, which spanned multiple categories.

Of these reviewers, 155, or 38.5% made reference to specific terminology related to bureaucracy and excessive bureaucracy. The number of comments is greater than that of the reviewers, as some respondents commented in more than one area and in that instance, were counted only once. The total number of comments recorded was 186. Overall, echoing the results for PS1, these below average reviews examined referenced a bureaucratic atmosphere. The level of "bureaucracy" and excessive bureaucracy, or bureaupathic behaviors were examined together, as laypersons often use the word "bureaucracy" with a negative connotation. Therefore, when examining employee comments, this was considered a negative term. Terminology attributed to bureaucracy included the words "red tape" and "government."

Here, the primary complaint centered on the limitations of their roles, in that there was little opportunity for advancement. In fact, many respondents said their roles were unchallenging, that management was largely aloof and disconnected from the "common worker." Many respondents also said management tended to be nepotistic in their hiring practices and that organizational connections were key to obtaining career growth.

General and specific references to attributes of bureaucracy and bureaupathic or excessive bureaucracy are presented in Tables 6.5 and 6.6.

As demonstrated, many respondents, 38.5%, made comments that were indicative of bureaucracy and bureaupathic conditions in their workplace. The most indicated category was general bureaucracy, which included reference to "red tape" and related terms.

Hotline Specification

PS2's hotline is called the "Ethics Hotline." Like PS1, third-party hotline provider, The Network, manages PS2's hotline. To understand how their hotline works, and to obtain their organizational data, an internal (PS2) Hotline Administrator ("HA2") and an employee from The Network who manages PS2's hotline ("NE1") was interviewed. The identities of these interview subjects are being withheld for privacy. They were interviewed on June 25, 2012 (HA2), and September 4, 2012 (NE1). According to HA2, PS2's internal hotline group is run by a managing director and has six regional offices and employs "Ethics Analysts." HA2 said these analysts are attorneys, and any and all hotline personnel employed by PS2 are always attorneys. Per HA2, there are five ways to reach the hotline, and calling is one of them. Additional methods of contact include web form, fax, e-mail, and regular mail. All are guaranteed to be confidential, and all tipsters, whether they are internal or external, do not have to give their name or any other identifying information.

In terms of triage, when complaints come to their office, their analyst/attorneys immediately determine whether the complaint suggests a legal, regulatory, or policy violation, which is assigned to an "ethics investigator," who could be a member of

Table 6.5   PS2 Social Media/Bureaucracy Analysis Summary

Attribute	Data	Analysis
Time frame	6/13/08–6/20/13	Five-year time period
Population	1,314	0.5% of all employees (260,000)
Sample set	403	31% of the population (1,314) 0.2% of all employees (260,000)
Respondents indicating bureaucracy or bureaupathic behaviors	155	38.5% of the sample set (403) 12% of the population (1,314) 0.06 % of all employees (260,000)
Total comments indicating bureaucracy and bureaupathology	186	112 Bureaucracy + 74 Bureaupathic
Bureaucracy	112	General (48) Hierarchy of authority (22) System of rules (7) Technical expertise (5) Career service (9) Insistence on the rights of office (21)
Bureaupathic	74	Impersonal treatment (16) Prolonged role enactment (19) Resistance to change (17) Resistance to interrogation and investigation (13) Strict reliance on organizational rules and procedures (9)

Table 6.6   PS2 Social Media/Bureaucracy Dataset

Count	Type	Attribute	Comment	Date
1.	Bureaupathic	Impersonal treatment	"It's genuinely possible for employees to completely disappear within the system"	5/9/13

(Continued)

Table 6.6 *(Continued)* **PS2 Social Media/Bureaucracy Dataset**

Count	Type	Attribute	Comment	Date
2.	Bureaupathic	Impersonal treatment	"No enthusiasm within the team"	1/9/13
3.	Bureaupathic	Impersonal treatment	"Stop treating employees like robots"	3/30/12
4.	Bureaupathic	Impersonal treatment	"Lack of opportunity to move"	2/24/12
5.	Bureaupathic	Impersonal treatment	"Stop hiring graduates with degrees in robot-manufacturing rather than in people-service management"	8/11/11
6.	Bureaupathic	Impersonal treatment	"I feel like a little mouse in this gigantic company"	6/10/11
7.	Bureaupathic	Impersonal treatment	"Your just a Peabody [sic]. Not much room for advancement"	3/9/11
8.	Bureaupathic	Impersonal treatment	"No one knows what's going on ever"	5/23/10
9.	Bureaupathic	Impersonal treatment	"Just another number"	2/18/10
10.	Bureaupathic	Impersonal treatment	"Robotic environment"	2/6/10
11.	Bureaupathic	Impersonal treatment	"You're pretty much chained to your desk while on the clock"	9/20/09
12.	Bureaupathic	Impersonal treatment	"You will feel like a cog in a machine"	7/9/09

(Continued)

Table 6.6 *(Continued)*   **PS2 Social Media/Bureaucracy Dataset**

Count	Type	Attribute	Comment	Date
13.	Bureaupathic	Impersonal treatment	"As an employee, you are just a number"	12/26/08
14.	Bureaupathic	Impersonal treatment	"I feel like another ant in this huge company"	10/9/08
15.	Bureaupathic	Impersonal treatment	"Employees are treated like cattle instead of human beings"	7/1/08
16.	Bureaupathic	Impersonal treatment	"You are just a number, one of the headcount"	6/13/08
17.	Bureaupathic	Prolonged role enactment	"Monkey trainable type of admin work"	6/17/13
18.	Bureaupathic	Prolonged role enactment	"Many positions have little to no advancement opportunities"	6/2/13
19.	Bureaupathic	Prolonged role enactment	"Transferring between departments was extremely difficult"	3/8/13
20.	Bureaupathic	Prolonged role enactment	"Career progression is slow"	3/1/13
21.	Bureaupathic	Prolonged role enactment	"Work is to [sic] heavy and boring"	9/18/12
22.	Bureaupathic	Prolonged role enactment	"Not [sic] opportunity to move up the ladder"	9/16/12
23.	Bureaupathic	Prolonged role enactment	"Very boring environment"	8/5/12
24.	Bureaupathic	Prolonged role enactment	"Jobs [are] quiet safe, routine and comfortable"	3/28/12

(Continued)

Table 6.6 *(Continued)* **PS2 Social Media/Bureaucracy Dataset**

Count	Type	Attribute	Comment	Date
25.	Bureaupathic	Prolonged role enactment	"You will be pidgeon-holed. Wherever you start.... expect to stay there, and at that salary"	12/2/11
26.	Bureaupathic	Prolonged role enactment	"Work is monotonous"	7/9/11
27.	Bureaupathic	Prolonged role enactment	"You can get paid decent money to work very little because there is so much redundancy in the organization. My brain atrophied and I had to leave"	4/14/11
28.	Bureaupathic	Prolonged role enactment	"Absolutely no growth"	11/25/10
29.	Bureaupathic	Prolonged role enactment	"Mundane, mind numbing set of job duties"	6/12/10
30.	Bureaupathic	Prolonged role enactment	"Depending on the department you are in, it could be a dead end area where there is no room for advancement or growth"	2/10/10
31.	Bureaupathic	Prolonged role enactment	"Virtually impossible to move to a different department without quitting the firm"	12/26/08

(Continued)

Table 6.6 *(Continued)*   **PS2 Social Media/Bureaucracy Dataset**

Count	Type	Attribute	Comment	Date
32.	Bureaupathic	Prolonged role enactment	"Extremely vertical groups, each group only does their thing, and nothing else. It's like wearing blinders to work"	11/21/08
33.	Bureaupathic	Prolonged role enactment	"Work is BORING AS ANYTHING"	11/12/08
34.	Bureaupathic	Prolonged role enactment	"If you want a run of the mill cruisy [sic] environment where mediocrity and sycophancy are tacitly encouraged then this place is for you"	10/15/08
35.	Bureaupathic	Prolonged role enactment	"The work once you learn is very repetitive like most jobs and very tedious"	9/10/08
36.	Bureaupathic	Resistance to change	"Systems are so antiquated"	5/11/13
37.	Bureaupathic	Resistance to change	"No willingness to improve in any aspect. Although management was told how to change processes and procedures, they did not care at all"	1/9/13
38.	Bureaupathic	Resistance to change	"Many systems are running 4–5 years behind current releases"	10/3/12
39.	Bureaupathic	Resistance to change	"Invest in…more up to date technology"	8/27/12

(Continued)

Table 6.6 *(Continued)*   **PS2 Social Media/Bureaucracy Dataset**

Count	Type	Attribute	Comment	Date
40.	Bureaupathic	Resistance to change	"80's technology"	7/5/12
41.	Bureaupathic	Resistance to change	"Stale company"	6/26/12
42.	Bureaupathic	Resistance to change	"Systems are medieval"	4/24/12
43.	Bureaupathic	Resistance to change	"Nothing [in terms of advice to management] you don't listen to employees current or past anyway"	2/24/12
44.	Bureaupathic	Resistance to change	"Outdated systems/ processes; very manual work for some departments"	9/20/11
45.	Bureaupathic	Resistance to change	"Not open to change"	4/16/11
46.	Bureaupathic	Resistance to change	"Very far behind the curve in systems and practices"	4/16/11
47.	Bureaupathic	Resistance to change	"In most positions you are working with older technology"	10/12/10
48.	Bureaupathic	Resistance to change	"[Uses] excuse[s] not to change"	6/3/10
49.	Bureaupathic	Resistance to change	"Antiquated systems"	3/7/10
50.	Bureaupathic	Resistance to change	"Middle management stuck in the stone age"	12/1/9
51.	Bureaupathic	Resistance to change	"The technology is outdated"	2/19/09

(Continued)

Table 6.6 *(Continued)*   PS2 Social Media/Bureaucracy Dataset

Count	Type	Attribute	Comment	Date
52.	Bureaupathic	Resistance to change	"Change is like moving a mountain"	9/7/08
53.	Bureaupathic	Resistance to interrogation and investigation	"Lack of ethics"	2/25/13
54.	Bureaupathic	Resistance to interrogation and investigation	"The amount of waste due to mismanagement is absolutely staggering"	2/22/13
55.	Bureaupathic	Resistance to interrogation and investigation	"Deep employee distrust in upper management"	1/18/13
56.	Bureaupathic	Resistance to interrogation and investigation	"[You have to] learn how to keep your mouth shut when you see something wrong/unethical"	1/8/13
57.	Bureaupathic	Resistance to interrogation and investigation	"Unethical at times"	10/23/12
58.	Bureaupathic	Resistance to interrogation and investigation	"Senior management lost its moral compass"	3/26/12
59.	Bureaupathic	Resistance to interrogation and investigation	"Managers are rewarded only on financial results, not based on how they achieved the results. Therefore, ethics and doing the right thing are sometimes secondary actions"	8/19/11

(Continued)

Table 6.6 *(Continued)* **PS2 Social Media/Bureaucracy Dataset**

Count	Type	Attribute	Comment	Date
60.	Bureaupathic	Resistance to interrogation and investigation	"Dishonest middle managers"	6/29/11
61.	Bureaupathic	Resistance to interrogation and investigation	"Management... prefers to hide ugly things under the carpet"	1/27/11
62.	Bureaupathic	Resistance to interrogation and investigation	"Management is evasive"	5/8/10
63.	Bureaupathic	Resistance to interrogation and investigation	"You lie and cheat your own employees"	10/29/09
64.	Bureaupathic	Resistance to interrogation and investigation	"Many seniors thinking they are above the law"	8/21/08
65.	Bureaupathic	Resistance to interrogation and investigation	"Low ethical standards"	7/14/08
66.	Bureaupathic	Strict reliance on organizational rules and procedures	"Work environment was very structured"	6/20/13
67.	Bureaupathic	Strict reliance on organizational rules and procedures	"The processes and systems make being productive very difficult"	3/16/13

(Continued)

Table 6.6 (*Continued*) PS2 Social Media/Bureaucracy Dataset

Count	Type	Attribute	Comment	Date
68.	Bureaupathic	Strict reliance on organizational rules and procedures	"Near dysfunctional in terms of getting things done. Extremely process heavy and inefficient"	2/25/13
69.	Bureaupathic	Strict reliance on organizational rules and procedures	"The processes were horrendously inefficient and time-consuming"	1/9/13
70.	Bureaupathic	Strict reliance on organizational rules and procedures	"Decision making is moribund, changes take forever and are generally no longer pertinent by the time they occur"	10/3/12
71.	Bureaupathic	Strict reliance on organizational rules and procedures	"Too many rules and restrictions"	3/30/12
72.	Bureaupathic	Strict reliance on organizational rules and procedures	"There are far too many 'channels' to go through to get anything of importance accomplished"	4/25/11
73.	Bureaupathic	Strict reliance on organizational rules and procedures	"Processes are speed bumps to achieving results as apposed to bridging or enabling results to be driven"	8/22/08

(Continued)

Table 6.6 (Continued) PS2 Social Media/Bureaucracy Dataset

Count	Type	Attribute	Comment	Date
74.	Bureaupathic	Strict reliance on organizational rules and procedures	"It is very hard to get things done. Lots of unnecessary and absurd procedures to follow. Some people only care about following company's procedures or policies and keep themselves out of trouble. It is so frustrating if you want to get something done"	6/29/08
75.	Bureaucracy	Career service	"Longterm employment"	6/3/13
76.	Bureaucracy	Career service	"Not many people are fired"	5/4/13
77.	Bureaucracy	Career service	"Get rid of old school dinosaurs that are ruining your organization"	12/4/12
78.	Bureaucracy	Career service	"It's virtually impossible to get fired for poor performance or even breaking fairly serious workplace rules"	11/22/12
79.	Bureaucracy	Career service	"Hard to get fired"	2/2/12
80.	Bureaucracy	Career service	"Easy to stay for a long time with the company"	1/11/11

(Continued)

Table 6.6 *(Continued)* **PS2 Social Media/Bureaucracy Dataset**

Count	Type	Attribute	Comment	Date
81.	Bureaucracy	Career service	"You will find more idiots who managed to stick around for 10–20 yrs and become your boss"	9/16/10
82.	Bureaucracy	Career service	"PS2 never sleeps because they are afraid of losing their jobs"	1/25/09
83.	Bureaucracy	Career service	"Lifers sitting in one job for too long"	9/24/08
84.	Bureaucracy	General bureaucracy	"Paralyzed by red tape"	6/14/13
85.	Bureaucracy	General bureaucracy	"Bureaucracy that rivals the federal government"	5/11/13
86.	Bureaucracy	General bureaucracy	"The company perfectly fits the stereotype of a massive decentralized organization characterized by stifling bureaucracy"	5/9/13
87.	Bureaucracy	General bureaucracy	"Too big and bureaucratic to be run efficiently"	4/11/13
88.	Bureaucracy	General bureaucracy	"It's a bureaucracy, like working for government"	3/16/13
89.	Bureaucracy	General bureaucracy	"Big bureaucratic machine"	3/10/13
90.	Bureaucracy	General bureaucracy	"Death by bureaucracy"	2/7/13

(Continued)

Table 6.6 *(Continued)* PS2 Social Media/Bureaucracy Dataset

Count	Type	Attribute	Comment	Date
91.	Bureaucracy	General bureaucracy	"Too centralized"	1/26/13
92.	Bureaucracy	General bureaucracy	"Bureaucratic, tyrannical mess of a company to work for. The right hand does not know what the left hand is doing"	1/17/13
93.	Bureaucracy	General bureaucracy	"Because of the companies size there are a number of layers to all positions—which makes the company extremely bureaucratic"	11/15/12
94.	Bureaucracy	General bureaucracy	"Burocratic [sic] environment...lots of red tape"	11/11/12
95.	Bureaucracy	General bureaucracy	"A bureaucratic maze"	8/16/12
96.	Bureaucracy	General bureaucracy	"Thick bureaucracy and red tape everywhere"	8/13/12
97.	Bureaucracy	General bureaucracy	"More bureaucratic than the post office"	8/11/12
98.	Bureaucracy	General bureaucracy	"Almost impossible to actually get things done"	8/11/12
99.	Bureaucracy	General bureaucracy	"Disorganized and beareaucratic [sic]"	4/14/12
100.	Bureaucracy	General bureaucracy	"Culture of bureaucracy"	3/28/12

(Continued)

Table 6.6 *(Continued)*   **PS2 Social Media/Bureaucracy Dataset**

Count	Type	Attribute	Comment	Date
101.	Bureaucracy	General bureaucracy	"Boring and bureaucratic"	3/26/12
102.	Bureaucracy	General bureaucracy	"I felt like I worked for a government agency"	3/4/12
103.	Bureaucracy	General bureaucracy	"The business is not streamlined"	1/11/12
104.	Bureaucracy	General bureaucracy	"Super siloed even within divisions"	11/29/11
105.	Bureaucracy	General bureaucracy	"Employees are robots and are expected to act like robots"	9/1/11
106.	Bureaucracy	General bureaucracy	"Takes too long to get anything done due to all the red tape"	6/24/11
107.	Bureaucracy	General bureaucracy	"...A nightmare of red tape"	5/7/11
108.	Bureaucracy	General bureaucracy	"Very bureaucratic"	3/13/11
109.	Bureaucracy	General bureaucracy	"Bureaucratic nonsense"	3/7/11
110.	Bureaucracy	General bureaucracy	"Bureaucratic nightmare"	2/9/11
111.	Bureaucracy	General bureaucracy	"Total bureaucracy"	2/1/11
112.	Bureaucracy	General bureaucracy	"Bureaucracy and politics peppered with manipulative tactics"	9/29/10

(Continued)

Table 6.6 *(Continued)* **PS2 Social Media/Bureaucracy Dataset**

Count	Type	Attribute	Comment	Date
113.	Bureaucracy	General bureaucracy	"[To work at PS2] you need to be comfortable with bureaucracy"	8/3/10
114.	Bureaucracy	General bureaucracy	"Very political and bureaucratic"	7/17/10
115.	Bureaucracy	General bureaucracy	"Bureaucratic"	7/10/10
116.	Bureaucracy	General bureaucracy	"Massive bureaucracy; massive entangled mess"	6/3/10
117.	Bureaucracy	General bureaucracy	"Extremely, extremely siloed. Moving from one department to another is akin to changing companies"	4/15/10
118.	Bureaucracy	General bureaucracy	"Full of bureaucracy"	3/14/10
119.	Bureaucracy	General bureaucracy	"There's a lot of bureaucracy in the organization"	2/15/10
120.	Bureaucracy	General bureaucracy	"Very slow moving, bureaucratic company"	12/15/09
121.	Bureaucracy	General bureaucracy	"Burocracy [sic] is literaly [sic] whats [sic] killing them, you may spend most of your day making sure that you follow the procedures, it leave [sic] no time for actual work"	9/27/09

(Continued)

Table 6.6 *(Continued)* **PS2 Social Media/Bureaucracy Dataset**

Count	Type	Attribute	Comment	Date
122.	Bureaucracy	General bureaucracy	"Bureaucracy"	9/12/09
123.	Bureaucracy	General bureaucracy	"Bureaucracy "	7/13/09
124.	Bureaucracy	General bureaucracy	"Lots of bureaucracy"	6/28/09
125.	Bureaucracy	General bureaucracy	"Bureaucracy"	5/19/09
126.	Bureaucracy	General bureaucracy	"Bureaucratic"	5/12/09
127.	Bureaucracy	General bureaucracy	"PS2 is a bureaucratic nightmare"	2/23/09
128.	Bureaucracy	General bureaucracy	"Too much bureaucracy"	8/20/08
129.	Bureaucracy	General bureaucracy	"Bureaucracy…large and bloated"	8/20/08
130.	Bureaucracy	General bureaucracy	"Unnecessary long [sic] bureaucracy"	8/1/08
131.	Bureaucracy	General bureaucracy	"Lots of bureaucracy	7/8/08
132.	Bureaucracy	Hierarchy of authority	"Vureaucracy, unnecessary management hierarchy"	10/9/12
133.	Bureaucracy	Hierarchy of authority	"To [sic] much hierarchy within the firm"	6/26/12
134.	Bureaucracy	Hierarchy of authority	"Very silo'ed [sic], segregated environment"	11/29/11
135.	Bureaucracy	Hierarchy of authority	"Too many layers of management"	11/15/11

(Continued)

Table 6.6 *(Continued)* **PS2 Social Media/Bureaucracy Dataset**

Count	Type	Attribute	Comment	Date
136.	Bureaucracy	Hierarchy of authority	"Lack of interaction and support from upper management"	11/14/11
137.	Bureaucracy	Hierarchy of authority	"Fundamentally superficial barriers inherent to the organizational hierarchy"	3/7/11
138.	Bureaucracy	Hierarchy of authority	"Extremely layered"	2/1/11
139.	Bureaucracy	Hierarchy of authority	"The sheer size of the company allows for pockets and layers of extremely poor management to thrive using outdated, archaic management practices and defeat all attempts to improve the company with new ideas and technology"	12/1/10
140.	Bureaucracy	Hierarchy of authority	"Too many layers"	9/20/10
141.	Bureaucracy	Hierarchy of authority	"Very hierarchical"	6/27/10
142.	Bureaucracy	Hierarchy of authority	"PS2 has many layers within the organization"	5/28/10
143.	Bureaucracy	Hierarchy of authority	"So big and full of silos that getting things done takes a small miracle every time"	3/14/10

(Continued)

Table 6.6 *(Continued)*   PS2 Social Media/Bureaucracy Dataset

Count	Type	Attribute	Comment	Date
144.	Bureaucracy	Hierarchy of authority	"Several levels/layers of hierarchy"	9/12/09
145.	Bureaucracy	Hierarchy of authority	"Too heavily matrixed, too siloed"	7/19/09
146.	Bureaucracy	Hierarchy of authority	"Working at PS2 teaches you to deal with bureaucracy and find your way through a maze of disconnected information to get an answer"	2/17/09
147.	Bureaucracy	Hierarchy of authority	"Departments work in silos"	1/16/09
148.	Bureaucracy	Hierarchy of authority	"Your title is your everything. You are treated a certain way based on your title and job level"	12/12/08
149.	Bureaucracy	Hierarchy of authority	"Eliminate layers"	12/10/08
150.	Bureaucracy	Hierarchy of authority	"Too many layers of management"	9/24/08
151.	Bureaucracy	Hierarchy of authority	"Layers of management that do not perform any job"	9/10/08
152.	Bureaucracy	Hierarchy of authority	"Layers upon layers of middle management"	8/20/08
153.	Bureaucracy	Hierarchy of authority	"Cut the incompetent layers"	7/8/08

(Continued)

Table 6.6 (Continued)   PS2 Social Media/Bureaucracy Dataset

Count	Type	Attribute	Comment	Date
154.	Bureaucracy	Insistence on the rights of office	"Managers essentially answer to no one"	5/9/13
155.	Bureaucracy	Insistence on the rights of office	"Managers really act like manager; [sic] you will definitely have the impression that you are 'managed'"	4/19/13
156.	Bureaucracy	Insistence on the rights of office	"Very few Indians and lots and lots of chiefs"	3/29/13
157.	Bureaucracy	Insistence on the rights of office	"Eliminate 50–75% of the staff from the level of Director up"	2/22/13
158.	Bureaucracy	Insistence on the rights of office	"Too many chiefs and no Indians"	2/13/13
159.	Bureaucracy	Insistence on the rights of office	"Managers use employees as shields, so they have people to blame when things go awry"	2/13/13
160.	Bureaucracy	Insistence on the rights of office	"Upper management extremely out of touch with the rest of the company"	1/18/13
161.	Bureaucracy	Insistence on the rights of office	"Fiefdoms"	1/6/13

(Continued)

Table 6.6 *(Continued)* PS2 Social Media/Bureaucracy Dataset

Count	Type	Attribute	Comment	Date
162.	Bureaucracy	Insistence on the rights of office	"People are promoted based on Senior Managers needing head count under them so they look important and don't lose their jobs"	1/4/13
163.	Bureaucracy	Insistence on the rights of office	"Upper management is very out of the loop"	12/1/12
164.	Bureaucracy	Insistence on the rights of office	"Management ignoring market trends and insisting in [sic] old model of banking"	4/24/12
165.	Bureaucracy	Insistence on the rights of office	"Generally disinterested, absent and self promoting management"	1/12/12
166.	Bureaucracy	Insistence on the rights of office	"Decisions made at top management level without employee insight"	1/20/11
167.	Bureaucracy	Insistence on the rights of office	"Management abuses power and if you are not a manager you have no say. Management has no communication with its employees"	1/9/11
168.	Bureaucracy	Insistence on the rights of office	"Senior leadership is too insulated from employees"	12/30/10

(Continued)

Table 6.6 *(Continued)*   **PS2 Social Media/Bureaucracy Dataset**

Count	Type	Attribute	Comment	Date
169.	Bureaucracy	Insistence on the rights of office	"Manager was allowed to run roughshod [sic] over the employees, insisted on pagers being answered 24/7"	8/9/10
170.	Bureaucracy	Insistence on the rights of office	"Arrogant management"	7/17/10
171.	Bureaucracy	Insistence on the rights of office	"Autocratic management styles	3/8/10
172.	Bureaucracy	Insistence on the rights of office	"My boss didn't know what I was employed to do"	11/27/9
173.	Bureaucracy	Insistence on the rights of office	"Senior management treated everyone below as dumb high school students"	12/13/08
174.	Bureaucracy	Insistence on the rights of office	"Fiefdoms"	11/21/08
175.	Bureaucracy	Systems of rules	"Successful sales also get a lot of scrutiny through compliance guidelines"	8/25/11
176.	Bureaucracy	Systems of rules	"Red tape associated with getting [IT-related] access, requesting a change etc."	4/18/11
177.	Bureaucracy	Systems of rules	"Streamline the many internal systems that exist"	3/5/11

(Continued)

Table 6.6 *(Continued)* **PS2 Social Media/Bureaucracy Dataset**

Count	Type	Attribute	Comment	Date
178.	Bureaucracy	Systems of rules	"Systems and business processes are very slow"	2/9/11
179.	Bureaucracy	Systems of rules	"The security protocols get in the way of real work at times"	1/31/11
180.	Bureaucracy	Systems of rules	"Access takes weeks before you can use software"	3/4/10
181.	Bureaucracy	Systems of rules	"Numerous systems existed that did not "talk" one another"	4/25/09
182.	Bureaucracy	Technical expertise	"Systems nightmare"	11/8/12
183.	Bureaucracy	Technical expertise	"Large and complex"	10/3/12
184.	Bureaucracy	Technical expertise	"Technology unit is hampered from delivering solutions to the business due to complex process and procedures"	8/11/12
185.	Bureaucracy	Technical expertise	"[Need] less processes"	3/4/12
186.	Bureaucracy	Technical expertise	"Very large distributed systems"	6/18/11

the Legal, Compliance, or Corporate Security and Investigations team, and tracked to resolution.

When asked whether Dodd–Frank changed the way their hotline is managed or advertised, HA2 said they reissued their Code of Conduct, and continue to provide ongoing awareness (via e-mail, internal intranet, training courses, etc.). For potential complainants, internal or external, looking to contact the hotline from home, as is the case with 41% of callers, the hotline contact information can be accessed easily—that is, if you know the hotline is called an "Ethics Hotline." According to The Network, as many as 41% of calls to hotlines come in after business hours and on weekends (Malone, 2003).

A Google search for "PS2 Ethics Hotline" yielded the actual hotline web page as the first result, which was complete with telephone number and all other contact information listed. However, if a complainant searches for "PS2 Fraud Hotline" the number is not easily located (on the seventh page of results, the PS2 Code of Conduct was linked where the hotline number could be located at the end of this lengthy document).

With respect to hotline best practices, HA2 further advised their golden sources for best practices included the Federal Sentencing Guidelines for Organizations and materials from such sources as the Ethics and Compliance Officers Association (ECOA), Ethics.org resource center and materials from The Network and Ethics Point, the two leading providers of third-party hotlines to public and private organizations (at the time). Today, they are all known as NAVEX Global.

With respect to the external communication of their hotline, in PS2's Schedule 14A (Form DEF 14A) filed March 12, 2010, PS2 discloses the existence and specifics of their hotline to shareholders. Schedule 14A is a disclosure required by the SEC for the proxy solicitation process, in advance of the shareholder voting process. Per their Schedule 14A:

Ethics Hotline

> PS2 strongly encourages employees to raise possible ethical issues. PS2 offers several channels by which employees and others may report ethical concerns or incidents, including, without limitation, concerns about accounting, internal controls or auditing matters. We provide an Ethics Hotline that is available 24 hours a day, seven days a week with live operators who can connect to translators in multiple languages, a dedicated e-mail address, fax line, a web-link and conventional mailing address. Individuals may choose to remain anonymous to the extent permitted by applicable laws and regulations. We prohibit retaliatory actions against anyone who, in good faith, raises concerns or questions regarding ethics, discrimination or harassment matters, or reports suspected violations of other applicable laws, regulations or policies. Calls to the Ethics Hotline are received by a vendor, located in the U.S., which reports the calls to PS2's Ethics Office for handling. (p. 15)

To further understand third-party hotline management, an employee of The Network (now NAVEX Global) NE1 was interviewed. By way of background, The Network is a technology company that provides an anonymous, confidential reporting hotline service. In a letter they wrote to the SEC in 2003, they self-reported as being "the nation's first outsourced employee 'hotline.'" At that time, they reported having over 1,000 clients, to include "many" of the Fortune 500. Today, according to available information, they have over 3,400 clients, including nearly half of the Fortune 500.

According to their website, their hotline center never closes and offers toll-free service in over 180 languages and their call center employees follow a "proprietary interview methodology" that offers "substantial incident reports." They also provide web intake with international web forms.

As for their client list, NE1 advised The Network handles the hotlines of "nearly all the financial industry" including PS2, J.P. Morgan Chase, Bank of America, and Wells Fargo, along with the Federal Reserve, to name a few. According to NE1, the names of these clients were revealed because they have expressly permitted The Network, in advance, to disclose this information. According to HE1, individuals can call hotlines and ask the identity of the administering organization, to learn the third-party provider of a specific hotline.

Other clients of The Network, who have been disclosed in the public domain, include various cities (GS3, California, Tulsa, Oklahoma, Mesa, Arizona, Sacramento, California) colleges and universities (Lafayette College in Pennsylvania, Arizona State University, Vanderbilt University, Purdue University, University of Texas at Dallas and San Antonio, University of Alabama), media organizations (Discovery Communications, the world's largest nonfiction media company), and travel companies, such as Norwegian Cruise Line.

When asked about the use of third-party hotline providers by the federal government, NE1 advised that the federal government tended to manage their hotlines internally, rather than use a third-party provider.

Regarding their competition, NE1 said their competitors, EthicsPoint and Global Compliance, are now all one company, NAVEX Global. When asked why a company should choose The Network over the competition, NE1 said they offer the most complete, in-depth reports with a more "detailed, technology assisted interview process" with calls lasting 15–20 minutes. While NE1 acknowledged EthicsPoint once said they had the best case management software, "banks didn't care about that" because they "have their own software." With respect to case management, NE1 said The Network offers "standard incident codes" and then banks often supplement these with their own codes.

As for information flow, NE1 advised their hotline tip intake process (via telephone) is as follows: The tipster makes the call to their unique hotline number (each client has their own number in each country). The hotline interviewer, called the "interview specialist" will learn the company and location of a given caller via a "pop up" on their "intake screen." For example, the interview specialist could see on their screen "PS2 caller from France." The interview specialist also manages the web tip intake process. There is one dedicated URL provided for this purpose, per client.

After the tip is logged, "within 15 minutes" a "triage team feeds [the tip] into the system" and an e-mail is sent to the client. Then, the client sends the tip to another internal designee for handling. The ultimate resolution of the tip is tracked via The Network's software.

When asked about the triage process for immediate matters, NE1 advised they have an "immediate escalation process for cases reported which are time sensitive [handled within 24 hours]." To escalate these matters, The Network is provided with telephone numbers of "key people" to be contacted by The Network in the event of urgent matters, such as "immediate threat of workplace violence, falsification, etc."

If the client wishes to communicate with the anonymous complainant, following the initial tip (i.e., to get further information), they will contact their contact at The Network who will make a note in the system to communicate their request for additional detail to the caller, if they call back. According to NE1, most callers do not call a second time.

When asked about their benchmarking report and the complete absence of prosecutions as a result of their services, NE1 said "PS2 and others often don't report back to them on resolution."

As for their employees, The Network's triage team is based in Atlanta, Georgia, where they have over 200 interview specialists. When I asked whether The Network would hire me, I was told I am "overqualified." Rather, according to NE1, they hire "entry level" personnel; some may come straight out of college, yet others are hired without a degree, as it is not required. Interview specialists are paid by the hour and are "incentivized based on quality of report." All candidates are subject to background checks (convicted felons are not hired) and have to sign a nondisclosure agreement.

A review of the The Network's website, on July 22, 2013, under the "careers" section yielded several job advertisements for Interview Specialists, which were described as personnel tasked with "answer[ing] inbound employee assistance-type calls from employees of out Fortune 500 client companies." The Network further said interview specialists "are responsible for accurately documenting these calls using PC and Windows-based applications."

At this time, seven postings for these positions were present on their careers page, where they were seeking speakers in the following languages (in addition to English language fluency): British/English, French, German, Mandarin Chinese, Portuguese, and Spanish. The stated candidate requirements were "A minimum of one year customer service experience; Call center experience preferred; Ability to read, write and speak fluently in English and [in the given language]." The job postings further say the candidate should demonstrate "Ability to conduct a structured interview; Minimum typing speed of 35+ WPM with 90% accuracy required; Excellent grammar, spelling and writing skills; and a pleasant and friendly phone presence."

As for the regional requirements and governing laws, NE1 advised they follow SOX and international laws, and that the laws governing their service are a "Hodgepodge." According to NE1, "in some countries, you cannot ask certain questions." For instance, using France as an example, NE1 advised in this region, certain questions cannot be asked, nor can information be recorded regarding certain matters. They employ a separate data privacy firm, Hunton & Williams, to handle/advise them on regional legal issues.

When asked about the volume of calls received by financial firms, NE1 said that "some financial firms rarely get a call." When asked why, NE1 responded "it is an issue of promotion of the hotline" and that "some say to use the hotline as a last resort. It's a cultural thing. Many want to keep the volume down." Incidentally, NE1 later revealed the cost of service "depends on volume."

As for the actual cost incurred to clients to have The Network manage their hotline, according to NE1, every "report taken [costs] between $40–60 per report" with an "average cost of $400–500 per year" with "additional cost for translation services, etc." and that "all in, companies can expect to pay between $30–100k per year with a minimum cost of $1k allowed [per year]."

When asked how the hotline reporting process changed following Dodd–Frank, NE1 said that Dodd–Frank "didn't change things much" except that "companies want to keep employees from reporting outside, otherwise more money in damages… [companies are] trying to get people to report internally."

Hotline Metrics

The hotline data for PS1 includes calls received to the hotline between 2004 and 2010 (Tables 6.7 and 6.8).

According to organizational documents, at PS2, 2004 was the first year of what they called their "Five Point Plan" where they increased their level of communication and transparency for employees into their fraud hotline process, by publicizing to employees the number of calls received per year by the hotline, the nature of complaints, and how they were handled (in the aggregate; in general terms). In this year, they received 1,619 complaints, which included calls from 25 different countries, where 42% of the contacts were anonymous. Most of the complaints received in this year (1,260) were categorized by the company as "HR-related" and were said to have been "handled by the appropriate areas." The 352 business and operational complaints were reportedly related to sales/service/operational practices, fraud, falsified or missing documents, conflict of interest and collections. The actions taken in 142 matters included "retraining or firings, reissuing policies, and even taking away contracts from vendors."

In 2005, they received 2,485 complaints, including calls from 44 different countries where 48% of the complainants remained anonymous. The issues raised involved mainly sales/service/operational practices (29%), fraud (15%), falsified or missing documents (10%), conflicts of interest (9%), and collections and information security (both at 7%). The actions taken in 259 matters included employee terminations, to lesser corrective actions, including training, reissuing policies, and strengthening controls.

Table 6.7 PS2 Hotline Metrics

Year	Total Complaints	Human Resources Related	Business/ Operational Issues	Action Taken
2004	1,619	1,267	352	142
2005	2,485	1,620	865	259
2006	2,405	1,424	981	350
2007	1,949	1,332	617	200
2008	2,277	1,383	894	373
2009	1,881	1,177	704	278
2010	2,031	1,290	741	268

Table 6.8 Complaint Type

Year / Complaint Type	2004	2005	2006	2007	2008	2009	2010
Complainants remaining anonymous	0.42	0.48	0.52	0.50	0.43	0.44	0.42
Accounting/Audit irregularities	N/A	—	—	0.01	0.02	0.02	N/A
AML/Terrorist financing	N/A	—	—	0.01	0.01	0.01	N/A
Bribery/Gifts	N/A	—	0.03	0.10	0.03	0.05	N/A
Collections	N/A	0.07	0.04	0.03	0.04	0.03	N/A
Conflicts of interest	N/A	0.09	0.05	0.05	0.03	0.04	N/A
Falsified or missing documents	N/A	0.10	0.11	0.16	0.12	0.08	N/A
Fraud	N/A	0.15	0.12	0.09	0.08	0.08	N/A
Information security/Privacy	N/A	0.07	0.09	—	0.14	0.15	N/A
Insider trading	N/A	—	—	—	0.01	—	N/A

(Continued)

Table 6.8 *(Continued)*   **Complaint Type**

Year	2004	2005	2006	2007	2008	2009	2010
Complaint Type							
Misuse of corporate assets	N/A	—	0.02	0.02	0.01	0.01	N/A
Other	N/A	—	0.09	0.06	0.04	0.04	N/A
Retaliation	N/A	—	0.07	0.13	0.10	0.10	N/A
Sales, service, and operational practices	N/A	0.29	0.38	0.34	0.36	0.38	N/A
Vendor practices	N/A	—	—	—	0.01	0.01	N/A
Total	N/A	100	100	100	100	100	N/A

Note: N/A, Not Available.

In 2006, 52% of the contacts were anonymous. The 2,405 reported matters in this year involved sales, service, and operational practices (38%); falsified or missing documents (11%); fraud (12%); information security (7%); retaliation (7%); privacy (2%); misuse of corporate assets (2%); conflicts of interest (5%); collections (4%); bribery/gifts (3%), and other (9%). These complaints were said to have originated from North America (42%), Asia Pacific (17%), Europe, Middle East and Africa (EMEA) (14%), Japan (13%), Mexico (9%), and Latin America (5%). Reported actions taken include recommending training, amending policies, and disciplinary action.

In 2007, of the 1,949 total complaints, 50% of complainants remained anonymous. Complaints included sales, service, and operational practices (34%); retaliation (13%); accounting/audit irregularities (1%); bribery/kickbacks (3%); collections (3%); conflicts of interest (5%); [falsification of expense reporting (2%), falsification of time sheets (6%), falsified or missing documents (8%) classified as 16% "falsified or missing documents"]; fraud/theft (9%); gifts/entertainment (7%); misuse of corporate assets (2%); and other (6%). Actions taken in 200 matters included recommending training, amending policies, and disciplinary action.

In 2008, of the 2,277 total complaints, 43% of complainants remained anonymous. In this year, complaints included sales, service, and operational practices (38%); information security/privacy (14%); retaliation (10%); fraud/theft (8%); [falsified or missing documents (6%), collections (4%), falsification of time reporting (4%), falsification of expense reporting (2%) classified as 12% "falsified or missing documents"]; bribery/kickbacks/gifts/entertainment (3%); conflicts of interest (3%); accounting/financial irregularities (2%); anti money laundering (AML)/terrorist financing (1%); other policy and regulatory violations (1%); vendor practices (1%); misuse of corporate assets (1%); insider trading (1%); and other (1%). Callers originated from North America (49%), Mexico (20%), EMEA (12%), Asia Pacific

(10%), Latin America (5%), and Japan (4%). Reported actions taken in 373 matters included recommending training, amending policies and business processes, and disciplinary action.

In 2009, of the 1,881 total complaints, 44% of complainants remained anonymous. Complaints included sales, service, and operational practices (38%); information security/privacy (15%); retaliation (10%); fraud/theft (8%); bribery/kickbacks/gifts/entertainment (5%); conflicts of interest (4%); [falsification of time reporting (4%), falsification of expense reporting (2%), falsified or missing documents (2%) classified as 8% "falsified or missing documents"]; additional policy and regulatory violations (3%) added to "other"; collections (3%); accounting/financial irregularities (2%); AML/terrorist financing (1%); misuse of corporate assets (1%); vendor practices (1%); and other (3%). Callers originated from North America (47%), Mexico (24%), Asia Pacific (10%), Latin America (7%), EMEA (7%), and Japan (5%). Reported actions taken in 278 of the matters included training, amendments to policies and business processes, and disciplinary action.

In 2010, 42% of contacts remained anonymous. As of 2010, detailed data breakdowns were no longer provided. It was noted that this reporting change coincided with a chance in departmental administration which occurred in this year, which could account for the change in policy. However, it was reported the 1,290 employment-related complaints were referred to "Employee Relations," which is presumably the human resources department. The 742 business and operational issues were said to have been handled by PS2's Ethics Office; the same department that internally manages the fraud hotline. According to available information, 268 of the complaints this year were handled with the use of training, amendments to policies and business practices, and disciplinary action.

To benchmark the hotline metrics, the 2009 and 2012 reports were consulted for their benchmarking data, as they are based on the analysis of calls received to their hotline between the relevant time periods, which are 2004–2008, 2007, and 2011, respectively.

Corporate Governance and Compliance Benchmarking Reports were consulted. The Network and BDO Consulting produce these reports on an annual basis. It should be noted that in their reporting, The Network groups the results for the financial industry along with that of the Construction and Real Estate industry. A request made to this organization to receive disaggregated data was denied. Per e-mail from The Network Employee (NE1) (the same employee who was interviewed on September 4, 2012 the contents of which are located in Chapter 3, "Third Party Hotline Process"), "To your question, we can only provide information in aggregated format to protect the anonymity of our clients. Even to break it down by the vertical can put our clients at risk since we dominate that vertical" (e-mail dated September 12, 2012). They also would not provide a client list. In response to this research request, the response from The Network was as follows: "Our benchmarking report is compiled from reports generated by our global client set. Because of our commitment to confidentiality, we do not divulge specific client information (nor do we track it outside of the client-specific database). We only show and track the total number of organizations, total number of employees, and numbers of organizations per employee size" (e-mail from The Network Employee 2 [NE 2], dated August 2, 2012).

According to their report, the hotline contact report rates per 1,000 employees for the financial industry, and for an organization of this size, during the relevant time periods were as shown in Table 6.9.

To summarize, in contrast with PS1, according to the data, the number of calls received by PS2 has met, and, at times, exceeded the benchmarking figures. However, when examined qualitatively, it is evident that the time with the greatest amount of fraud, the 2007–2009 time period immediately preceding Dodd–Frank, we see that PS2 actually experienced a decline in the number of tips they received. Also, the number of frauds being reported is low, in light of the complaint volume.

To this end, according to the same benchmarking report, not a single complaint, out of all their clients analyzed (they are the hotline administrator for over 3,000 public and private sector clients) between 2004 and 2011 resulted in a prosecution.

As a result, it is clear that organizations must look at not just the number of complaints received, and whether that comports with benchmarking figures, but to look at the quality of tips received, especially during particular time periods, such as those with a proven increase in fraud in the given industry.

Also, it would seem that organizations may want to examine these benchmarking reports qualitatively and ask their hotline provider a series of probing questions, such as how it is possible that no prosecutions have ever resulted based on data received to their hotline. In other words, this means that none of the complaints they handled have ever resulted in an employee being charged with a crime? Then the organization must consider whether they have had employee prosecutions during this time. If the answer is yes, then this either means meaningful data are not being reported to this hotline, or the hotline may not be handling or triaging the calls appropriately.

Historical Context

The time period between 2007 and 2009, when PS2's hotline calls actually declined, was considered to be the financial crisis. Again, during this time, according to the Federal Deposit Insurance Corporation (FDIC), 366 U.S. banks failed. PS2 was also seriously affected by this crisis. Indeed, PS2 was recapitalized by the U.S. government in November 2008.

Fraud Metrics

According to the information available in the public domain, there is a lot of employee fraud occurring in this organization. What follows is a sample set of employee crimes that occurred at the hands of PS2 employees during the relevant time period (2004–2010), which were made available to the public.

Table 6.9 Hotline Metrics

Time Period FY January–December	Number of Employees (PS2's Annual Reports 2004–2010)	Average Benchmarking Figure Size, Industry	Number of Actual Complaints Received	Complaints Expected per Benchmarking	Delta	Percentage of Actual versus Benchmarking
FY 2004	294,000	8.3, 3.17 = 6	1,619	1,764	145	92%
FY 2005	307,000	9.5, 5.61 = 8	2,485	2,456	+29	101%
FY 2006	337,000	8.5, 6.06 = 7	2,405	2,359	+96	102%
FY 2007	387,000	9.30, 4.90 = 7	1,949	2,709	760	72%
FY 2008	326,900	8.60, 7.93 = 8	2,277	2,615	338	87%
FY 2009	269,000	7.66, 8.28 = 8	1,881	2,152	271	87%
FY 2010	260,000	7.19, 6.52 = 7	2,031	1,820	+211	112%

One noteworthy insider fraud case in recent years was the case of Gary Foster—one that has been dubbed by *The Wall Street Journal* as "the ultimate inside job" (Bray, 2011). Foster, legally blind, stole approximately $19.2 million from PS2 in a scheme that lasted for a year and a half (May, 2009–December, 2010). During this time, Foster, a vice president who monitored derivative contracts, wired himself the money in a series of transactions from PS2 corporate accounts to his own personal bank account at another institution (Bray, 2011; Dye, 2011).

Although the amount stolen here is enough to say this was an egregious crime, what makes it especially problematic is that Foster, despite making less than $100,000 per year from PS2, lived lavishly and flaunted this wealth to coworkers. Foster owned three luxury cars (a Maserati, a BMW, and a Ferrari) and owned six homes, including one in Englewood Cliffs, New Jersey, that had a $500,000 entertainment system, to include bathroom mirrors that doubled as video screens (Bray, 2011). Despite his flagrant display of wealth relative to his position, Foster was not caught until a routine PS2 audit.

Foster, who had worked for PS2 since 1999, was arrested in June 2011 and charged with bank fraud and pleaded guilty to the crime. In June 2012, he was sentenced to 8 years in prison.

In 2011, it was reported that a PS2 employee, a wealth manager in Indonesia, was detained by police on theft charges after stealing an estimated $2 million. PS2 reportedly admitted this theft took place (Reuters, May 7, 2011). At this time, a parallel investigation ensued into PS2's debt collection practices after a local resident died following questioning by PS2 debt collectors for a delinquent credit card bill (Reuters, May 7, 2011)

Following this crime, while Indonesian authorities investigated, the bank was barred from adding new credit card clients in this country for 2 years, and from taking new private wealth clients for 1 year. Authorities said if they determined PS2 committed crimes they would revoke their operating license (Reuters, May 7, 2011). The wife of the man who died also filed a lawsuit against PS2 for $347 million in damages (Reuters, 2011).

In 2010, it was reported several employees of PS2 in India, including relationship manager Shivraj Puri, stole between $67 and $89 million from the bank's wealthy Indian clients using forged documents (Wachtel, 2010). At least 30 PS2 clients were affected by these frauds, and it was unclear at the time of the reporting whether the clients would be compensated for their loss (Wachtel 2010; Wilson, 2010). The scheme was perpetrated only a few months (Wachtel, 2010).

In 2011, it was reported that a PS2 employee pleaded guilty to stealing nearly $750,000 from 22 PS2 clients and faced 120 years in prison (Dremann). According to the report, Tamara Moon, a registered general securities representative and sales assistant, over the course of 8 years, from 2000 to 2008, unlawfully traded in customers' accounts. This theft was especially troubling, as Moon purposely targeted clients who, she believed would be least likely to notice her crime, due to their elderly age, or poor health status (Dremann, 2011).

Moon admitted to the thefts in her plea application, where she documented how she created fake authorization letters and transferred client money into her own account. It was further reported Moon used this money to invest in real estate and remodel her home (Dremann, 2011).

As a result of this crime, PS2 was fined by the Financial Industry Regulatory Authority (FINRA) $500,000 for failing to detect and investigate the "red flags" that were produced over the course of this employee's thieving transactions.

In PS2's Form 10K filed in 2010, they disclosed criminal charges were brought against a PS2 subsidiary (CBB) and three current or former employees in Belgium. The court convicted all defendants under the Prospectus Act, finding they did not follow their conditions/standards for issuers who offer securities to the public, and convicted CBB under Fair Trade Practices legislation. CBB was fined 165,000 Euro (approximately USD$218,000), and the individual defendants were also fined 427.50 Euro. PS2 was further ordered to compensate over 60 civil claimants, who didn't settle their disputes, for 2.4 million Euro (approximately USD$3.17 million). CBB appealed the judgment, and in their 2012 10K, PS2 reported on May 21, 2012, the Belgian appellate court dismissed all criminal charges against CBB, and the public prosecutor appealed this decision to the Belgian Supreme Court.

In 2011, Reuters reported PS2 was fined $770,000 for failing to identify a Ponzi scheme that was orchestrated by an employee in Hong Kong. According to the Securities and Futures Commission (SFC), between 2004 and 2009, a PS2 employee defrauded 13 PS2 Asia clients by taking their money, which was supposed to be invested in financial products. The SFC found that PS2 was aware of the crime, yet did not report it to authorities in a timely manner. As a result, they vowed to hire an external expert to examine their operational practices (Reuters, October 3, 2011).

In cases of employee fraud at PS2, it was discovered that several occurred that involved collusion with multiple employees. In one such case in New York, in 2006, several PS2 employees conspired to steal client account numbers in what the media dubbed a "three woman fraud ring" (SecurityWeek News, 2001).

In this case, the subject employees stole over $1 million from clients by stealing their credit card numbers and using the cards to buy luxury merchandise. In furtherance of the crimes, the employees changed the home addresses on the client's accounts to retrieve the merchandise. The employees, Lisa Reid, Sophia Grant, and Mahogani Graves, received sentences ranging from 21 to 30 months in prison and were ordered to make restitution.

In one of the more egregious fraud matters reported in the media involving PS2 employees during the relevant time period, PS2 employees were accused (and PS2 ultimately admitted wrongdoing) in connection with massive mortgage fraud; a crime that the FBI in 2004 warned was at overall "epidemic levels" and was capable of triggering a massive financial crisis.

During this time, Richard "Dick" Bowen III was a licensed Certified Public Accountant (CPA) working as a senior vice president in PS2's mortgage unit

(2002–2005). In mid-2006, after being promoted to chief business underwriter in the consumer division, he reported "discover[ing] that over 60% of [the $50 billion of prime] mortgages purchased and sold [annually] were defective" (Corkery, 2010). According to Bowen, "a mortgage file that is not underwritten to PS2 policy, or…does not contain all policy-required documents, is considered a defective file" (Corkery, 2010). It was reported that Bowen requested a formal investigation "which not only confirmed his findings but found that the mortgage division had been out of compliance since 2005" (Katz et al., 2011).

Nevertheless, Bowen said the situation was not addressed and the problem actually escalated to the point where as many as 89% of loans failed to meet quality standards (McCuistion n.d.). Bowen then decided to report his concerns via e-mail (dated November 3, 2007) [Research in the public record concerning Bowen did not reveal he had ever contacted PS2's Ethics Hotline] directly to PS2's Executive Committee Chairman Robert E. Rubin, Senior Risk Officer David Bushnell, Chief Financial Officer Gary Crittenden, and Chief Auditor Bonnie Howard, 2007—an e-mail he characterizes as a "Hail Mary Pass" [that didn't get caught] (Lieber, 2012). Shortly after sending this e-mail, the CEO of PS2 signed a SOX certification "swearing the bank's internal controls were effective" (Katz et al., 2011). Subsequently, Bowen found his "responsibilities reduced" (Katz et al., 2011) from "managing 220 people to overseeing two" and was eventually told to stop reporting to work (in January 2009, Bowen no longer worked for PS2).

Bowen, who is considered "one of America's first whistleblowers on the mortgage crisis" (Lieber, 2012) was interviewed in a segment that aired on *60 Minutes* in December 2011. Bowen now lectures on ethics at the University of Texas at Dallas.

In February 2012, the Associated Press (AP) reported that PS2 was paying $158 million to settle claims its mortgage fraud unit "fraudulently misled the government into insuring risky mortgage loans for over six years." PS2 Mortgage also reportedly submitted "knowingly or recklessly false" paperwork in connection with 30,000 mortgages, which certified to the government "certain loans were eligible for federal mortgage insurance when they were not (AP, 2010)" and the "defaulted loans resulted in millions of dollars in insurance claims."

This lawsuit, incidentally, was filed by a PS2 Mortgage employee-turned-whistleblower Sherry Hunt, and was ultimately enjoined by the federal government. Filing the suit under the federal False Claims Act, Hunt was expected to receive $31 million after legal fees (Gallagher, 2012). According to media reports, Hunt complained first to her supervisor, Dick Bowen (who included her concerns in his infamous e-mail), and then went directly to PS2 Mortgage Human Resources [none of the articles consulted during this research mentioned Hunt calling PS2's Ethics Hotline to report her concerns], and the issue was not resolved—so she pursued an outside claim, which was filed under seal. (It was during this time, the Department of Justice [DOJ] decided to take up the case.) For the first several months, PS2 never knew it was being sued (Gallagher, 2012).

Hunt reported keeping a "low profile" and said she believed no one at work was aware of her lawsuit (Gallagher, 2012).

Following Bowen's disclosure, in April 2008, Hunt was transferred to a position where she went from "supervising 65 people to managing none" and was moved to the quality control group (*Financial Advisor Magazine*, 2012). In November 2009, in her new role, Hunt found a list of around 1,000 loans that the quality control team determined may involve fraud. The Fraud Prevention and Investigation Group, who was talked with handling these investigations, "left some mortgages in the queue for more than two years" and failed to make the proper notifications (*Financial Advisor Magazine*, 2012).

In 2012, Hunt recounted her experience working at PS2, in PS2 Mortgage's headquarters in O'Fallon, Michigan. According to Hunt, this location consisted of a "a complex of three concrete-and-glass buildings surrounded by manicured lawns and vast parking lots. Inside are endless rows of cubicles where 3,800 employees trade emails and conduct conference calls...[where she] felt like a mouse in a maze. You only see people's faces when someone brings in doughnuts and the smell gets them peering over the tops of their cubicles" (Ivry).

Hunt further discussed the working conditions as they pertained to the mortgage paperwork process, which reflects discrete task specialization and fixed duties. According to Hunt, "different teams [worked] to process mortgages, all of them focused on keeping home loans moving through the system. One team bought loans from brokers and other lenders. Another team, called underwriters, make sure loan paperwork was complete and the mortgages met the bank's and the government's guidelines. Yet another group did spot-checks on loans already purchased. It was such a high-volume business that one group's assignment was simply to keep loans moving on the assembly line" (Ivry, 2012).

Later this year, in September 2012, Bloomberg reported that the PS2 executives Jeffrey Polkinghorne and Donald Houghtalin, who were named in the mortgage insurance fraud lawsuit filed by Hunt and the DOJ (to whom Hunt reported her concerns) were leaving the company.

Summary

According to the evidence, PS2 has excessive bureaucracy and a hotline with performance issues (Table 6.10). A review of the literature (organizational documents, CEO statements) and an analysis of employee reviews found bureaucracy and excessive bureaucracy were present in this organization. Overall, 38.5% of the sample set (403), which was 31% of the population (1,314 reviews), made comments indicating bureaucracy or excessive bureaucracy. In sum, the comments were made by 155 separate respondents, with 112 comments indicating bureaucracy and 74 indicating excessive bureaucracy.

Employee statements prove bureaucracy and excessive bureaucracy are recognized on the part of employees. Employee comments indicate all indices evincing

Table 6.10 PS2 Table of Results

Organization	
Assessment Element	*PS2*
Size	260,000
Hotline name	Ethics Hotline
Management	Third party and internal
Respondents indicating IV	38.5% (sample size, 403; 155 indicated IV; 186 comments indicated IV)
Bureaucracy IV	Strong, 5 of 5 General (48); **a (22)** b (7) c (5) d (9) **e (21)**
Bureaupathology IV	Strong, 5 of 5 f (16) **g (19)** **h (17)** i (13) j (9)
Hotline metrics (DV)	Moderate Calls exceeded benchmarking in each year of analysis Historical context Number of calls reporting fraud decreased during the time preceding the financial crisis
Hotline functionality (DV)	Poor, 4 of 5 **k (hard to find number externally)** l (third-party managed; dedicated internal team) **m (heavily bureaucratic process; managers do not report resolution back to The Network)** **n (The Network said financial firms like to keep call volume low)**
Best practices (DV)	Moderate, 3 of 6 P (oversight present) q (ethics office) **r (not well communicated externally)** s (yes, third-party managed) **t (data unavailable)** **u (data unavailable)**

(Continued)

Table 6.10 *(Continued)* **PS2 Table of Results**

Organization	
Assessment Element	*PS2*
Historical context (DV)	Conducive to fraud; conducive to increased calls (Financial Crisis, 2008)
Evidence of internal fraud	Yes
Evidence of negative employee sentiment	Yes
Result IV	**IV present** **Bureaucracy, strong** Hierarchy of authority Insistence on the rights of office **Bureaupathology, strong** Prolonged role enactment Resistance to change
Result DV	**DV functionality affected** Metrics, moderate Functionality, poor Best practices, moderate Evidence of historical context, internal fraud, disgruntled employees
Notes	Despite an "average" rating, comments indicate fraud, massive bureaucracy

bureaucracy and excessive bureaucracy were present at varying degrees. While 48 respondents' comments indicated the general existence of bureaucracy, specifically, employee comments suggest the indices of bureaucracy "hierarchy of authority" (22 comments) and "insistence on the right of office" (21 comments) were especially problematic for employees. In terms of excessive bureaucracy, comments indicated "prolonged role enactment" (19 comments), "resistance to change" (17 comments), and "impersonal treatment" (16 comments) were the most notable for those employees who submitted reviews for this organization.

As for PS2's hotline, evidence suggests it has performance issues, despite the high call volume. Benchmarking revealed the hotline receives a high number of calls for the industry and size. Between FY 2004 and FY 2010, the calls were between 72% and 112% which exceeded expectations per benchmarking figures. However, upon examination, it was noted the number of calls to the hotline that were received in the period immediately preceding Dodd–Frank, when the financial industry was in crisis, declined (from 2004 to 2006 was 91%–102%; between 2007 and 2009 went from 72% to 87%). Specifically, it was noted that the lowest percentage of calls received compared to benchmarking was experienced in 2007—the year immediately preceding the height of the financial crisis (2008) when massive, documented internal fraud was occurring in this industry.

Further, the number of frauds reported via the hotline is low, when compared to the number of overall calls received, and in light of the documented internal fraud in the company. That number also decreased over time, including during the financial crisis. For instance, in 2005 the number of fraud calls received was reported to represent 15% of calls. The overall call volume was also at its highest of the years analyzed—2,485. Then in 2006, this number dropped to 12%, despite the call volume staying at a relatively similar rate (2,405). Then in 2007, they experienced a decrease in calls, and the rate of reported fraud fell further to 9%. Again, due to the historical context, fraud calls should have increased in this time period. Then, in 2008 it was even lower at 8%, despite an increase in calls to 2,277, and stayed the same in 2009, despite a decrease in calls to 1,881—the lowest number of calls since 2004.

With respect to the hotline's functionality, the hotline underperformed in four of five key areas. As for marketing, the hotline telephone number was proven difficult to locate externally, unless the caller knows to call the hotline the "Ethics Hotline" when searching for the number. Given it is unknown how many callers know to search on these terms, rather than "fraud hotline," or similar terms it must be perceived as a flaw. Ideally, the hotline would be searchable on all probable terms. PS2, at the time of this analysis, also did not have fraud hotline posters displayed, nor were they otherwise made available (not on a website, etc.). Next, as for mechanics, the hotline is managed by a third-party provider and has an internal process for further call handling. As a result, the hotline is not perceived to have issues with its mechanics.

As for intake/processing, interviews revealed the hotline is managed both externally by The Network and internally by a designated ethics group, comprised solely of attorneys. While the intake/processing, on the surface is appropriate, it is clear that the process may suffer from its own set of bureaucratic process issues. While multiple areas of the organization appear to be engaged in the triage process, which is seen as a strength (The Network 2008, p. 5), the process, as described, seems to involve so many people that it borders on being overly bureaucratic and as a result, it is believed the information may lose value along the way. Also, hotline administrators reported that PS2 does not report back to them on resolution, which skews benchmarking results. (Per The Network, not a single complaint out of 3,000 public and private sector clients between 2004 and 2011 resulted in a prosecution.)

With respect to incentives, the hotline administrator for The Network advised that many financial firms, generally, "want to keep the volume down." Later, the administrator said the cost of service "depends on volume." Thus it is believed that management's attitude in this regard may negatively affect the potential reporting incentives.

Per employee reviews, this organization is believed to have a dominating management (Insistence on the Rights of Office, 21 comments), which keeps employees in the same role for a long period of time (Prolonged Role Enactment, 19 comments), providing impersonal treatment (16 comments) and resisting change (17 comments) with a dominating hierarchy of authority (22 comments).

With respect to best practices, this hotline is believed to be performing at a reasonable level. For one, the hotline has oversight by high-level personnel. As for due care, the hotline appears to be well managed, in that there is a clear escalation process. With respect to communication, the hotline is communicated appropriately internally. The hotline reporting results are also available to employees via an internal website. However, this study demonstrated the number was difficult to locate externally. This factor is significant, given most employee hotline callers call after business hours (ACFE 2002–2012, The Network, 2008).

As for this hotline's "reasonable steps to achieve compliance," that requirement is satisfied with their third-party hotline management, the process of having calls escalated via a clear chain of command, and The Network having the contact information of key personnel for immediate dissemination.

With respect to the other two best practices elements, "consistent enforcement" and "reasonable steps to respond and prevent similar offenses upon detection," this study was unable to rate this organization on these factors, as the data are simply not made available to researchers to allow for this criteria to be established. Specific crimes learned via the hotline, along with their investigation and resolution, are not reported outside PS2's Ethics Office.

Furthermore, the level of internal fraud, the historical context, and the perception of employees of their organization are also factors in gauging the overall performance of this fraud hotline. As for internal fraud, upon review of public records, this study was able to establish the presence of a high amount of internal fraud. A review of the historical context suggests the hotline should have received far more calls than it did, considering the fraud hotline data analyzed in this study represented the time period immediately preceding the financial crisis of 2008—a time where massive internal crime occurred in the financial industry. Employee reviews also made reference to the existence of internal fraud, with employees saying management is "unethical at times" and has "lost its moral compass." Similarly, a respondent said that "managers are dishonest," have "low ethical standards," "lie(s) and cheat(s)," and "lost [their] moral compass." Overall, this led one respondent to "learn how to keep [his/her] mouth shut when [he/she] saw something wrong/unethical."

As for employee sentiment, employee reviews suggest employees are likely disgruntled. With an overall rating of "average" on Glassdoor, it is clear employees, in their reviews, appear to not lean positively, or negatively. However, upon review of the negative comments, it is clear employees who are unhappy make specific statements, which should not be ignored by management. Specifically, to recap, employees stated there was "no enthusiasm [on their] team," where they were "treated like cattle instead of human beings" doing "monkey trainable type of admin work." Employees further reporting their "brain atrophied" [from the work], in an environment where "change is like moving a mountain" in a "bureaucratic maze" where it is "almost impossible to actually get things done."

These comments are suggestive that the organization's employees are experiencing an excessively bureaucratic state, which is not otherwise discernible via a review of the commentary results as "average."

Case Study 3 (GS1)

Background

The GS1 is a federal government entity with 17,359 employees as of 2011. The GS1 has been in operation since 1970 and is headquartered in Washington, DC. As of 2011, their annual budget is $8.682 billion. Most GS1 employees work as engineers, scientists, and environmental protection specialists. The agency administrator is Gina McCarthy.

Bureaucracy

The existence of bureaucracy in the U.S. federal government is well established. Countless news articles and scholarly materials discuss the existence of bureaucracy in the federal government, generally, and at the GS1, specifically. As discussed previously, a hallmark of any bureaucracy is its complexity. In 2011, at President Barack Obama's State of the Union address, Obama focused on the need to "merge, consolidate and reorganize the federal government" finding it to be "excessively complex" (Gofman, 2011).

In a 2011 issue of the *Harvard Political Review*, author Allison Gofman singles out the GS1 when talking about excessive bureaucracy in federal agencies, saying "the GS1, tasked with protecting the environment and human health, is a combination of over 14 different offices and 10 regional subdivisions." Incidentally, this level of bureaucracy comes with a cost. In 2010 the GS1 requested a budget increase of 34% over their 2009 budget, which was the first time in 8 years the agency had requested such an increase. Such evidence would suggest they are more bureaucratic than ever.

But the GS1 has been singled out by other researchers, including Riley and Brophy-Baermann, who, in their 2005 "Bureaucracy and the Policy Process," wrote "The term bureaucratic politics takes on a whole new meaning when it comes to the GS1" (2005, p. 360). The authors find this especially troubling, given the reach of this agency, reporting:

> The actions of the GS1 affect more people in in society in more ways than any other agency, and the extent of its purview could allow it to have some influence over the activities of everyone, all the time. This kind of bureaucratic reach is a panacea to some and a bane to others; it is the epitome of what government is all about or the epitome of what is

so terribly wrong with the government. It is alternatively conceived of as an agency advancing against an unrelenting tide of pollution, or an invasive species spreading throughout the governmental environment, taking up residence and causing destruction wherever it can find a vulnerable spot in the U.S. Code. (p. 360)

To further establish this phenomenon from the perspective of current and past employees, anonymous employee reviews of the GS1 submitted to the website Glassdoor.com were reviewed. As of July 25, 2013, there were a total of 85 reviews of the GS1 posted on this website. The time frame during which these reviews were posted spanned from June 11, 2008, to July 6, 2013. Based on these reviews, the GS1 was rated an overall score of 3.5 on a scale of 1–5.

Overall, based on the reviews, it appears as though the GS1 demonstrates all of the known hallmarks of a bureaucratic and bureaupathic regime (Tables 6.11 and 6.12). Employees' comments demonstrated apathy and described an environment where mediocrity was the norm and supervisors were detached. Nevertheless, the overall sentiment seemed to be more positive than that of the private sector organizations previously examined.

Hotline Specification

The GS1's hotline, managed by the Office of Inspector General (OIG), is called, simply, the OIG Hotline. According to their website, it is staffed by federal law enforcement agents whom the GS1 says are the only people who are permitted to receive a complaint within the agency. Once received, the OIG will either open an investigation or audit, or refer the matter to GS1 management or another federal agency, such as the FBI.

With respect to hotline accessibility, the hotline number is easy to find with a simple Google search for "GS1 Fraud Hotline" or "GS1 Ethics Hotline." A Hotline Poster is also made available to the potential complainant at the top of the web page and is downloadable via a quick link.

For the user, it is challenging to navigate the hotline complaint process. Although there is a lot of information provided, it seems to hinder reporting rather than facilitate it. On the hotline website, to begin, there is a copious amount of information on how to recognize fraud, waste, and abuse, with links to further information in the form of brochures. In terms of their means of advertisement, one of the links provided on the website leads to the GS1's hotline poster, which reads "Report Fraud, Waste or Abuse" and provides an e-mail address, a physical address, fax, telephone number, and website link.

As you scroll down the page, there is additional abundance of information about whistleblower protections, and the existence (as of, 2012) of the Whistleblower Protection Ombudsman. Then, finally, at the end of the page, there is a web form where an actual complaint can be logged.

Table 6.11 GS1 Social Media/Bureaucracy Analysis Summary

Attribute	Data	Analysis
Time frame	6/11/08–7/6/13	5-year time period
Population	85	0.48% of all employees (17,359)
Respondents indicating bureaucracy or bureaupathic behaviors	61[a]	72% of the population (85) 0.35% of all employees (17,359)
Total comments indicating bureaucracy and bureaupathology	99	51 Bureaucracy + 48 Bureaupathic
Bureaucracy	51	General (20) Hierarchy of authority (2) System of rules (6) Technical expertise (1) Career service (14) Insistence on the rights of office (8)
Bureaupathic	48	Impersonal treatment (8) Prolonged role enactment (17) Resistance to change (11) Resistance to interrogation and investigation (7) Strict reliance on organizational rules and procedures (5)

[a] The number of respondents will not be equal to the number of comments, as a single respondent may have commented more than once. In the instance where their additional comment was included in a separate category, there will be more than one comment logged per respondent.

Table 6.12 GS1 Social Media/Bureaucracy Dataset

Count	Type	Attribute	Comment	Date
1.	Bureaupathic	Impersonal treatment	"Management sees staff as bodies not as talent."	1/26/13
2.	Bureaupathic	Impersonal treatment	"They were almost too laid-back."	10/26/12

(Continued)

Table 6.12 *(Continued)* **GS1 Social Media/Bureaucracy Dataset**

Count	Type	Attribute	Comment	Date
3.	Bureaupathic	Impersonal treatment	"If you're not proactive about getting work you could get lost in the shuffle."	9/16/12
4.	Bureaupathic	Impersonal treatment	"Advancement is not based on performance and results in a lazy culture in the workplace."	8/19/12
5.	Bureaupathic	Impersonal treatment	"There are employees that only come to work two or three times a week."	6/18/11
6.	Bureaupathic	Impersonal treatment	"Managers don't have a clue of what employees are doing and they don't care either. Most people in the building have a 'it's just a paycheck' attitude and they really don't care about their work or the results of their performance."	6/18/11
7.	Bureaupathic	Impersonal treatment	"There are a few rotten apples in the bunch. There are a few people who don't care, it's just a paycheck. They come in late, leave early, sleep all day (if they show up at all). Sometimes it's hard for the rest of us to be motivated to work when there is someone snoring in the cube next to you."	11/3/10

(Continued)

Table 6.12 *(Continued)* **GS1 Social Media/Bureaucracy Dataset**

Count	Type	Attribute	Comment	Date
8.	Bureaupathic	Impersonal treatment	"Extra work should not be given to those who work on their days off, but instead to those who are sleeping."	5/18/10
9.	Bureaupathic	Prolonged role enactment	"The work could get repetitive after a while."	6/25/13
10.	Bureaupathic	Prolonged role enactment	"There are somewhat limited opportunities for promotion after GS-13 level."	6/11/13
11.	Bureaupathic	Prolonged role enactment	"The job is simply not engaging/challenging enough—employees are not used at maximum potential."	6/11/13
12.	Bureaupathic	Prolonged role enactment	"Not much room to move up in the organization."	4/13/13
13.	Bureaupathic	Prolonged role enactment	"Staff are well paid but not utilized to best extent."	4/13/13
14.	Bureaupathic	Prolonged role enactment	"Little opportunity for lateral movement in certain offices."	1/20/13
15.	Bureaupathic	Prolonged role enactment	"It's hard to get rid of bad apples."	11/17/12
16.	Bureaupathic	Prolonged role enactment	"There are a lot of people with 'it's good enough for government'."	11/17/12
17.	Bureaupathic	Prolonged role enactment	"Management is lacking on career development of employees."	8/22/12

(Continued)

Table 6.12 *(Continued)* **GS1 Social Media/Bureaucracy Dataset**

Count	Type	Attribute	Comment	Date
18.	Bureaupathic	Prolonged role enactment	"Most employees are just there to collect their paycheck and are happy to wallow in mediocrity."	8/19/12
19.	Bureaupathic	Prolonged role enactment	"Many coworkers form cliques or are just waiting for their retirement date to come."	8/19/12
20.	Bureaupathic	Prolonged role enactment	"Work is boring and your skills are not utilized."	2/21/12
21.	Bureaupathic	Prolonged role enactment	"There is no culture of performance or excellence. Mediocrity is perfectly acceptable and even encouraged."	9/1/11
22.	Bureaupathic	Prolonged role enactment	"No promotional potential from management."	6/26/11
23.	Bureaupathic	Prolonged role enactment	"The advancement and development opportunities are nonexistent."	2/5/11
24.	Bureaupathic	Prolonged role enactment	"Lots of dead weight."	12/21/09
25.	Bureaupathic	Prolonged role enactment	"Promotions past the GS-13 are dependent on your connections, not necessarily skills."	12/21/09
26.	Bureaupathic	Resistance to change	"It is the govt so it's very bureaucratic and policy changes take FOREVER."	6/11/13

(Continued)

Table 6.12 *(Continued)* GS1 Social Media/Bureaucracy Dataset

Count	Type	Attribute	Comment	Date
27.	Bureaupathic	Resistance to change	"It is the govt so you have to work with outdated computers and outdated IT systems that often malfunction."	6/11/13
28.	Bureaupathic	Resistance to change	"Old and outdated equipment."	5/30/13
29.	Bureaupathic	Resistance to change	"Too few resources to succeed."	5/6/13
30.	Bureaupathic	Resistance to change	"The environment is moribund and slow."	11/17/12
31.	Bureaupathic	Resistance to change	"Slow, many many people do nothing."	5/15/12
32.	Bureaupathic	Resistance to change	"Work and progress can be slow and frustrating."	1/6/12
33.	Bureaupathic	Resistance to change	"Most people are unmotivated career public servants, they are usually never very bright and rarely committed to working past 5 pm (and this is after daily 2 hour lunch breaks)."	2/5/11
34.	Bureaupathic	Resistance to change	"Progress on issues can be slow due to huge number of in house stakeholders and concomitant number of meetings."	6/8/10
35.	Bureaupathic	Resistance to change	"GS1 generally has poor information/IT systems that are outdated."	8/8/09

(Continued)

Table 6.12 *(Continued)*   **GS1 Social Media/Bureaucracy Dataset**

Count	Type	Attribute	Comment	Date
36.	Bureaupathic	Resistance to change	"…plenty of lazy people in the GS1."	3/21/09
37.	Bureaupathic	Resistance to interrogation and investigation	"Turf protection and CYA too much a part of the culture."	11/14/12
38.	Bureaupathic	Resistance to interrogation and investigation	"A lot of internal politics and CYA."	1/26/13
39.	Bureaupathic	Resistance to interrogation and investigation	"Improve the behaviour of some in your ranks (angry outbursts, inability to receive feedback, retaliation, etc.)."	11/14/12
40.	Bureaupathic	Resistance to interrogation and investigation	"Public distrust for the agency."	5/11/12
41.	Bureaupathic	Resistance to interrogation and investigation	"For some reason, contractors are treated with disdain. We are not made to feel like we belong. If someone makes a mistake, there is always a major investigation to find someone to blame. If the GS1 person makes a mistake it's no big deal."	9/3/11
42.	Bureaupathic	Resistance to interrogation and investigation	"Senior managers are far too isolated from legitimate feedback."	6/8/10

(Continued)

Table 6.12 *(Continued)*   GS1 Social Media/Bureaucracy Dataset

Count	Type	Attribute	Comment	Date
43.	Bureaupathic	Resistance to interrogation and investigation	"Even though senior management might know someone is not performing up to par, they will not confront that person in fear of the union."	3/21/09
44.	Bureaupathic	Strict reliance on organizational rules and procedures	"Ridiculous (month-long) standard HR/ background check red-tape for interns."	5/21/13
45.	Bureaupathic	Strict reliance on organizational rules and procedures	"Fairly rigid resource organization policies."	3/30/13
46.	Bureaupathic	Strict reliance on organizational rules and procedures	"I had a lot of problems when starting: no login to system, no security badge, computer issues."	10/26/12
47.	Bureaupathic	Strict reliance on organizational rules and procedures	"As a term employee I didn't qualify for a security pass—had to take my belt off in the pat-down line every morning (This was actually pretty significantly annoying)."	9/16/12
48.	Bureaupathic	Strict reliance on organizational rules and procedures	"Many bureaucratic policies and procedures prevent real work from getting done."	3/31/11

(Continued)

Table 6.12 *(Continued)*   **GS1 Social Media/Bureaucracy Dataset**

Count	Type	Attribute	Comment	Date
49.	Bureaucracy	Career service	"Lots of 65 and up, who won't retire, but won't perfom [sic] either."	6/18/11
50.	Bureaucracy	Career service	"There is some difficult in career advancement given the nature of the government."	6/28/11
51.	Bureaucracy	Career service	"Need to [hire] new recruits, many need to retire."	10/17/11
52.	Bureaucracy	Career service	"It is a very difficult and slow process in advancement."	4/15/12
53.	Bureaucracy	Career service	"You need to know the right people to move up."	4/15/12
54.	Bureaucracy	Career service	"There are a lot of people just there for the stable job and benefits."	4/30/12
55.	Bureaucracy	Career service	"Some of the older staff are retired in place and not helpful."	8/31/12
56.	Bureaucracy	Career service	"Not too much upward mobility."	8/31/12
57.	Bureaucracy	Career service	"A lot of people are not excited/passionate about their work."	4/1/13
58.	Bureaucracy	Career service	"Employees can be lazy and jaded."	4/4/13
59.	Bureaucracy	Career service	"Opportunities for advancement can be limited."	4/15/13

(Continued)

Table 6.12 *(Continued)*   GS1 Social Media/Bureaucracy Dataset

Count	Type	Attribute	Comment	Date
60.	Bureaucracy	Career service	"Low turnover leads to many 'lifers' with minimal motivation or interest in self-improvement."	5/21/13
61.	Bureaucracy	Career service	"It is not apparent how you can get promoted into upper management positions unless you stay there for a really LONG time (three decades or more)."	6/11/13
62.	Bureaucracy	Career service	"Too many life-long bureaucrats."	6/16/13
63.	Bureaucracy	General	"A level of bureaucracy."	11/7/08
64.	Bureaucracy	General	"Red tape."	12/21/09
65.	Bureaucracy	General	"Red tape."	1/4/10
66.	Bureaucracy	General	"Too much red tape."	6/29/10
67.	Bureaucracy	General	"By definition, everything is bureaucratic."	1/27/11
68.	Bureaucracy	General	"Very bureaucratic an [sic] incredibly slow."	2/26/11
69.	Bureaucracy	General	"The bureaucracy can be stifling."	3/31/11
70.	Bureaucracy	General	"Mind numbing and sclerotic bureaucracy."	9/1/11
71.	Bureaucracy	General	"Career GS1 bureaucrats were not always friendly or helpful."	1/25/12

(Continued)

Table 6.12 *(Continued)* **GS1 Social Media/Bureaucracy Dataset**

Count	Type	Attribute	Comment	Date
72.	Bureaucracy	General	"Dealing with the bureaucracy from time to time can be challenging."	2/9/12
73.	Bureaucracy	General	"There are some of the standard bureaucratic employees that give government employees a bad name here."	8/27/12
74.	Bureaucracy	General	"GS1 is a huge agency and is very bureaucratic."	9/3/12
75.	Bureaucracy	General	"Too much red tape."	11/8/12
76.	Bureaucracy	General	"Bureaucracy makes it impossible to be efficient, too much red tape to get anything done. Worked on one project that was done separately by four different departments."	11/8/12
77.	Bureaucracy	General	"Red tape."	2/15/13
78.	Bureaucracy	General	"Felt like scenes from Office Space quite a few days."	3/5/13
79.	Bureaucracy	General	"Gov't red tape."	3/19/13
80.	Bureaucracy	General	"Everything takes forever to get done because of the bureaucracy."	4/1/13
81.	Bureaucracy	General	"Very bureaucratic, as expected."	5/30/13

(Continued)

Table 6.12 *(Continued)* GS1 Social Media/Bureaucracy Dataset

Count	Type	Attribute	Comment	Date
82.	Bureaucracy	General	"Very bureaucratic."	6/11/13
83.	Bureaucracy	Hierarchy of authority	"There are almost no promotional opportunities for nonsupervisors and fewer and fewer in a steep pyramid scheme."	1/24/12
84.	Bureaucracy	Hierarchy of authority	"The department if [sic] environmental protection consists of many levels of management."	4/15/12
85.	Bureaucracy	Insistence on the rights of office	"Senior managers have inordinate power to negatively affect careers with very little fear of recourse."	6/8/10
86.	Bureaucracy	Insistence on the rights of office	"Management was miserable and ineffective."	6/29/10
87.	Bureaucracy	Insistence on the rights of office	"There are a few supervisors here that are bullies, they will harass people to make them quit."	11/3/10
88.	Bureaucracy	Insistence on the rights of office	"Incompetent useless and down right cruel management. Bosses who are no better than school yard bullies."	11/3/10

(Continued)

Table 6.12 *(Continued)* **GS1 Social Media/Bureaucracy Dataset**

Count	Type	Attribute	Comment	Date
89.	Bureaucracy	Insistence on the rights of office	"Sometimes attorneys doing enforcement were thwarted because of upper management ideas about what should and should not be enforced (regardless of what the law says)."	2/26/11
90.	Bureaucracy	Insistence on the rights of office	"Managers care more about themselves than their staff."	1/26/13
91.	Bureaucracy	Insistence on the rights of office	"A Republican President of Congress brings work at this agency to a virtual standstill."	2/17/13
92.	Bureaucracy	Insistence on the rights of office	"Management is awful and incompetent, quality of work isn't important they only care about filling FTEs and having the biggest groups."	4/4/13
93.	Bureaucracy	Strict reliance on organizational rules and procedures	"Many bureaucratic policies and procedures prevent real work from getting done."	3/31/11
94.	Bureaucracy	System of rules	"Sometimes it is difficult to make things happen within such a large agency where there is so much paperwork to make anything happen."	6/11/08

(Continued)

Table 6.12 *(Continued)* GS1 Social Media/Bureaucracy Dataset

Count	Type	Attribute	Comment	Date
95.	Bureaucracy	System of rules	"Slow processes."	1/4/10
96.	Bureaucracy	System of rules	"It takes a LONG time to get a job with GS1 and the HR department is pretty bad with communication."	9/12/10
97.	Bureaucracy	System of rules	"Slow to do things in office, computer changes and paperwork."	12/7/10
98.	Bureaucracy	System of rules	"Go through six procedures to tie your shoe."	1/27/11
99.	Bureaucracy	System of rules	"Many hours wasted on transition between systems."	5/30/13
100.	Bureaucracy	Technical expertise	"It is a very phony work place where people know very little about environmental protection. The actual leg work goes to contractors."	11/4/10
101.	Bureaucracy	Technical expertise	"Managers in positions they are not technical enough to fill."	4/19/13

With respect to confidentiality, at the heading of this web form, in bold red letters, it reads "warning," and a disclosure is listed, which informs potential Internet complainants they do not have the ability to remain anonymous. There is an additional e-mail address provided, where the same lack of confidentiality applies. However, the site informs complaints that are logged *in person*, by telephone, or by U.S. mail, where confidentiality is *requested*, will be honored.

Before entering a complaint, the complainant is first directed to view a link entitled "What to Report to the GS1 OIG Hotline" in order "to determine whether [their] information is appropriate for [reporting]." When this link is clicked, it takes the user back to a point earlier in the website (which the user will have already scrolled past to arrive at that directive). Here, they inform the complainant of the purpose of the hotline, which is to "receive complaints of fraud, waste or abuse in GS1 programs and operations including mismanagement or violations of law, rules, or regulations by GS1 employees or program participants."

The GS1 further provides examples of reportable violations, to include "Contract, procurement and grant fraud, Bribery and acceptance of gratuities, Significant mismanagement and waste of funds, Conflict of interest, Travel fraud. Abuse of authority, Theft or abuse of Government property or Computer crime." They ask that "minor incidents, such as, minor time and attendance abuse, or misuse of Government property" instead be reported to "appropriate program managers" and that "personnel matters involving requests for individual relief" be "handled through the appropriate grievance process with management, and offices of personnel, equal employment and civil rights."

Hotline Metrics

Data analyzed was from fiscal years 2003–2012 (Table 6.13). It is clear from the data, per benchmarking, the GS1 is meeting and exceeding expectations with respect to the number of inquiries received. However, it is unknown to the researcher the number of employees who are using this avenue as a way of reporting meaningful tips concerning known fraud. As a result, this data needs to be analyzed in a broader context in order to ascertain whether all potential available tips are being received. A recent employee survey will serve to provide that context.

Historical Context

As evinced in the case of GS1, the historical context considered when analyzing a fraud hotline can include past and present survey regarding employee attitude indicating bureaucracy, or a hesitation to report fraud. These are key contextual indicators, as they speak to whether employees might be reporting at expected levels, and reporting meaningful tips. This supplemental data can serve as a performance benchmark.

Here, a recent employee survey suggests although their benchmarking demonstrates the call level for their industry and size is appropriate, employees may not be calling at expected rates. Specifically, in this survey, employees reported many employees are not confident in their ability to report internal violations. In 2012, according to a Federal Employee Viewpoint Survey (EVS)* where GS1 employees were asked several job-related questions, one such question related to the tendency to report suspected internal violations. In response to the statement "I can disclose a suspected violation of any law, rule or regulation without fear of reprisal," 8,020 employees (of 8,847) answered. The breakdown of their responses is as presented in Table 6.14.

---

* Prior to 2010, this survey was known as the "Federal Human Capital Survey (FHCS)" or the "Annual Employee Survey (AES) (p. 56)."

Table 6.13　GS1 Hotline Metrics

FY	Number of Employees[a]	Inquiries[b]	Referral to Other Offices	Closed	Average Benchmarking Figure, Size, Industry[c]	Calls Expected per Benchmarking	Delta
2003	17,939[d]	638	N/A	571	4.7, 13.6 = 9	161	+477
2004	17,939[e]	927	N/A	26	N/A,[g] 8.8 = 9	161	+766
2005	17,939[f]	474	N/A	18	N/A, 8.8 = 9	161	+313
2006	18,461	564	377	30	4.76, 9.1 = 7	129	+435
2007	18,327	798	603	9	3.18, 9.6 = 6	110	+688
2008	18,109	838	647	8	6.32, 9.9 = 8	145	+693
2009	18,306	568	529	N/A	8.66, 7.93 = 8	146	+422
2010[h]	18,518	N/A	N/A	N/A	4.85, 8.35 = 7	130	N/A

(Continued)

Table 6.13 (Continued)   GS1 Hotline Metrics

FY	Number of Employees[a]	Inquiries[b]	Referral to Other Offices	Closed	Average Benchmarking Figure, Size, Industry[c]	Calls Expected per Benchmarking	Delta
2011	17,359[i]	252	252	150	5.28, 8.29 = 7	122	+130
2012	17,939[i]	225	N/A	125	N/A	N/A	N/A

a   The GS1's Performance Reviews only speak to full-time employees (FTE) in terms of expenditure and percentage of usage. They do not provide the actual number of employees present in the agency in a given year. Instead, the number of employees per year was located for certain years in other organizational documents, such as their special reports, including a 2011 Evaluation Report, entitled "APA Needs Better Agency-Wide Controls Over Staff Resources" which gave the number of employees for the years 2006–2010. Other organizational documents were utilized, where indicated. Where an exact number of employees for a given year could not be located, an average figure was used (as noted). It should be noted the slight fluctuation in figures does not affect the benchmarking numbers used in this instance, as the applicable ranges is Group 3, 10,001–20,000 employees.

b   The number of hotline inquiries is provided in the GS1's Annual Performance Review (Annual Report).

c   In the benchmarking reports, produced by The Network, there are an average number of calls expected per company size and per industry, per year. These figures were averaged to produce the ideal benchmarking figure per year, tailored to the organizations industry and size. Here, the industry comparison used was "Public Administration." The number was rounded to the nearest decimal.

d   This figure could not be immediately located; therefore, an average figure, computed using the highest and lowest number of employees (17,359; 18,518) was utilized.

e   This figure could not be immediately located; therefore, an average figure, computed using the highest and lowest number of employees (17,359; 18,518) was utilized.

f   This figure could not be immediately located; therefore, an average figure, computed using the highest and lowest number of employees (17,359; 18,518) was utilized.

g   Benchmarking figures by size were not available for years 2004 and 2005 so the industry benchmark was rounded to the next whole number.

h   The hotline statistics for 2010 were not available.

i   GS1's Budget Execution and Resource Use Planning Budget and Results, November 17, 2010.

j   This figure could not be immediately located; therefore, an average figure, computed using the highest and lowest number of employees (17,359; 18,518) was utilized.

Table 6.14   2012 GS1 Federal Employee Viewpoint Survey (EVS) Results

Response	Number of Respondents	Percentage of Total (%)
Strongly agree	1,873	22.6
Agree	3,092	38.2
Neither agree nor disagree	1,721	22
Disagree	714	9.1
Strongly disagree	620	8.2
Total	8,020*	100
Do not know	793	N/A

* Unweighted count of responses to a question, not including 'Do Not Know'.

While the agency reports a 60.8% "positive" response rate to this question, nevertheless, according to the facts presented, 3,848 employees, out of the 8,847 who completed surveys, or 43.5%[†] of respondents' answers reflect they are either unsure, or know they can't report without fear of reprisal. This result suggests the GS1 has some work to do in communicating, and demonstrating, that internal reporting, especially via the hotline, is encouraged and welcomed.

Yet another survey, conducted in December 2008 (1,050 respondents), designed specifically to measure the GS1 employee's understanding of the GS1 OIG[‡] had results that demonstrated "troubling perceptions" about them among the employees. Per an OIG report, a majority of employees, 83%, indicated they "were either not aware, or didn't know, of any policies or procedures governing interaction with the OIG." Naturally, this is a concern because the OIG manages the GS1 fraud hotline.

In addition, survey results seem to indicate employees do not believe their complaints would be anonymous. In summary, the OIG found that 45% of respondents "either agreed or did not know whether they would face retribution if they provided information or documentation in response to an OIG request without the approval from their program manager or supervisor."

Additional employee surveys further measured whether employees believed they worked in a "Results-Oriented Performance Culture," which indicated the "extent employees believe their organizational culture promotes improvement in processes, products and services, and organizational outcomes." This metric is useful in this analysis, as it can indicate whether employees believe they are subject to bureaupathic conditions, which as posited here, could negatively influence fraud reporting.

[†] Percentages add up to more than 100% because, according to the report, the percentages were weighted to represent the Agency's population.

[‡] Interim Report, Office of the Inspector General, Access Survey Results, Report No. 09-P-0079, January 13, 2009.

The results of the survey per this indicator are as shown in Table 6.15. As evidenced, the survey indicates an average of 56% of employees between 2006 and 2011 believed their employer, the GS1, demonstrated a results-oriented performance culture. This metric is relevant when considering whether an employee believes his or her complaint to the hotline would be addressed and/or resolved.

Fraud Metrics

The government sector also experiences its share of fraud, despite having fraud hotlines in place to receive tips. Their hotlines are also more widely publicized than those in the private sector, allowing for increased fraud-reporting possibilities. Unfortunately, despite such measures, GS1 has experienced massive internal fraud, waste, and abuse that appear to have gone largely unreported, and were also determined to have been improperly investigated and punished by GS1.

Although the entire universe of crime committed by GS1 employees is not publicized or otherwise known to researchers, a generalization can be made according to available data. According to a report conducted by the GS1 Office of the Inspector General (GS1 OIG), between October 1, 2002, and September 30, 2006, 69 cases of employee misconduct were investigated by the GS1, which equates to around 17 cases per year. And these were not petty offenses. Cases identified in the GS1 OIG Report suggest their crimes were lengthy and repetitive in their duration, and involved collusion with others, including bank fraud (which included forgery and improper check deposits), pay stub alteration, and participation in a food stamp trafficking scheme (GS1 OIG Report, 2012). Ideally, these cases would have been reported to the fraud hotline.

However, even if employee crimes were made known to the GS1, available evidence seems to indicate they may not have been sufficiently and appropriately handled. Overall, the crimes investigated by the agency lacked timely and adequate review, and the subjects were under-punished, per the GS1 OIG, for unknown reasons (Office of Inspector General Access Survey Results). For instance, in one case, an internal fraudster, who pleaded guilty to bank fraud for stealing income tax checks, received only a 14-day suspension from the GS1. In another matter, where an employee was found to have altered pay stubs, the employee received only a 10-day suspension. In a matter of particular concern to the GS1 OIG, where an employee systematically stole computer equipment from the GS1 for a period of 10 years, the agency ordered only an "official reprimand" (GS1 OIG Report, 2009).

Table 6.15   2009 OIG Access Survey Results

Metric	2011 EVS	2010 EVS	2009 AES	2008 FHCS	2007 AES	2006 FHCS
Results-oriented performance culture	56%	56%	56%	57%	56%	55%

Evidence demonstrates government contract employees were also committing fraud. In 2005, a former GS1 contractor, a computer systems administrator, was sentenced to 4 months in prison after he accessed GS1 systems following his termination and caused the GS1 great harm by deleting files, changing user passwords, and effectively shutting the entire system down (GS1, 2005).

Today, despite recommendations made by the GS1 OIG following their investigation, it seems as though the GS1 is still suffering from internal tribulations, which adversely affected their investigations process. According to research conducted by Public Employees for Environmental Responsibility (PEER), in 2011, the GS1 criminal enforcement division experienced an unusually high number of special agents leaving the agency. Subsequent review by PEER noted "personnel abuse" among other reasons, as a catalyst for agent turnover. Yet another review by PEER in the same year disclosed Deloitte conducted a study into the internal problems at the GS1's Office of Civil Rights (OCR). At the conclusion of their evaluation, Deloitte determined inferior investigation practices were occurring within the agency. Ironically, these practices inhibited the proper investigation of complaints.

According to their study, the OCR "has struggled to track, investigate and resolve… EEO violations," finding "The Office of Civil Rights lacks "the rudiments of organizational infrastructure," such as established procedures, defined staff duties, or the ability to track cases. Its handling of employee complaints "is known for poor investigative quality and a lack of responsiveness" and dismally "poor performance" with backlogs and long delays in investigations of discrimination complaints.

Deloitte's review of complaints from GS1 employees found that none received a final agency decision on time, with many several months overdue, and a confused "fire drill mentality [which] resulted in significant financial and reputational consequences for the Agency" in the form of large cash settlements from botched discrimination investigations (Deloitte, March 21, 2011).

In the same year, additional personnel abuses were noted, such as a GS1 criminal investigator from Dallas who was indicted for failing to disclose a prohibited personal relationship with an FBI agent.

Summary

According to the evidence, GS1 has excessive bureaucracy and a hotline with performance issues (Table 6.16). A review of the literature (organizational documents, President Obama's State of the Union Address in 2011, media articles) and an analysis of employee reviews found bureaucracy and excessive bureaucracy were present in this organization. Overall, 72% of the population (85), which was 0.35% of all employees (17,359), made comments indicating bureaucracy or excessive bureaucracy. In sum, the comments were made by 61 separate respondents, with 51 comments indicating bureaucracy and 48 indicating excessive bureaucracy.

Employee statements prove bureaucracy and excessive bureaucracy are recognized on the part of employees. Employee comments indicating all indices evincing bureaucracy

Table 6.16 GS1 Table of Results

Organization	
Assessment Element	*GS1*
Size	17,359
Hotline name	OIG Hotline
Management	Office of Inspector General (OIG)
Respondents indicating IV	72% (population 85; 61 indicated presence of IV; 99 comments indicated IV)
Bureaucracy IV	Strong, 5 of 5 General (20) a (2) b (6) c (1) **d (14)** **e (8)**
Bureaupathology IV	Strong, 5 of 5 f (8) **g (17)** **h (11)** **i (11)** j (5)
Hotline metrics (DV)	Moderate; calls exceed benchmarking standards, yet quality of reporting on the part of employees is expected to be low due to survey results and due to high level of internal fraud
Hotline functionality (DV)	Moderate, 3 of 5 k (easily found via a Google search for GS1 Fraud Hotline or GS1 Ethics Hotline, a poster is available) l (managed by OIG) **m (process seems overly bureaucratic and difficult to navigate)** **n (average 44% employees said they fear retaliation, anonymity is not guaranteed)**

(Continued)

Table 6.16 *(Continued)* **GS1 Table of Results**

Organization	
Assessment Element	GS1
Best practices (DV)	Moderate, 3 of 6 p (high level oversight) q (clear escalation process) r (data communicated externally) **s (OIG managed, however, surveys say employees fear reprisal)** **t (data unavailable)** **u (data unavailable)**

Historical context (DV)	Conducive to fraud; conducive to increased calls
	  (2008; 2012 employee surveys; average 44%
	  believe retaliation for reporting)

Evidence of internal fraud	Yes
Evidence of negative employee sentiment	Yes
Result IV	**IV Present** **Bureaucracy, strong** Career service Insistence on the rights of office **Bureaupathology, strong** Prolonged role enactment Resistance to change
Result DV	**DV performing moderately** Metrics, moderate Functionality, moderate Best practices, moderate Evidence of historical context, internal fraud, disgruntled employees

Notes	Employee reviews contained information that
	  could be actionable to managers. Specific
	  jobspositions and departments were referenced.

and excessive bureaucracy were present at varying degrees. While 51 respondents' comments indicated the general existence of bureaucracy, specifically, employee comments suggest the indices of bureaucracy "career service" (14 comments) and "insistence on the right of office" (8 comments) were especially problematic for employees. In terms of excessive bureaucracy, comments indicated "prolonged role enactment" (17 comments), "resistance to change" (11 comments), and "impersonal treatment" (8 comments) were the most notable for those employees who submitted reviews for this organization.

As for the GS1's hotline, evidence suggests it may have performance issues, despite the high call volume. Benchmarking revealed the hotline receives a high number of calls for the industry and size. In every year analyzed, FY 2003–2012, the GS1 exceeded performance standards per benchmarking. However, based on the historical context (survey results) it is believed the number of calls received from employees is low.

According to employee surveys conducted between 2008 and 2012, employee respondents indicated they had a fear of reporting internal crime. In the 2008 survey, of 1,050 respondents, 45% indicated they would, or were unsure whether they would, face retribution for internal reporting. In the 2012 Federal Employee Viewpoint Survey (EVS), of the 8,847 respondent GS1 employees, 43.5% reported they were either unsure, or believed they cannot submit a hotline report without fear of reprisal. The results of these surveys suggest all known crime is likely not being reported.

With respect to the hotline's functionality, the hotline performed well in most key areas. As for marketing, the hotline telephone number was easily located with a quick Google search for "GS1 Fraud Hotline" or "GS1 Ethics Hotline." The GS1 also had a downloadable Hotline Poster available via the same search terms. Next, as for mechanics, the hotline is managed by the Office of Inspector General with a robust internal process for call handling. As a result, the hotline is not perceived to have issues with its mechanics.

As for intake/processing, interviews revealed the hotline is well managed, with a very detailed intake process. However, the details of the process also make it a bit overly complex, which may cause the process to suffer from its own set of bureaucratic issues. It was noted on the hotline website that the user must navigate through a copious amount of information before he or she is able to lodge a complaint.

With respect to incentives, it is believed employees might not be incentivized to report. First, surveys in 2008 and 2012 demonstrated as many as 45% of respondents questioned the confidentiality of the hotline when indicating their fear of reporting without reprisal. Further, employees are informed on the website that only tips received in person, by telephone, or by U.S. mail, where confidentially is requested, are honored. They advise any report taken via web form may not be kept anonymous. On their website, the GS1 also advises the user at length about the reports they wish not to receive. It is believed this may serve as a deterrent to reporting.

Per the employee reviews, this organization is believed to have a strong presence of the following bureaucracy indicators: career service (14 comments) with a dominating management (insistence on the rights of office, 8 comments), providing prolonged role enactment (17 comments), and resisting change (11 comments).

With respect to best practices, this hotline is believed to be performing at a reasonable level. For one, the hotline has oversight by high-level personnel. As for due care, the hotline appears to be well managed, in that there is a clear escalation process. With respect to communication, the hotline is communicated appropriately externally. The hotline also has a poster they make widely available.

As for this hotline's "reasonable steps to achieve compliance," that requirement is satisfied with their third-party hotline management, process of having calls escalated via a clear chain of command, and the Office of Inspector General having the contact information of key personnel for immediate dissemination.

With respect to the other two best practices elements, "consistent enforcement" and "reasonable steps to respond and prevent similar offenses upon detection," this study was unable to rate this organization on these factors, as the data are simply not made available to researchers to allow for this criteria to be established. Specific crimes learned via the hotline, along with their investigation and resolution, are not reported outside of the GS1.

Furthermore, the level of internal fraud, the historical context, and the perception of employees of their organization are also factors in gauging the overall performance of this fraud hotline. As for internal fraud, upon review of public records, this study was able to establish the presence of a high amount of internal fraud. A review of the historical context suggests the hotline might not be receiving the level of employee calls that it should, due to the perception of retaliation for reporting.

As for employee sentiment, employee reviews suggests there are some disgruntled employees at GS1. While an overall rating of 3.5 out of 5 on Glassdoor, which could be construed as "above average" (overall evaluation not provided by Glassdoor), suggests that employees, in their reviews, appear to lean slightly positively. However, upon review of the negative comments, it is clear employees who are unhappy make specific statements, which should not be ignored by management. Specifically, to recap, employees stated there was "lots of dead weight" and "most [employees] are unmotivated career public servants" subjected to "fairly rigid resource organization policies," which "prevent real work from getting done." Indeed, one respondent said working for the GS1 "felt like scenes from [the movie] Office Space most days."

These comments suggest that the organization's employees are experiencing an excessively bureaucratic state, which is not otherwise discernible via a review of the commentary results as "above average."

Case Study 4 (GS2)

Background

According to the U.S. Census, GS2, a state government entity, had 70,891 workers as of March 2011. Located in the Midwest, GS2 is the 20th most populous state. The largest city in GS2 is Milwaukee and their capital is Madison. GS2 is known as "America's Dairyland" due to their high level of dairy production. Most GS2 residents were reportedly born in the state. At this writing, the governor of GS2 is Scott Walker.

Bureaucracy

As a state government agency, a certain level of bureaucracy might be assumed to exist in the state of GS2, and several articles have been written to this effect

("Republicans Destroy Local Control, Create Massive Partisan Regulatory Bureaucracy, June 28, 2013; At a Loss: The State of GS2 After Eight Years Without the Public Intervenor's Office" Winter, 2004). However, one way to understand the specifics as to the organizational condition from the unique perspective of a state employee is through their candid reviews. The employees of the state of GS2 reviewed their employer on Glassdoor.com. Overall, 29 employees submitted a review of the agency, where they overall evaluated their employer at a 3.5 rating, on a scale from 1 to 5. What was particularly unique about this organization with respect to their Glassdoor.com review results is that only 7% of respondents indicated they "approve" of the "CEO" who in this case is the governor, Scott Walker.

The respondents' comments were submitted between March 12, 2010, and March 27, 2013 (Tables 6.17 and 6.18). To summarize, the reviewer sentiment

Table 6.17 GS2 Social Media/Bureaucracy Analysis Summary

Attribute	Data	Analysis
Time frame	3/12/10–3/27/13	3-year time period
Population	29	0.04% of state employees (70,891)
Respondents indicating bureaucracy or bureaupathic behaviors	18[a]	64% of the population (29) 0.03% of state employees (70,891)
Total comments indicating bureaucracy and bureaupathology	32	15 Bureaucracy + 17 Bureaupathic
Bureaucracy	15	General (4) Hierarchy of authority (3) System of rules (0) Technical expertise (0) Career service (3) Insistence on the rights of office (5)
Bureaupathic	17	Impersonal treatment (7) Prolonged role enactment (3) Resistance to change (3) Resistance to interrogation and investigation (3) Strict reliance on organizational rules and procedures (1)

[a] The number of respondents will not be equal to the number of comments, as a single respondent may have commented more than once. In the instance where their additional comment was included in a separate category, there will be more than one comment logged per respondent.

Table 6.18 GS2 Social Media/Bureaucracy Dataset

Count	Type	Attribute	Comment	Date
1.	Bureaucracy	General	"Government bureaucracy"	9/22/11
2.	Bureaucracy	General	"Red tape"	9/22/11
3.	Bureaucracy	General	"We function in a large bureaucracy"	4/10/12
4.	Bureaucracy	General	"Red tape, red tape, red tape"	10/2/12
5.	Bureaucracy	Hierarchy of authority	"Legislature should reduce depth of management employees"	2/25/11
6.	Bureaucracy	Hierarchy of authority	"No more collective bargaining for state workers"	5/12/11
7.	Bureaucracy	Hierarchy of authority	"The top management is not in touch with the real world. The things that come down from there is [sic] laughable"	12/27/11
8.	Bureaucracy	Career service	"Most careers have a long shelf life"	5/12/12
9.	Bureaucracy	Career service	"Stable employer, virtually no chance of a layoff"	11/13/12
10.	Bureaucracy	Career service	"Stop paying those who don't work and just suck up the money"	6/18/10
11.	Bureaucracy	Insistence on the rights of office	"Too often people are appointed to their positions and do not have the right experience"	9/3/10

(Continued)

Table 6.18 *(Continued)* **GS2 Social Media/Bureaucracy Dataset**

Count	Type	Attribute	Comment	Date
12.	Bureaucracy	Insistence on the rights of office	"People in positions they aren't qualified to be in"	9/22/11
13.	Bureaucracy	Insistence on the rights of office	"Upper management dislike and distrust you"	12/2/11
14.	Bureaucracy	Insistence on the rights of office	"Promotions and other opportunities based on personal relationships and who you know"	1/18/12
15.	Bureaucracy	Insistence on the rights of office	"Decisions at high levels are made primarily with a focus on political outcomes/ advantages not because they make good business sense"	4/10/12
16.	Bureaupathic	Impersonal treatment	"Poor internal talent development"	8/3/10
17.	Bureaupathic	Impersonal treatment	"Sometimes [performance] reviews do not take place for 3–5 years"	11/9/10
18.	Bureaupathic	Impersonal treatment	"You better have a thick skin"	12/1/11
19.	Bureaupathic	Impersonal treatment	"You have to have a thick skin"	4/10/12
20.	Bureaupathic	Impersonal treatment	"Basically chained to your desk/phone. Don't ask if I'm on break when I go to the bathroom"	11/28/12

(Continued)

Table 6.18 *(Continued)* **GS2 Social Media/Bureaucracy Dataset**

Count	Type	Attribute	Comment	Date
21.	Bureaupathic	Impersonal treatment	"You better have thick skin"	2/27/13
22.	Bureaupathic	Impersonal treatment	"Trust employees"	2/27/13
23.	Bureaupathic	Prolonged role enactment	"Not much room for growth"	11/9/10
24.	Bureaupathic	Prolonged role enactment	"Not much chance for upward mobility since most employees have been there so long they never leave and gradually work their way up in management based on seniority not performance [sic]"	12/14/12
25.	Bureaupathic	Prolonged role enactment	"Repetitive work"	3/27/13
26.	Bureaupathic	Resistance to change	"Culture is too relaxed, no impetus to get things done"	12/26/11
27.	Bureaupathic	Resistance to change	"Change is slow to occur"	8/3/10
28.	Bureaupathic	Resistance to change	"Quantity and quality of work unimportant"	1/18/12
29.	Bureaupathic	Resistance to interrogation and investigation	"Waste a lot of money, typical government run facility"	6/18/10
30.	Bureaupathic	Resistance to interrogation and investigation	"No real threat of disciplinary action for anything less than a felony"	1/18/12

(Continued)

Table 6.18 *(Continued)*   **GS2 Social Media/Bureaucracy Dataset**

Count	Type	Attribute	Comment	Date
31.	Bureaupathic	Resistance to interrogation and investigation	"Some negative coworkers since the whole budget issue. Dealing with criminal is its own can of worms"	6/14/12
32.	Bureaupathic	Strict reliance on organizational rules and procedures	"Paperwork is almost impossible to keep current"	3/12/13

is largely one that indicates a tough working environment. Several respondents cautioned any future applicants they must have "thick skin" in order to tolerate the job. Many also indicated they were not trusted, nor were they treated fairly in several respects. One even hinted at internal crime issues, describing coworkers as "criminals."

As demonstrated, a majority of respondents, 64%, made comments that were indicative of bureaucracy and bureaupathic conditions in their workplace. The most indicated categories included "insistence on the rights of office" and "impersonal treatment."

Hotline Specification

The GS2 Act 126 established the GS2 state hotline, managed by the GS2 Legislative Audit Bureau, in 2007. The hotline is called the "Fraud, Waste and Mismanagement Hotline." The toll-free hotline number has been operational since April 2008. The hotline telephone number, containing the word "fraud," is provided on their hotline website (1-877-FRAUD-17). This website was easily located with an Internet search for the terms "GS2 Fraud Hotline." According to the website, their hotline is staffed "primarily by a Certified Fraud Examiner." In terms of reporting popularity, in their 2008 report, the state auditor advised that most tips to their hotline are received via telephone.

In 2009, a secure web-based form was also created. This form is available on their hotline website, along with a form that can be printed and mailed. The printed form guides respondents by suggesting examples of how to include the major elements of a complaint (i.e., who, what, when, where, how, and why). The state auditor logs and tracks all hotline reports, regardless of how they are received.

The website further guides complaints by providing a brief set of "tips for callers" to include the suggested complaint parameters (complaint should involve state government), and requests complaints be as specific and inclusive of facts as possible. Complainants are also urged to supply a name and telephone number for follow-up, and are reminded this information will remain confidential by law.

Hotline Metrics

The State of GS2 produces biennial special reports that summarize their hotline activity. Data are also included in their regular biennial reporting. Data concerning the performance of the State of GS2's hotline were obtained for the years 2008–2012. In their 2008 report, they specify 75 out of 140 hotline reports "involved state programs, agencies, employees or contractors." This report was part of their regular, biennial reporting. In the following year, 2009, and again in 2012, the state created a separate, dedicated hotline report (Table 6.19).

Overall, benchmarking demonstrates the hotline receives a low number of reports for their size, and their industry. It was also noted that the number of tips received regarding Employee Misconduct and Agency Mismanagement have recently increased.

Historical Context

By all accounts, the state employees in GS2 are extremely upset about Governor Scott Walker's cuts to public employee rights and benefits. In March 2011, Walker confirmed that collective bargaining would end for most public workers. In that year, state workers also didn't receive a pay increase (AP). According to state documents, for the 2009–2011 biennium, state workers were further subjected to hour reductions and furloughs, also implemented by the governor, to decrease state expenditures. These furloughs applied to all state employees, full and part time. Articles in *The New York Times* discussed the "unrest" and "protests" that were mounting in this state, and spreading to others as fear of similar cuts among those employees worsened (Cooper, 2011).

Generally, the public outrage over the policy changes made by Walker and other state lawmakers has resulted in an unprecedented amount of public discontent and counterattacks. Media articles report ammunition being found outside the GS2 state capitol, death threats sent to Republican state senators, and thefts and boycotts of businesses that made contributions to Walker's campaign (FoxNY.com, 2011; Murdock, 2011; Newby, 2011).

Several protests also occurred, including one at the GS2 state capitol, which police estimated was larger than protests during the Vietnam era, containing up to 100,000 people in a single demonstration (Kelleher, 2011). In fact, *USA Today* reported GS2 state police said the March 26, 2011, protest was the largest they had ever seen (Contorno, Benson & Jones, 2011).

Table 6.19 GS2 Hotline Metrics

FY	Number of Employees	Inquiries	Unfounded/ No Action	Resolved	Pending	Average Benchmarking Figure, Industry,[a] Size	Calls Expected per Benchmarking	Delta
2008[b]	70,891[c]	140[d]	30	22	23	6.32, 8.60 = 7	496	–356
2009		79[e]	18	16	19	8.66, 7.66 = 8	567	–488
2010[f]		87[g]	30	19	9	4.85, 7.19 = 6	425	–338
2011		79[h]	38	46	28	5.28, 7.52 = 6	425	–346
2012[i]		83[j]				5.28, 7.52[k] = 6	425	–342

[a] Here, the industry category is Public Administration.

[b] For their 2008 report, the reporting began in April 2008, which was the advent of the hotline.

[c] U.S. Census. March 2011. This figure was used for all benchmarking, as detailed, historical state employee breakdowns were not immediately available. Nevertheless, for benchmarking purposes, any number of workers over 50,000 is considered in the same category range.

d Of these, the majority, 41, pertained to Waste/Inefficiency issues, next, 17, related to Agency Mismanagement, 5 dealt with Ineligible Beneficiaries, 5 dealt with Vendor/Contractor Issues, 4 were categorized as "other," and 3 were allegations related to Employee Misconduct. (It is unclear from the data provided which complaints were classified, and which were not, as the figures do not add up to the total number of reports.)

e Of these, the majority 30, pertained to Waste/Inefficiency issues, next, 12 related to Agency Mismanagement, 7 dealt with Vendor/Contractor Issues, 2 were allegations related to Ineligible Beneficiaries, and 2 were categorized as "other." (It is unclear from the data provided which complaints were classified, and which were not, as the figures do not add up to the total number of reports.)

f Since these reports are produced biennially, and 2009 hotline figures were provided in a special report, the 2010 figures were deduced by subtracting the 2009 figures from the 2009/2010 biennial reports.

g Since these reports are produced biennially, and 2009 hotline figures were provided in a special report, the 2010 figures were deduced by subtracting the 2009 figures from the 2009/2010 biennial reports.

h Of these, the majority 18, dealt with Ineligible Beneficiaries, next, 17 related to Agency Mismanagement, 15 pertained to Waste/Inefficiency issues, 5 were allegations related to Employee Misconduct, and 3 were categorized as "other." (It is unclear from the data provided which complaints were classified, and which were not, as the figures do not add up to the total number of reports.)

i Since these reports are produced biennially, and 2011 hotline figures were provided separately, the 2012 figures were deduced by subtracting the 2011 figures from those provided in the 2011/2012 biennial report.

j Since these reports are produced biennially, and 2011 hotline figures were provided separately, the 2012 figures were deduced by subtracting the 2011 figures from those provided in the 2011/2012 biennial report. Of these, the majority, 19, pertained to Waste/Inefficiency issues, next, 16 were allegations related to Ineligible Beneficiaries, 10 were related to Agency Mismanagement, 7 dealt with Vendor/Contractor Issues, and 7 were categorized as "other." (It is unclear from the data provided which complaints were classified, and which were not, as the figures do not add up to the total number of reports.)

k Since 2012 benchmarking figures are unavailable, and since the data for 2011/2012 were aggregated in their reporting, the 2011 benchmarking figures were used for both datasets.

Such negative employee sentiment is likely to continue. Although state employees recently received a pay increase (as of July 26, 2013; 1%), this raise is unlikely to satisfy most state workers, who have not received an increase in 4 or 5 years. According to the Associated Press, democrats have called this increase "paltry" in light of "increased pension and healthcare costs over the past two years, [which] equated to a 12–14% pay cut" (Bauer, 2013). Incidentally, the governor's own salary increase was double that of the average state employee, rising from $144,423 to $147,328 (rising by $2,905, a 2% increase).

Overall, it is well known that disgruntled employees, generally, tend to commit more workplace crime. The state of unrest, which exists in the state of GS2, should be considered when marketing and evaluating the fraud hotline.

Fraud Metrics

According to the U.S. Census, as of July 2011, the state of GS2 had a population of just over 5.7 million, and 5% of those residents are serving GS2 as public workers. Although they represent a relatively small percentage of the overall population, their crimes against the state are especially egregious, as they are persons whom residents should be able to trust. Despite having a fraud hotline in place, which is designed to receive tips from state workers and residents alike, the fraud, waste, and abuse on the part of public workers is ongoing.

A review of the news archives reveals the state of GS2 has had its share of public employee theft, waste, and mismanagement on the part of former governors, among other officials, dating back to the 1800s. Such scandals caused the author to caution state residents that "power corrupts" and to "always keep a watchful eye over the public servants whom they hire" (GS2 Historical Society, 2006).

A recent theft by a trusted GS2 employee demonstrates the harm capable by workers who are trusted by state residents with important business tasks. In July 2012, this employee, who was a public worker for 7 years, was indicted on federal fraud charges after using an assumed name, fake social security number, and a falsified passport, among other fabricated documentation, to fraudulently obtain a home in a low income housing complex intended for more deserving residents. In all, the worker stole at least $18,000 worth of benefits (Mohr).

To make matters worse, this employee worked in the secretary of state's office, where she would have been tasked with accurately and securely maintaining important state records, including municipal records, state laws, and deeds, dating back 100 years. To have such a crime committed in his office is obviously contrary to the professional philosophy of the current secretary of state, which is, to "[be] there when you need help" (SOS Website). Unfortunately, it seems the secretary of state's office may be the one most deserving of "help" with respect to their employee vetting process, as this particular employee obtained her job using an alias (Mohr, 2012).

In yet another even more egregious case of public employee crime in GS2, between 2008 and 2011, three employees of the Milwaukee County Department of Health Services systematically stole more than $350,000 from the state's food assistance program, FoodShare. During that time, the workers opened benefits accounts in the names of persons who were fictitious, incarcerated, or otherwise ineligible for benefits, and used the benefits for themselves, and sold the cards to others for profit. The scheme was complicated and involved outside collaborators, all of whom sold fraudulent cards, falsified records, bribed residents, and stole cash (Garza, 2011). In all, the two complaints filed against the workers document 30 charges with multiple counts, including fraud, forgery, and misconduct in a public office.

When the offending employees' homes were searched, a treasure trove of nearly 1,000 social security numbers and other personally identifiable information was retrieved (Garza, 2011). And their crime was well known to many state residents. One resident reported paying the women $50 per month to extend his own FoodShare benefits and advised they were bribing countless other residents in the same manner, telling investigators they "had the whole east side hooked up" (Garza, 2011).

Again, this was a crime by trusted, long-term employees who abused their position to obtain benefits for which they were not otherwise eligible. Collectively, according to state records, the three thieving workers had logged over 60 years of service to the state of GS2, and each collected salaries that were the cost of living equivalent to making $60,000 in New York City. What's equally as troubling is it seemed to be a crime of which many people were aware—both internally and externally.

In yet another more recent case, in late July 2012, a trusted Milwaukee official was arrested for misconduct after it was learned she embezzled money from the state in collusion with an outside party. According to the search warrant, this employee, in her capacity as director of Milwaukee County's Community Business Development Partners Agency (CBDP), is believed to have created fake contracts and incurred erroneous expenses that were billed to the federally funded program and made payable to her and the accomplice (DeLong, 2012). She also double-billed accounts and received kickback money (WTMJ News, 2012). Ironically, this person was tasked with contract oversight, which would have entailed the prevention and avoidance of such theft. The employee, again, was a trusted, long-term public worker (nearly 10 years) who made $89,000 per year (the cost of living equivalent of $157,000 in New York City).

Most importantly, this case further called into question the hiring practices of Governor (and former Milwaukee County Executive) Scott Walker. Walker, who hired this worker, has been the target of a separate, long-term, massive probe into his administration as county executive, which has spanned over 2 years, and includes shocking allegations, to include "campaign finance malfeasance, embezzlement of veterans funds, bid-rigging, and even child enticement" (Schultze, July 24, 2012) (Table 6.20).

Table 6.20 GS2 Table of Results

Organization	
Assessment Element	*GS2*
Size	17,891
Hotline name	Fraud, Waste and Mismanagement Hotline
Management	GS2 Legislative Audit Bureau
Respondents indicating IV	64% (population 29; 18 indicated presence of IV; 32 comments indicated IV)
Bureaucracy IV	Moderate to high, 3 of 5 General (4) **a (3)** b (0) c (0) **d (3)** **e (5)**
Bureaupathology IV	Strong, 5 of 5 **f (7)** **g (3)** **h (3)** **I (3)** **J (1)**
Hotline metrics (DV)	Low, calls received are far below benchmarking figures
Hotline functionality (DV)	Poor, 4 of 5 k (easily located externally) **l (hotline only has a single person handling calls)** **m (a single actor adds a perceived reporting and process bias)** **n (employees especially disgruntled due to historical context)**
Best practices (DV)	Good, 2 of 6 p (high level oversight) **q (escalation process is unclear)** r (data are communicated externally) **s (a single staffer is noted)** t (reports indicate enforcement) u (reports indicate escalation)

(Continued)

Table 6.20 *(Continued)* **GS2 Table of Results**

Organization	
Assessment Element	*GS2*
Historical context (DV)	Conducive to fraud; conducive to increased calls (2011 end of collective bargaining; unprecedented level of protests and other demonstrations during this time)
Evidence of internal fraud	Yes
Evidence of negative employee sentiment	Yes
Result IV	**IV Present** **Bureaucracy, moderate to high** Hierarchy of authority Career service Insistence on the rights of office **Bureaupathology, strong** Impersonal treatment Prolonged role enactment Resistance to change Resistance to interrogation and investigation
Result DV	**DV metrics, functionality affected** Metrics, low Functionality, poor Best practices, good Evidence of historical context, internal fraud, disgruntled employees
Notes	The historical context suggests employees of the state of GS2 at this time would be especially disgruntled—a condition that is known to give rise to fraud and can further inhibit fraud reporting.

According to his website, Governor Walker was elected Milwaukee County Executive in 2002 "to reform the scandal-ridden city government" (ScottWalker. org). In 2010, while Walker was campaigning to become governor, a "John Doe" investigation was quietly launched into Walker's administration, after $60,000 went missing in connection with an annual event that Walker sponsors to benefit area veterans (Schultze, July 20, 2012). Since then, it expanded as additional issues surfaced, including allegations of criminal activity on the part of key workers in his administration (during his tenure as Milwaukee County Executive). Originally, six people were charged with 15 felonies; one person, who turned himself in to prosecutors, was convicted on 2 counts (Bottari, 2011). In all, six people were charged, including three key members of Walker's staff, including former Milwaukee County deputy chiefs of staff Kelly Rindfleisch and Tim Russell, and constituent services director Darlene Wink, convicted of wrongdoing (Hall & Spicuzza, 2013). This investigation expanded to the state level before it was ultimately closed in March 2013. Although the investigation uncovered "illegal campaign contributions to Walker's campaign, illegal campaign activity by [Walker's] taxpayer-funded staffers and embezzlement of veterans' funds and other misdeeds….since…before [Walker] was elected governor in November 2010," the investigation closed without finding sufficient evidence of wrongdoing beyond those charged (Hall & Spicuzza, 2013).

Despite the lack of official charges, there are many critics who say Walker evaded prosecution with expensive legal defense (Hall & Spicuzza, 2013). Now that the scandal is behind him, sources have said Walker may now be preparing to run for additional offices, including reelection to his current post in 2014 and a possible presidential run in 2016 (Hall & Spicuzza, 2013).

Summary

According to the evidence, GS2 has excessive bureaucracy and a hotline with performance issues. A review of the literature (organizational documents, media articles) and an analysis of employee reviews found bureaucracy and excessive bureaucracy were present in this organization. Overall, 64% of the population (29), which was 0.03% of all employees (70,891), made comments indicating bureaucracy or excessive bureaucracy. In sum, the comments were made by 18 separate respondents, with 15 comments indicating bureaucracy and 17 indicating excessive bureaucracy.

Employee statements prove bureaucracy and excessive bureaucracy are recognized on the part of employees. Employee comments indicating three of five indices evincing bureaucracy and five of five indices indicating excessive bureaucracy were present at varying degrees. While 15 respondents' comments indicated the general existence of bureaucracy, specifically, employee comments suggest the indices of bureaucracy "insistence on the rights of office" (5 comments) as having the strongest presence, followed by "career service" (3 comments) and "hierarchy of authority" (3 comments). The remaining comments (4) were suggestive of the general existence of bureaucracy. With respect to bureaupathology, all five indices were present, especially "impersonal treatment" (7 comments).

As for GS2's hotline, evidence suggests it may have performance issues. Benchmarking revealed the hotline receives a low number of calls for the industry and size. In every year analyzed, FY 2008–2012, GS2's hotline performance was substandard per benchmarking.

With respect to the hotline's functionality, the hotline performed moderately. As for marketing, the hotline telephone number was easily located with a quick Google search for "GS2 Fraud Hotline." Next, as for mechanics, the hotline is reportedly managed by a single person, a Certified Fraud Examiner (CFE).

This suggests this hotline is not available 24/7 and assistance is not provided in multiple languages, due to understaffing. As a result, this hotline may not be operating well from a mechanics perspective.

As for intake/processing, organizational records reveal the hotline only has one person handling calls. As a result, the intake and processing is performed by a single actor, which suggests the potential for a perceived reporting and process bias. However, it is positive aspect that the employee handling the calls is experienced in fraud (a CFE). The website offers clear reporting guidelines that are not overly bureaucratic. Confidentiality is also assured. The state auditor also logs and tracks all hotline reports.

The historical context suggests employees of the state of GS2 at this time would be especially disgruntled—a condition that is known to give rise to fraud and can further inhibit fraud reporting. In 2011, Governor Scott Walker announced collective bargaining would end for most public workers. Many state employees also reportedly went a long time (4–5 years) without a pay increase and were subject to hour cuts and furloughs. Poor employee sentiment resulted in a number of unprecedented public demonstrations (Contorno, Benson & Jones, 2011).

In addition, per the employee reviews, this organization is believed to have a dominating management ("insistence on the rights of office," 5 comments), providing "impersonal treatment" (7 comments).

With respect to best practices, this hotline is believed to be lacking in several areas. For one, the hotline does not appear to have a clear, reported oversight process conducted by high-level personnel. As for due care, the hotline does not appear to have a well-managed, clear escalation process. With respect to communication, the hotline is communicated appropriately externally. The hotline does not make a poster available to external parties. It is unknown whether a poster is provided internally.

As for this hotline's "reasonable steps to achieve compliance," that requirement is satisfied with their third-party hotline management, process of having calls escalated via a clear chain of command, and the Office of Inspector General having the contact information of key personnel for immediate dissemination.

With respect to the other two best practices elements, "consistent enforcement" and "reasonable steps to respond and prevent similar offenses upon detection," this study was unable to rate this organization on these factors, as the data are simply not made available to researchers to allow for this criteria to be established. Specific crimes learned via the hotline, along with their investigation and resolution, are not reported outside of the state of GS2.

Furthermore, the level of internal fraud, the historical context, and the perception of employees of their organization are also factors in gauging the overall performance of this fraud hotline. As for internal fraud, upon review of public records, this study was able to establish the presence of a high amount of internal fraud. Furthermore, employee reviews on Glassdoor also indicated the presence of internal fraud, with one respondent describing his or her coworkers as "criminals."

As for employee sentiment, employee reviews suggest employees are likely disgruntled. With an overall rating of 3.5 out of 5 on Glassdoor, which could be construed as "above average" (overall evaluation not provided by Glassdoor), their reviews could be interpreted as leaning slightly positively. However, when specific comments and other indicators are considered, it is clear the organization's employees are experiencing an excessively bureaucratic state. For example, a separate metric on Glassdoor indicates only 7% of the population of respondents (29) indicated they "approve" of Governor Walker. This statistic suggests employees are generally unhappy with the regime, despite having potentially indicated they might be satisfied with their job.

Employees who submitted reviews to Glassdoor document a highly bureaucratic environment, which affects their ability to advance in the organization. Specifically, indicating "people are in positions they are not qualified to be in" and "promotions are based on personal relationships and who you know" and there is "not much room for growth" "since most employees have been there so long they never leave and gradually work their way up in management based on seniority not performance."

Further, employees who submitted negative comments on Glassdoor say the organizational bureaucracy has created poor working conditions and organizational waste and mismanagement. Respondents warn potential future employees to "have a thick skin," "upper management dislike(s) and distrust(s) you," you are "basically chained to [your] desk/phone," and an organization that "waste[s] a lot of money."

When the historical context is evaluated in light of comments posted to Glassdoor, it is clear that the current political climate had a negative effect on employees. Employee respondents indicated there was low morale due to Governor Walker's removal of the collective bargaining process ("some negative co-workers since the whole budget issue"). This comment validates that employees were disgruntled, a condition giving rise to fraud and also inhibiting fraud hotline reporting per the Theory of Bureaucracy. Per Caiden, excessive bureaucracy conditions "promote organizational sabotage" (1985, p. 25).

Case Study 5 (GS3)

Background

GS3 is a city government entity. According to the GS3 website, they have 19,500 employees working for the city. GS3 is located in Southern California and is one of their major cities. GS3 is the eighth largest city in the United States, and the second largest in California. Their primary economy is driven by the military, tourism, and manufacturing. According to the *Farmer's Almanac*, GS3 has one of the top 10 best climates. The interim mayor of GS3 is Todd Gloria.

Bureaucracy

News articles have documented the presence of massive bureaucracy in GS3's city government. However, more recently, the issue moved to the forefront, indicating the city bureaucracy had become especially problematic. In a press release dated November 15, 2011, with the headline "Local Businesses List Top Solutions To Cut City Red Tape," it was reported, for the first time in 10 years, a special forum was held for interested parties to voice their concerns regarding the city's bureaucracy directly to the city council. During this meeting, one speaker likened the city's bureaucratic red tape to "trying to get into a speakeasy with the wrong password" (Awbry, 2011).

Additional articles chronicle the city's bureaucracy, with titles such as "Insane ... Mindless Bureaucracy,"[*] where residents discuss their inability to park overnight in front of their apartment complex due to city restrictions, "The Bureaucracy of the 'Awful Tower,'"[†] which discusses the "the city of GS3's bureaucratic morass slow[ing] down road and other infrastructure repairs" and "Government Bureaucracy Impedes Growth in the Construction Industry,"[‡] which discussed how challenges relating to "bonding, workers' compensation and government regulations" were raised by construction officials at a recent roundtable discussion (Dillon, 2011; Rico, 2012 ; Uy, 2010).

To gain a unique insight into the presence of bureaucracy and bureaupathic conditions, as they are observed by city employees, the website Glassdoor.com was reviewed, where 18 past and present employees provided detailed, unsolicited reviews of their employer (Tables 6.21 and 6.22). Overall, the 18 respondents rated their employer an average of 3.1, on a scale of 1–5. These reviews were provided between February 20, 2009, and July 8, 2013.

Hotline Specification

GS3's fraud hotline is called a "Fraud, Waste and Abuse Hotline." An Internet search for "GS3 Fraud Hotline" easily results in their hotline page, which is the first search result. One notable quality of this website is how the city immediately (third sentence) tells the user they would prefer they reported their concern in person, by saying, "Face to face reporting is always the best form of communication, although that is not always feasible. Current City procedures and/or department instructions state that all complaints should be sent through the chain of command."

The city auditor manages GS3's hotline. However, the city auditor uses a third-party hotline provider, namely, The Network, to manage their fraud hotline. This fact is disclosed on their hotline webpage. Similar to the GS2 state

---

[*] GS3 Reader 2010.
[†] The Voice of GS3 2011.
[‡] *The Daily Transcript* 2012.

Table 6.21   GS3 Social Media/Bureaucracy Analysis Summary

Attribute	Data	Analysis
Time Frame	2/20/09–7/8/13	4-year time period
Population	18	0.09% of city employees (19,500)
Respondents indicating bureaucracy or bureaupathic behaviors	12[a]	0.06% of city employees (19,500) 67% of the population (18)
Total comments indicating bureaucracy and bureaupathology	22	11 Bureaucracy + 11 Bureaupathology
Bureaucracy	11	General (1) Hierarchy of authority (3) System of rules (1) Technical expertise (1) Career service (1) Insistence on the rights of office (4)
Bureaupathic	11	Impersonal treatment (3) Prolonged role enactment (2) Resistance to change (3) Resistance to interrogation and investigation (1) Strict reliance on organizational rules and procedures (2)

[a] The number of respondents will not be equal to the number of comments, as a single respondent may have commented more than once. In the instance where their additional comment was included in a separate category, there will be more than one comment logged per respondent.

Table 6.22   GS3 Social Media/Bureaucracy Dataset

Count	Type	Attribute	Comment	Date
1.	Bureaucracy	General	"Bureaucratic"	12/10/12
2.	Bureaucracy	Hierarchy of authority	"Top heavy in upper management"	12/21/11
3.	Bureaucracy	Hierarchy of authority	"Top heavy"	2/7/13

(Continued)

Table 6.22 *(Continued)*   **GS3 Social Media/Bureaucracy Dataset**

Count	Type	Attribute	Comment	Date
4.	Bureaucracy	Hierarchy of authority	"Very structured and hierarchical"	3/6/13
5.	Bureaucracy	System of rules	"Poor upper management, they [sic] regulations they put out seem un-compeditive [sic]"	12/21/11
6.	Bureaucracy	Technical expertise	"Top heavy salaries in IT"	10/17/12
7.	Bureaucracy	Career service	"Seniority kind of sucks. You don't have to do a good job..."	8/22/10
8.	Bureaucracy	Insistence on the rights of office	"Top management plays favorites"	3/16/09
9.	Bureaucracy	Insistence on the rights of office	"Hiring departments conduct interviews, but they already have someone in mind for them to hire, and its usually the person they want to promote within their department"	4/14/10
10.	Bureaucracy	Insistence on the rights of office	"The city salary is top heavy for appointments by the Mayor and Council. So many upper management making over $100,000 a year. The Union/Classified employees are going without to support upper management pay"	10/17/12

(Continued)

Table 6.22 (Continued) GS3 Social Media/Bureaucracy Dataset

Count	Type	Attribute	Comment	Date
11.	Bureaucracy	Insistence on the rights of office	"Senior management with big egos that don't like to have their opinions challenged"	5/7/13
12.	Bureaupathic	Impersonal treatment	"Un-friendly [sic] area managers that do no [sic] do anything"	12/21/11
13.	Bureaupathic	Impersonal treatment	"Terrible management that don't know how to interact with and communicate with employees"	6/8/13
14.	Bureaupathic	Impersonal treatment	"Don't ignore [employees] and treat them like they are invisible"	7/8/13
15.	Bureaupathic	Prolonged role enactment	"Lack of promotional opportunities"	5/11/10
16.	Bureaupathic	Prolonged role enactment	"They do not hire very often"	4/6/12
17.	Bureaupathic	Resistance to change	"Hard to make a successful program, City really just want [sic] to offer the basics and not anything more"	12/21/11
18.	Bureaupathic	Resistance to change	"Allow the free flow of ideas"	1/15/12
19.	Bureaupathic	Resistance to change	"Limiting on creativity"	12/10/12
20.	Bureaupathic	Resistance to interrogation and investigation	"Increasing mistrust"	12/10/12

(Continued)

Table 6.22 *(Continued)*   GS3 Social Media/Bureaucracy Dataset

Count	Type	Attribute	Comment	Date
21.	Bureaupathic	Strict reliance on organizational rules and procedures	"It's all paperwork for the City"	3/27/09
22.	Bureaupathic	Strict reliance on organizational rules and procedures	"Pools are restricted from serving their individual community needs, instead have to operate as a whole which really doesn't work cause some programs work better in communities than others"	12/21/11

hotline, GS3 provides materials and other guidance for users to guide them through the complaint process, including a list of sample "fraud," "waste," and "abuse" issues. On their hotline website, they also have a link to more information about The Network, which is a largely promotional piece, where they advise potential users The Network is "the leading provider of hotlines to complex organizations." In addition to The Network, callers can submit complaints to the city auditor, direct. According to city documents, as of 2008, they were contracted to pay The Network $12,000 per year for these services (GS3 Office of the City Auditor, 2008).

According to their organizational documents, the hotline was established on December 2, 2005, per GS3 Municipal Code §26.1703(c). After some organizational transitioning, the Office of the City Auditor assumed responsibility for the hotline as of July 21, 2008, and it was opened to the public on August 25, 2008.

In terms of triage, it is reported that The Network sends the city auditor "instant email notification of all complaints" to the city auditor, audit manager, and audit analyst (GS3 Office of the City Auditor October 20, 2008). Then, the city auditor conducts investigations on "all material complaints received related to fraud, waste, and abuse" (Luna, 2008). Any nonfraud-related complaints go before the City Auditor's Hotline Intake and Review Committee (city auditor, personnel director, Office of Ethics and Integrity designee, and labor relations director). This committee, which meets every 2 weeks, is tasked with reviewing the complaints and deciding whether further investigation is warranted. In this instance, referrals are made via written memorandum to the appropriate department director, who must, in turn, provide written proof back to the city auditor the matter was handled (Luna, 2008).

Hotline Metrics

In FY 2009, the average number of calls received was 12 per month. During this time, the hotline was exceeding its expected level of calls via benchmarking. However, from 2010 forward, a significant drop in calls is noted, bringing them under the expected call levels (Table 6.23).

Historical Context

The city auditor publishes quarterly reports documenting the performance of their fraud hotline. They also provide special reports in response to request, and in response to certain investigations conducted, which will be discussed later in this work. Data concerning the performance of the hotline date back to 2006.

One detail that was noted in their first (publically available) hotline performance report, which was dated October 16, 2008 (and provides a summary of call volume dating back to, 2006), was a suggested limit placed on call volume by The Network. Specifically, in this report, it reads "In 2008, we estimate 176 complaints will be made to the hotline if the quarterly trend continues. Based on the estimated number of complaints that will be filed in 2008, the Network's limit of 288 calls per year will not be exceeded. However, if the number of complaints per month averages more than 24 in 2009, the complaint cap limit will be exceeded" (Luna, Q1 2009, p. 3).

In an interview with a representative from The Network (NE1), we learned organizations were charged on a "per report" basis. Now this information suggests that "caps" are further placed on volume, presumably to keep within a certain service guideline. This pricing model seems to work against the spirit of the hotline, which is to foster open communication for the purpose of reducing internal fraud.

In addition, in a designated section of this report, the city auditor discussed the value of the reporting received, yet says it has created a strain on internal resources:

Number of Fraud Complaints

From the Hotline's inception in December 2005 through June 2008, the City received 13 fraud complaints (3 percent of all complaints), including accounting or audit irregularities complaints. Since assuming responsibility for the Hotline in July 2008, we have received ten calls in the first three months that require investigation by City Auditor staff.

Table 6.23 GS3 Hotline Metrics

FY	Number of Employees	Inquiries	Fraud, Waste, and Abuse	Average Benchmarking Figure, Industry[a] Size	Calls Expected per Benchmarking	Delta
2006[b]	19,500[c]	180	N/A	13.6, 4.7 = 9	175	+5
2007[d]		140	N/A	3.18, 9.6 = 6	117	+23
2008[e]		176	N/A	6.32, 9.9 = 8	156	+20
2009[f]		140	17	8.66, 7.93 = 8	156	+16
2010		61	N/A	4.85, 8.35 = 7	136	−75
2011		76	N/A	5.28, 8.29 = 7	136	−60
2012		115	19	5.28, 8.29 = 7[g]	136	−21

[a] Here, the industry category is Public Administration.

[b] Reported for the calendar year.

[c] Since annual breakdowns are difficult to obtain due to their fiscal year reporting schedule, the most recent figure is being used for this analysis. For benchmarking purposes, slight fluctuations are not material to the outcome. Here, they are in group 3 (10,001–20,000 employees).

[d] Reported for the calendar year.

[e] Reported for the calendar year.

[f] July 2008–June 2009.

[g] 2012 figures are not yet available. As a result, 2011 figures were used, since they are the most recent numbers, and similar economic conditions, and thus most likely to be similar.

During the first quarter of fiscal year 2009, fraud-related complaints requiring City Auditor investigation represent 15 percent of all complaints filed. There has been a significant increase in the number of fraud-related complaints compared to previous years. The number of fraud and accounting complaints made in the first quarter is of concern in terms of the number hours required to investigate these complaints. Based on the 13 fraud and accounting complaints filed in 2006 and 2007, we estimated allocating 600 staff hours in fiscal year 2009 to investigate up to 15 fraud complaints or about 40 hours per complaint. If the number of fraud and accounting complaints received in the first quarter continues to trend for the remainder of the fiscal year, we estimate receiving a total of 40 fraud-related complaints and exceeding our planned staff hours by 1,080 hours. As of October 3, 2008, we had used approximately 147 of 600 staff hours investigating complaints. (Luna, Q1 2009 October 16, 2008, p. 5)

The budgetary constraint with respect to the hotline was further noted later in their report, where they conclude their discussion of resource issues with a value proposition, saying that "if the current trend in the number of complaints continues, the Auditor's Office will be required to either reduce the number of hours spent on planned performance audits, or hire an investigator to examine the fraud related complaints received" (Luna, October 16, 2008, p. 6). This statement suggests an unfortunate trade-off must occur, where city administrators must make a decision of whether to investigate fraud hotline tips or conduct audits, both of which are top ways that organizational fraud is discovered, per the Association of Certified Fraud Examiners (2002–2016).

This fact is especially troubling, considering this hotline, per their own reports, appears to be generating valid and actionable complaints (Table 6.24). There are 17* special reports posted in the public domain that document investigations conducted following hotline complaints. These reports are provided publically per California Government Code § 53087.6(e)(2).† Overall, there were four reports created in 2012, three in 2011, two in 2010, and eight in 2009. Of these, 82% of the allegations (14) on which the reports were based were substantiated.

In city documentation, it was reported they planned to expand their fraud hotline marketing efforts in Q3 2012, to "remind employees of their obligation under the City's Administrative Regulation 95.60"‡ and "increase the level of employee

---

* There are 18 reports in total, but 2 pertain to the same issue and were thus counted as 1 report for clarity.

† Stating substantiated allegations, and others, which contain information "deemed necessary [for disclosure] to serve the interests of the public" are made publically available. All others are kept confidential.

‡ This regulation encourages employees to fulfill their own moral obligations to the city by disclosing improper governmental activities within their knowledge.

Table 6.24 GS3 Hotline Reports

Count	Report Date	Details	Status	Notes
1.	6/18/12	A city employee was accused of conflict of interest; conducting a side business at a city location for profit.	Unsubstantiated	N/A
2.	6/4/12	An allegation was submitted regarding the improper use of special use permits for personal gain.	Unsubstantiated	Oversight weaknesses were discovered and addressed as part of this investigation.
3.	1/29/09	A city facility was accused of mishandling scrap metal.	Unsubstantiated	Although this allegation was unsubstantiated, certain recommendations were made based on conditions discovered upon inspection.
4.	8/21/12	A city convention center was accused of inflating attendance numbers to justify a recent expansion.	Substantiated	N/A

(Continued)

Table 6.24 *(Continued)* **GS3 Hotline Reports**

Count	Report Date	Details	Status	Notes
5.	3/29/12	A city employee was reported for using the city Internet to conduct noncity business.	Substantiated	Five city employees were recommended for discipline.
6.	12/15/11	An allegation was submitted that a city department was operating in violation of its contract with the city.	Substantiated	N/A
7.	10/25/11	It was alleged a nonprofit organization filed to receive a false reimbursement from the city.	Substantiated	The city was erroneously billed for $20,000, and a demand for the return of funds was initiated.
8.	3/3/11	A city employee was accused of stealing money, making false accounting entries, and concealing/ destroying associated records.	Substantiated	Missing funds totaled $100,998.
9.	11/5/10	A complaint alleged contract administration abuse.	Substantiated	N/A

(Continued)

Table 6.24 *(Continued)*   **GS3 Hotline Reports**

Count	Report Date	Details	Status	Notes
10.	7/21/10	A city employee was accused of selling city scrap metal to fund employee events.	Substantiated	It was determined official procedures surrounding the sale of such metals didn't exist. Consistent records regarding the sale of $21,000 worth of such metals between 2004 and 2010 could not be located.
11.	11/23/09	A city employee was accused of submitting false information to fraudulently receive health benefits.	Substantiated	Issue highlighted greater weaknesses in benefit documentation submission process.
12.	6/30/09	It was alleged a city employee stole items from a city inspection site.	Substantiated	N/A
13.	6/29/09	A city nonprofit organization was accused of accounting irregularities and possible misuse of city funds.	Substantiated	Duplicate billings in the amount of $112,070 were located, and the city sought restitution.

(Continued)

Table 6.24 *(Continued)* **GS3 Hotline Reports**

Count	Report Date	Details	Status	Notes
14.	5/28/09	A city program was accused of delaying fundraiser money deposits.	Substantiated	N/A
15.	4/7/09	A city organization was accused of accounting irregularities, misuse of funds, and assault.	Substantiated	The city employee had two civil judgments filed against him/her, and $1,085 was paid using city funds.
16.	2/23/09	The city was performing duplicate and unnecessary replacement of water meter boxes.	Substantiated	Ninety-two potential water meter boxes replacements were avoided, saving the city $30,728.
17.	1/16/09	A city employee was accused of misusing his/her position to obtain confidential documents for personal gain.	Substantiated	N/A

Note: N/A, Not Available.

confidence in [the] Fraud Hotline as a viable means to address fraud, waste and abuse in City operations." Such efforts include (1) posting a link of the CityNet webpage to the Fraud Hotline Quarterly Report; (2) sending a broadcast e-mail to all employees reminding them that the Fraud Hotline is a viable method of reporting fraud, waste, and abuse; and (3) mailing a memo, business card, and Fraud Hotline Brochure titled "Doing What's Right" to employees (Luna, 2008, p. 1).

Fraud Metrics

As of 2010, the population of the city of GS3 was approximately 1.3 million, making it the eighth largest city in the United States. In the same year, GS3 was lauded as one of the "Top 10 Safest cities in the U.S." by *Forbes* magazine (Levy n.d.). However, despite this designation, which was bestowed upon GS3 due to their low rate of violent crime, research reveals this city is not immune to fraud, waste, and abuse. In fact, certain crimes previously committed by GS3's city employees have been so egregious, they were viewed as a contributory factor in the city's financial crisis of 2002–2003. Moreover, the fraud committed on the part of GS3 city officials was so unique, in October 2010, it culminated in a "first" for the SEC—never before had the SEC ever secured financial penalties against city officials in a municipal bond fraud case.

The 2010 recovery on the part of the SEC represented a long-awaited measure of individual justice for crimes that had occurred in the city of GS3 at the hand of its high-ranking officials 8 years ago. Specifically, according to their complaint, the SEC found that from 2002 to 2003, GS3 officials, knowing the city had financial challenges, misrepresented the financial health of the city's pension funds and health plans, thereby misleading investors.

On April 7, 2008, the SEC filed securities fraud charges against the high-ranking GS3 city officials responsible for this fraud, including the former Deputy City Manager, Treasurer, Auditor and Comptroller, and Finance Manager. On October 27, 2010, the SEC announced that four of the employees agreed to pay financial penalties for their crimes. The City of GS3, as a collective, had been previously charged in 2006 with this crime. At that time, experts expressed displeasure with the fact the individual employees—who were directly responsible for the violations—were not charged (Walsh, 2006).

Unfortunately, this was not the first time a high-ranking GS3 employee was charged with a crime that inflicted great financial damage and brought disgrace to city government. In 2012, the city was forced to relive the embarrassment caused by their former city officials, council member Ralph Inzunza, and Deputy Mayor Michael Zucchet, who in 2005 were forced to resign from the city council in a salacious scandal that was coined "Stripper-Gate" (Moran, 2012). In 2005, Inzunza and Zucchet were convicted of extortion, wire fraud, and conspiracy after they were caught accepting bribes from a local strip club owner in exchange for using their political influence to repeal "no touch" laws, which had lowered strip club profits (Moran, 2012). In June 2005, the two resigned in disgrace from their political positions.

After being sentenced to 21 months in federal prison, despite overwhelming evidence of his guilt, Inzunza drew further ire from the community as he remained free on bail while he continued to file appeals for the next six and a half years. Finally, after the Supreme Court declined to hear his case, in January 2012 he was sent to a minimum-security satellite camp at Atwater Federal Prison, where he was said to remain until August 2013 (Moran, 2013). Earlier this year, it was reported Inzunza was being transferred to a halfway house where he will serve out the remainder of his sentence (Moran, 2013).

For the residents of GS3, unfortunately, Ralph Inzunza was not the first of the Inzunza lineage to bring disgrace to local politics. His brother, Nick Inzunza, former mayor of National City in GS3 County, also resigned in shame in 2006 after a news report revealed his low-income rental properties, containing 100 units, had serious health code violations (CBS8.com, 2009). Inzunza responded to the press, blaming these violations on his owner-wife, to whom he had transferred 2 of 10 units in the previous week (Branscomb & Sierra, 2005). Residents of the units, who complained of vermin, lack of heat and hot water, and nonworking appliances, among other problems, were often evicted shortly following their complaint (Branscomb & Sierra, 2005).

Despite his past, Nick was brought on to serve as chairman of GS3 county's Hispanic Chamber of Commerce (SDCHCC). The SDCHCC reported having no concern over Nick's past, when their interim president told the GS3 *Union Tribune* "he has a lot of experience with finances, and that could be really helpful right now" (Soto, 2009). The SDCHCC was recently subject to massive financial crime at the hands of an internal fraudster, who recently stole $70,000 from the organization's bank accounts (Soto, 2009).

More recently, in March 2011, a Parks and Recreation Department (PRD) employee with fiduciary responsibility for the agency was arraigned on charges of grand theft by an employee for stealing more than $100,000 from various recreation centers from 2004 to 2008. In collusion with another employee, who was later charged with two counts of felony charges of creating false accounts with public money, the two wrote themselves checks and swiped reimbursement payments, membership fees, and other payments intended for the PRD (Gustafson, 2011).

Ironically, one of the perpetrators, a 30-year city veteran, was featured positively in news article about city budget cuts (Gustafson, 2011). He portrayed as a good employee and thus a potential tragic casualty of a waning city budget. Now instead, following his fraud, the news articles are a mea culpa; critical of the city's inability to suspend his pension eligibility, despite defrauding the city.

As a result of this and other city employee–perpetuated crimes, the new pension reforms were amended in June 2012 under Proposition B, to "eliminate pension benefits for City officers or employees convicted of a felony related to their employment, duties or obligations as a City officer or employee." Incidentally, a hotline tip revealed this crime (The GS3 Union Tribune, 2011).

Summary

According to the evidence, the city of GS3 has excessive bureaucracy and a hotline with performance issues (Table 6.25). A review of the literature (organizational documents, media articles) and an analysis of employee reviews found bureaucracy

Table 6.25 GS3 Table of Results

Organization	
Assessment Element	*GS3*
Size	19,500
Hotline name	Fraud, Waste and Abuse Hotline
Management	Third party and city auditor
Respondents indicating IV	67% (population 18; 12 respondents indicating presence of IV; 22 comments indicated IV)
Bureaucracy IV	5 of 5 General (1) **a (3)** b (1) c (1) d (1) **e (4)**
Bureaupathology IV	5 of 5 **f (3)** g (2) **h (3)** I (1) J (2)
Hotline metrics (DV)	Low, exceeded benchmarking for 4 years, until 2010 (Dodd–Frank period) calls declined to levels below benchmarking
Hotline functionality (DV)	Great, 3 of 4 k (easily located externally) l (third-party provider) m (third-party provider and internal handling process; process well documented) **n (reporting discouraged; potential callers urged to report in person)**
Best practices (DV)	Great, 3 of 6 p (high-level oversight) q (escalation process is clear) **r (data are reported externally, calls are discouraged; no poster)** s (third-party provider with internal escalation process) t (reports indicate enforcement) u (reports indicate escalation)

(Continued)

Table 6.25 *(Continued)* **GS3 Table of Results**

Organization	
Assessment Element	GS3
Historical context (DV)	Conducive to fraud; conducive to increased calls (calls declined after 2009 hotline report said there was a cap on the hotline calls received by the provider)
Evidence of internal fraud	Yes
Evidence of negative employee sentiment	Yes
Result IV	**IV present** **Bureaucracy, strong** Hierarchy of authority Insistence on the rights of office **Bureaupathology, strong** Impersonal treatment Resistance to change
Result DV	**DV metrics affected** Metrics, low Functionality, moderate Best practices, great Evidence of historical context, internal fraud, disgruntled employees
Notes	Evidence that an internal crime was reported via the hotline; according to one report, from 2010 to 2012, 82% of their complaints received were substantiated

and excessive bureaucracy were present in this organization. Overall, 67% of the population (18), which was 0.09% of all employees (19,500), made comments indicating bureaucracy or excessive bureaucracy. In sum, the comments were made by 18 separate respondents, with 11 of their comments indicating bureaucracy and 11 indicating excessive bureaucracy.

Employee statements prove bureaucracy and excessive bureaucracy are recognized on the part of employees. Employee comments indicating five of five indices evincing bureaucracy and five of five indices indicating excessive bureaucracy were present at varying degrees. Employee comments suggest the indices of bureaucracy "insistence on the rights of office" (4 comments) as having the strongest presence, followed by "hierarchy of authority" (3 comments). With respect to bureaupathology, all five indices were present, especially "impersonal treatment" (3 comments) and "resistance to change" (3 comments).

As for GS3's hotline, evidence suggests it may have performance issues. Benchmarking revealed the hotline was performing as expected per benchmarking estimates between 2006 and 2009. Suddenly, in 2010, the calls fell sharply below benchmarking estimates (–75) and remained below estimates in the ensuing years up to 2012.

A review of the historical context provided a possible reason for this decline. Upon reviewing organizational documents (internal reports), it was learned this drop occurred immediately following documented budgetary concerns over call volume in light of The Network's imposed limits. Although their hotline shows evidence of being well operated, the limitation on reporting placed by The Network, and emphasis to employees to report in person, may have caused their hotline to fall short of expectations.

With respect to the hotline's functionality, the hotline performed great. As for marketing, the hotline telephone number was easily located with a quick Google search for "GS3 Fraud Hotline." With respect to mechanics, the hotline is managed by a third-party provider and has an internal process for further call handling. As a result, the hotline is not perceived to have serious issues with its mechanics.

However, communication of the hotline is a concern. The hotline website appears to discourage hotline reporting. In fact, one of the first statements on the hotline website tells the user it is preferable to report in person. Although organizational documents state the hotline plans to expand its marketing efforts, this effort might be futile if their website deters potential complainants. As a result, overall, this hotline may not be operating as well as it could from a mechanics perspective.

As for intake/processing, organizational records reveal the hotline is managed by a third-party provider, The Network. As a result, the intake and processing are regulated. Organizational documents also outline a clear process for handling calls from their receipt by The Network to closure by the city auditor. The hotline website also provides a clear statement about their adherence to Whistleblower Protection Laws and commitment to protecting against whistleblower retaliation. It is further reported the GS3 Office of the City Auditor logs and tracks all hotline reports. The website also makes their hotline data readily available to the public, via a link to their hotline reports and statistics.

The historical context, as documented in organizational documents, suggests their hotline is subject to a "complaint cap" by The Network, which limits the number of reports their hotline can receive. In organizational documents, the city expressed great concerns over the "significant increase in the number of fraud related complaints" in light of this cap. This fact is problematic, considering their hotline generates actionable tips. According to one report, from 2010 to 2012, 82% of their complaints received were substantiated.

In addition, per the employee reviews, this organization is believed to have a dominating management ("insistence on the rights of office," 4 comments), providing "impersonal treatment" (3 comments).

With respect to best practices, this hotline is believed to perform reasonably well. For one, the hotline has a clear, reported oversight process conducted by high-level personnel. As for due care, the hotline has a well-managed, clear escalation process. With respect to communication, the hotline is communicated appropriately externally. However, as noted previously, the complaint cap and the website language deterring reporting are problematic. The hotline does not make a poster available to external parties. It is unknown whether a poster is provided internally.

As for this hotline's "reasonable steps to achieve compliance," that requirement is satisfied with their third-party hotline management, process of having calls escalated via a clear chain of command, and the office of the city auditor having a documented triage process.

With respect to the other two best practices elements, "consistent enforcement" and "reasonable steps to respond and prevent similar offenses upon detection," this hotline outperformed all others examined in that this aspect could be evaluated. The city auditor posted reports in the public domain, which documented the investigations conducted following hotline complaints and any resolution/remediation, which followed thereafter.

Furthermore, the level of internal fraud, the historical context, and the perception of employees of their organization are also factors in gauging the overall performance of this fraud hotline. As for internal fraud, upon review of public records, this study was able to establish the presence of a high amount of internal fraud. From the city's hotline reports, we learned a majority of the complaints received via the hotline are substantiated, and that 41% involved a city employee (seven reported matters). In one matter, the employee had stolen over $100,000. Furthermore, employee reviews on Glassdoor also indicated the presence of disgruntled employees, with one respondent saying there was an atmosphere of "increasing mistrust."

Glassdoor reviews also indicate employee sentiment is poor. With an overall rating of 3.1 out of 5 on Glassdoor, which could be construed as "above average" (overall evaluation not provided by Glassdoor), their reviews could be interpreted as leaning slightly positively. However, when specific comments and other indicators are considered, it is clear the organization's employees are experiencing an excessively bureaucratic state. For example, a separate metric on Glassdoor indicates only 7% of the population of respondents (29) indicated they "approve" of Governor Walker. This statistic suggests employees are generally unhappy with the regime, despite having potentially indicated they might be satisfied with their job.

Employees who submitted reviews to Glassdoor document a highly bureaucratic environment, whose organizational structure inhibits growth and advancement. Specifically, they indicated it is "very structured and hierarchical" with "poor upper management" where you "don't have to do a good job" to gain seniority. Comments also suggest internal communication might be lacking. One reviewer said, "terrible management [does not] know how to interact with and communicate with employees" and yet another reported the city's "senior management with big egos…don't like to have their opinions challenged."

Case Study 6 (NP1)

Background

The subject of this case study, hereinafter known as NP1, is a nonprofit organization, which is named by *Forbes* as one of the top 200 largest charities (Barrett, 2006). Incorporated in 1905, in the District of Columbia, they have over 500 chapters with a stated purpose "to prevent and alleviate human suffering in the face of emergencies by mobalizing the power of volunteers and the generosity of donors". According to their 2012 tax return, they generated over $3 billion in total revenue and have 31,000 employees. The president and CEO, and the highest paid executive, make a combined annual salary totaling over $1 million (BBB, 2012). NP1 is a tax-exempt organization, as defined under 501(c)(3) of the Internal Revenue Code. In their 2012 Form 990, they reported they were not aware of a "significant diversion" of their agencies assets during that fiscal year.

As of fiscal year ending June 30, 2011, NP1's program expenses were to include expenditures for international relief and development services, domestic disaster services, health and safety services, community services, and services to armed forces (BBB, 2012). In the same year, NP1 collected over $600 million in charitable donations.

This charity also meets the Better Business Bureau's (BBB) 20 Standards for Charity Accountability, earning a "meets standards" grade in all subcategories within the broad categories of governance and oversight (board oversight, board size, board meetings, board compensation, conflict of interest), measuring effectiveness (effectiveness policy, report), finances (program expenses, fund raising expenses, accumulating funds, audit report, detailed expense breakdown, accurate expense reporting, budget plan), and fund raising and informational materials (truthful materials, annual report, website disclosures, donor privacy, cause marketing disclosures, complaints) (BBB, 2003).

Bureaucracy

The state of bureaucracy at NP1 is well documented. In the case of NP1, particular problems with organizational hierarchy were noted, which were accompanied by an apparent resistance to inspection and review. Per organizational theorist Victor Thompson, this is an indicator of organizational bureaupathology (1961, p. 155). One such article, dating back to August 7, 1990, titled "[NP1] Hindered by Bureaucracy," described "A lumbering bureaucracy, onerous regulations and a complicated chain of command hinder [NP1] from rushing to the scene when disaster hits" (*Observer-Reporter*). As evidence, the author cites a survey of 100 emergency management officials undertaken by the publication where over half of the respondents reported "significant problems regarding who was in charge when [NP1] was involved in an operation" (*Observer-Reporter* 1990). More recently, NP1 has been subject to federal citations due to their bureaucratic structure, which appears to lack adequate processes for inspection and review. In 2006, the U.S. Food and Drug Administration (FDA) announced they fined NP1 $4.2 million for multiple breaches of federal laws and FDA regulations. In their consent decree, NP1 was asked to "establish clear lines of managerial control" (FDA, 2006), In this and other press releases, it was announced the FDA placed NP1 under a consent decree in 1993, which was amended in 2003 to allow the FDA to impose "significant fines for failure to comply with agency regulations" (FDA, 2010). Overall, between 2003 and 2006, the FDA sent NP1 seven letters and assessed a total of $5.7 million in penalties. In 2010, the FDA fined NP1 another $16 million for "mismanagement" among other agency problems. In their press release dated June 17, 2010, the FDA reported the conducted inspections of NP1 in 2008 and 2009, which revealed a failure to "identify problems" and "adequately investigate." As of that time, the FDA said it had sent 12 letters to NP1 and imposed a total of $21 million in fines, under the 2003 consent decree.

Then, in 2012, the Department of Health and Human Services (HHS) intervened and assessed an additional $9.5 million penalty. In a letter dated January 13, 2012, they documented the previous inspections of the FDA of 16 different U.S. facilities and determined multiple violations. The decree violations outlined included the following: Inadequate Managerial Control, Inadequate QA, Failure to Comply with Reporting Requirements, Inadequate Problem Management (including Lookback Investigations), a Failure to Follow Standard Operating Procedure, Inadequate Training and Staffing Levels, and Inadequate Record Keeping. In response to these findings, the head of compliance of the Center for Biologics Evaluation and Research (CBER) at the FDA stated the problems NP1 experienced were "partly attributed to a lack of continuity in the organization's leadership team". Critics said the fines against NP1 should have been even higher (Kolvea, 2012).

NP1 appears to have taken measures to rectify their massive bureaucracy in the past. In 1991, NP1 an oversight committee planned a massive overhaul, to include "replacing the top-heavy Washington- dominated structure with a regional operation." Overall, the committee noted a condition of "mistrust and lack of accountability to be central problems" (*San Francisco Examiner* 1991).

Although the true effects of the committee's efforts are unknown, the recent actions of NP1 workers would suggest the negative effects of bureaucracy still exist. According to recent reports, 4,500 NP1 workers walked out on their jobs and protested due to agency bureaucracy, which they blamed for inadequate wages (Clarke, 2013; Ward, 2013).

President Obama also acknowledged the issue of bureaucracy as it pertained to this organization. When speaking to the public from an NP1 location in 2012, following Hurricane Sandy, President Obama warned "no bureaucracy, no red tape" (The White House, 2012).

It is believed, due to a lack of organizational documentation, the bureaucratic structure of NP1 is so massive that it cannot be easily elucidated or depicted. In terms of a formal organization structure, NP1 doesn't make this clear in their public facing materials. On their website, they have a Congressional Charter and a list of corporate officers. Once such document entitled "Governance for the 21st Century" was over 145 pages long and didn't include a chart. Likewise, a search of their website for "Organization Chart" and "Organization Structure" didn't yield any charts, documents, or other materials that might clarify the overall organizational makeup. Few organization charts were immediately located, and they tended to reflect small factions of the agency, such as the Office of Development Service, and one depicting a particular service offered by NP1, which was dated November 1942.

To examine the perception of bureaucracy on the part of NP1 employees, company reviews were examined on Glassdoor. On Glassdoor, as of February 21, 2014, 457 reviews of NP1 were posted by anonymous sources that identified as current and past NP1 employees. Overall, NP1 received an average rating of a 3.1 on a 5-point scale. The reviews analyzed for this examination were limited to those reviews where the respondents "rated" the company to be "below average," or in this case, rated it under three stars. This limited the number of reviews included for examination to 170, which constituted approximately 37% of all reviews.

Of these reviewers, 150, or 88% made reference to specific terminology related to bureaucracy and excessive bureaucracy. The number of respondents and comments are not equivalent, because in certain cases, respondents' comments were counted more than once when their comments spanned multiple categories. The total number of comments was 343. The comments examined were posted to the website between June 12, 2008, and February 21, 2014.

General and specific references to attributes of bureaucracy and bureaupathic or excessive bureaucracy were as presented in Tables 6.26 through 6.28.

Hotline Specifications

NP1 operates two hotlines, both managed by a third-party vendor, Global Compliance Inc (now NAVEX Global). Of these hotlines, the Concern Connection Line (hereinafter referred to as "hotline") is dedicated to receiving complaints regarding fraud, waste, abuse, safety concerns, and unethical conduct. NP1 also operates a second hotline, which is used to handle complaints of a specific nature, relative to a commodity supplied by the business. The statistics concerning the

Table 6.26   NP1 Hotline Metrics

Fiscal Year	Time Period	Number of Employees	Average Benchmarking Figure: Size, Industry	Calls Expected per Benchmarking	Delta
2013	July 1, 2012–June 30, 2013	31,000	7.61 per 1,000 9.94 per 1,000 = 8.78 (9)	279	+481

Table 6.27   NP1 Social Media/Bureaucracy Summary

Attribute	Data	Analysis
Time frame	6/11/08–2/21/14	1.5% of all employees (31,000)
Population	457	37% of the population (457)
Sample set	170	0.55% of all employees (31,000)
Respondents indicating bureaucracy or bureaupathic behaviors	150	88% of the sample set (170) 33% of the population (457) 0.50% of all employees (31,000)
Total comments indicating bureaucracy and bureaupathology	343	99 Bureaucracy 244 Bureaupathic
Bureaucracy	99	General (6) Hierarchy of authority (23) System of rules (20) Technical expertise (2) Career service (14) Insistence in the rights of office (34)
Bureaupathic	244	Impersonal treatment (113) Prolonged role enactment (15) Resistance to change (35) Resistance to interrogation and investigation (79) Strict reliance on organizational rules and procedures (2)

number of calls made to either hotline are not externally publicized but were provided upon request for research purposes.

Based on information provided by NP1, although their hotline was implemented following the Sarbanes–Oxley Act of 2002, there was no connection. According to an employee of NP1, the hotline was implemented in 2003 "primarily due to the increase in fraud cases due to the 911 fund being established. [NP1] needed a mechanism for the public as well as employees to report fraud, waste and abuse." Reason being, per the NP1 employee, "As a nonprofit, we do not officially fall under SOX, but we actually do follow all the prescribed recommendations as closely as possible i.e. ...report quarterly to the audit committee of our board" (2013).

On NP1's website, the hotline contact information is accessible to employees and the public from their "Contact Us" page, where there is a link for "Reporting fraud,

Table 6.28 NP1 Social Media/Bureaucracy Dataset

Count	Type	Attribute	Comment	Date
1.	Bureaucracy	General	"Bureaucracy hampers productivity"	6/12/08
2.	Bureaucracy	Technical expertise	"Technology used to control and monitor employees rather than enable them to be more productive"	6/12/08
3.	Bureaupathology	Resistance to interrogation and investigation	"They [senior management] don't take advice, I wouldn't bother"	6/12/08
4.	Bureaupathology	Impersonal treatment	"Management expects you to be available 100% of the time because you are working for a voluntary agency"	6/18/08
5.	Bureaucracy	System of rules	"A simple business that overcomplexifies itself to the point to dysfunction"	7/7/08
6.	Bureaucracy	System of rules	"Overcomplexification of processes makes work overproceduralized and dehumanizing"	7/7/08
7.	Bureaupathology	Impersonal treatment	"Always on call"	7/7/08
8.	Bureaupathology	Strict reliance on organizational rules and procedures	"Trust employees. Stop trying to document every second of the workday and let people do their jobs"	7/7/08

(Continued)

Table 6.28 *(Continued)* **NP1 Social Media/Bureaucracy Dataset**

Count	Type	Attribute	Comment	Date
9.	Bureaupathology	Impersonal treatment	"Employee morale is low, turnover is high and employee recognition and work life balance is bad"	7/8/08
10.	Bureaucracy	Career service	"Any employee with seniority is seen as part of the problem, and therefore is discounted, ignored or displaced"	7/9/08
11.	Bureaupathology	Resistance to change	"Significant change is required to save the business, and new regimes fail to study the situation before they enact solutions, which are always misdirected"	7/9/08
12.	Bureaucracy	Hierarchy of authority	"Inability to empower staff to make their own decisions so we have to go up to the senior vice president sometimes for a routine question"	7/11/08
13.	Bureaupathology	Resistance to interrogation and investigation	"Lack of accountability"	7/11/08
14.	Bureaupathology	Resistance to interrogation and investigation	"Tell us what you know. Don't let rumors circulate for months before saying anything"	7/11/08
15.	Bureaupathology	Prolonged role enactment	"Paying unnecessary management"	8/12/08

(Continued)

Table 6.28 *(Continued)* **NP1 Social Media/Bureaucracy Dataset**

Count	Type	Attribute	Comment	Date
16.	Bureaupathology	Resistance to investigation and interrogation	"There is a 'waste' of donated income"	8/12/08
17.	Bureaupathology	Resistance to interrogation and investigation	"Our financial situation is terrible (and getting worse)"	8/21/08
18.	Bureaupathology	Resistance to interrogation and investigation	"Increase communication about the financial solvency of the organization to employees and to the public"	8/21/08
19.	Bureaupathology	Resistance to interrogation and investigation	"Misuse of funds is causing [NP1] to go under"	9/17/08
20.	Bureaupathology	Resistance to interrogation and investigation	"The public has lost trust in [NP1] with all the scandals both nationally and locally"	9/17/08
21.	Bureaucracy	Career service	"Much dead wood is still afloat within the organization"	9/28/08
22.	Bureaucracy	Insistence on the rights of office	"Several key executives are grossly unqualified and lack basic management and leadership skills"	9/28/08
23.	Bureaupathology	Resistance to interrogation and investigation	"There is a lot of nepotism and favoritism to go around"	9/28/08

(Continued)

Table 6.28 *(Continued)* NP1 Social Media/Bureaucracy Dataset

Count	Type	Attribute	Comment	Date
24.	Bureaupathology	Resistance to interrogation and investigation	"Evidence of long term patterns of malfeasance, discrimination, and even corruption"	10/1/08
25.	Bureaupathology	Resistance to interrogation and investigation	"Misallocation of donor monies and volunteer time"	10/1/08
26.	Bureaupathology	Resistance to interrogation and investigation	"Repeated violations of key federal and state regulations"	10/1/08
27.	Bureaupathology	Resistance to interrogation and investigation	"Expensive use of PR to stifle criticism and dodge accountability"	10/1/08
28.	Bureaupathology	Resistance to interrogation and investigation	"Deep structural cronyism"	10/1/08
29.	Bureaupathology	Resistance to interrogation and investigation	"Management desperately needs strict oversight, rigorous training in governance, transparency and service delivery"	10/1/08
30.	Bureaupathology	Resistance to interrogation and investigation	"Left to flounder when called to defend your work, not defended by your direct manager"	10/2/08
31.	Bureaupathology	Resistance to interrogation and investigation	"Malfeasance, incompetence, cronyism and arrogance"	10/2/08

(Continued)

Table 6.28 *(Continued)* **NP1 Social Media/Bureaucracy Dataset**

Count	Type	Attribute	Comment	Date
32.	Bureaupathology	Impersonal treatment	"It is the most thankless job out there, management does not care about you at all"	10/25/08
33.	Bureaupathology	Resistance to interrogation and investigation	"Incompetent leadership, lack of performance benchmarks, lack of accountability to the public, lack of oversight"	11/18/08
34.	Bureaupathology	Resistance to interrogation and investigation	"[NP1] needs regulatory help"	11/19/08
35.	Bureaupathology	Resistance to interrogation and investigation	"The consent decree and constant warnings from the FDA make the work environment difficult and destroys morale. I suspect senior management is incapable of leading the company out of its regulatory crisis. I mean it's been 22 years on the consent decree"	11/19/08
36.	Bureaucracy	Insistence on the rights of office	"Management governs by fear and innuendo when no one is looking...otherwise it treats employees, volunteers and like a used car salesman, not a philanthropic organization with a serious life saving job to do"	12/16/08

(Continued)

Table 6.28 *(Continued)* **NP1 Social Media/Bureaucracy Dataset**

Count	Type	Attribute	Comment	Date
37.	Bureaupathology	Resistance to interrogation and investigation	"We need a charity cop to save the organization from itself"	12/16/08
38.	Bureaupathology	Resistance to interrogation and investigation	"[NP1] It's run like a mob pizza restaurant where the cops eat free…[senior management] turn yourselves in"	12/16/08
39.	Bureaupathology	Resistance to interrogation and investigation	"Within 3 months of working here, even the most naïve and well-intentioned state wondering how the management goes on collecting paychecks and perks like energizer bunnies without ever being held to account [sic] by their superiors in DC or the IRS"	12/16/08
40.	Bureaupathology	Resistance to change	"The culture and embedded leadership make it difficult to move the organization into the current and necessary climate. Institutionalized inertia"	1/3/09
41.	Bureaucracy	General	"There is a lot of red tape; it's a top heavy organization"	1/16/09
42.	Bureaupathology	Resistance to change	"Lazy about change"	1/25/09

(Continued)

Table 6.28 *(Continued)*   **NP1 Social Media/Bureaucracy Dataset**

Count	Type	Attribute	Comment	Date
43.	Bureaupathology	Resistance to interrogation and investigation	"Come for the mission, leave because of the ethics"	1/25/09
44.	Bureaucracy	General	"Excuse people who weigh the organization down with negative attitudes, political red tape and drama"	2/4/09
45.	Bureaucracy	Insistence on the rights of office	"In many way NP1 is another company with politics that hinder productivity, egos that hinder effectiveness and stubbornness that hinders success"	2/4/09
46.	Bureaucracy	Insistence on the rights of office	"Practice what you preach"	2/4/09
47.	Bureaupathology	Resistance to change	"The executives at headquarters are change resistant and disengenous"	2/4/09
48.	Bureaucracy	Insistence on the rights of office	"Road staff held responsible for poor communications and errors of management; little appreciation"	3/7/09
49.	Bureaupathology	Impersonal treatment	"Never any positive feedback from employers, you're only aware of your job performance when something is wrong, and then it is probably too late"	3/7/09

(Continued)

Table 6.28 (Continued)   NP1 Social Media/Bureaucracy Dataset

Count	Type	Attribute	Comment	Date
50.	Bureaupathology	Impersonal treatment	"Treat people how you want us to treat the public"	3/7/09
51.	Bureaucracy	Career service	"Lack of growth potential, no encouragement to succeed"	3/11/09
52.	Bureaupathology	Impersonal treatment	"Total lack of respect [for employees]	3/11/09
53.	Bureaupathology	Resistance to change	"The organization is also stuck in the past, refusing to move along with the times"	3/11/09
54.	Bureaupathology	Resistance to change	"There are no consequences for toxic employees"	7/22/09
55.	Bureaucracy	Career service	"Promotions are basically not an option"	12/22/09
56.	Bureaupathology	Impersonal treatment	"Inability to accommodate a life outside of work"	12/22/09
57.	Bureaupathology	Impersonal treatment	"A place where you are taken for granted"	12/22/09
58.	Bureaupathology	Impersonal treatment	"Treat all employees with respect"	12/22/09
59.	Bureaupathology	Resistance to change	"Update equipment"	12/22/09
60.	Bureaupathology	Resistance to change	"Equipment is in poor condition and technology is outdating"	12/22/09
61.	Bureaupathology	Resistance to interrogation and investigation	"Misuse of company funds"	12/22/09

(Continued)

Table 6.28 *(Continued)* **NP1 Social Media/Bureaucracy Dataset**

Count	Type	Attribute	Comment	Date
62.	Bureaupathology	Resistance to interrogation and investigation	"Manager [sic] money more efficiently"	12/22/09
63.	Bureaupathology	Resistance to change	"Start listening to folks doing the actual work"	1/18/10
64.	Bureaucracy	Career service	"People are promoted based on longevity and politics rather than merit and ability"	3/31/10
65.	Bureaupathology	Impersonal treatment	"It is common for managers to be verbally abusive—I will never forget the weekly, day-long meetings for which management planned nothing but kept employees captive for 8 hours. They would bluster, threaten, cajole, insult, abuse, argue, swear at, stomp around and pontificate to employees. Most employees either lost their temper, threatened to quit or cried at work at one time or another. All of the staff at every level were openly frustrated and sarcastic, and appropriately so. It was the most dysfunctional,	3/31/10

(Continued)

Table 6.28 *(Continued)*   **NP1 Social Media/Bureaucracy Dataset**

Count	Type	Attribute	Comment	Date
			abusive work environment I've ever encountered and ruined what could have otherwise been the most rewarding job imaginable"	
66.	Bureaucracy	Insistence on the rights of office	"Management tries to get you to work harder by using guilt and fear"	7/1/10
67.	Bureaucracy	System of rules	"Rules, rules, rules, rules, rules"	7/1/10
68.	Bureaucracy	System of rules	"Staff are treated as children, with constant micromanagement, and tons of rules, by management that has absolutely no idea how the process works"	7/1/10
69.	Bureaupathology	Impersonal treatment	"Staff are treated as children, with constant micromanagement"	7/1/10
70.	Bureaupathology	Impersonal treatment	"Rarely does someone compliment you on your hard work, most people looks at us like gears in a machine"	7/1/10
71.	Bureaucracy	Career service	"People have been here so long that they do not have innovation or energy"	7/13/10
72.	Bureaucracy	General	"Bureaucracy"	7/13/10

(Continued)

Table 6.28 *(Continued)* **NP1 Social Media/Bureaucracy Dataset**

Count	Type	Attribute	Comment	Date
73.	Bureaupathology	Impersonal treatment	"My job is not what was discussed in interviews. In fact, there was a switcheroo after I started which is incredibly unprofessional and speaks to weak organization and communication skills"	7/13/10
74.	Bureaucracy	Career service	"Long time staff are entrenched in a culture of operational loss"	8/21/10
75.	Bureaucracy	Career service	"In this job market, there should be no problem hiring top talent to purge the current employ of the dead wood that permeates the organization. We have plenty of people locally that are hanging on for retirement. Put them out to pasture"	8/21/10
76.	Bureaupathology	Resistance to change	"Current national HQ operational policies are outdated and unmaintained"	8/21/10
77.	Bureaupathology	Resistance to interrogation and investigation	"Accountability is no where to be found"	8/21/10
78.	Bureaucracy	System of rules	"Very complicated place to work"	9/14/10

(Continued)

Table 6.28 *(Continued)* **NP1 Social Media/Bureaucracy Dataset**

Count	Type	Attribute	Comment	Date
79.	Bureaupathology	Resistance to change	"If you try to bring in fresh ideas, watch out"	9/14/10
80.	Bureaupathology	Resistance to change	"…Chapter leaders, many of which have been there FOREVER—do not have the skill set to change"	9/14/10
81.	Bureaupathology	Impersonal treatment	"Constantly working overtime and horrible managers"	9/25/10
82.	Bureaupathology	Impersonal treatment	"No career growth, no career advancement, low pay, horrible hours, nonsupportive management"	11/17/10
83.	Bureaupathology	Impersonal treatment	"Provide balance between work and life"	11/17/10
84.	Bureaupathology	Resistance to interrogation and investigation	"Management is 100% inflexible. There is a very strong "Good Ole' Boys (mostly gals) network which protects itself, and harasses people who question them or defend themselves against them. The Human Resources Department exists solely for the protection of the organization and is mean spirited, ruthless and dishonest to the employees.	12/19/10

(Continued)

Table 6.28 *(Continued)*   **NP1 Social Media/Bureaucracy Dataset**

Count	Type	Attribute	Comment	Date
			Even if you have had excellent job performance and multiple promotions, questioning the wrong person or the wrong policy will set you on a course which will in one way or another cause your employment to end"	
85.	Bureaupathology	Resistance to interrogation and investigation	"Be honest. Ask yourself how many times you have had to compromise your principles to be where you are today"	12/19/10
86.	Bureaucracy	Hierarchy of authority	"Complete lack of professionalism permeates executive management team, which filters down and translates into extremely low employee morale and high attrition rate"	1/14/11
87.	Bureaupathology	Impersonal treatment	"No work/life balance including limited PTO/ sick time"	1/14/11
88.	Bureaupathology	Resistance to change	"Lack of new ideas"	2/22/11
89.	Bureaucracy	Insistence on the rights of office	"At the mercy of a regional vice presidents whims"	3/11/11

(Continued)

Table 6.28 *(Continued)* **NP1 Social Media/Bureaucracy Dataset**

Count	Type	Attribute	Comment	Date
90.	Bureaupathology	Impersonal treatment	"[The company] needs to value their employees. They treat me like I am a number"	3/17/11
91.	Bureaupathology	Impersonal treatment	"Management showed lack of caring for employees"	3/23/11
92.	Bureaupathology	Impersonal treatment	"Misled in interview"	4/16/11
93.	Bureaupathology	Resistance to interrogation or investigation	"If there were issues or problems no one took responsibility for their mistakes"	4/16/11
94.	Bureaucracy	Insistence on the rights of office	"Management threats with disdain"	5/20/11
95.	Bureaupathology	Impersonal treatment	"Not realistic or up-front AT ALL about the real hours or activities involved in this position...increase professionalism. Be honest with new hires"	6/7/11
96.	Bureaupathology	Impersonal treatment	"Poor management, lack of respect for employees"	6/8/11
97.	Bureaucracy	Insistence on the rights of office	"The managers are not rulers or leaders who show no respect for the dedication of the employees"	6/22/11

(Continued)

Table 6.28 *(Continued)* **NP1 Social Media/Bureaucracy Dataset**

Count	Type	Attribute	Comment	Date
98.	Bureaupathology	Resistance to interrogation and investigation	"This organization is corrupted by nepotism and waste"	6/22/11
99.	Bureaupathology	Resistance to interrogation and investigation	"You are not accountable for anything"	7/14/11
100.	Bureaupathology	Resistance to interrogation and investigation	"Extremely inefficient, often does not live up to the public trust. Not a lot of accountability"	8/3/11
101.	Bureaupathology	Impersonal treatment	"If you want to work somewhere were people treat you like a child, step right up"	8/14/11
102.	Bureaupathology	Impersonal treatment	"Management treats you like a child"	8/14/11
103.	Bureaupathology	Resistance to change	"Technology is terrible"	8/14/11
104.	Bureaupathology	Resistance to change	"Sales methodologies and attitudes are very dated"	8/14/11
105.	Bureaupathology	Prolonged role enactment	"Dead end with no stability"	8/25/11
106.	Bureaupathology	Prolonged role enactment	"No scope for upward mobility"	8/25/11
107.	Bureaupathology	Impersonal treatment	"Constant harassment and incompetence"	9/21/11

(Continued)

Table 6.28 *(Continued)* **NP1 Social Media/Bureaucracy Dataset**

Count	Type	Attribute	Comment	Date
108.	Bureaupathology	Impersonal treatment	"The collections department is not allowed to have breaks longer than 30 minutes, even when working long shift, which seems as though it is illegal"	9/21/11
109.	Bureaupathology	Resistance to interrogation and investigation	"I heard jokes and offensive comments...I spoke up and nothing was done"	9/21/11
110.	Bureaupathology	Resistance to interrogation and investigation	"If you don't do something serious, someone is going to file a lawsuit for a hostile work environment soon"	9/21/11
111.	Bureaucracy	Insistence on the rights of office	"Management seems to only want money"	10/4/11
112.	Bureaupathology	Impersonal treatment	"Learn to be nice and helpful—not mean and controlling"	10/4/11
113.	Bureaucracy	Insistence on the rights of office	"Had to deal with egotistical attitudes of the senior staff who felt they knew everything and could do everything better than anyone else"	10/6/11

(Continued)

Table 6.28 *(Continued)* **NP1 Social Media/Bureaucracy Dataset**

Count	Type	Attribute	Comment	Date
114.	Bureaucracy	System of rules	"So much pressure on doing everything right that you can't get anything done and one you mess up or potentially make them [sic] upper management mad then say good bye to your job"	10/26/11
115.	Bureaupathology	Impersonal treatment	"They treat you as if you can be easily replaced. No respect for anyone"	10/26/11
116.	Bureaucracy	Insistence on the rights of office	"Take some customer service classes. Hire and retain efficient and caring workers instead of those who just agree with you"	11/22/11
117.	Bureaucracy	Insistence on the rights of office	"Many senior management.....play politics and don't really care about helping the customer"	11/22/11
118.	Bureaupathology	Impersonal treatment	"There is absolutely no respect for personal/family time"	12/6/11
119.	Bureaupathology	Impersonal treatment	"Abusive and unhealthy management practices toward employees"	12/6/11
120.	Bureaupathology	Impersonal treatment	"No respect for employees"	1/25/12

(Continued)

Table 6.28 *(Continued)* **NP1 Social Media/Bureaucracy Dataset**

Count	Type	Attribute	Comment	Date
121.	Bureaupathology	Resistance to interrogation and investigation	"HR staff is not aware of half the things that management does"	1/25/12
122.	Bureaupathology	Resistance to change	"Untold $millions have been wasted in a revolving door of consultants with elaborate and unworkable 'solutions' which have either never been implemented or are only partially installed, and less efficient and less effective than prior systems, methods"	2/26/12
123.	Bureaupathology	Resistance to change	"Alleged 'experts' both consultants and senior leadership are clueless at identifying root causes of problems, developing expedient solutions and implementing needed changes"	2/26/12
124.	Bureaupathology	Resistance to interrogation and investigation	"Leadership that wastes money, resources and opportunities"	2/26/12
125.	Bureaupathology	Resistance to interrogation and investigation	"Long term employees are pushed aside, or terminated for presenting realistic assessments of the ongoing failures and weaknesses of the most fashionable 'transformation'"	2/26/12

(Continued)

Table 6.28 *(Continued)*   **NP1 Social Media/Bureaucracy Dataset**

Count	Type	Attribute	Comment	Date
126.	Bureaucracy	Hierarchy of authority	"HQ senior management and board of governors tragically clueless"	3/1/12
127.	Bureaupathology	Prolonged role enactment	"Political, very less [sic] opportunities for growth"	3/24/12
128.	Bureaupathology	Resistance to interrogation and investigation	"And lower those crazy salaries that CEOs are making. [current CEO] makes over 1.2 million a year!!!??? Ridiculous for a non profit"	3/24/12
129.	Bureaupathology	Prolonged role enactment	"Quit promotion your friends and buddys [sic] and promote people that have worked their way up from the bottom"	4/1/12
130.	Bureaucracy	Hierarchy of authority	"Do something to allow the most senior management to listen directly to the concerns and frustrations of the front-line employees, without having to filter everything through the insulating layers of management."	4/13/12
131.	Bureaupathology	Impersonal treatment	"Long hours, few breaks"	4/28/12
132.	Bureaupathology	Impersonal treatment	"Put caring for staff above the almighty dollar"	4/28/12

(Continued)

Table 6.28 *(Continued)*   NP1 Social Media/Bureaucracy Dataset

Count	Type	Attribute	Comment	Date
133.	Bureaupathology	Impersonal treatment	"Treat others how you would like to be treated"	4/28/12
134.	Bureaupathology	Impersonal treatment	"Chapter CEO was more concerned in how [sic] their image reflected to volunteers and community rather than taking care of the people within the organization."	4/30/12
135.	Bureaupathology	Impersonal treatment	"No recognition for achievements, rewards only to the 'favorites' and not to people that deserve it, whether it is an employee or volunteer"	4/30/12
136.	Bureaupathology	Resistance to interrogation and investigation	"Little circles within employees looking out for their own agendas (promotions, career advancements, etc.) that trampled the code of conduct and the mission of an organization asa [sic] whole"	4/30/12
137.	Bureaupathology	Prolonged role enactment	"Low morale, high turnover; refuse to fire underperforming/unprofessional staff; few opportunities for professional growth and advancement"	5/8/12

(Continued)

Table 6.28 *(Continued)* **NP1 Social Media/Bureaucracy Dataset**

Count	Type	Attribute	Comment	Date
138.	Bureaucracy	System of Rules	"Morale is at an all time low, and tech's are sick and tired of getting written up or talked to by problem management. Makes us want to work slower and more careful so we don't make mistakes."	6/9/12
139.	Bureaupathology	Resistance to interrogation and investigation	"Consent decree for almost 20 years, are you kidding the American public??ANY private company would shut the heck down by now"	6/9/12
140.	Bureaupathology	Resistance to interrogation and investigation	"Lots of restructuring needed here. I can name management but I'm sorry, I need my job to provide for my family"	6/9/12
141.	Bureaupathology	Resistance to change	"Very old fashioned ideals and practices"	6/18/12
142.	Bureaupathology	Prolonged role enactment	"No advancement for most employees. However, that may depend on the location and if you 'belong' to the right click [sic]"	6/25/12

(Continued)

Table 6.28 *(Continued)*   NP1 Social Media/Bureaucracy Dataset

Count	Type	Attribute	Comment	Date
143.	Bureaucracy	Career service	"No respect for the worker-ants. If you are the manager and above you will get promotions with the exact same responsibilities and tasks, others will stay in the same spot forever"	6/28/12
144.	Bureaucracy	Career service	"If you don't 'shake the boat' you can [sic] some job stability for a few yrs"	6/28/12
145.	Bureaucracy	Insistence on the rights of office	"Upper management does not inspire any respect or trust"	6/28/12
146.	Bureaupathology	Resistance to change	"Management very poor—not technologically inclined or smart, egoistic, lazy and can get envious of staff trying to rise [sic]"	6/28/12
147.	Bureaupathology	Resistance to interrogation and investigation	"Frequent layoffs and they will target people…who have made valid concerns about the process, waste, etc."	6/28/12
148.	Bureaupathology	Impersonal treatment	"In the last 5 years, there have been repeated rounds of restructuring and layoffs, resulting in insane amounts of turn-over and a staff is more worried about their jobs than service delivery"	7/1/12

(Continued)

Table 6.28 *(Continued)* **NP1 Social Media/Bureaucracy Dataset**

Count	Type	Attribute	Comment	Date
149.	Bureaupathology	Impersonal treatment	"You are yelled at almost daily and degraded"	7/27/12
150.	Bureaupathology	Strict reliance on organizational rules and procedures	"Most direction is given by email so that a person can track their request because they have a lack of trust in each other"	7/27/12
151.	Bureaupathology	Resistance to interrogation and investigation	"Lots of CYA and no accountability"	8/3/12
152.	Bureaucracy	System of rules	"Way too many changes result in disorganized execution and trying to make one size fits all results in many, many lost opportunities"	8/9/12
153.	Bureaucracy	System of rules	"Stop the silos and kingdom building and work as one organization not little kingdoms inside an organization"	8/9/12
154.	Bureaupathology	Prolonged role enactment	"Take the shackles off staff and let them do the jobs they are hired to do"	8/9/12
155.	Bureaupathology	Resistance to change	"They do not listen or value [employee] input at a professional level"	8/9/12

(Continued)

Table 6.28 *(Continued)*   **NP1 Social Media/Bureaucracy Dataset**

Count	Type	Attribute	Comment	Date
156.	Bureaucracy	Hierarchy of authority	"Confusing reporting structure and divisive relationship between chapters"	9/17/12
157.	Bureaucracy	Hierarchy of authority	"Internal competition destroys the morale"	9/17/12
158.	Bureaucracy	Insistence on the rights of office	"[To CEO] your immediate staff sends the message internally that you are scary and should be feared"	9/17/12
159.	Bureaucracy	System of rules	"Break down the silos and get people communicating"	9/17/12
160.	Bureaupathology	Resistance to interrogation and investigation	"Stop putting underperformers and problem employees who lack experience in management positions"	9/17/12
161.	Bureaupathology	Impersonal treatment	"60–70 hour workweek is not only common, but expected"	10/13/12
162.	Bureaupathology	Impersonal treatment	"Absolutely no work life balance"	10/13/12
163.	Bureaupathology	Impersonal treatment	"The pressure is constant and employees regularly go weeks without one day off"	10/13/12
164.	Bureaupathology	Impersonal treatment	"The leave policy in my division is this: the only excusable leave is bereavement leave"	10/16/12
165.	Bureaupathology	Impersonal treatment	"They treat their employees horribly"	11/2/12

(Continued)

Table 6.28 *(Continued)*   NP1 Social Media/Bureaucracy Dataset

Count	Type	Attribute	Comment	Date
166.	Bureaupathology	Impersonal treatment	"This organization strips you of your work ethic and degrades your skills"	11/2/12
167.	Bureaupathology	Impersonal treatment	"A revolving door and most of those going out are key talent that management should strive to retain"	11/2/12
168.	Bureaupathology	Resistance to interrogation and investigation	"Very wasteful of the resources they have and not open to very simple changes to improve"	11/2/12
169.	Bureaucracy	Insistence on the rights of office	"Loading the upper management with overpaid Directors and getting rid of the folks who do the actual work"	11/15/12
170.	Bureaupathology	Impersonal treatment	"There is no work/life balance. If you have young children, keep looking"	12/1/12
171.	Bureaupathology	Impersonal treatment	"Learn how to improve work/life balance"	12/4/12
172.	Bureaucracy	Insistence on the rights of office	"Local management was abrasive with employees and offered little support"	12/12/12
173.	Bureaupathology	Impersonal treatment	"VERY poor work life balance as you are always expected to respond on a moment's notice"	12/12/12

(Continued)

Table 6.28 *(Continued)*   **NP1 Social Media/Bureaucracy Dataset**

Count	Type	Attribute	Comment	Date
174.	Bureaupathology	Impersonal treatment	"Employees work very long hours and often 7 days a week. Employees are expected to answer their phones and emails immediately at all hours"	12/14/12
175.	Bureaucracy	Hierarchy of authority	"No empowerment between line staff and management"	1/10/13
176.	Bureaupathology	Prolonged role enactment	"Promotions are hard to come by and they don't reward top talent"	1/10/13
177.	Bureaupathology	Impersonal treatment	"Anyone who gives notice to terminate is harassed and has it held over their head until they leave"	1/11/13
178.	Bureaupathology	Prolonged role enactment	"Horrible career development opportunities and room for growth"	1/11/13
179.	Bureaupathology	Resistance to interrogation and investigation	"No accountability"	1/13/13
180.	Bureaupathology	Resistance to interrogation and investigation	"Executives making sweeping changes based on politics, then falsify numbers to look good"	1/13/13
181.	Bureaupathology	Resistance to interrogation and investigation	"Good ol' [sic] boy hotel"	1/13/13

(Continued)

Table 6.28 *(Continued)*   NP1 Social Media/Bureaucracy Dataset

Count	Type	Attribute	Comment	Date
182.	Bureaucracy	General	"Lots of tension between departments"	2/5/13
183.	Bureaucracy	Hierarchy of authority	"It was impossible to get departments to talk and coordinate"	2/21/13
184.	Bureaupathology	Impersonal treatment	"Management treats you like a worthless commodity"	2/22/13
185.	Bureaupathology	Impersonal treatment	"There is no work/life balance"	2/22/13
186.	Bureaupathology	Impersonal treatment	"Employee turnover is high, many employees hired simply to be a body to fit scheduling purposes"	2/22/13
187.	Bureaucracy	Hierarchy of authority	"Hardworking loyal paid staff have no voice"	2/25/13
188.	Bureaupathology	Impersonal treatment	"Long hours kills family life"	2/25/13
189.	Bureaupathology	Resistance to change	"Slow to respond to change"	2/25/13
190.	Bureaupathology	Resistance to interrogation and investigation	"Good ole [sic] boy network at its best!"	2/25/13
191.	Bureaupathology	Impersonal treatment	"Treat you like little kids"	2/28/13
192.	Bureaupathology	Resistance to interrogation and investigation	"Basically keep your mouth shut and never ask questions"	2/28/13

(Continued)

Table 6.28 *(Continued)* NP1 Social Media/Bureaucracy Dataset

Count	Type	Attribute	Comment	Date
193.	Bureaupathology	Impersonal treatment	"The people who do the work come with extensive knowledge and should be valued more than they are currently"	3/9/13
194.	Bureaucracy	System of rules	"It is a high risk, low rewards type environment with bosses always hounding you for not doing work to their standards"	3/14/13
195.	Bureaucracy	Career service	"Career development is challenging and difficult"	3/27/13
196.	Bureaucracy	Hierarchy of authority	"Upper management is disconnected"	3/27/13
197.	Bureaupathology	Resistance to change	"Great mission often overshadowed by overwhelming internal concerns and inability to adapt to change"	3/27/13
198.	Bureaupathology	Resistance to change	"Very slow to adapt to changing technologies and trends"	3/27/13
199.	Bureaucracy	Hierarchy of authority	"Loaded with upper level management"	4/26/13
200.	Bureaucracy	Insistence on the rights of office	"No leadership accountability"	4/26/13
201.	Bureaupathology	Impersonal treatment	"Communications— either there are very little or it is misleading or incorrect"	4/26/13

(Continued)

Table 6.28 *(Continued)* **NP1 Social Media/Bureaucracy Dataset**

Count	Type	Attribute	Comment	Date
202.	Bureaupathology	Impersonal treatment	"they treat you like you are in high school"	4/27/13
203.	Bureaucracy	System of rules	"You will be micromanaged"	4/27/13
204.	Bureaupathology	Impersonal treatment	"If you are a mindless sheep, then you will like it there"	4/27/13
205.	Bureaupathology	Resistance to interrogation and investigation	"Clean house fast! This company has a bunch of lawsuits waiting to happen"	4/27/13
206.	Bureaucracy	Career service	"No procedures for removing nonperforming employees leaving everyone else stuck cleaning up the mess"	5/8/13
207.	Bureaucracy	Insistence on the rights of office	"Not the best management and long hours. They expect you to be on their call no exceptions"	5/16/13
208.	Bureaupathology	Impersonal treatment	"Very vague management that used corporate buzz words instead of providing clear and concise instructions"	5/16/13
209.	Bureaupathology	Impersonal treatment	"This organization once made me feel like I was making a difference and now I feel like I'm a cash cow and all they care about is the money coming in"	5/22/13

(Continued)

Table 6.28 *(Continued)*   NP1 Social Media/Bureaucracy Dataset

Count	Type	Attribute	Comment	Date
210.	Bureaucracy	Hierarchy of authority	"CEO completely out of touch"	5/24/13
211.	Bureaucracy	System of rules	"Decisions are made in a vacuum"	5/24/13
212.	Bureaupathology	Impersonal treatment	"No sense of neutrality and objectivity"	5/24/13
213.	Bureaupathology	Impersonal treatment	"Give everyone a chance to be heard and express their ideas. Let people feel included and part of the decision making process when possible"	5/24/13
214.	Bureaupathology	Resistance to change	"HR practices have historically been corrupt"	5/24/13
215.	Bureaupathology	Resistance to interrogation and investigation	"Only those that suddenly fall out of the favorites list get investigated or reprimanded"	5/24/13
216.	Bureaupathology	Resistance to interrogation and investigation	"I have seen many good, ethical people leave out of disgust"	5/24/13
217.	Bureaupathology	Resistance to interrogation and investigation	"Do not turn a blind eye when you know someone is doing something wrong. Hold ethics above all else. Hold everyone accountable equally"	5/24/13

(Continued)

Table 6.28 *(Continued)* **NP1 Social Media/Bureaucracy Dataset**

Count	Type	Attribute	Comment	Date
218.	Bureaupathology	Impersonal treatment	"[Changes] made for a fun job to just being treated like a 'widget' making $$$$$ for them"	6/15/13
219.	Bureaucracy	Career service	"…Many 'lifers' left"	6/15/13
220.	Bureaucracy	Insistence on the rights of office	"Stop barking orders"	6/15/13
221.	Bureaupathology	Impersonal treatment	"Stop exploiting your workforce's dedication"	6/15/13
222.	Bureaupathology	Impersonal treatment	"Have loyalty to employees"	6/15/13
223.	Bureaupathology	Resistance to change	"Management quickly angered by feedback provided or when asked for help"	6/15/13
224.	Bureaupathology	Resistance to change	"Take the time to strategize with employee feedback how to create change"	6/15/13
225.	Bureaupathology	Resistance to interrogation and investigation	"With [CEO] making over $600k+ extensive benefit package and any managers/board meetings having catered lunches, among other wasted expenses, how do you expect anyone to donate to NP1 thinking its going to a good cause?"	6/15/13

(Continued)

Table 6.28 *(Continued)*   **NP1 Social Media/Bureaucracy Dataset**

Count	Type	Attribute	Comment	Date
226.	Bureaucracy	Insistence on the rights of office	"Daily added unnecessary pressure from management above what is required to do the job"	6/17/13
227.	Bureaucracy	Insistence on the rights of office	"Superiors were hypocrites, expected me to be their slave…"	6/18/13
228.	Bureaucracy	General	"Now being run like a giant corporation"	6/24/13
229.	Bureaupathology	Resistance to change	"Outdated equipment (computers, software)"	6/24/13
230.	Bureaupathology	Resistance to change	"A lack of resources to invest in infrastructure"	7/1/13
231.	Bureaupathology	Impersonal treatment	"Be more passionate to your employees"	7/11/13
232.	Bureaupathology	Prolonged role enactment	"They say you can move up in the company but that's not true"	7/11/13
233.	Bureaupathology	Resistance to interrogation and investigation	"They are misleading to tell you the donations are for a nonprofit, that's a lie"	7/11/13
234.	Bureaucracy	Career service	"There seems to be a heavy concentration in middle management of people staff that have been there a long time and do not seem qualified"	7/19/13

(Continued)

Table 6.28 *(Continued)* **NP1 Social Media/Bureaucracy Dataset**

Count	Type	Attribute	Comment	Date
235.	Bureaucracy	Hierarchy of authority	"Top heavy"	7/19/13
236.	Bureaucracy	Hierarchy of authority	"The org charts by region are amazingly top heavy"	7/19/13
237.	Bureaucracy	Insistence on the rights of office	"People only talk to people with the right title"	7/19/13
238.	Bureaucracy	System of rules	"One of the constant aspects is change; there is constant change and micromanagement like no private sector company I have ever worked with"	7/19/13
239.	Bureaupathology	Impersonal treatment	"Constant fear of reorganization & layoffs as they happen frequently, and if you're not in the right little group, you are outta there!"	7/19/13
240.	Bureaupathology	Impersonal treatment	"I believe they abuse the collections staff"	7/19/13
241.	Bureaupathology	Resistance to interrogation and investigation	"Do a better job of saving money"	7/19/13
242.	Bureaucracy	Hierarchy of authority	"There are no opportunities for career growth"	7/20/13
243.	Bureaucracy	Hierarchy of authority	"The chain of command and my responsibilities changed monthly"	7/26/13

(Continued)

Table 6.28 *(Continued)*   NP1 Social Media/Bureaucracy Dataset

Count	Type	Attribute	Comment	Date
244.	Bureaupathology	Impersonal treatment	"Poor treatment of employees"	7/26/13
245.	Bureaupathology	Impersonal treatment	"Employees are not treated as people, but as another cog in the machine"	7/26/13
246.	Bureaucracy	Insistence on the rights of office	"Employees have had to sue the company because of their prejudices, the management tyrades [sic], the fear felt by the employees personal, emotional and mental, we never knew if we were going to have a job that day or be terminated by the choice of management"	7/27/13
247.	Bureaupathology	Resistance to interrogation and investigation	"Management needs to take staff complaints seriously and address problems instead of ignoring them. If an employee expresses concern about working in a hostile environment, management and HR should address these concerns instead of targeting the staff and allow future retaliation to the point the staff want to leave their job"	7/31/13

(Continued)

Table 6.28 *(Continued)* **NP1 Social Media/Bureaucracy Dataset**

Count	Type	Attribute	Comment	Date
248.	Bureaucracy	Insistence on the rights of office	"Practice what you preach. I saw people get written up for the smallest of infractions and for things I saw managers doing themselves"	8/7/13
249.	Bureaucracy	System of rules	"Quit with the micro management and all the 'write ups'"	8/7/13
250.	Bureaupathology	Impersonal treatment	"Managers playing favorites with some employees and conversely very unfairly punitive with other employees"	8/7/13
251.	Bureaupathology	Impersonal treatment	"The leadership in the company is comprised of fallout from companies that had failed. Now not surprisingly the company had turned into the most unhumanitarian humanitarian organization."	8/7/13
252.	Bureaupathology	Impersonal treatment	"If you don't mind lying to people and being programmed like a robot, well this would be a great position for you"	8/7/13

(Continued)

Table 6.28 *(Continued)*   **NP1 Social Media/Bureaucracy Dataset**

Count	Type	Attribute	Comment	Date
253.	Bureaupathology	Resistance to interrogation and investigation	"Seek sturdy and trustworthy leadership with a proven record of success to try and save the company before the current leadership runs it into the ground"	8/7/13
254.	Bureaupathology	Resistance to interrogation and investigation	"Fiscally irresponsible and failing fast....I would not be surprised to see the company gone in 5 years"	8/7/13
255.	Bureaucracy	Hierarchy of authority	"Departments work in silos and lack communication with others that would allow better functionality"	8/14/13
256.	Bureaucracy	Insistence on the rights of office	"High level positions are mismanaged resulting in layoffs and constant changes"	8/14/13
257.	Bureaupathology	Impersonal treatment	"The decrease in revenue caused senior management to pressure the employees to the point of verbal abuse"	8/14/13
258.	Bureaupathology	Impersonal treatment	"Formal complaints to HR not acknowledged or resolved"	8/14/13

(Continued)

Table 6.28 *(Continued)* NP1 Social Media/Bureaucracy Dataset

Count	Type	Attribute	Comment	Date
259.	Bureaupathology	Resistance to interrogation and investigation	"Provide opportunities for employer [sic] growth instead of finding ways to hinder their performance and looking out for your own back"	8/14/13
260.	Bureaucracy	Insistence on the rights of office	"Most of the 'power' to affect decision-making, along with career growth opportunities are seated with those working at regional or national levels"	9/3/13
261.	Bureaupathology	Impersonal treatment	"There is little appreciation from top management"	9/3/13
262.	Bureaucracy	System of rules	"Pay is low for the perfection the company demands"	9/8/13
263.	Bureaupathology	Impersonal treatment	"Position responsibilities should have been explained better at hiring"	9/8/13
264.	Bureaucracy	Hierarchy of authority	"No communication between departments"	9/11/13
265.	Bureaucracy	Hierarchy of authority	"Top heavy management"	9/11/13
266.	Bureaucracy	Insistence on the rights of office	"Staff pay is very low, yet our regional CEO made $500,000"	9/11/13

(Continued)

Table 6.28 *(Continued)*   **NP1 Social Media/Bureaucracy Dataset**

Count	Type	Attribute	Comment	Date
267.	Bureaucracy	System of rules	"Management and scheduling act like a crime has taken place if you already made plans and can't conform to their every demand"	9/11/13
268.	Bureaupathology	Impersonal treatment	"Crazy hours and white lies"	9/11/13
269.	Bureaupathology	Impersonal treatment	"Impossible to have a life outside of work"	9/11/13
270.	Bureaucracy	Insistence on the rights of office	"Elitist management that is only concerned about their tails and how they appear"	9/24/13
271.	Bureaucracy	Insistence on the rights of office	"Management is very self-serving"	9/24/13
272.	Bureaucracy	Insistence on the rights of office	"Senior management needs to stop leading by fear, everyone is afraid of losing his or her jobs [sic]"	9/24/13
273.	Bureaupathology	Impersonal treatment	"Does not care about workers"	9/24/13
274.	Bureaupathology	Impersonal treatment	"Favoritism with management"	9/24/13
275.	Bureaupathology	Impersonal treatment	"They need to appreciate the workers in the field more and stop treating them as disposable and replaceable"	9/24/13

(Continued)

Table 6.28 *(Continued)*   **NP1 Social Media/Bureaucracy Dataset**

Count	Type	Attribute	Comment	Date
276.	Bureaupathology	Impersonal treatment	"Stop intimidating people so they can work"	9/24/13
277.	Bureaupathology	Impersonal treatment	"Low pay, little room for advancement, uncertain future, favoritism"	9/24/13
278.	Bureaupathology	Prolonged role enactment	"No room for advancement unless you are a favorite, it doesn't matter your education or work ethic"	9/24/13
279.	Bureaupathology	Resistance to interrogation and investigation	"Horrible management with too much favoritism and unethical actions taken"	9/24/13
280.	Bureaupathology	Resistance to interrogation and investigation	"Learn to be fair and ethical"	9/24/13
281.	Bureaupathology	Resistance to interrogation and investigation	"Scheduling department is unethical, by giving friends the good hours and shifts"	9/24/13
282.	Bureaupathology	Resistance to interrogation and investigation	"Wasteful with resources and money"	9/24/13
283.	Bureaupathology	Resistance to interrogation and investigation	"Wasteful with resources and money"	9/24/13

(Continued)

Table 6.28 *(Continued)* **NP1 Social Media/Bureaucracy Dataset**

Count	Type	Attribute	Comment	Date
284.	Bureaupathology	Impersonal treatment	"Management sets unrealistic gols [sic] work till you drop atmosphere. They treat employees with no respect and micromanage them. Work mandatory long hours. I won't be here too long"	9/25/13
285.	Bureaucracy	Insistence on the rights of office	"Senior management gets bonuses based on profit management rather than client outcomes"	9/26/13
286.	Bureaupathology	Resistance to interrogation and investigation	"Stop the bleeding"	9/26/13
287.	Bureaupathology	Impersonal treatment	"Underpaid and unappreciated"	10/2/13
288.	Bureaucracy	Hierarchy of authority	"Work to narrow the vast communication void between senior management and those actually in the trenches"	10/4/13
289.	Bureaupathology	Prolonged role enactment	"Spend months and years unraveling poor decisions"	10/4/13
290.	Bureaupathology	Impersonal treatment	"Your stomach twists and you feel sick"	10/6/13
291.	Bureaupathology	Impersonal treatment	"If you want stability of any kind, do not work for NP1"	10/6/13

(Continued)

Table 6.28 *(Continued)*   **NP1 Social Media/Bureaucracy Dataset**

Count	Type	Attribute	Comment	Date
292.	Bureaupathology	Resistance to change	"The best people are leaving because they don't want to deal with the endless financial mess and the never ending layoffs"	10/6/13
293.	Bureaupathology	Resistance to interrogation and investigation	"Financial mess with incompetent and entrenched executive management that are accountable to no one"	10/6/13
294.	Bureaupathology	Resistance to interrogation and investigation	"Management hides the true financial disaster of the company because they are afraid it will hurt donations"	10/6/13
295.	Bureaupathology	Resistance to interrogation and investigation	"Tell the public the true financial situation"	10/6/13
296.	Bureaupathology	Impersonal treatment	"Sweatshop"	10/12/13
297.	Bureaupathology	Prolonged role enactment	"No room for advancement unless someone leaves or die [sic]"	10/12/13
298.	Bureaupathology	Prolonged role enactment	"Please get rid of your worthless directors, CEOs and VPs"	10/12/13
299.	Bureaupathology	Resistance to change	"IT systems are a wreck"	10/12/13
300.	Bureaucracy	Hierarchy of authority	"Way too much management and very political"	10/13/13

(Continued)

Table 6.28 *(Continued)* **NP1 Social Media/Bureaucracy Dataset**

Count	Type	Attribute	Comment	Date
301.	Bureaucracy	Hierarchy of authority	"Decrease the layers—way too many"	10/13/13
302.	Bureaupathology	Impersonal treatment	"Long hours (60+ per week)"	10/17/13
303.	Bureaupathology	Resistance to interrogation and investigation	"Admit you are bankrupt due to your practices and fold"	10/17/13
304.	Bureaupathology	Resistance to interrogation and investigation	"Huge mismanagement and wasteful spending with very few dollars actually getting to clients"	10/17/13
305.	Bureaucracy	Insistence on the rights of office	"Only company where you can keep losing money and get a promotion"	10/23/13
306.	Bureaupathology	Impersonal treatment	"Beware, working here is only for the strong"	10/23/13
307.	Bureaucracy	Insistence on the rights of office	"Inappropriate comments often made [by management]"	11/4/13
308.	Bureaucracy	System of rules	"Took over 3 months and numerous calls to HR to be paid for last month's work"	11/4/13
309.	Bureaupathology	Impersonal treatment	"HR department is hard to reach and does not respond to employee"	11/4/13
310.	Bureaupathology	Impersonal treatment	"Information is not shared so employees are often left in the dark"	11/4/13

(Continued)

Table 6.28 *(Continued)* NP1 Social Media/Bureaucracy Dataset

Count	Type	Attribute	Comment	Date
311.	Bureaupathology	Impersonal treatment	"It is sad how negative the culture can be at times"	11/4/13
312.	Bureaupathology	Resistance to change	"Change seems near impossible"	11/4/13
313.	Bureaupathology	Resistance to change	"Hire more people from outside the current organization"	11/4/13
314.	Bureaupathology	Impersonal treatment	"Long hours, little pay, very poor management, work every weekend"	11/11/13
315.	Bureaupathology	Impersonal treatment	"Very sad place to be a part of"	11/11/13
316.	Bureaupathology	Impersonal treatment	"All management cares about is numbers and uses natural disasters to push their numbers"	11/11/13
317.	Bureaupathology	Impersonal treatment	"When hired you might want to train or tell the new employees what the job they are actually doing is"	11/11/13
318.	Bureaupathology	Resistance to interrogation and investigation	"A lot of politics in the office"	11/11/13
319.	Bureaupathology	Resistance to change	"Lacking modern information technology"	11/13/13

(Continued)

Table 6.28 *(Continued)* **NP1 Social Media/Bureaucracy Dataset**

Count	Type	Attribute	Comment	Date
320.	Bureaucracy	Technical expertise	"The latest bone headed move is [sic] to allow more appointments to be made than we have staff to process"	11/17/13
321.	Bureaupathology	Impersonal treatment	"Horrendous hours— there is no balance. People dread each day and turnover is ongoing"	11/17/13
322.	Bureaupathology	Impersonal treatment	"There are a lot who are lazy, inept and uncaring"	11/17/13
323.	Bureaucracy	Hierarchy of authority	"Extremely top-heavy"	12/31/13
324.	Bureaupathology	Impersonal treatment	"I don't feel that they care about their people like they should"	12/31/13
325.	Bureaupathology	Impersonal treatment	"Poor management, treat your staff better and try not to overwork them"	1/4/14
326.	Bureaupathology	Resistance to interrogation and investigation	"Company in constant state of flux due to poor financial management"	1/13/14
327.	Bureaupathology	Resistance to interrogation and investigation	"Focus on where money goes in regards to unnecessary travel expenses"	1/13/14
328.	Bureaupathology	Impersonal treatment	"No incentives for employees, very low moral [sic]"	1/18/14

(Continued)

Table 6.28 *(Continued)* **NP1 Social Media/Bureaucracy Dataset**

Count	Type	Attribute	Comment	Date
329.	Bureaupathology	Impersonal treatment	"Low pay, no room for growth, the mentality is to use employees as much as possible before they move on to a better job"	1/18/14
330.	Bureaupathology	Resistance to change	"[Get your] head out of the clouds and listen to your employees, we have great ideas"	1/18/14
331.	Bureaupathology	Impersonal treatment	"Terrible management. No concern for the employees"	1/21/14
332.	Bureaupathology	Resistance to interrogation and investigation	"When they repeatly [sic] get fines, it's only the workers fault never management"	2/3/14
333.	Bureaupathology	Resistance to interrogation and investigation	"Their unprofessional skills of running a business have been on FDA's radar for years"	2/3/14
334.	Bureaupathology	Resistance to interrogation and investigation	"Take accountable [sic] for your own actions"	2/3/14
335.	Bureaupathology	Impersonal treatment	"Treated like a piece of crap"	2/6/14
336.	Bureaupathology	Impersonal treatment	"Job security is a joke"	2/6/14
337.	Bureaupathology	Impersonal treatment	"I don't believe they care about the volunteers"	2/11/14

(Continued)

Table 6.28 *(Continued)* **NP1 Social Media/Bureaucracy Dataset**

Count	Type	Attribute	Comment	Date
338.	Bureaucracy	System of rules	"The atmosphere is very strict. You are expected to do everything right the first time or there will be meetings and consequences about it for weeks"	2/19/14
339.	Bureaupathology	Impersonal treatment	"Work life balance is absolutely non existent"	2/19/14
340.	Bureaupathology	Impersonal treatment	"A greater amount of respect for employees would be greatly appreciated"	2/19/14
341.	Bureaucracy	System of rules	"Micro-managed"	2/21/14
342.	Bureaupathology	Impersonal treatment	"The nonprofit is run like a middle school"	2/21/14
343.	Bureaupathology	Resistance to change	"New ideas are not accepted and are ignored by 'old timers'"	2/21/14

waste or abuse." On this page, the potential tipster is informed the website enables the user to "report [his/her] concern in a confidential and anonymous manner".

On the "Submit a New Report" page, the user is prompted to select a "primary issue" he or she is reporting. The available choices are as follows: EEO/Diversity Issues; Environment, Health, Safety and Security; HR Administration and Actions; Legal and Regulatory Issues; Other—Nonallegations; Other—Violations or Concerns; Protecting Company Assets and Workplace Conduct Issues.

According to their organizational literature, employees are encouraged to report concerns internally, first. Specifically, in their "New Employee and Volunteer Orientation and Participant Guide," "Employees and volunteers are requested to first notify their supervisor, human resources representative, or any manager with whom they feel comfortable in the event a questionable situation arises in the workplace. If attempts to resolve the issue at the local level are unsuccessful, the Concern Connection Line is the next step" (NP1, 2006).

Hotline Metrics

The hotline metrics for NP1 are repeated in Table 6.29.

Table 6.29 NP1 Hotline Metrics

Fiscal Year	Time Period	Number of Employees	Average Benchmarking Figure: Size, Industry	Calls Expected per Benchmarking	Delta
2013	July 1, 2012– June 30, 2013	31,000	7.61 per 1,000 9.94 per 1,000 = 8.78 (9)	279	+481

Historical Context

During the time period of the hotline data provided, Hurricane Sandy occurred (October, 2012). Hurricane Sandy was one of the most destructive and costly hurricanes in U.S. history. According to the Federal Emergency Management Agency (FEMA), more than $1.4 billion in individual assistance has been provided, and $3.2 billion in emergency work was approved. It has been reported that NP1 provided as much as $15 million in relief in connection with this event (NP1 and Hurricane Sandy Relief Fund Give $15.2 Million, 2013).

It was also reported following Hurricane Katrina in August 2005, NP1 employees engaged in fraud. According to FBI press releases, NP1 employees and other members of the public were charged in at least 30 separate frauds between 2009 and 2012 for crimes committed in 2005. Therefore, it is anticipated there will be additional frauds against NP1 reported in connection with Hurricane Sandy in the near future. As a result, the number of calls to NP1's hotline was expected to be above average in terms of volume for this time period, which it was.

Fraud Metrics

According to media reports, employee fraud has occurred in this organization during the time period of the hotline data provided (FY, 2013). On October 31, 2013, local news outlets in Florida reported an NP1 employee had been systematically stealing from a local NP1 chapter since 2011. Overall, this employee reportedly stole over $200,000 by creating fraudulent benefit cards using another employee's username and password (ABC WCJB TV, 2013). In this news report, a statement from NP1 was published, where they acknowledged this fraud, which they said was uncovered during an examination of one of their business operations. It should be noted that according to Form 990 standards, this event should be disclosed in their next filing.

Summary

The presence of bureaucracy (IV) was established, which has affected the performance of the hotline (DV) creating performance issues. A review of the literature and an analysis of employee reviews found bureaucracy and excessive bureaucracy were present in this organization. In sum, the comments were made by 150 separate respondents. Of their responses, 99 comments indicated bureaucracy and 244 indicated excessive bureaucracy (Table 6.30).

Employee statements prove bureaucracy and excessive bureaucracy are recognized on the part of employees. Employee comments indicating all indices evincing bureaucracy and excessive bureaucracy were present at varying degrees. Specifically, employee comments suggest the indices of bureaucracy "insistence on the right of office" (34 comments) and "hierarchy of authority" (23 comments) were especially problematic for employees. In terms of excessive bureaucracy, comments indicated "impersonal treatment" (113 comments) and "resistance to interrogation and investigation" (79 comments) were the most notable for those employees who submitted reviews for this organization.

As for the hotline's metrics, the hotline is receiving a number of calls, surpassing benchmarking estimates. Specifically, in FY 2013, it received 760 calls, which is above the benchmarking figure of 279. However, a limitation is that this study is unable to determine from the data provided the number of calls made my employees, as opposed to the general public.

With respect to the hotline's functionality and best practices, the hotline performed moderately. Again, a lack of available data hindered research efforts. However, it should be noted that NP1 could make more of their hotline data available to the general public, and to researchers, if they desired. Here, additional data was requested but the researcher was told that it would not be made available.

Overall, the hotline's specifications demonstrate the potentially negative effect of organizational bureaucracy on the fraud hotline. This resistance by administrators to provide data demonstrated a "resistance to investigation and interrogation" as indicated by a majority of employees. The act of directing employees to speak to their manager, rather than call the hotline, is further evidence of "hierarchy of authority" and "insistence on the rights of office," which results in poor hotline functionality. Employees who wish to not report to an internal party are thus discouraged from calling. The demand for employees to report internally rather than call the hotline further evinces a dominating management who insists reports come through them, rather than another channel. This demand is against the hotline's purpose, which is to receive fraud tips, and is thus evidence of bureaupathology.

Overall, per the employees who provided reviews, this organization is believed to have a dominating management ("insistence on the rights of office") who freely exercises their authority ("hierarchy of authority"), providing "impersonal treatment" (113 comments) and "resisting interrogation and investigation" (79 comments). It is believed that these conditions give rise to internal fraud and also hinder employee fraud reporting to the hotline.

Comments further indicated the presence of disgruntled employees. On a positive note, employees were very enthusiastic about the mission of their organization, which they found overall to be very rewarding. However, it was clear

Table 6.30 NP1 Table of Results

Organization	
Assessment Element	NP1
Size	31,000
Hotline name	Concern Connection Line
Management	Third party and internal
Respondents indicating IV	88% (sample size 170; 150 indicated IV; 343 comments indicated IV)
Bureaucracy IV	Strong, 5 of 5; general (6) **a (23)** b (20) c (2) d (14) **e (34)**
Bureaupathology IV	**f (113)** g (15) h (35) **I (79)** J (2)
Hotline metrics (DV)	Great; calls exceed benchmarking; historical context (conducive to fraud, yet calls were above benchmarking levels during a relevant time period)
Hotline functionality (DV)	Moderate, 3 of 5 **Marketing (employees are encouraged to contact manager first) Mechanics (not enough parties engaged)** Intake (third-party managed) Processing (third-party managed) **Incentives (administrator didn't understand value of hotline)** Moderate, 3 of 6 Oversight (internal oversight) Due care (clear process) **Effective communication (well communicated, but employees discouraged from calling)** Reasonable steps to achieve compliance (yes, third-party managed) **Consistent enforcement (data unavailable)** **Reasonable steps to respond and prevent similar offenses (data unavailable)**

(Continued)

Table 6.30 *(Continued)*   **NP1 Table of Results**

Organization	
Assessment Element	*NP1*
Best practices (DV)	
Historical context (DV)	
Evidence of internal fraud	Yes
Evidence of negative employee sentiment	Yes
Result IV	**IV** **Present bureaucracy strong** 　Hierarchy of authority 　Insistence on the rights of office **Bureaupathology** 　Impersonal treatment 　Resistance to interrogation and investigation
Result DV	**DV metrics, functionality, and best practices affected** Metrics, great Functionality, moderate Best practices, moderate Evidence of historical context, internal fraud, disgruntled employees
Notes	Despite an "average" rating, comments indicate fraud, massive bureaucracy

that employees felt they were mistreated. Many employees complained about the working hours, which were well beyond that of normal positions. Employees also negatively discussed the "CEO salary" and compared it to their own low wages. They also expressed concern over the constant organizational change, "lack of communication" within the organization, the "poor management," and resulting "low morale."

As a result of the negative employee sentiment, which overwhelmingly indicated "impersonal treatment" and "resistance to interrogation and investigation," it is believed that not all employees who are aware of fraud are reporting it to the hotline.

As for internal fraud, upon review of public records, this study was able to establish the presence of internal fraud during the relevant time period. A review of the historical context suggests the hotline should have future internal fraud reported due to Hurricane Sandy. Employee reviews also made reference to the existence of internal fraud, with employees saying there was "waste of donated income," "misuse of funds," with "repeated violations of key federal and state regulations," and the "financial situation was terrible."

Conclusions

This work asked, "Does organizational bureaucracy affect the fraud hotline process?" To answer this question, this work examined the fraud hotline in six subject organizations, which included a vast array of organization types—one medium-sized private sector organization; one large, private sector organization; three public sector organizations (one federal, one state, and one city government); and one nonprofit organization.

This central question was divided into a series of subquestions. In answering those subquestions, this work identified and isolated specific indicators to measure the subject organizations' fraud hotline performance:

1. Does organizational bureaucracy exist in the six subject organizations?
2. Do employees perceive organizational bureaucracy in the six subject organizations?
3. Does organizational bureaucracy result in a low number of hotline calls?
4. Does organizational bureaucracy result in a low hotline functionality?
5. Does organizational bureaucracy result in reduced best practices compliance?
6. Does organizational bureaucracy result in fraud, waste, and abuse?

The first two questions established whether the organization had bureaucracy conditions present and whether they were perceptible by employees. To measure the above, the following conditions were established: (1) state of organizational bureaucracy in each of the subject organizations; (2) perception of employees as to bureaucracy in their organizations; (3) the number of hotline calls received by the subject organization; (4) the functionality of the hotline; (5) the level of adherence of best practices compliance by the subject organization; and the (6) state of internal fraud, waste, and abuse in the subject organization.

First, the presence of bureaucracy and bureaupathology in all of the subject organizations was established. Overall, employees perceived agency bureaucracy, which in the case of this study, had reached bureaupathic levels. The strongest bureaucracy indicator present was "insistence on the rights of office." The strongest bureaupathology indicator present was "impersonal treatment."

One organization studied was determined to have great functionality and best practice adherence, despite the presence of bureaupathology. As a result, it is possible for organizations to have well-functioning hotlines despite organizational bureaucracy. It is believed that if organizations identify their areas of concern by conducting similar analysis as conducted in this study, it is possible for them to prevent organizational bureaupathology from affecting their hotline.

One reason that hotlines underperformed was due to a lack of information sharing, at all levels. This is a sign of bureaupathology, where individual workers can have a tendency to withhold information.

Organizations can also potentially reduce bureaupathology by addressing the specific conditions identified. Bureaupathology theory holds that individual managers can overcome these conditions. According to the Theory of Bureaucracy, individual managers have the ability to control the factors that contribute to the employee perception of excessive bureaucracy (Tompkins, 2005).

Here, the strongest bureaucracy indicator was "insistence on the rights of office," and the strongest bureaupathology indicator present was "impersonal treatment." Both conditions can be the result of poor management and can also be rectified with keen management practices.

Accessibility

This study determined that private sector hotline numbers were not as readily accessible as their public sector and nonprofit sector counterparts. One reason for this is that the public sector and nonprofit organizations are assuming callers will originate externally, whereas private sector callers do not. However, most hotline callers will call from outside the organization. Thus, organizations should make their hotline numbers readily accessible to external users. According to available statistics, most employee callers call hotlines from outside the office and outside of business hours. In addition, callers can be third parties (i.e., vendors, or other suppliers) who will also likely seek the number externally.

Information

Certain organizations didn't make available the data concerning their hotlines, nor did they make available the outcomes of any reporting or investigations. For some organizations, their general hotline data were not easily located in the public domain (PS1, PS2, and NP1). For most all of the organizations, data regarding hotline outcomes was also unavailable (PS1, PS2, GS1, NP1). This practice, which is contrary to best practices, also indicates bureaupathology. This practice is also consistent with bureaupathology theories, which say that employees conceal information. Organizations should make sure their data are being made available, despite the tendency of some employees to conceal these data. The data should be available to the public to give confidence in the operation of the hotlines. The data and information regarding outcomes also give confidence to the public that the organization is well managed from an antifraud perspective.

Cost

This study learned that several organizations consciously keep call volume low to reduce costs. This practice should be examined more thoroughly.

Name

Hotlines in this study had many naming conventions. While individual organizations have latitude to select the names for their hotlines, it made it more challenging for the number to be located. Some hotlines, when the term "fraud hotline" was searched, didn't return a result because the hotline, despite being a "fraud hotline" by definition, was known by a different name. Hotlines should consider embedding keywords in their hotline webpages or otherwise which will allow for searches for "fraud hotline" and similar to return their hotline page.

Users

Overall, potential users of hotlines should feel encouraged to report. In this study, it was learned that hotline processes, either purposely or inadvertently, deterred users from reporting. Organizations should review their hotline materials in this regard.

In one case (GS1), employees said in an organizational survey they feared retaliation for hotline reporting. In this instance, organizations should make especially clear to their employees that hotline reporting is encouraged and is something to be celebrated by the organization, rather than feared.

A summary of complete research results is presented in Table 6.31.

Discussion

There were some important takeaways from this work, regarding hotline functionality and crime, the concept of organizations as victims, and the employees as clients.

This study demonstrated benchmarking alone might not tell an organization how well their hotline is actually functioning to prevent and detect crime. Organizations may need to conduct more comprehensive examinations of their hotline, to include known crime and external or historical factors to determine the true health of their hotline. But today, only the organizations can determine their own true hotline functionality, as they are the only party with access to their organizational crime data.

It is possible that organizations might have a false sense of security about their own hotlines. Organizations may assume, after benchmarking, their hotlines are functioning well, so they are protected against internal crime. However, as demonstrated in this study, a hotline functionality assessment may not have a consistent relationship with internal crime levels.

Overall, hotlines will always be unique in that the organization's primary clients are also their employees. This factor provides a unique challenge for hotlines, in that the bureaupathology of the organization cannot be easily separated from the client.

Table 6.31 Full Research Results

Organization						
Assessment Element	PS1	PS2	GS1	GS2	GS3	NP1
Org Type	Private sector	Private sector	Federal government	State government	City government	Nonprofit
Size	48,256	260,000	17,359	17,891	19,500	31,000
Hotline name	Integrity Hotline	Ethics Hotline	OIG Hotline	Fraud, Waste and Mismanagement Hotline	Fraud, Waste and Abuse Hotline	Concern Connection Line
Management	Third party and internal	Third party and internal	Office of inspector general (OIG)	GS2 legislative audit bureau	Third party and city auditor	Third party and internal
Respondents indicating IV	23% (sample size 195; 45 indicated IV; 54 comments indicated IV)	38.5% (sample size, 403; 155 indicated IV; 186 comments indicated IV)	72% (population 85; 61 indicated presence of IV; 99 comments indicated IV)	64% (population 29; 18 indicated presence of IV; 32 comments indicated IV)	67% (population 18; 12 respondents indicating presence of IV; 22 comments indicated IV)	88% (sample size 170; 150 indicated IV; 343 comments indicated IV)

(Continued)

Table 6.31 (Continued) Full Research Results

Organization						
Assessment Element	PS1	PS2	GS1	GS2	GS3	NP1
Bureaucracy IV	5 of 5 general (12); **a (4)** b (3) c (3) d (3) **e (6)**	5 of 5 general (48); **a (22)** b (7) c (5) d (9) **e (21)**	5 of 5 general (20) a (2) b (6) c (1) **d (14)** e (8)	3 of 5 general (4) a (3) b (0) c (0) **d (3)** e (5)	5 of 5 general (1) a (3) b (1) c (1) d (1) **e (4)**	5 of 5 general (6) **a (23)** b (20) c (2) d (14) **e (34)**
Bureaupathology IV	f (6) g (9) h (1) i (5) j (2)	f (16) g (19) h (17) i (13) j (9)	f (8) **g (17)** **h (11)** **i (11)** j (5)	f (7) g (3) **h (3)** i (3) j (1)	f (3) g (2) **h (3)** i (1) j (2)	**f (113)** g (15) h (35) **i (79)** j (2)
Hotline metrics (DV)	Low; below benchmarking	High; above benchmarking	High; above benchmarking	Low; below benchmarking	Low, exceeded benchmarking for 4 years, until 2010	High; calls exceed benchmarking

(Continued)

Table 6.31 (Continued) Full Research Results

Organization						
Assessment Element	PS1	PS2	GS1	GS2	GS3	NP1
Hotline functionality (DV)	Poor, 3 of 4 **k (number hard to find internally and externally)** **l (not enough parties engaged)** m (third-party managed) **n (managers didn't understand value of hotline)**	Poor, 3 of 4 **k (hard to find number externally)** l (third-party managed; dedicated internal team) **m (heavily bureaucratic process; managers do not report resolution back to The Network)** **n (The Network said financial firms like to keep call volume low)**	Moderate, 2 of 4 k (easily found via a Google search for GS1 "Fraud Hotline" or GS1 "Ethics Hotline"; a poster is available) l (managed by OIG) **m (process seems overly bureaucratic and difficult to navigate)** **n (average 44% employees said they fear retaliation, anonymity is not guaranteed)**	Poor, 4 of 5 k (easily located externally) **l (hotline only has a single person handling calls)** **m (a single actor adds a perceived reporting and process bias)** **n (employees especially disgruntled due to historical context)**	Great, 3 of 4 k (easily located externally) l (third-party provider) **m (third-party provider and internal handling process; however, believed to be suffering due to below)** **n (reporting discouraged; potential callers urged to report in person)**	Moderate, 2 of 4 k (number located easily) **l (not enough parties engaged)** m (third-party managed) **n (administrator didn't understand value of hotline)**

(Continued)

Table 6.31 (Continued) Full Research Results

Organization		PS1	PS2	GS1	GS2	GS3	NP1
	Assessment Element						
Best practices (DV)		Weak, 4 of 6 **p (1 delegate only)** q (clear process) **r (not well communicated)** s (yes, third-party managed) **t (data unavailable) u (data unavailable)**	Moderate, 3 of 6 P (oversight present) q (ethics office) **r (not well communicated externally)** s (yes, third-party managed) **t (data unavailable) u (data unavailable)**	Moderate, 3 of 6 p (high level oversight) q (clear escalation process) r (data communicated externally) s (OIG managed, however, surveys say employees fear reprisal) **t (data unavailable) u (data unavailable)**	Good, 2 of 6 p (high level oversight) **q (escalation process is unclear)** r (data are communicated externally) **s (a single staffer is noted)** t (reports indicate enforcement) u (reports indicate escalation)	High, 6 of 6 p (high level oversight) q (escalation process is clear) **r (data are reported externally, calls are discouraged; no poster)** s (third-party provider with internal escalation process) t (reports indicate enforcement) u (reports indicate escalation)	Moderate, 3 of 6 Oversight (internal oversight) Due care (clear process) **Effective communication (well communicated, but employees discouraged from calling)** Reasonable steps to achieve compliance (yes, third-party managed)

(Continued)

Table 6.31 (Continued) Full Research Results

Organization						
Assessment Element	PS1	PS2	GS1	GS2	GS3	NP1
						Consistent enforcement (data unavailable) Reasonable steps to respond and prevent similar offenses (data unavailable)
Historical context (DV)	Conducive to fraud; conducive to increased calls (Financial Crisis, 2008)	Conducive to fraud; conducive to increased calls (Financial Crisis, 2008)	Conducive to fraud; conducive to increased calls (2008; 2012 employee surveys; average 44% believe retaliation for reporting)	Conducive to fraud; conducive to increased calls (2011 end of collective bargaining; unprecedented level of protests and other demonstrations during this time)	Conducive to fraud; conducive to increased calls (calls declined after 2009 Hotline report said there was a cap on the hotline calls received by the provider)	Conducive to fraud; conducive to increased calls (Hurricane Sandy)

(Continued)

Table 6.31 (*Continued*) Full Research Results

Organization						
Assessment Element	PS1	PS2	GS1	GS2	GS3	NP1
Evidence of internal fraud	Yes	Yes	Yes	Yes	Yes	Yes
Evidence of negative employee sentiment	Yes	Yes	Yes	Yes	Yes	Yes
Result IV Bureaucracy Strongest presence	Hierarchy of authority Insistence on the rights of office	Hierarchy of authority Insistence on the rights of office	Career service Insistence on the rights of office	Hierarchy of authority Career service Insistence on the rights of office	Hierarchy of authority Insistence on the rights of office	Hierarchy of authority Insistence on the rights of office
Bureaupathology	Impersonal treatment Prolonged role enactment	Prolonged role enactment Resistance to change	Prolonged role enactment Resistance to change	Impersonal treatment Prolonged role enactment Resistance to change Resistance to interrogation and investigation	Impersonal treatment Resistance to change	Impersonal treatment Resistance to interrogation and investigation

(Continued)

Table 6.31 (Continued) Full Research Results

Organization						
Assessment Element	PS1	PS2	GS1	GS2	GS3	NP1
Result DV	**Metrics, functionality and best practices affected** Metrics, poor Functionality, poor Best practices, weak Evidence of historical context, internal fraud, disgruntled employees	**DV functionality affected** Metrics, moderate Functionality, poor Best practices, moderate Evidence of historical context, internal fraud, disgruntled employees	**DV performing moderately** Metrics, moderate Functionality, moderate Best practices, moderate Evidence of historical context, internal fraud, disgruntled employees	**DV metrics, functionality affected** Metrics, low Functionality, poor Best practices, good Evidence of historical context, internal fraud, disgruntled employees	**DV metrics affected** Metrics, low Functionality, great Best practices, great Evidence of historical context, internal fraud, disgruntled employees	**DV metrics, functionality and best practices affected** Metrics, great Functionality, moderate Best practices, moderate Evidence of historical context, internal fraud, disgruntled employees

(Continued)

Table 6.31 (Continued) Full Research Results

Organization Assessment Element	PS1	PS2	GS1	GS2	GS3	NP1
Notes	Despite an "average" rating, comments indicate fraud, massive bureaucracy	Despite an "average" rating, comments indicate fraud, massive bureaucracy	Employee reviews contained information that could be actionable to managers. Specific job positions and departments were referenced	The historical context suggests employees of the state of GS2 at this time would be especially disgruntled—a condition that is known to give rise to fraud and can further inhibit fraud reporting	Evidence that an internal crime was reported via the hotline; According to one report, from 2010 to 2012, 82% of their complaints received were substantiated	Despite an "average" rating, comments indicate fraud, massive bureaucracy

This study determined organizational bureaucracy does not have a consistent relationship to hotline performance. The literature said organizational bureaucracy could have resulted in decreased hotline performance. That was not consistently proven in this study. Rather, the stronger the level of bureaucracy in an agency, the better the hotline performed from a metrics, functionality, and best practices perspective.

This means that the media reports that posited that the SEC hotline is suffering due to excessive bureaucracy may be false. However, those reports said the complainants might believe, due to excessive bureaucracy, their complaints are not being handled appropriately. Here, it was learned that perception could be an outcome of the lack of communication to complainants about the process, which was a noted shortcoming of many hotlines, even in those hotlines that followed best practices.

This study further established the value of reviewing the historical context when analyzing a fraud hotline. In several instances in this study, a subject hotline "benchmarked" appropriately. A full evaluation of the historical context and the state of organizational fraud was often the sole indicator that the hotline potentially may not be performing according to expectations.

Here, the strongest bureaucracy indicator was "insistence on the rights of office," and the strongest bureaupathology indicator present was "impersonal treatment." Both conditions gave rise to better hotline performance, but may also give rise to internal fraud.

This study considered social media in evaluating fraud hotlines. In their "Recommended Practices for Office of Inspector General Hotlines," the Department of Homeland Security advances the use of social media in fraud hotlines (2010).

This work set forth a hotline assessment methodology that can be replicated in any organization. This study used a holistic approach to analyze fraud hotlines that included several unique factors, such as historical context and social media analysis of employee sentiment. This methodology is advanced with the end goal of all organizations evaluating their present fraud hotlines, for effectiveness, and their organizations, for internal fraud.

Further hotline assessments will serve to further build the general body of knowledge regarding fraud hotlines. In Patrick Scott's work, *Examining Red Tape in Public and Private Organizations*, he suggests as "one of the most effective strategies to advance the state of knowledge is to continue to expand the use of different methodologies (both qualitative and quantitative) and different populations to study red tape" (2002, p. 481).

Global Hotlines

International Hotline Callers

On July 21, 2010, President Obama signed legislation permitting foreign nationals to collect money rewards for reporting bribery per the Foreign Corrupt Practices Act (FCPA) (NWC).

According to recent reports, international whistleblowers are being actively sought by U.S. authorities. Their tips are highly desired by U.S. hotline administrators. It is believed people outside the United States may have knowledge of many frauds being perpetuated against the U.S. government, such as false billings, tax evasion, and securities fraud involving U.S. companies (McCormack, Pike & Mahendranathan, 2016).

It is important to know that whistleblower hotlines that are based in the United States welcome all tipsters. Callers to hotlines do not have to be American citizens, nor must they reside in the United States. According to the SEC, 10% of all their tips come from individuals in 67 countries outside the United States (Thomas, 2016).

Any caller to the SEC Whistleblower Hotline is also eligible to receive an award. To date, the SEC has awarded four such awards to persons living outside the United States (McCormack, Pike & Mahendranathan, 2016). In fact, the largest award the SEC Whistleblower Program has awarded to date ($30 million, September 22, 2014), was awarded to a whistleblower living in a foreign country (SEC, 2014). Overall, the SEC reports that 24% of all their award recipients in fiscal year 2016 were foreign nationals (Thomas, 2016).

International tipsters can collect rewards under the False Claims Act (FCA). The FCA is a U.S. law that was established in 1863. It allows private citizens to bring claims forward, on behalf of the U.S. government. In return, they receive between 15% and 30% of recoveries (McCormack, Pike & Mahendranathan, 2016).

Outside the United States, the laws and regulations regarding hotline reporting vary. For some countries, the process is similar to that in the United States. For others, it can be very different. As a result, it is important when establishing a global hotline to take note of that area's specific rules and requirements.

For instance, Canadian regulations governing hotlines are similar to those in the United States. Their 2003 Canadian Security Commission Administrators (SCA) Multilateral Instrument 52-110 2004 is similar to that of SOX in the United States (The Network, n.d., p. 7). In Canada, hotlines, replete with anonymous reporting capabilities, are required in publicly listed companies.

However, in France, their rules governing hotlines are very different. There, since 2009, hotline reporting is "strictly restricted in scope to financial and accounting issues, with no exceptions" (The Network, n.d., p. 10). Also, anyone seeking to establish a hotline must first obtain permission from the Commission Nationale de l'Informa que et des Libertes (The Network, n.d., p. 10). Another big difference is that anonymous reporting to a hotline in France is generally not permitted (The Network, n.d., p. 10).

To illustrate these differences, Table 6.32 depicts the variances in whistleblower protection standards in various locations across the globe.

Protections for whistleblowers can also vary, depending on the location. For instance, in the Republic of Namibia, Southwest Africa, whistleblower protections do not exist, but whistleblowers in other parts of South Africa are protected under the "Protected Disclosures Act" (Rajgopal, 2016).

Table 6.32 Global Whistlewblower Protection Standards

	United States	United Kingdom	Germany	France	Netherlands	Hong Kong	Japan	China	Australia	South Africa
Overall protection rating	c	c	b	b	b	a	c	c	b	c
Express laws	✓	✓	X	X	X	X	✓	✓	✓	✓
General dismissal laws	X	✓	✓	✓	✓	✓	✓	✓	✓	✓
Protection against retaliation	✓	✓	✓	✓	X	✓	✓	✓	✓	✓
External reporting encouraged	✓	X	X	X	X	X	X	✓	✓	X
Internal reporting encouraged	✓	✓	✓	X	X	X	X	X	✓	✓
Consultation on whistleblowing procedures required	X	X	✓	✓	X	X	X	X	X	X

(Continued)

Table 6.32 (Continued)   Global Whistlewblower Protection Standards

	United States	United Kingdom	Germany	France	Netherlands	Hong Kong	Japan	China	Australia	South Africa
Board/ management investigation of disclosures required	✓	X	X	X	X	X	✓	X	X	X
Government/ regulatory incentives to disclose	✓	X	X	X	X	X	X	✓	X	X

Source: DLA Piper 2014, 4.

a Little or no protection.
b Some protection through general laws.
c Express protection.

Despite these differences, it is possible for a single hotline to satisfy multiple regional requirements. Typically, a global the hotline webpage will offer various sets of instructions and links to regional-specific web forms that address the individual requirements.

In the last several years, whistleblower hotline programs have been enacted in other countries. Yet experts say they are unlikely to have the same success as the SEC hotline because they offer little to no incentive to callers (Kelton, 2012).

Hotline in Senegal

In 2014, this author was contacted to assist the Senegalese equivalent of the U.S. Inspector General in the development of their new fraud hotline.

When I worked with the Senegalese government in the creation of their fraud hotline, I learned how cultural differences can impact hotline design. For example, the Senegalese were concerned about callers potentially spending too much time talking to hotline agents. This interested me, as hotline designers would typically be concerned about excessive call volume, or getting callers to speak more, rather than less. Yet in this case, the Senegalese culture could account for this difference. In Senegal, it was explained, cell phones, and thus telephone conversations, are rare for the citizens of Senegal. To encourage callers, the hotline was free of charge, as is customary. But due to the rarity of phones and calls, the Senegalese government feared citizens would call the hotline, just to chat, perhaps at length, resulting in increased costs.

Policy Implications

Overall, this study will facilitate policy decisions. Some of the key factors that affect those decisions might include the following.

Employees Are Rational Actors Who Will Report Fraud

The Theory of Bureaucracy assumes that employees are rational actors. This study determined employees in a wide range of sectors are exposed to excessive bureaucracy. As rational actors, it is assumed employees are making a conscious decision to withhold information from the company concerning known internal fraud. Per Caiden, employees who are exposed to excessive bureaucracy will respond by "not inform[ing] on wrongdoing" (Caiden, p. 25). The policy implication of this finding is that employees can be persuaded or conditioned to report internal fraud.

Individual Managers Can Control Excessive Bureaucracy

So how can an organization persuade an employee to report internal fraud, knowing excessive bureaucracy makes employees inclined against reporting? How can an organization alleviate the negative effects of excessive bureaucracy on their hotline reporting processes? According to the Theory of Bureaucracy, individual managers have the ability to control the factors that contribute to the employee's perception of excessive bureaucracy (Tompkins, 2005).

Yet other researchers advance individual managers as the arbiters of bureaucracy, who are empowered to monitor organization conditions and alleviate any known excess. In "Organization Theory and Public Management," Tompkins tells managers their "task is to adjust structural variables continually as internal and external conditions change" (2005, p. 65). Yet other researchers, such as Giblin, in "Bureaupathology: The Denigration of Competence" sets forth the specific steps that managers can take to control organizational bureaupathology (Giblin, 1981).

Organizational theorists offer guidance for managers in accomplishing this task. Downs (1964) argues that "bureaucratic pathologies can be corrected by finding the proper mix of agency personnel types, adopting extra organizational means such as reorganization, obtaining feedback on its performance from outside sources, or creating overlapping administrative responsibilities to encourage competition and discourage subordinate collusion" (Meier, 2003, p. 7). Perez and Barkhurst (2012) further say companies can "have an inflexible accountability mechanism" to control excessive bureaucracy (p. 168).

Cost Concerns Might Affect Hotline Reporting Levels

This study determined cost concerns might be affecting hotline reporting. An interview with the third-party hotline provider confirmed there is a cost per hotline report. The GS3 hotline administrators, managed by this provider, documented a "complaint cap" in their organizational documents and immediately following, the number of reports received to their hotline dropped. It is unknown whether management implicitly or explicitly discouraged future reporting, and how this reduction was achieved. However, the data show that the concerns expressed by management immediately preceded a steep reporting decline.

Managers Can Affect Hotline Reporting Levels

In the case of GS3, it is believed that management somehow deterred hotline reporting, resulting in a lower instance of calls. Organizational documents showed memos citing hotline cost concerns. Immediately following, calls went down. While it is unclear exactly how management may have discouraged hotline reporting, it is an important research finding that hotline reporting can, potentially, be controlled by management. This finding suggests management could also work inversely, potentially increase the level, and quality of hotline reports received by their organization.

Conclusion

The topic of fraud hotlines is timely and important. Now, more than ever, organizations are wise to ensure their hotlines are functioning well to receive fraud tips. The Theory of Bureaucracy sheds light on the possible reasons for hotline performance problems, as evinced in the SEC Whistleblower Program. Social media data can be used to provide insight into employee perception of bureaucracy, which may affect their hotline. In their Recommended Practices for Office of Inspector General Hotlines, the Department of Homeland Security recommends the use of social media in fraud hotlines (2010). Hotline performance evaluations incorporating the use of this data are timely and are in line with industry recommendations.

Chapter 7

Special Topics

Hotlines in the Nonprofit Sector

By all accounts, fraud in the nonprofit sector is a growing problem. According to the 2013 Report to the Nations, a semi-annual report by the Association of Certified Fraud Examiners (ACFE), the frequency of fraud occurring in this sector has risen since 2010, climbing from 9.6% to 10.4% in the cases they examined, with a median loss increasing to $100,000 (p. 25). Further confirming this upward trend, a recent investigation by the *Washington Post* revealed specific instances of nonprofit employee fraud, which occurred at the hands of employees.

This study, published in October, exposed the "significant diversion" of assets indicated in the Forms 990 filings with the IRS of more than 1,000 nonprofit entities, resulting in hundreds of millions of dollars of loss (Stephens, 2013). In one of the more egregious examples cited in the study, the American Legacy Foundation, a nonprofit dedicated to smoking danger awareness, lost an estimated $3.4 million due to an employee embezzler (Devaney et al., 2013; Post, 2013; Stephens, 2013). Overall, it was reported as much as a half-billion dollars was misappropriated from 10 nonprofits alone, between 2008 and 2012, due to "theft, investment fraud, embezzlement and other unauthorized uses of funds" (Stephens, 2013).

While this is an alarming figure, lawyers say the instance of employee fraud is a known reality in this industry, due to the tendency of these employers to be "trusting of employees" and have "less stringent financial controls" than other sectors (Devaney et al., 2013). In light of this loss, it is prudent to examine internal fraud prevention efforts in this sector. To thwart the instance of this fraud, lawyers recommend nonprofits "encourage whistleblowing" as a preventative measure (Devaney et al., 2013). This recommendation is aligned with studies by the ACFE conducted since 2002, which have found tips were the way that fraud is most often detected in all sectors. Therefore, it is prudent to examine the current use of fraud hotlines in the nonprofit sector.

Then this work examines the use of hotlines in the nonprofit sector by looking at the status of their use in 20 of the 200 largest U.S. charities, as reported in their IRS Form 990 (Forbes, 2006). Then, this work presents the case study of one of these charity's hotlines, to determine individual performance. Ultimately, this work highlights the need for additional research in this area and calls for more widespread use of hotlines in the nonprofit sector.

Nonprofits presently lose a lot of money to fraud. Fraud in nonprofits is estimated to cost as much as $40 billion annually, representing 13% of donations (Greenlee, 2007, p. 2).

Fraud in the nonprofit sector is increasing. According to the Association of Certified Fraud Examiners (ACFE), from 2010 to 2014, fraud in this sector increased by 12.5%, and the median loss increased 20% to $108,000 per incident (p. 24). In fact, today, nonprofits are the second most susceptible organization to embezzlements, other than the financial industry (Venable LLP, 2013) (Stephens & Flaherty, 2013).

Lawyers cite several reasons nonprofit entities are susceptible to employee fraud. Nonprofits have "less stringent financial controls" than other businesses (Devaney et al., 2013). Experts say nonprofit employees are usually more "trusted" due to the emphasis on "altruistic program activities" and "constrained staffing levels at most nonprofits...mak[ing] segregation of duties more difficult" (Sol, 2011).

Today, hotlines are recommended, but are not required, in nonprofit entities. It is important to understand which nonprofits are using hotlines. Organizations with hotlines are more likely to catch fraud. Studies also suggest that fraud in these organizations is less costly, in part, due to early detection (ACFE, 2014, p. 4).

Recent inquiries have called attention to accountability in nonprofit organizations. In 2007, a "string of high-profile financial scandals" led to an investigation into the spending habits of the leaders of six religious organizations claiming nonprofit status (Haverluck, 2007; Stephens & Flaherty, 2013). Allegations included the purchase of private jets, cosmetic surgery, and opulent furnishings, including a $23,000 "commode with marble top" (Haverluck, 2007). Although this investigation was closed without significant findings of wrongdoing, it called attention to the finances of organizations claiming a tax exempt status.

Recent investigative research has increased awareness of the fraud occurring in nonprofits. The IRS and the *Washington Post* recently examined IRS Form 990 filings, filed by organizations exempt from income tax.

Since 2008, the IRS has required nonprofits to report known fraud, meeting certain criteria, in the Form 990 (Kalick, 2014). Per the IRS, this fraud is considered a "significant diversion," and they are required to report the full amount lost, and details of the crime.

The IRS Form 990 requires organizations to report known fraud as follows: "The governance section (Part IV) of Form 990 asks whether there has been a *significant diversion* of assets. Filing instructions direct nonprofits to disclose a *diversion of assets* defined as any unauthorized conversion or use of the organization's assets, other than for the organization's authorized purposes, including embezzlement or theft" (IRS, 2013; Stephens & Flaherty, 2013).

The IRS adds further guidance for organizations as to what should be reported as a "significant diversion of assets" as follows:

> Report diversions by the organization's officers, directors, trustees, employees, volunteers, independent contractors, grantees (diverting grant funds), or any other person, even if not associated with the organization other than by the diversion. A diversion of assets does not include an authorized transfer of assets for FMV consideration, such as to a joint venture or for-profit subsidiary in exchange for an interest in the joint venture or subsidiary. For this purpose, a diversion is considered significant if the gross value of all diversions (not taking into account restitution, insurance, or similar recoveries) discovered during the organization's tax year exceeds the lesser of (1) 5% of the organization's gross receipts for its tax year, (2) 5% of the organization's total assets as of the end of its tax year, or (3) $250,000. (IRS, 2013, p. 21)

Fraud meeting the threshold to warrant disclosure includes "diversions of more than $250,000 or those identified as having exceeded 5 percent of an organization's annual gross receipts or total assets."

Therefore, per the IRS, if an organization experiences employee theft of $250,000 or more, in total, they are required to disclose this fact by indicating "yes" in the Governance Section 5 of their Form 990. As of 2012, nonprofits must explain "the nature of the diversion, amounts or property involved, corrective actions taken to address the matter, and the pertinent circumstances" in Schedule O of the Form 990 (Christopher, 2012).

In 2012, the IRS reviewed the tax filings and publically available information of 285 organizations reporting a significant diversion of assets, in 2009, when they began collecting governance data from 1,300 nonprofit organizations. As a result of this effort, the IRS determined approximately $170 million was lost in "significant diversions" as reported in Part VI, Section A, Item 5 (Panetta, 2012). There, the respondent is asked "Did the organization become aware during the year of a significant diversion of the organization's assets?" Most reported cases involved theft or embezzlement, although it was said "there were many other cases whether the taxpayer did not explain the significant diversion as Schedule O requires" (Lerner, 2012; Panetta, 2012).

As a result of their initial review in 2012, Lois Lerner, Director of the Exempt Organizations Division of the IRS, announced their intent to "conduct an examination program in the area".

Later, in 2013, the *Washington Post* conducted a broader examination into the Form 990. They reviewed over 1,000 IRS Form 990s filed between 2008 and 2012 and determined over a half-billion dollars was misappropriated from 10 nonprofits alone, due to "theft, investment fraud, embezzlement and other unauthorized uses of funds" (Stephens & Flaherty, 2013). The *Post* found half of all organizations reporting fraud (p. 500) were not transparent about the fraud in their Form 990, leaving out the total amount stolen, which is contrary to federal disclosure requirements (Stephens & Flaherty, 2013).

In one of the more egregious examples cited in the study, the American Legacy Foundation, a nonprofit dedicated to smoking danger awareness, lost an estimated $3.4 million due to an employee embezzler (Devaney, 2013; Post, 2013; Stephens & Flaherty, 2013).

The increase in volume and awareness of nonprofit fraud has subjected this sector to additional scrutiny. As part of their investigation, the *Washington Post* created a publicly available, searchable database of their findings. Congress and state attorneys general have been reviewing the material, and launched investigations, and additional government inquiries are expected (Loya, Montano, Martin & Tenenbaum, 2015, p. 2; Stephens & Flaherty, 2013).

As a result, accountants, such as CliftonLarsonAllen, are recommending nonprofits "provide a way for individuals to anonymously report suspicious activities" (Trimner, 2013). The primary way this is conducted is via a fraud hotline.

Fraud hotlines have been advanced by legislation as a method of fraud prevention and detection since the passage of the Sarbanes–Oxley Act of 2002 (SOX). SOX requires all publicly listed companies to operate a confidential reporting mechanism where employees can report fraud occurring in their workplace. The use of fraud hotlines in the private sector was later reinforced by Dodd–Frank in 2010. Dodd–Frank was instituted in response to major corporate fraud, which contributed to the world financial crisis of 2008–2012.

Hotlines are valued due to their ability to receive anonymous tips, and their ability to receive such tips from internal sources. Employees are the primary callers of fraud hotlines. Employees are also said to be aware of fraud occurring in their organization. According to a 2011 National Business Ethics Survey, over half (52%) of Fortune 500 employees polled said they observed misconduct in their workplace (Ethics Resource Center, 2012). In their 2012 Report to the Nations, the ACFE reported over half of their fraud hotline tips came from employees (p. 33).

Fraud hotlines are used in all sectors. Government agencies have used them since the late 1970s, following the Civil Service Reform Act of 1978 (CSRA). The CSRA was the first piece of legislation to increase the legal protections of federal employees who reported misconduct in the workplace (Shimabukuro &

Whitaker, 2012). However, their use became more prevalent following President George Bush's signing of the Whistleblower Protection Act (WPA). The WPA is a federal law that protects government whistleblowers from retaliation by their employer for reporting wrongdoing in the workplace.

Since SOX, fraud hotlines have been recommended, but are not required, in nonprofits. (Andrews & LeBlanc, 2013; GrossMendelsohn, 2013) Lawyers recommend them as a way of "encourag[ing] whistleblowing" to prevent fraud (Devaney et al., 2013). Per SOX, all entities, including nonprofit organizations, are prohibited from, and can be held criminally liable for, retaliating against whistleblowers and impeding an investigation (American Bar Association, 2013). Thus, nonprofits that currently operate fraud hotlines are using them as a matter of best practices, to demonstrate a commitment to encouraging whistleblowers.

Today, due to the lack of reporting requirements, it is largely unknown how many nonprofits currently operate fraud hotlines. It is believed that many nonprofits may operate fraud hotlines today as a best practice. Only estimates exist. In a 2007 study by Greenlee, Fischer, Gordon, and Keating, 40% of nonprofits operated a fraud hotline.

Evidence suggests hotlines are successful at catching fraud in nonprofits. Nonprofits that use The Network,* (now NAVEX Global) one of the largest third-party hotline providers, report an "extremely high percentage" of corruption and fraud, representing 13% of all cases in the "Public Administration" sector (a category containing some, but not all, of their nonprofit clients), which has been "consistent over the last four years" (2013, p. 13).

News reports have confirmed employees will use hotlines to report nonprofit fraud. One fraud at the Red Cross, reported in their Form 990, was originally detected via an anonymous tip to their hotline (News 4 JAX, 2013).

As discussed earlier, nonprofit entities are not required to use fraud hotlines. Today, it is difficult to determine which ones are currently using them because there is no single source containing this information. As a result, this author conducted an examination to determine the use of fraud hotlines by the *Forbes* list of 50 largest U.S. charities.

Methodology

To determine potential usage, each organization's website was reviewed for the page containing their hotline information. Ideally, the hotline is well advertised externally, as most callers to hotlines call from home and after business hours (Andrews & Leblanc, 2013). If a hotline was not located on the website, the organization was contacted by telephone and asked if they had a hotline. For those organizations employing hotlines, the researcher documented the name of the hotline,

---

* Overall, this assessment is based on 64 organizational clients of The Network, with a total of 468,966 employees.

whether it was managed internally or externally, and whether the number was easily located externally.

Next, of the organizations with hotlines, their fraud disclosures were examined for information suggesting the fraud was learned via the hotline. The fraud disclosures examined were taken from their Form 990 disclosures and the studies by the IRS and the *Washington Post*, which examined the Form 990s for nonprofits filed in 2008–2012. First, the organization was researched in a database created by the *Washington Post*, reporting the results of their analysis. If the organization was not located, then their Form 990s were independently examined during the same time period (2008–2012) to determine any reported diversions. Their 2013 Form 990, if available, was also reviewed. The Form 990 disclosure was reviewed closely to determine, if reported, whether it was revealed to the organization via a hotline tip.

Reports of the fraud documented in the Form 990 were also researched in the media, to determine whether the fraud reported was determined via a hotline tip.

The organization's website was also reviewed to determine whether they independently disclose any fraud captured from their hotline to the public.

Dataset

The organizations examined in this work, from the *Forbes* December 2014 list of the largest charities in the U.S. are as follows: American Cancer Society, American Heart Association, American Jewish Joint Distribution Committee, American National Red Cross, AmeriCares Foundation, Boy Scouts of America, Boys & Girls Clubs of America, Brother's Brother Foundation, Campus Crusade for Christ, CARE USA, Catholic Charities USA, Catholic Medical Mission Board, Catholic Relief Services, ChildFund International, Compassion International, Cross International, Dana-Farber Cancer Institute, Direct Relief, Father Flanagan's Boy's Home, Feed the Children, Feeding America, Food for the Poor, Good 360, Goodwill Industries International, Habitat for Humanity International, Kingsway Charities, Leukemia & Lymphoma Society, Lutheran Services in America, Make-A-Wish Foundation of America, MAP International, Marine Toys for Tots Foundation, Mayo Clinic, Memorial Sloan-Kettering Cancer Center, Nature Conservancy, Operation Blessing International Relief & Development, Planned Parenthood Federation of America, Population Services International, Salvation Army, Samaritan's Purse, Save the Children Foundation, St. Jude Children's Research Hospital, Step Up for Students, Susan G. Komen for the Cure, Task Force for Global Health, Teach for America, The Y-YMCA, United Service Organizations, United States Fund for UNICEF, United Way and World Vision.

Results

The 10 organizations employing hotlines are as follows: (1) American Cancer Society, (2) American National Red Cross, (3) Feed the Children, (4) Habitat for

Humanity International, (5) Mayo Clinic, (6) Memorial Sloan-Kettering Cancer Center, (7) St. Jude Children's Research Hospital, (8) The YMCA, (9) United Way, and (10) World Vision.

Assessments of eight of these organizations are as follows:

The American Cancer Society (ACS) is a charitable organization based out of Austin, Texas. According to their website, ACS has operated a fraud hotline since 2005. Their hotline is operated by Ethics Point, a major third-party supplier of hotline services. The ACS didn't disclose any reports about any fraud detected via their hotline.

In 2009, the American Cancer Society reported a diversion. They reported a former employee engaged in a fraud "related to telecommunications" and the "amount of property involved $1,517,057." According to their disclosure, "The theft was investigated though our internal Audit Services Department and their findings were reported to the authorities." This employee was prosecuted, convicted, and sentenced. It was not reported whether this fraud was learned via a hotline tip. From 2010 to 2013, they didn't report any significant diversions on their Form 990.

In 2013, the American National Red Cross reported a significant diversion of assets. They reported an employee in their Texas office stole $300,000, which they explain is "less than 0.00008 of total American Red Cross assets" (2012 Form 990).

According to media records, that was not the only fraud to occur that year. According to 2013 news reports, a Red Cross employee in Florida reportedly stole over $200,000 from the organization since 2011. She stole funds intended for victims of disasters. To perpetrate her fraud, she stole the credentials of another employee and used her "approvals" to authorize debit account payments to herself. Her fraud was uncovered due to an employee tip to the hotline (News 4 JAX, 2013). In April 2014, she was sentenced to 6 months in jail and ordered to return $88,000 in restitution (Cordeiro, 2014).

Overall in their 2012 Form 990, the Red Cross reported $640,000 in total losses in two separate incidents. The Red Cross advised that amount is "less than 0.00017 of total American Red Cross assets."

In their 2012 Form 990, they reported discovering $220,000 missing from their chapter in Tennessee. It was discovered these funds were being used in Russia. They said $88,000 was recovered, which is similar to the case above, yet it is unclear whether this report is describing the same incident.

In the same Form 990, they reported an employee stole $420,000 by taking excessive payroll payments. This employee was arrested and charged with embezzlement. The Red Cross reported receiving restitution, though they did not say how much.

In their Form 990s from 2008 to 2011, they didn't report any significant diversions.

Feed the Children is a scientific organization based out of Oklahoma City, Oklahoma. Also in 2009, Feed the Children disclosed their facility in Elkhart, Indiana, was "stripped" sometime between 2005 and 2007 resulting in "a minimum" of $3,000,000 in damages. They reported this fraud was the subject of litigation, to recover the funds. In this year, their reported revenue was $1.18 billion. In their Form 990s from 2010 to 2013, they didn't report any significant diversions.

On their website, Feed the Children did not disclose the data from their fraud hotline. Also, when called, it was determined their hotline did not work (on February 23, 2015). This organization said their hotline was "managed by an independent firm," but they didn't say which one.

For the Mayo Clinic, their Form 990s from 2010 to 2012 were available for review. They do not provide copies of their Form 990 on their website, like many other charities. Instead, they require a written request to their chief legal officer to receive their Form 990. A review of their available Form 990s didn't report any significant diversions of assets.

Habitat for Humanity's 2013 Form 990 reported a significant diversion of assets. Specifically, $350,000 worth of inventory was stolen or diverted by former staff and third-party service providers. Form 990s from 2010 to 2012 didn't report any significant diversions.

Memorial Sloan Kettering Cancer Center, in their 2010 Form 990, reported $4,000,000 in supplies were stolen in a multiyear fraud. According to the *Wall Street Journal*, an employee ordered toner-ink cartridges in bulk, and diverted them to himself and sold them for profit. This employee, who earned $37,000 per year, was said to live a lavish lifestyle, with an apartment in Trump Tower and a BMW that he paid for with cash (El-Ghobashy, 2010). The organization reported recovering the stolen funds from insurance.

St Jude's Form 990s from 2009 to 2013 didn't report any significant diversion of assets.

As for the YMCA, their 2010 Form 990 reported an employee embezzled $16,386 in cash. It was reported the organization received restitution from the insurance company in the full amount of the fraud, lest a $1,000 deductible.

Their 2008 Form 990 reported the chief executive officer (CEO) was "removed from his office under accusations of fiscal and operational impropriety, including nepotism. The COO [chief operating officer], CFO [chief financial officer] and Senior Program Director, all of whom were related to the CEO, were asked to resign their positions in connection to the investigation into financial and operational misconduct of the CEO." The YMCA said the case was presently under investigation by the Westchester County DA and the Department of Housing and Urban Development.

According to a March 7, 2008, news report, the CEO was under investigation for misuse of funds. The article further reported the CEO and his family members were accused of "us[ing] cars leased by the organization" (ABC NEWS 7, 2008). Further research identified the former executive director as Gregory du Sablon. The allegations included "questionable purchases" made by the CEO. These purchases were reportedly "approved" by a fellow board member, but that person claims to have not provided approval and that his signature was forged (News 12 Westchester, 2008). The DA was also looking into home repairs at Sablon's residence, that were alleged to have been conducted with YMCA materials and performed by YMCA personnel.

Conclusion

In his work "Empowering Employees to Prevent Fraud in Nonprofit Organizations," John Bradley says that given the effectiveness of hotlines, "employers would be advised to implement more [of them]" (Bradley, 2014, p. 12). Legislation enacted following similar crimes in publicly listed companies have resulted in the required use of fraud hotlines. It will be of interest to note whether this will happen in the nonprofit sector.

In the meantime, increased transparency of hotline data in this sector would be helpful to consumers from an antifraud perspective. Ideally, organizations operating hotlines will report their hotline data to the public to provide confidence their tips are heard and handled appropriately.

Hotlines and Cybercrime Prevention in the Financial Industry

Called the "The Bank Robberies of the Future," cybercrimes represent the future of bank crime, where "bank robbers...don't need guns, and they don't wear masks. Instead, they hide behind their computer screens and cover their digital tracks" (Lobosco, 2013). As a result of this change in the nature of the crime, the bank criminal has also evolved, innovating to adapt to "fast-evolving technologies and changing methodologies...[which is] presenting a significant challenge for investigators" (Interpol, 2014).

This chapter examines the applicability of a traditional crime prevention approach to prevent and detect cybercrime in the financial industry. Although bank crime has become more technical, nontechnical approaches to this type of crime seem to provide useful resiliency. In fact, a 2013 E&Y study indicated that as much as 80% of cybersecurity solutions are nontechnical in nature, involving "good governance" (p. 21). One such approach from a governance perspective is the fraud hotline.

Fraud hotlines, which are present in most banks following the Sarbanes–Oxley Act of 2002, show considerable promise in thwarting cybercrime. Since 2002, studies have proven that tips are the primary way that corporate crime is detected (ACFE, 2002–2016). Ironically, cybercriminals are most likely to be tipsters to such hotlines, due to their knowledge of current and planned crimes in this space, vast network, and desire/need for money.

This chapter considers the use of money rewards to incentivize tipsters. While bank hotlines do not typically offer reward money to callers, it is an approach worth considering in light of the benefits of increased detection and prevention of cybercrime. A case study of a hotline that presently offers rewards to callers is explored to gauge the potential value of this approach.

Problem Statement

By all accounts, cybercrime is a significant national threat. President Obama has informed the nation that it is "one of the most serious economic and national security challenges we face" (WhiteHouse gov., n.d.). One of the reasons cybercrime is so threatening to a business is its potential for economic harm. In fact, a single act of cybercrime could destabilize the United States and global economy, causing "billions of dollars in losses to the Nation's financial infrastructure" (National Security Council, 2011; United States Government Accountability Office Report, 2007).

Cybercrime is most prevalent and damaging in the financial industry. Cybercrime accounts for 38% of economic crime in the financial services sector, which is more than double that of other sectors (Ashford, 2012). Banks also face other unique risks, such as a loss of customers, brand value, and overall reputation (Ashford, 2012).

The financial industry is particularly vulnerable to cybercrime. A recent Depository & Trust Clearing Corp. report called cybercrime the "top systemic threat" to this industry. Key persons with significant insight into the cybercrime problem have warned financial institutions of the ongoing threat (Lokshin, n.d.), and the Federal Bureau of Investigation (FBI) and the CEO of JPMorgan Chase cautioned banks to be especially vigilant (Raval, 2014; The Associated Press, 2014).

Financial institutions are also losing a large amount of money to cybercrime. According to recent estimates, cyberattacks are costing banks as much as $500 million per year in the United States alone (McAfee, 2013). These losses are expected to increase over time. According to a 2013 study by the Ponemon Institute, cybercrime costs to the victim organization have increased by 78% since 2009 (Greenberg, 2013).

History

Fraud hotlines have been used in the government sector since the late 1970s, following the Civil Service Reform Act of 1978 (CSRA). The CSRA was the first piece of legislation to increase the legal protections of federal employees who reported misconduct in the workplace (Shimabukuro & Whitaker, 2012). In both the public and private sectors, the widespread use of hotlines began in 1989 and thereafter, following President George Bush's signing of the Whistleblower Protection Act (WPA). The WPA is a federal law that protects government whistleblowers from retaliation by their employer for reporting wrongdoing in the workplace.

Hotlines were required in publicly listed companies following the implementation of the Sarbanes–Oxley Act of 2002 (SOX). SOX is federal law created to strengthen the internal controls of publically listed companies, following the revelation of several internal frauds (e.g., Enron, Arthur Andersen, Adelphia Communications, ImClone, WorldCom). SOX provisions require that companies have an "anonymous reporting mechanism" for employees to report fraud, and fraud hotlines became the generally accepted way of receiving those tips, and satisfying the regulatory requirement.

The use of fraud hotlines in the private sector was later reinforced by the Dodd–Frank Wall Street Reform and Consumer Protection Act of 2010 ("Dodd–Frank"). Dodd–Frank was a policy response to corporate crime, which occurred despite SOX (e.g., Madoff) causing the Global Financial Crisis of 2008–2012. Dodd–Frank is a U.S. federal statute that is said to represent the most comprehensive change to financial regulations since the Great Depression (Greene, 2011). Dodd–Frank required regulators to create 243 new rules, designed to enhance accountability and transparency within the financial system (Davis Polk, 2010).

As part of that reform, Dodd–Frank added a money reward for hotline tipsters. Dodd–Frank expanded whistleblower provisions in SOX and the Securities and Exchange Act of 1934 (SEA) to provide tipsters, who report violations of certain laws to federal authorities, a reward based on the amount of money recovered by the SEC. Overall, the tipster is promised between 10% and 30% of recoveries over $1 million.

Hotlines and Cybercrime Prevention

Hotlines are seen as an important fraud prevention tool. Studies support the use of hotlines as a method of receiving organizational fraud tips. As a case in point, the Association of Certified Fraud Examiners has determined via corporate surveys, over the last decade, tips are the primary way that organizational fraud is discovered (ACFE, 2002–2012).

Hotlines are also proven to reduce loss due to fraud. Research has placed this savings as high as 50% (Buckhoff, 2003). These statistics have given executives confidence in the use of hotlines as a fraud prevention tool. In fact, in a recent American Institute of Certified Public Accountants (AICPA) Forensic and Valuation Services Trend Survey, over half of executives declared "internal whistleblower hotlines [will] lead to improvements in preventing fraud in the next two to five years" (Andrews and LeBlanc, 2013).

Cybercrime Prevention

Now that we have established the value of fraud hotlines in crime prevention efforts, it is important to review their potential value for cybercrime. Research demonstrates crime prevention theorists strongly support preventative efforts, which consider specific cybercriminal attributes (United Nations Office on Drugs and Crime [UNODC], 2013, p. 39). Hotlines that provide money reward are believed to provide an incentive that is especially attractive to these callers. According to the literature, cybercrime perpetrators are often underemployed (UNODC, 2013, p. 9).

Cybercrimes can also tend to have a large number of participants, which can result in a lot of potential callers. Overall, 80% of cybercrime acts are said to be organized, and perpetrated, by large criminal groups (UNODC, 2013, p. 18). As a result, it can be inferred that there are many "witnesses" to an average cybercrime— and thus, many potential tipsters—who could be persuaded to report crime, in exchange for the promise of money rewards.

The SEC Hotline

When considering the value of offering money rewards for tips, it is important to review a hotline that currently employs that method. One such hotline is the SEC hotline, established by Dodd–Frank in 2010. The SEC hotline, which offers money rewards to callers, receives a high volume of tips. In 2012, their first year of operation, they received 3,001 reports (SEC, p. 1). That number is steadily increasing. In 2013 they received 3,238 reports, representing an 8% increase (SEC, p. 8).

Tipsters to this hotline are receiving sizable awards. On November 15, 2013, the SEC awarded $14 million, in exchange for an actionable tip. SEC says more awards like this are forthcoming. News of these payouts is expected to results in an increased number of calls, and increased confidence in the hotline.

While the volume of tips is increasing, critics suggest the "success" rate of the hotline, to date, is low. Of these tips, as of October 2013, six were deemed to have been "high-quality" by the OWB, in that they resulted in an award to the tipster (SEC, p. 14). With 6,573 tips provided to the hotline, this means the program has a 0.09% "success rate." However, the SEC has said additional payouts are planned, and experts say more time is needed before the hotline can be properly evaluated (Murphy, 2012).

Hotlines and Cybercrime

Based on the evidence, hotlines are expected to be ideal vehicles to receive intelligence information concerning cybercrime. As demonstrated, the SEC hotline is successful in its ability to attract callers. Cybercriminals have knowledge of impending crime and may be incentivized to provide tips with the promise of money reward.

Thus, it is important to consider whether hotlines would be good vehicles for cyber-crime reporting in the financial industry.

Other industries are currently using hotlines to elicit cybercrime tips. One such hotline is The IC3 (The Internet Crime Complaint Center), which is a partnership between the FBI and the National White Collar Crime Center. On a local level, agencies such as the Sangamon County Sheriff's Office in Illinois recently created a cybercrime hotline (Reynolds, 2014). While these hotlines do not offer money rewards to callers, it is clear they see the value of marketing hotlines to receive cybercrime tips.

Yet other government hotlines are presently offering such rewards. Some agencies have even recently increased their reward amounts. New York State recently started a hotline to receive tips about illegal guns. This hotline offers a $500 reward (FOX News, 2013). Since 1982, Kansas City has operated a hotline that pays callers for their tips regarding felony crime. Recently, they announced the doubling of their potential payout to callers, from $1,000 to $2,000 (2014).

The financial industry has the potential to provide hotlines that offer rewards. While it would represent a new focus for this industry, as demonstrated, it is not a new concept. However, it would be easy to implement. The financial industry has hotlines in place to receive crime tips, and they can market them internally and externally for use in thwarting cybercrime, and provide a reward to callers.

Today, bank hotlines are typically marketed internally. While they are available to external callers, they are often not well marketed to this audience. Therefore, external marketing campaigns would be required.

Potential internal callers (current employees with knowledge of cybercrime) are currently the primary audience of hotlines. However, financial industry hotlines are commonly not marketed to receive cybercrime tips. Nevertheless, this is an easy fix. Current hotline marketing efforts could easily be augmented to invite potential employee callers to report any knowledge of potential cybercrime incidents, or current departmental conditions giving rise to cyber incidents.

The offer of reward money is also an element that may increase reporting both internally and externally. As evinced with the SEC hotline, rewards certainly lead to a high volume of calls. Given the great potential for loss due to incidents of cybercrime, a cost-benefit analysis may certainly prove to be cost effective to banks that offer reward money in exchange for tips. Like the SEC hotline, individual firms can conduct analyses over time to gauge the return on investment, in terms of quality of information gleaned in exchange for reward money paid.

Policy Implications

One consideration for this approach will be the cost benefit. However, one of the key benefits of this program is that firms can leverage their existing hotline to reduce operational costs. However, there might be a start-up cost associated with preparing the hotline for cybercrime-specific callers. For example, the staff assigned to receive these calls may require highly specialized training in order to understand and respond to the tip/threat. This training would include education into the psychology of the potential callers (which could be either an employee, third party, or the cybercriminal themselves) and how to best elicit information from each caller. If the firm is using a third-party hotline provider, their staff could be augmented at the direction of the client bank to include such personnel.

Another possible outcome is a high volume of calls, as seen with the SEC hotline. Lawyers warn that when money rewards are offered, a certain number of tipsters will call with *any* information, just for a chance to "hit the lottery" (Carney, 2013; Healy, 2013). If that happens, the hotline could become unwieldy without proper advance planning.

There are two potential implications of high call volume. It can increase expenses and also reduce hotline functionality. In terms of expense, some third-party providers charge their clients based on the number of tips received, or "reports." Both internal and external hotlines may also require additional personnel and training, as discussed, both resulting in potential increased costs. This increase should be considered as part of the potential expense of the program. If the call volume increases dramatically, it could also make the hotline more bureaucratic, which has challenged the SEC hotline. Unmanageable call volumes can impede the hotline's ability to produce meaningful results.

This was evinced in the SEC's hotline. Upon evaluation, inspectors found several shortcomings indicative of a potentially unmanageable program. One such oversight was a lack of agency performance metrics (SEC, 2013, p. 20–22) which the evaluators determined "may result in the degradation in performance and unnecessary long response times" (p. 21).

Another unintended consequence of an unmanageable hotline is call avoidance. It is possible that potential callers have avoided the SEC hotline due to perceived agency bureaucracy. Recent media reports have said the SEC hotline was not properly vetting complaints (Singer, 2013; Tobe, 2013). Experts believe tipsters with valid claims may be avoiding the hotline "because they are intimidated by the length of the bureaucratic process," one that *Forbes* called "ponderous" (Singer, 2013; Tobe, 2013). However, careful advance planning can reduce the likelihood of these problems.

Also, to confirm value and utility of the hotline to the organization, a careful program evaluation should be conducted following the first full year of operation. In conducting their cost-benefit analysis, program evaluators should also consider the reputational benefits. While it may be difficult to fully monetize crime averted, the statistics regarding the average cybercrime loss, and the noted reduction in incidents can be calculated and evaluated for effectiveness.

Another possible benefit of this program, which is difficult to measure, is increased public confidence. When hotlines are marketed externally, the public can become more aware of a bank's efforts to prevent and detect crime, which can result in an increased reputation for that firm. This increase in confidence could result in increased business. The firm could measure these potential benefits, by noting certain increases in this regard following the introduction of the external hotline marketing efforts.

Conclusion

Cybercrime is a major problem for financial institutions. If the industry was to provide money in exchange for tips, which could serve to prevent and detect this crime, the value could be significant. Similar to the SEC's program, actionable tips are expected to result. Despite the potential policy implications, evidence supports the use of hotlines to receive cybercrime tips. Increased reputation of the firm, and associated business, could also be realized. While there are costs involved, the cost due to cybercrime is expected to far outweigh the potential program costs. With cybercrime costing the average firm $11 million every 10 months (Ponemon Institute, 2013), it seems wise for firms to explore the possibility of purposing their existing hotlines to receive cybercrime tips.

Marketing Fraud Hotlines to Prevent Crime

Will dedicated hotlines increase cybercrime reporting? Yes, according to one New Jersey lawmaker's recent proposal to introduce a Cyber Fraud Hotline. The story behind this proposal illustrates a growing public need for cybercrime reporting mechanisms.

Research suggests that would-be tipsters across the globe are often aware of cybercrime yet don't know how to report it. It is important to understand the history behind the use of fraud hotlines to receive crime tips and the present use of this reporting mechanism to receive tips about cybercrime.

In New Jersey, Assembly Republican Leader Jon Bramnick learned that his constituents had knowledge of cybercrimes but didn't know how to report them. He also determined that he, himself, didn't know how to report them. Thus, he concluded New Jersey needed "one-stop shopping" for cyber fraud reporting.

Across the globe, in Mumbai, India, research suggests their residents experienced similar reporting challenges. A 2010 KPMG Survey revealed that most respondents, 79%, did not know how to report cybercrime.

In response to their cyber-reporting challenges, Australia recently implemented a cyber hotline at the national level, the Australian Cybercrime Online Reporting Network (ACORN). ACORN is expected to revolutionize cybercrime reporting by "enable[ing] police to access a national picture of the cybercrime affecting Australians and Australian businesses, enabling them to develop improved tactical and strategic responses to key cybercrime threats."

Naturally, for entities deciding to implement a similar hotline, cost may be a concern. However, some are able to implement their cybercrime hotline at no cost to taxpayers. For the Sangamon County Sheriff's Office, the hotline was implemented "at no cost to taxpayers...[by] us[ing] a line that was already owned by the sheriff's office and hook[ing] up a voice mail to it."

While cybercrime hotlines are not always easy to implement, it is clear that governments are recognizing their value in the fight against cybercrime.

References

ABC News. (2012, Jan. 10). Former councilman in 'stripper-gate' headed to prison. *ABC News*. Retrieved from http://www.10news.com/news/former-councilman-in-stripper-gate-headed-to-prison

ABC News. (2008, Mar. 7). Westchester DA probes YMCA director. *ABC News*. Retrieved from http://abc7ny.com/archive/6005309/

ABC News. *(n.d.)* State employee charged with social security fraud. (n.d.). *ABC News*. Retrieved from http://www.wqow.com/category/140922/more-local-news

ABC News. (2013, Oct.31). Former Morgan Stanley employee accused of fraud. *ABC News*.

AICPA Antifraud Programs and Controls Task Force. (2010, June). Audit committee considerations for whistleblower hotlines. *Journal of Accountancy*.

Alam, P., & Pearson, M.A., & Makar, S. (2004, Apr.). Earnings management revisited: further suggestions in the wake of corporate meltdowns. *Fraud Magazine*. Association of Certified Fraud Examiners. Retrieved from https://www.acfe.com/article.aspx?id=4294967804

American Bar Association. (2013, Apr. 8). Nonprofits and Sarbanes Oxley. Retrieved from https://www.americanbar.org/groups/probono_public_service/resources/program_management/nonprofits_sarbanes_oxley.html

American Institute of CPAs (AICPA). (2011, May 25). House financial services panel looks at Dodd-Frank whistleblowing rules. Retrieved from https://www.aicpa.org/advocacy/cpaadvocate/2011/pages/housepanellooksatdodd-frankwhistleblowing.aspx

American Red Cross. (2006, Aug.). Governance for the 21st Century.

American Red Cross. (2012). IRS Form 990.

American Red Cross. (2013, Oct. 30). Red Cross and hurricane sandy relief fund give $15.2 million. Retrieved from http://www.redcross.org/news/article/nj/princeton/Red-Cross--Hurricane-Sandy-NJ-Relief-Fund-Give-152-Million-to-Rebuild

American Red Cross Employee. (2013, Dec. 16). EMail.

Andrews, C. P., & LeBlanc, B. P. (2013, Aug.). Fraud hotlines: Don't miss that call. *Journal of Accountancy*. Retrieved from http://www.journalofaccountancy.com/issues/2013/aug/20127043.html

Anechiarico, F., & Jacobs, J. B. (1996). *The pursuit of absolute integrity*. London: University of Chicago Press.

Anti-Fraud Collaboration. (2014, Nov. 17). The fraud resistent organization: tools, traits, and techniques to deter and detect financial reporting fraud. *Center for Audit Quality*. p. 44. Retrieved from http://www.thecaq.org/fraud-resistant-organization

Arnall, D., & Herman, C. (2008, Sept. 25). FDIC: WaMu the 'largest bank failure ever. *ABC News*. Retrieved from http://abcnews.go.com/Business/story?id=5889501

Asian Development Bank. (2009). Global financial turmoil and emerging market economies: Major contagion and a shocking loss of wealth. *Asian Development Bank*. Retrieved from http://www.maths-fi.com/Major-Contagion-and-a-shocking-loss-of-wealth-032009.pdf

Association of Certified Fraud Examiners (ACFE). (2002–2012). Report to the nations on occupational fraud and abuse. *ACFE*. Retrieved from https://ACFE.com

Association of Certified Public Accountants (AICPA). (2007). The sarbanes oxley act. *AICPA*. Retrieved from http://fmcenter.aicpa.org/Resources/Traditional/Sarbanes-Oxley+Act.htm

Association of Government Accountants. (2009, Feb. 19). Fraud prevention controls "hotline best practices". Retrieved from https://www.agacgfm.org

Augar, P. (2008, Sept.). Do not exaggerate investment banking's death. *Financial Times*. Retrieved from https://www.ft.com/content/daae00b6-88bc-11dd-a179-0000779fd18c

Awbry, M. (2011, Nov. 15). Navigating city bureaucracy 'is like trying to get into a speakseasy with the wrong password.' *San Diego Rostra*. Retrieved from https://sdrostra.com/matt-awbrey/navigating-city-bureaucracy-is-like-trying-to-get-into-a-speakeasy-with-the-wrong-passoword/

Bandler, J. & Hechinger, J. (2003, June 6). Six former Xerox executives will pay $22 Million to SEC. *The Wall Street Journal*. Retrieved from https://www.wsj.com/articles/SB105482351065879700

Barkas, S. (2016, May 11). Palm desert may set up employee whistleblower hotline. *The Desert Sun*. Retrieved from http://www.desertsun.com/story/news/local/palm-desert/2016/05/11/palm-desert-city-council-ethics-hotline/84178954/

Barnard, A. (2012, Mar. 8). Rising G.O.P. star from Staten Island draws on political gifts to fend off critics. *The New York Times*. Retrieved from https://mobile.nytimes.com/2012/03/09/nyregion/michael-grimm-gop-congressman-fights-critics.html?mcubz=0

Barnett, C. (2000). Measurement of white collar crime using uniform white collar reporting (UCR) data. Retrieved from https://archives.fbi.gov/archives/news/pressrel/press-releases/white-collar-crime-study

Barr, M. S. (2016, Dec. 8). Trump's dismantling of Dodd-Frank would be 2008 all over again. *Fortune*. Retrieved from http://fortune.com/2016/12/08/trump-dodd-frank-2008-financial-crisis-steve-mnuchin/

Barrett, D. (2002, July 24). Rigas arrested, charged with conspiracy. *USA Today*. Retrieved from https://usatoday30.usatoday.com/sports/hockey/stories/2002-07-24-rigas-arrested_x.htm

Barrett, W. P. (2014, Dec. 10). The largest U.S. charities for 2014. *Forbes*. Retrieved from https://www.forbes.com/sites/williampbarrett/2014/12/10/the-largest-u-s-charities-for-2014/#35ce41613675

Bartholomew, C., & S. Nilson. (2012). *The SEC's whistleblower program. Weil, Gotshal & Manges LLP*. Retrieved from https://www.weil.com/-/media/files/pdfs/Whistleblower_Powerpoint_Fed_Sec.pdf

Bauer, S. (2013, June 26). Wisconsin panel OKs pay raise for state, UN workers. *Associated Press*.

BBC News. (2002, July 24). Adelphia execs arrested for fraud. *BBC News*. Retrieved from http://news.bbc.co.uk/2/hi/business/2149956.stm

BBC News. (2002, Oct. 15). Ex-Imclone boss admits fraud. *BBC News*. Retrieved from http://news.bbc.co.uk/1/hi/business/2330649.stm

BBC News. (2009, Jan. 28). Global job losses 'could hit 51 million'. *BBC News*.

Beresford, D. R., N. deB Katzenbach, & C. B. Rogers, Jr. (2003). Report of investigation by the Special Investigative Committee of the Board of Directors of WorldCom Inc http://www.concernedshareholders.com/CCS_WCSpecialReport.Exc.pdf.

Bernard, H. R. (2012). *Social research methods: Qualitative and quantitative approaches.* Sage.

Better Business Bureau. (2013). Charity study. *BBB.* Retrieved from https://www.bbb.org/new-york-city/charity-study-paper/

Better Business Bureau. (2003). *Standards for charity accountability.* Retrieved from https://www.bbb.org/us/storage/0/Shared%20Documents/Standards%20for%20Charity%20Accountability.pdf

Biegelman, M. T. (2004). Designing a robust fraud prevention program. *Fraud Magazine.* ACFE. Retrieved from http://www.fraud-magazine.com/article.aspx?id=4294967803

Bishop, J. T., & Temkin, D. J. (2007). Benchmarking your whistleblower hotline. *American Lawyer Media Law Journal , 14* (8).

Blau, J. (2003, July 7). WorldCom malfeasance revealed. *CBS News.* Retrieved from http://www.cbsnews.com/news/worldcom-malfeasance-revealed/

Blau, P.M. (1964). *Exchange and power in social life.* New York: Wiley.

Bloomberg BusinessWeek. (2013, July). Company overview of Glassdoor, Inc. Retrieved from http://investing.businessweek.com/research/stocks/private/snapshot.asp?privca pId=42888542

Bloomberg News. (2004, Mar. 16). Actress tells of flying on Adelphia's planes. *Los Angeles Times.* Retrieved from http://articles.latimes.com/2004/mar/16/business/fi-adelphia16

Bookman, Z. (2007). Convergences and omissions in reporting corporate and white collar crime. *DePaul Bus & Comm. LJ, 6* (347).

Bosworth, M. H. (2007, Apr. 5). Former Morgan Stanley employee arrested on data theft charges. Retrieved from https://www.Consumeraffairs.com.

Bottari, M. (2011, Sept. 25). Is Scott Walker john doe? *Huffington Post.* Retrieved from http://www.huffingtonpost.com/mary-bottari/scott-walker-john-doe_b_978770.html

Bouchard, S. E., & Linthorst, T. A. (2010, July 20). Congress passes sweeping changes to labor and employment whistleblower protections. *Moran Lewis.* Retrieved from http://www.morganlewis.com/index.cfm/publicationID/fb1bf169- 849e-4325-8ecl-e35002b2d5ca/fuseaction/publication.detail

Bozeman, B., & Rainey, H. G. (1998). Organization rules and the 'bureaucratic personality'. *American Journal of Political Science, 42* (1), 163–189.

Bradley, J. M. (2014, Sept. 18). Empowering employees to prevent fraud in nonprofit organizations. *Penn Law: Legal Scholarship Repository.* Retrieved from http://scholarship.law.upenn.edu/faculty_scholarship/1446/

Branscomb, L. W., & Sierra, T. (2005, Dec. 15). Landlord of opportunity (democratic mayor of National City is a slumlord). *San Diego Tribune.*

Bray, C. (2011, June 28). Arrest in alleged Citi fraud. *The Wall Street Journal.*

Brennan, J. (2015). Having an ethics hotline is a really really bad idea (really?). Society of Corporate Compliance and Ethics. Retrieved from http://complianceandethics.org/having-an-ethics-hotline-is-a-really-really-bad-idea-really/

Briggs & Veselka. (2015). 6 Answers to the most frequently asked questions about Sarbanes Oxley. Briggs & Veselka Co.

Buckhoff, T. A. (2003, July). The benefits of a fraud hotline. *The CPA Journal.* Retrieved from http://archives.cpajournal.com/2003/0703/dept/d076203.htm

Budman, S. (2013, July 19). Glassdoor: 5 companies with best work-life balance sit in bay area. *NBC.* Retrieved from http://www.nbcbayarea.com/news/tech/Glassdoor-Top-5-Companies-with-Best-Work-Life-Balance-216237971.html

Bukhari, J. (2017, Jan. 24). 3 More scandals that will have you saying 'WTF Wells Fargo'. *Fortune.* Retreived from http://fortune.com/2017/01/24/wells-fargo-scandals/

Bush, G. W. (2002). Statement on signing the Sarbanes Oxley Act of 2002. The American Presidency Project.

Caiden, G. E. (1969). *Administrative reform.* Chicago: Adeline Publishing Company, pp. 114–115.

Caiden, G. E. (1985). Excessive bureaucratization: The J curve theory of bureaucracy and Max Weber through the looking glass. *Dialogue, 7* (4), 21–33.

Caiden, G. E. (1991). *Administrative reform comes of age.* de Gruyter Studies in Organization.

Caiden, G. E. (1991). What really is public maladministration. *Public Administration Review,* 51 (6), 486–493.

Calsyn, C., Grayson, S., Cohen, J., & Berkowitz, P. (2013). Whistleblower update 2013: Complying with an evolving, growing & increasingly enticing government program. Corporate Law Advisory. *Lexis Nexis Webinar.* Retrieved from http://lexisnexis.com/in-house-advisory/fullArticle.aspx?Bid=62488

Carney, J. J., & Wangsgard, K. E. (2013, Oct. 8). "Show me the money" or 14 million reasons to upgrade your compliance program. Retrieved from https://www.*Lexology.com.*

Carney, L. (2016). Staff Report: Approve the creation of an "ethics hotline" for the City of Palm Desert. City of Palm Desert. Retrieved from http://cityofpalmdesert.granicus.com/MetaViewer.php?view_id=2&clip_id=252&meta_id=47488

Carton, B. (2010, Sept. 9). Pitfalls emerge in Dodd-Frank whistleblower bounty provision. *Compliance Week.* Retrieved from https://www.complianceweek.com/blogs/bruce-carton/pitfalls-emerge-in-dodd-frank-bounty-provision#.WYCvwRPytxg

CBS. (2009, Apr. 28). Nick Inzunza voted hispanic chamber of commerce chairman. *CBS.* Retrieved from http://www.cbs8.com/global/story.asp?s=10265396.

CFPB. (2016). Consumer financial protection bureau fines Wells Fargo $100 million for widespread illegal practice of secretly opening unauthorized accounts. Consumer Financial Protection Bureau. Retrieved from https://www.consumerfinance.gov/about-us/newsroom/consumer-financial-protection-bureau-fines-wells-fargo-100-million-widespread-illegal-practice-secretly-opening-unauthorized-accounts/

Chacón, D. J. (2015, Mar. 12). Santa Fe launches fraud, waste and abuse hotline for city employees. *Santa Fe New Mexican.* Retrieved from http://www.santafenewmexican.com/news/blogs/local_news/santa-fe-launches-fraud-waste-and-abuse-hotline-for-city/article_b0324cc2-c8ff-11e4-a477-4f656a3ab77a.html

Chacón, D. J. (2017, Jan. 17). As slow-moving fraud case continues, efficiency of city hotline questioned. *Sante Fe New Mexican.*

Chan, A. (2010, Sept. 9). FDIC insurance limit of $250,000 is now permanent. *Boston.com.*

Chartered Global Management Accountant (CGMA). (2015). Managing responsible business. *CGMA.* Retrieved from http://www.cgma.org/Resources/Reports/DownloadableDocuments/2015-07-21-Managing-Responsible-Business.pdf

Chinn, L., Mufson, H., & Dueltgen, J. (2013, November 19). Record breaking $14 million payout highlight of SEC's annual report. Proskauer. Retrieved from http://www.whistleblower-defense.com/2013/11/19/record-breaking-14m-payout-highlight-of-secs-annual-report/

Christopher, J. (2012). Part IV of the new form 990: New requirements for reporting governance practices and policies. *Fraternal Law Newsletter.*

Chung, J. (2010, June 1). Driver in deadly Long Island crash was speeding and unlicensed. Gothamist. Retrieved from http://gothamist.com/2010/06/01/driver_in_deadly_li_crash_was_speed.php

Ciancio, Nick. (2013). Utilizing hotline benchmarking data to improve ethics and compliance program effectiveness. Austin, TX: Association of Certified Fraud Examiners (ACFE). Retrieved from http://www.acfe.com/uploadedfiles/acfe_website/content/canadian/2013/presentations/2b-nick-ciancio.pdf

Clarke, P. (2013, Dec. 11). Red cross personal support workers go on strike. *The Toronto Star*.

CNN. (2002, Sept. 12). Three Tyco execs indicted for fraud. *CNN.com*. Retrieved from http://edition.cnn.com/2002/BUSINESS/asia/09/12/us.tyco/

CNNMoney. (2002, Sept. 17). Tyco wants its money back. Retrieved from http://money.cnn.com/2002/09/17/news/companies/tyco/index.htm

Coenen, T. (2008). *Essentials of corporate fraud*. Hoboken: John Wiley and Sons.

ComputerWeekly.com. (2012, Mar. 27). Cybercrime a growing threat to financial sector says PWC. Retrieved from http://www.computerweekly.com/news/2240147503/Cybercrime-a-growing-threat-to-financial-sector-says-PwC

Connecticut Department of Children and Families. (n.d.). Questions and answers. http://www.ct.gov/dcf/cwp/view.asp?a=2534&q=314388#Sued.

Conner, Cheryl. (2012, July 23). The power of the sisgruntled employee. *Forbes*. Retrieved from https://www.forbes.com/sites/cherylsnappconner/2012/07/23/the-power-of-the-disgruntled-employee/#44b8f3e86ced

Contorno, S., Benson, D., & Jones, B. (2011, Feb. 27). Police: Wisconsin protest Saturday 'one of largest'. *USA Today*. Retrieved from https://usatoday30.usatoday.com/news/nation/2011-02-26-wisconsin-saturday-rally_N.htm

Cook, N. (2009, Sept. 13). What happened to Lehman's employees? *Newsweek*. Retrieved from http://www.newsweek.com/what-happened-lehmans-employees-79593

Cooper, M., & Seeley, K. Q. (2011, Feb. 18). Wisconsin leads way as workers fight state cuts. *New York Times*. Retrieved from http://www.nytimes.com/2011/02/19/us/politics/19states.html

Cordeiro, M. (2014, Apr. 16). Ex-red cross official gets jail for over $200,000 in theft. *The Gainsville Sun*. Retrieved from http://www.gainesville.com/article/LK/20140416/News/604135344/GS/

Corkery, M. (2010, Apr. 7). Meet a Citigroup whistleblower: Richard M. Bowen III. *The Wall Street Journal*. Retrieved from https://blogs.wsj.com/deals/2010/04/07/meet-a-citigroup-whistleblower-richard-m-bowen-iii/

Corkery, M. (2016). Wells Fargo fined $185 million for fraudulently opening accounts. *The New York Times*, September 8.

Crozier, M. (1964). *The bureaucratic phenomenon*. Chicago: University of Chicago Press.

Dash, E., & Timmons, H. (2007, Mar. 27). Citigroup to cut at least 10,000 in overhaul. *The New York Times*. Retrieved from http://query.nytimes.com/gst/fullpage.html?res=9C00EED71230F934A15750C0A9619C8B63&pagewanted=all

Davis Polk. (2010). Summary of the Dodd Frank Wall Street Reform and Consumer Protection Act: *Davis Polk*. Retrieved from https://www.davispolk.com

Delikat, M., Phillips, R., Muoio, R., & Myers, J. (2013, Oct. 8). United States: Take heart, companies can win whistleblower cases: Two key victories in SOX and Dodd-Frank cases. Retrieved from http://www.mondaq.com/unitedstates/x/267822/Whistleblowing/Take+Heart+Companies+Can+Win+Whistleblower+Cases+Two+Key+Victories+Last+Week+in+SOX+and+DoddFrank+Cases

Deloitte. (2004). Antifraud whitepaper. Retrieved from http://www.deloitte.com/assets/Dcom- Shared%20Assets/Documents/us_assur_Antifraud%20whitepaper.pdf

Deloitte. (2011). CFO insights: Whistleblowing after Dodd-Frank: New risks, new responses. Retrieved from http://www.corpgov.deloitte.com/binary/com.epicentric.contentman-agement.servlet.ContentDeliveryServlet/USEng/Documents/Audit%20Committee/Antifraud%20Programs%20and%20Controls/cfo_whistleblowers_022211.pdf

Deloitte. (2011, Mar. 21). Evaluation of the EPA office of civil rights. Retrieved from https://assets.documentcloud.org/documents/723416/epa-ocr-audit.pdf

Deloitte. (2014). Lead by example: Making whistleblowing programs successful in corporate India. Deloitte Forensic India, Deloitte. Retrieved from https://www2.deloitte.com/content/dam/Deloitte/in/Documents/finance/in-fa-whistleblowing-survey-2014-noexp.pdf

Deloitte. (2004). Taking control: A guide to compliance with section 404 of the Sarbanes-Oxley Act of 2002. Retrieved from https://www.iasplus.com/en/binary/dttpubs/0407takingcontrol.pdf

Deloitte. (2007, Nov.). Ten things about fraud control: How executives view the fraud control gap. Deloitte Forensic Center. Retrieved from http://www.kahsa.org/files/public/financetoolkit/FRAUDTen.pdf

Deloitte. (2010). Whistleblowing and the race to report. Deloitte Forensic Center. Retrieved from https://www.slideshare.net/DeloitteForensicCenter/whistleblowing-and-the-new-race-to-report-deloitte-forensic-center-062512

DeLong, K. (2012, July 24). County employee Frieda Webb accused of misconduct in office. *Journal Sentinel.* Retrieved from http://fox6now.com/2012/07/24/county-employee-frieda-webb-accused-of-misconduct-in-office/amp/

Denney, A. (2016). Court expands whistleblower law to apply to private citizens. *New York Law Journal.* Retrieved from http://www.newyorklawjournal.com/id=1202770746326/Court-Expands-Whistleblower-Law-to-Apply-to-Private-Citizens?slreturn=20170710181220

Desio, P. An overview of the organizational guidelines. *United States Sentencing Commission.* Retrieved from https://www.ussc.gov/sites/default/files/pdf/training/organizational-guidelines/ORGOVERVIEW.pdf

Deutsch, C.H. (2001, June 1). Auditor finds no fraud in Xerox's annual report. Retrieved from http://www.nytimes.com/2001/06/01/business/auditor-finds-no-fraud-in-xerox-s-annual-report.html

Devaney, W.H., Martin, .S., Buell, N. & Tenenbaum J. (2013, Nov. 8). Preventing fraud and embezzlement in your nonprofit organization. Retrieved from http://www.Mondaq.com.

Dienst, J., & Forkin, J. (2013, Oct. 1). Whistleblower gets record $14 million payout from SEC. *NBC News.* Retrieved from http://www.nbcnews.com/news/other/whistleblower-gets-record-14-million-payout-sec-f8C11311621

Dillon, L. (2011, Nov. 10). Fact check: The bureaucracy of the 'awful tower'. *Voice of San Diego.* Retrieved from http://www.voiceofsandiego.org/mayor-2012/fact-check-the-bureaucracy-of-the-awful-tower/

DLA Piper. (2015). Whistleblowing: An employer's guide to global compliance. Employment Group, DLA Piper, p. 48. Retrieved from https://www.dlapiper.com/en/us/insights/publications/2015/06/whistleblowing-law-2015/

Dowling, J. D. (2011, Nov.). Global whistleblower hotline toolkit: How to launch and Operate a legally-compliant international workplace report channel. Retrieved from https://whitecase.com

Dowling, J. D. (2012, Jan.). Launching a global whistleblower hotline - Beyond Europe. *White & Case.*

Downs, A. (1964). *Inside bureaucracy*. Rand Corporation.

Dremann, S. (2011, Aug. 12). Fraud at Palo Alto branch costs Citigroup $500k. *Palo Alto Online*. Retrieved from http://www.paloaltoonline.com/weekly/story.php?story_id=15357

Dunkle, R. H. H., II. (2015, Apr. 23). Best practices for employee hotlines. *Accounting Today*.

Dye, J. (2011, June 27). Former Citigroup vice president charged with embezzling $19 million. *Huffington Post*. Retrieved from http://www.huffingtonpost.com/2011/06/27/citigroup-vice-president-embezzle-bank-fraud_n_885288.html

Egan, M. (2009, Aug. 21). Demystifying the bank closure process. *FOX Business*.

Egan, M. (2016, Sept. 9). 5,300 Wells Fargo employees fired over 2 million phony accounts. *CNN Money*. Retrieved from http://money.cnn.com/2016/09/08/investing/wells-fargo-created-phony-accounts-bank-fees/index.html

Egan, M. (2016, Sept. 21). I called the Wells Fargo ethics line and was fired. *CNN Money*. Retrieved from http://money.cnn.com/2016/09/21/investing/wells-fargo-fired-workers-retaliation-fake-accounts/index.html

Egan, M. (2016, Sept. 27). Fired Wells Fargo workers fight back with federal lawsuit. *CNN Money*. Retrieved from http://money.cnn.com/2016/09/26/investing/wells-fargo-fake-accounts-worker-lawsuit/index.html

Egan, M. (2017, Jan. 27). Elizabeth Warren asks why federal Wells Fargo complaint site has vanished. *CNN Money*. Retrieved from http://money.cnn.com/2017/01/27/investing/elizabeth-warren-wells-fargo-website-trump/index.html

Ehrlich, B., & J. C Boggs. (2017, Jan. 28). The next repeal and replace: Dodd-Frank. *Forbes*. Retrieved from https://www.forbes.com/sites/realspin/2017/01/28/the-next-repeal-and-replace-dodd-frank/#7dff0f845cd7

Eisinger, J. (2013, Jan. 23). Financial crisis suit suggests bad behavior at Morgan Stanley. *Dealbook NY*. Retrieved from https://dealbook.nytimes.com/2013/01/23/financial-crisis-lawsuit-suggests-bad-behavior-at-morgan-stanley/

El-Ghobashy, T. (2010). Almost like printing money. *The Wall Street Journal*. Retrieved from https://www.wsj.com

Ensign, R. L. (2013, Oct. 18). Another court rules in favor of internal whistleblower. *Wall Street Journal*. Retrieved from https://blogs.wsj.com/riskandcompliance/2013/10/18/another-court-rules-in-favor-of-internal-whistleblower/

Ensign, R. L. (2013, Oct. 21). Judge says whistleblower protections don't apply abroad. *Wall Street Journal*.

Environmental Protection Agency (EPA). (2012, Nov. 30). EPA annual survey. Retrieved from http://www.epa.gov/ohr/annual_survey.htm

Environmental Protection Agency, Office of Inspector General. (2009). Access survey results. Interim Report. Retrieved from https://www.epa.gov/office-inspector-general/report-office-inspector-general-access-survey-results

Ernst & Young. (2004). Fraud: real solutions to a real risk. E&Y Global Investigations & Dispute Advisory Group. Retrieved from https://www.ey.com

Ernst & Young. (2008). Corruption or compliance-Weighing the costs. 10th global fraud survey. Retrieved from http://www.ey.com/Publication/vwLUAssets/global_fraud_survey_2008/$FILE/EY_10TH_GLOBAL_FRAUD_SURVEY_2008.pdf

Ernst & Young. (2013). 16th annual global information security survey. Retrieved from http://www.ey.com/Publication/vwLUAssets/EY_-_2013_Global_Information_Security_Survey/$FILE/EY-GISS-Under-cyber-attack.pdf

Ernst & Young. (2013, May). Navigating today's complex business risks. Europe, Middle East, India and Africa Fraud Survey 2013. Retrieved from http://www.ey.com/Publication/vwLUAssets/Navigating_todays_complex_business_risks/$FILE/Navigating_todays_complex_business_risks.pdf

Ethicspoint. (2007). Beyond compliance: Implementing effective whistleblower hotline reporting systems. EthicsPoint Inc. Retrieved from http://touroinstitute.com/Beyond_Compliance.pdf

Ethics Resource Center. (2012). 2011 National business ethics survey. *Berkley Center for Religon, Peace & World Affairs, Georgetown University.* Retrieved from https://berkleycenter.georgetown.edu/publications/2011-national-business-ethics-survey-workplace-ethics-in-transition

Exall, M. (n.d.). Dodd-Frank and SOX: A whistleblower comparison. *The Network.*

Feder, B. J. (2002, June 29). Turmoil at Worldcom: The executives; bonuses once meant to retain talent now risk outrage. *The New York Times.* Retrieved from http://www.nytimes.com/2002/06/29/business/turmoil-worldcom-executives-bonuses-once-meant-retain-talent-now-risk-outrage.html

Federal Bureau of Investigation. (2001) Crime in the United States 2000. Retrieved from https://ucr.fbi.gov/crime-in-the-u.s/2000

Federal Bureau of Investigation. (2011) Financial crimes report to the public 2010–2011. Retrieved from https://www.fbi.gov/stats-services/publications/financial-crimes-report-2010-2011

Federal Deposit Insurance Corporation (FDIC). (n.d.). Failed bank list. Retrieved from Federal Deposit Insurance Corporation: http://www.fdic.gov/bank/individual/failed/banklist.html

Federal Deposit Insurance Corporation (FDIC). (2005, Aug. 16). Guidance on implementing a fraud hotline. Financial Institution Letters. Retrieved from https://www.fdic.gov/news/news/financial/2005/fil8005.html

Financial Crisis Inquiry Commission. (2011, Feb. 25). The financial crisis inquiry report. Retrieved from https://www.gpo.gov/fdsys/pkg/GPO-FCIC/pdf/GPO-FCIC.pdf

Flanagan, J. C. (1954). The critical incident technique. *Psychological Bulletin, 41* (4), 327–355.

Flesher, D. L. (1999). Attitudes toward whistle-blowing hotlines. *National Forum* 79(2): 5.

Forbes. (2006). The 200 largest U.S. charities. Retrieved from https://www.forbes.com/2005/11/18/largest-charities-ratings_05charities_land.html

Foti, C. (2013, Oct. 2). Employers Beware: Will the SEC be a saftey net for terminated whistleblowers? *Forbes.* Retrieved from https://www.forbes.com/sites/insider/2013/10/02/employers-beware-will-the-sec-be-a-safety-net-for-terminated-whistleblowers/#31074a7216c8

FOX News. (2013, Mar. 21). New York offers $500 reward for reporting illegal gun owners. *Fox News Politics.* Retrieved from http://www.foxnews.com/politics/2013/03/21/new-york-state-offers-500-reward-for-reporting-illegal-gun-owners.html

Frank, R. & Solomon D. (2002, May 24). Adelphia and Rigas family had a vast network of business ties. *The Wall Street Journal.* Retrieved from https://www.wsj.com/articles/SB1022168448423792680

Freudenheim, M. (2004, Sept. 2004). Court backs higher valuation of Healthsouth investors' loss. *The New York Times.* Retrieved from http://www.nytimes.com/2004/09/29/business/court-backs-higher-valuation-of-healthsouth-investors-loss.html

Frieden, T. (2004, Sept. 17). FBI warns of mortgage fraud epidemic. *CNN.com.* Retrieved from http://www.cnn.com/2004/LAW/09/17/mortgage.fraud/

Furguson, C., C. BeckC, & A. Bolt. (2010). *Inside Job.* Directed by Charles Furguson. Produced by Sony Pictures Classics.

Gallagher, J. (2012, Feb. 26). Why Sherry Hunt blew the whistle at Citi mortgage. *St. Louis Post Dispatch*. Retrieved from http://www.stltoday.com/business/local/why-sherry-hunt-blew-the-whistle-at-citimortgage/article_6fd9a0f6-5e3d-11e1-b5f2-0019bb30f31a.html

Garrett, S. (2011, May 11). Garrett chairs subcommittee hearing to review Dodd-Frank whistleblower provisions. Retrieved from http://garrett.house.gov/News/DocumentSingle.aspx?DocumentID=240758

Garza, J. (2011, Aug. 18). Five charged with fraud in foodshare program. *Journal Sentinel*. Retrieved from http://archive.jsonline.com/news/crime/128043253.html/

Geewax, M. (2016, Nov. 10). Trump team promises to 'dismantle' Dodd-Frank bank regulations. *The Two-Way*. Retrieved from http://www.npr.org/sections/thetwo-way/2016/11/10/501610842/trump-team-promises-to-dismantle-dodd-frank-bank-regulations

George, B. (2008, Nov. 19). Failed leadership caused the financial crisis. *U.S. News and World Report*. Retrieved from https://www.usnews.com/opinion/articles/2008/11/19/failed-leadership-caused-the-financial-crisis

Getter, D.E. (2014, Apr. 22). Federal deposit insurance for banks and credit unions. *Congressional Research Service*. Retrieved from https://fas.org/sgp/crs/misc/R41718.pdf

Giang, V. (2013, Mar. 29). Companies can now use Glassdoor to track job seekers. *Business Insider*. Retrieved from http://www.businessinsider.com/employers-can-now-use-glassdoor-to-track-their-competition-2013-3

Giblin, E. J. (1981, Dec. 1). Bureaupathology: The denigration of competence. *Human Resource Management*. Wiley Periodicals, Inc. A Wiley Company. Vol. 20, Issue 4, pp. 22-25.

Global Compliance Inc. (n.d.). Red Cross web reporting site. Retrieved from www.integrity-helpline.com/redcross

Gofman, A. (2011, Oct. 24). Under the hood: The cost of bureaucracy. *Harvard Political Review*. Retrieved from http://harvardpolitics.com/arusa/under-the-hood-the-cost-of-bureaucracy/

Goldman, R. (2008, Mar. 19). Bear Sterns calls in grief counselors. *ABC News*. Retrieved from http://abcnews.go.com/Business/story?id=4476286

Goldstein, M. (2007, June 20). Criminal probe snares Morgan Stanley VP. *Bloomberg*. Retrieved from https://www.bloomberg.com/amp/news/articles/2007-06-20/criminal-probe-snares-morgan-stanley-vpbusinessweek-business-news-stock-market-and-financial-advice

Golson, J. (2016, Mar. 14). Fired employee says Volkswagen deleted data about emissions scandal. *The Verge*. Retrieved from https://www.theverge.com/2016/3/14/11222478/volkswagen-diesel-scandal-lawsuit-deleted-data

Government Accountability Project. (2016, Jan. 28). Why whistleblowers wait: Recommendations to improve the Dodd-Frank Law's SEC Whistleblower awards program. Retrieved from https://www.whistleblower.org/sites/default/files/GAP_Report_Why_Whistleblowers_Wait.pdf

Greenberg, A. (2013, Oct. 8). Study: The cost of cybercrime continues to rise. *SC Magazine*. Retrieved from https://www.scmagazine.com/study-the-cost-of-cyber-crime-continues-to-rise/article/542712/

Greene, E. F. (2011). Dodd-Frank and the future of financial regulation. Harvard Business Law Review. Retrieved from https://www.hblr.org/2011/10/greene-symposium-dfa/

Greenlee, J., Fischer, M., Gordon, T., & Keating, E. (2007). An investigation of fraud in nonprofit organizations: Occurrences and deterrents. *Nonprofit and Voluntary Sector Quarterly*. Retrieved from http://journals.sagepub.com/doi/abs/10.1177/0899764007300407?journalCode=nvsb

Griffin, D. A. (2012, Sept. 18). Citi execs depart after mortgage fraud settlement. American Banker. Retrieved from https://www.americanbanker.com/news/citi-execs-depart-bank-after-mortgage-fraud-settlement

Griffin, E. (1997). *A first look at communication theory.* New York: The McGraw-Hill Companies.

Grimm, M. (2011). Reps. Grimm, Garrett, Campbell, and Stivers introduce whistleblower improvement act. *States News Service.* Retrieved from https://www.highbeam.com/doc/1G1-261186171.html

GrossMendelsohn. (Winter 2013). Nonprofit Insider. Retrieved from http://www.gma-cpa.com/wp-content/uploads/Nonprofit-Newsletter-2013-Winter.pdf

Gusdorf, M. (2008). Employment law-A learning module in six segments. *Society for Human Resource Management (SHRM).* Retrieved from https://www.shrm.org/aca-demicinitiatives/universities/TeachingResources/Pages/EmploymentLaw.aspx

Gustafson, C. (2011, Oct. 27). Former parks worker repays $40,000. *The San Diego Union-Tribune.* Retrieved from http://www.sandiegouniontribune.com/news/watchdog/sdut-former-parks-worker-repays-40000-2011oct27-htmlstory.html

Hagenbaugh, R. L. (2003, Aug.). Current issues: Corporate governance and Sarbanes Oxley-what you need to know. *Fraud Magazine.* Association of Certified Fraud Examiners.

Hall, D. J., & Spicuzza, M. (2013, Mar. 2). Prosecutor closes john doe investigation into Scott Walker aides. *Wisconsin State Journal.* Retrieved from http://host.madison.com/wsj/news/local/crime_and_courts/prosecutor-closes-john-doe-investigation-into-for-mer-scott-walker-aides/article_5952999e-8283-11e2-b977-001a4bcf887a.html

Hamiliton, J. (2012). House holds hearings on legislation revising Dodd-Frank whistleblower provisions. *Jim Hamilton's World of Securities Regulation.* Wolters Kluwer. Retrieved from http://jimhamiltonblog.blogspot.com/2011/05/house-holds-hearings-on-legislation.html

Harkay, P. (2009, Aug. 24). What options to solve the systemic banking crisis. *Universiteit Maastricht.*

Haverluck, M. F. (2007, Nov. 17). Televangelists face intense federal probe. *CBN News.* Retrieved from http://www.cbn.com/cbnnews/us/2007/November/Televangelists-Face-Intense-Federal-Probe/?Print=true

Healy, T. (2013, Oct. 16). Bold and unrelenting enforcement from the SEC: A six month review. *Reed Smith.* Retrieved from https://www.reedsmith.com/en/perspectives/2013/10/bold-and-unrelenting-enforcement-from-the-sec-a-si

Hirst, S. (2010). Investor protection provisions of the Dodd-Frank Act. *Harvard Law School.* Retrieved from https://corpgov.law.harvard.edu/2010/07/11/investor-protection-provisions-of-the-dodd-frank-act/

Holzer, J. (2012, Aug. 21). SEC pays $50,000 in first whistleblower award. *The Wall Street Journal.* Retrieved from https://www.wsj.com/articles/SB1000087239639044385580 4577603320771833802

Institute of Internal Auditors (IIA), The American Institute of Certified Public Accountants (AICPA), Association of Certified Fraud Examiners (ACFE). (2008, June) Managing the business risk of fraud: A practical guide. Retrieved from https://www.acfe.com/uploadedFiles/ACFE_Website/Content/documents/managing-business-risk.pdf

Interpol. (2014). Interpol national cybercrime training. http://www.interpol.int/About-INTERPOL/The-INTERPOL-Global-Complex-for-Innovation/Events2/INTERPOL-National-Cybercrime-Training-Seminar.

Ivry, Bob. (2012, May 31). Woman who couldn't be intimidated by Citigroup wins $31 million. *Bloomberg Markets.* Retrieved from https://longform.org/posts/woman-who-couldn-t-be-intimidated-by-citigroup-wins-31-million

Jenkins, R. (2014). The problem with ethics hotlines. *ChronicleVitae.* Retrieved from https://chroniclevitae.com/news/324-the-problem-with-ethics-hotlines

Jetter, D. (2015). 5 years later: Dodd-Frank continues to cripple small business, kill American jobs. *Americans for Tax Reform.* Retrieved from https://www.atr.org/5-years-later-dodd-frank-continues-cripple-small-business-kill-american-jobs

Johnson, D. (2015). Ethics at work 2015 survey of employees. Institute of Business Ethics, p. 22. Retrieved from http://www.ibe.org.uk/userassets/publicationdownloads/ibe_survey_eawl5_britain.pdf

Joseph, A. (2012, Jan. 10). Whistleblower bill draws lobbying. *Government Executive.* Retrieved from http://www.govexec.com/oversight/2012/01/whistleblower-bill-draws-lobbying/35798/

Kalick, L. (2014). Reporting on form 990. *The Center for Association Leadership (ASAE).* Retrieved from https://www.asaecenter.org/resources/articles/an_magazine/2014/may-june/reporting-fraud-on-form-990

Kashton, A. (2011, Apr. 26). Canada: The benefits and banes of fraud hotlines. Crowe Soberman LLP. *Mondaq.* Retrieved from http://www.mondaq.com/unitedstates/x/130412/White+Collar+Crime+Fraud/The+Benefits+And+Banes+Of+Fraud+Hotlines

Katz, Marshall & Banks. (2011, Mar. 12). Up to 100,000 protest Wisconsin law curbing unions. *Reuters.* Retrieved from http://www.reuters.com/article/us-wisconsin-protests-idUSTRE72B2AN20110313

KCPD Chief. (2014, Feb. 7). TIPS hotline reward doubles to up to $2000. Retrieved from KCPD Chief's Blog. http://kcpdchief.blogspot.com/2014/02/tips-hotline-reward-doubles-to-up-to.html.

Kelleher, J. B. (2011, Mar. 12). Up to 100,000 protest Wisconsin law curbing unions. Reuters. Retrieved from http://www.reuters.com/article/us-wisconsin-protests-idUS-TRE72B2AN20110313

Kelly, B. (2009, Feb. 18). Morgan Stanley executive charged with $25 million fraud. *Investment News.*

Kelton, E. (2013, June 26). SEC whistleblower rewards: Larger ones are coming. Forbes. Retrieved from https://www.forbes.com/sites/erikakelton/2013/06/26/sec-officials-on-whistleblower-rewards-the-best-is-yet-to-come/#399b4e197373

Kelton, E. (2012, Mar. 1). Seven ingredients for a successful whistleblower program. Forbes. https://www.forbes.com/sites/erikakelton/2012/03/21/seven-ingredients-for-a-successful-whistleblower-program/#64bbfb37390c

Kentouris, C. (2009, July 20). How a Morgan Stanley executive may have committed the perfect operations crime. Neh, almost. *Securities Technology Monitor.*

Kerschberg, B. (2011, Apr. 14). The Dodd Frank Act's robust whistleblowing incentives. Forbes. Retrieved from https://www.forbes.com/sites/benkerschberg/2011/04/14/the-dodd-frank-acts-robust-whistleblowing-incentives/

King, R. (2013, May 14). Glassdoor report surveys Facebook workforce sentiment one year after IPO. Retrieved from http://www.zdnet.com/article/glassdoor-report-surveys-facebook-workforce-sentiment-one-year-after-ipo/

King, R. (2013, May 17). Glassdoor: Google ranked top company with best business outlook. ZD Net. Retrieved from http://www.zdnet.com/article/glassdoor-google-ranked-top-company-with-best-business-outlook/

Klein, J. S., & N. J. Pappas. (2015). Circuit split on Dodd-Frank whistleblower retaliation. *New York Law Journal.* Retrieved from http://www.newyorklawjournal.com/id=1202744046986/Circuit-Split-on-DoddFrank-Whistleblower-Retaliation

Kling, M. (2013, Apr. 28). SEC's whistleblower program runs into crosswinds. Newsmax Finance. Retrieved from http://www.newsmax.com/Finance/StreetTalk/SEC-Whistleblower-Program-Crosswinds/2013/04/28/id/501687/

Kocieniewski, D. (2012, Sept. 11). Whistleblower awarded $104 million by IRS. *New York Times*.

Koehler, M. (2010). Dodd-Frank whistleblower provisions leading to one tip per day. Corporate Compliance Insights.

Kolhatkar, S. (2014, Jan. 28). Finance gadfly Sheila Bair takes a banking job. Bloomberg. Retrieved from https://www.bloomberg.com/news/articles/2014-01-28/sheila-bair-takes-the-revolving-door-to-a-seat-on-santander-board

Koleva, G. (2012, Feb. 17). Red Cross fined $9.6 million for unsafe blood collection. *Forbes*. Retrieved from https://www.forbes.com/sites/gerganakoleva/2012/01/17/american-red-cross-fined-9-6-million-for-unsafe-blood-collection/#4a87c51970ec

Koppel, N. (2010, Dec. 2010). Corporate America is no fan of the new whistleblower law. *Wall Street Journal*. Retrieved from https://blogs.wsj.com/law/2010/12/15/corporate-america-is-no-fan-of-new-whistleblower-law/

Kovacs, E. (2012, Nov. 23). ENISA releases report on the use of honeypots to detect cyber-attacks. *Softpedia News*. Retrieved from http://news.softpedia.com/news/ENISA-Releases-Report-on-the-Use-of-Honeypots-to-Detect-Cyberattacks-309270.shtml

KPMG. (2009). Integrity survey 2008-2009. *KPMG Forensic*. Retrieved from https://www.ice.gov/doclib/aml/pdf/2009/leary.pdf

KPMG. (2013). Fraud risk management: Developing a strategy for prevention, detection and response. *KPMG*. Retrieved from http://www.kpmg.com/US/en/IssuesAndInsights/ArticlesPublications/Documents/fraud-risk-management-whitepaper.pdf.

KPMG. (2013). Integrity survey. *KPMG Forensic*. Retrieved from https://assets.kpmg.com/content/dam/kpmg/pdf/2013/08/Integrity-Survey-2013-O-201307.pdf

Krisher, T., & D. McHugh. (2017). VW emissions-cheating deal could put employees in hot seat. Associated *Press*. Retrieved from http://www.businessinsider.com/ap-vw-emissions-cheating-deal-could-put-employees-in-hot-seat-2017-1

Kroll. (2013/2014). Global fraud report. *Kroll and the Economist Intelligence Unit*. Retrieved from https://www.eiuperspectives.economist.com/strategy-leadership/global-fraud-report-2013-2014

Kroll, K. (2012, July 24). Hotline benchmarking report reveals insight into compliance. *Compliance Week*. Retrieved from https://www.complianceweek.com/news/news-article/hotline-benchmarking-report-reveals-insight-into-compliance#.WY0jOsaZM0Q

Kumagai, J. (2004, Apr. 1). The whistle-blower's dilemma. *IEEE Spectrum*. Retrieved from http://spectrum.ieee.org/at-work/tech-careers/the-whistleblowers-dilemma

Kusserow, R. P. (2012). Developing and operating a hotline. *Compliance Resource Center*. Retrieved from https://www.complianceresource.com/wp-content/uploads/2013/03/0.2.2-Developing-and-Operating-a-Compliance-Hot-Line.pdf

LaCroix, K. M. (2013, Apr. 26). Will obstacles deter the SEC's Dodd Frank whistleblower program? The D&O Diary. Retrieved from http://www.dandodiary.com/2013/04/articles/securities-litigation/will-obstacles-deter-the-secs-dodd-frank-whistleblower-program/

La Cross Tribune Staff. Public Workers by the Numbers. (2011, Feb. 2). *La Crosse Tribune*. Retrieved from http://lacrossetribune.com/news/local/public-workers-by-the-numbers/article_d89a1ae2-3a5a-11e0-a028-001cc4c002e0.html

Lerner, L. (2012, Apr. 19). Prepared remarks of Lois Lerner, director, exempt organizations. *Georgetown University Law School.* Retrieved from http://op.bna.com.s3.amazonaws. com/hl.nsf/r%3FOpen%3dbyul-94erkh

Levy, F. (2010, Oct. 11). America's safest cities. *Forbes.com.* Retrieved from https://www.forbes. com/2010/10/11/safest-cities-america-crime-accidents-lifestyle-real-estate-danger.html

Libit, B., T. Frier, and W. Draney. (2014, Oct. 25). Elements of an effective whistleblower hotline. *Harvard Law School Forum on Corporate Governance and Financial Regulation.* Retrieved from https://corpgov.law.harvard.edu/2014/10/25/ elements-of-an-effective-whistleblower-hotline/

Liebelson, D. (2012, June 7). Study crushes one argument for Rep. Grimm's so-called whistleblower 'Improvement' act. *The Project on Government Oversight (POGP).* Retrieved from http://pogoblog.typepad.com/pogo/2012/06/study-crushes-argument-for-rep-grimms-so-called-whistleblower-improvement-act.html

Lieber, D. (2012, July 2). Whistleblower Richard Bowen hits Citigroup, then federal government. *Watchdog Nation.* Retrieved from https://watchdognation.com/ whistleblower-richard-bowen-hits-citigroup-then-federal-government/

Lighthouse. (2016). Why ethics hotlines are considered a best practice. *Lighthouse.* p. 14. Retrieved from https://www.lighthouse-services.com/documents/Why%20Ethics%20 Hotlines%20Are%20Considered%20a%20Best%20Practice.pdf

Lloyds Banking Group. (2015). Code of personal responsibility. Retrieved from http://www. lloydsbankinggroup.com/globalassets/our-group/responsible-business/download-centre/lloyds-banking-group_code-of-personal-responsibility_v3_2015.pdf

Lobosco, K. (2013, July 9). Cyberattacks are the bank robberies of the future. *CNN. com* Retrieved from http://money.cnn.com/2013/07/09/technology/security/ cybercrime-bank-robberies/

Lokshin, M. (2013, Aug. 20). With cyber threat to financial services, questions loom about role of regulation. Bloomberg Law. Retrieved from https://www.bna.com/ with-cyber-threats-to-financial-services-questions-loom-about-role-of-regulation/

Loser, C. M. (2009, May 1). Global financial turmoil and emerging market economies: Major contagion and a shocking loss of wealth? *Global Journal of Emerging Market Economies.* 1(2), 137–158.

Lowe, S. (2011, Mar. 3). Former San Diego Employee Accused in Theft of $100K from Park and Recreation Department. *Rancho Bernardo Patch.* Retrieved from https:// patch.com/california/ranchobernardo-4sranch/former-san-diego-city-employee-accused-in-theft-of-10c8162bf713

Loya, E. J., Jr., Montano, S.A., Martin, D.S., &Tenenbaum. (2015, Feb. 19). A primer on detecting, preventing, and investigating fraud, embezzlement, and charitable diversion. *Venable LLP.* Retrieved from https://www.venable.com/ files/Publication/1df8ab63-6f13-48d2-984a-38ebfe30d0ba/Presentation/ PublicationAttachment/c0ea21eb-372e-4bc0-a99c-5674d384bf2a/A-Primer-on-Detecting-Preventing-and-Investigating-Fraud-Embezzlement-and-Charitable-.pdf

Luna, E. (2008). City auditor letter to members of the audit committee. City Auditor's Quarterly Fraud Hotline Report. *City of San Diego.*

Luna, E. (2008, Oct. 16). Quarterly fraud hotline report Q1 2009. *San Diego City Auditor.*

Malone, T., & Childs, R. (2005). *Best practices in ethics hotlines, a framework for creating an effective anonymous reporting mechanism. The Network.* Retrieved from http://la-acfe. org/images/downloads/Resources/bestpracticesinethics2005.pdf

Malone, T. (2003, Jan. 29). Letter from The Network to the SEC. *The Network.*

Marley, P. (2013). Most state workers will see 1% pay increases beginning next month. *Journal Sentinel*. Retrieved from http://archive.jsonline.com/news/statepolitics/most-state-workers-will-see-1-pay-hikes-beginning-next-month-b9942534z1-213144061. html/

Marshall, M. N. (1996). Sampling for qualitative research. *Family Practice, 13* (6), 522-525.

Martin, J. (2013, July 19). Glassdoor: Digital exuberance hampers work-life balance. *Forbes. com*. Retrieved from https://www.forbes.com/sites/work-in-progress/2013/07/19/glassdoor-digital-exuberance-hampers-work-life-balance/#1879bf5d6b77

Maxwell, J. A. (1992). Understanding and validity in qualitative research. *Harvard Educational Review, 62* (3), 279.

McAfee. (2013, July). The economic impact of cybercrime and cyber espionage. *Center for Strategic and International Studies*. Retrieved from https://www.mcafee.com/uk/resources/reports/rp-economic-impact-cybercrime.pdf

McCool, G., & Graybow, M. (2009, Mar. 13). Madoff pleads guilty, is jailed for $65 billion fraud. *Reuters*. Retrieved from http://www.reuters.com/article/us-madoff-idUSTRE52A5JK20090313

McCormack, T., Pike, R. & Mahendranathan H. (2016). United States rewards international whistleblowers for help in uncovering fraud. *Huffington Post*. Retrieved from http://www.huffingtonpost.com/tim-mccormack/united-states-rewards-int_b_10004880.html

McCuistion, N. N. (n.d.). Whistleblowers: Inside the mortgage meltdown. Retrieved from www.frtv.org.

McHard, J.M. & Mohr, B.A. (2011, July/Aug.). Hotlines for heroes: Making a fraud hotline accessible and successful. *Fraud Magazine*. Association of Certified Fraud Examiners. Retrieved from http://www.fraud-magazine.com/article.aspx?id=4294970025

Meier, K. J., & Krause, G. A. (2003). The scientific study of bureaucracy: An overview. *Politics, policy, and organizations: Frontiers in the scientific study of bureaucracy*, 1–19.

Merkel, R. (2015, Sept. 29). Where were the whisleblowers in the Volkswagen emissions scandal? *The Conversation*. Retrieved from http://theconversation.com/where-were-the-whistleblowers-in-the-volkswagen-emissions-scandal-48249

Merriam, S. B. (1995). What can you tell from an N of 1: Issues of validity and reliability in qualitative research. *PAACE Journal of Lifelong Learning , 4*, 51–60.

Merriam-Webster Dictionary. (2014, Apr.). "Organization".

Merton, R.K. (1940). Bureaucratic structure and personality. *Social Forces*. Vol. 18, No. 4, 560–568.

Merton, R. K. (1957). *Social theory and social structure*. Glencoe, Illinois: Free Press.

Missouri Department of Social Services. (2012) Child welfare manual. Retrieved from https://dss.mo.gov/cd/info/cwmanual/section2/ch4/sec2ch4sub3_10.htm.

Mohr, E. (2012, July 17). State employees indicted in federal fraud charges. *TwinCities.com*. Retrieved from http://www.twincities.com/localnews/ci_21094458

Mohr, E. (2012, July 18). Washington county attorney: No new charges for state worker accused of fraud. *TwinCities.com*. Retrieved from http://www.twincities.com/ci_21101680/washington-county-attorney-no-new- charges-state-worker

MoneyScience. (2012, June 11). The whistleblower who sued Citibank and won. Retrieved from MoneyScience.com: http://www.moneyscience.com/pg/blog/TheFinancialServicesClub/read/368766/the-whistleblower-who-sued-citibank-and-won

Moran, G. (2013, Apr. 15). Ex-Councilman goes to halfway house. *The San Diego Union-Tribune.* Retrieved from http://www.sandiegouniontribune.com/sdut-ex-council-man-goes-to-halfway-house-2013apr15-story.html

Moran, G. (2012, Jan. 18). Ralph Inzunza told to report to prison by Jan 30. *The San Diego Union-Tribune.* Retrieved from http://www.sandiegouniontribune.com/sdut-inzuna-told-report-prison-jan-30-2012jan20-story.html

Morgan, Lewis & Brockius LLP. (2010, Aug.). Financial reform legislation: A guide to the employment-related provisions. White Paper. Retrieved from https://www.morganlewis.com/pubs/financial-reform-legislation-a-guide-to-the-employment-related-provisions

Morgan Stanley. (2006–2012). Form 10k Annual Report. New York: Securities and Exchange Commission.

Murdock, D. (2011, Mar. 18). Death threats by the dozen in Wisconsin. *National Review Online.* Retrieved from http://www.nationalreview.com/articles/262428/death- threats-dozens-wisconsin-deroy-murdock

National Security Council. (2011). Strategy to combat transnational organized crime. *The White House.* Retrieved from https://obamawhitehouse.archives.gov/sites/default/files/Strategy_to_Combat_Transnational_Organized_Crime_July_2011.pdf

NAVEX Global. (2007). Does your ethics and compliance program meet the federal sentencing guidelines?

NAVEX Global. (2008, Jan.). Legal brief: Detailed FAR training requirements. Retrieved from https://www.Navexglobal.com

NAVEX Global. (2013). Translation and interpretation services. NAVEX Global. Retrieved from http://www.navexglobal.com/en-us/file-download canonical? file=/NAVEXGlobal_LanguageSupport.pdf&file name=NAVEXGlobal_LanguageSupport.pdf

NAVEX Global. (2014). Hotline benchmarking methodology. Retrieved from https://www.Navexglobal.com

NAVEX Global. (2014, Feb. 25). NAVEX Global's 2014 hotline benchmarking report shows increasing quality of internal "whistleblower" reporting programs. Retrieved from Navexglobal.com

NAVEX Global. (2015) Ethics & compliance hotline benchmark report. Retrieved from https://www.Navexglobal.com

NBC News. (2006, May 26). Enron sentences will be tied to investor losses. *Associated Press. NBC News.* Retrieved from http://www.nbcnews.com/id/12993408/ns/business-corporate_scandals/t/enron-sentences-will-be-tied-investor-losses/

Newby, J. (2011, Mar. 11). Wisconsin unions threaten local businesses with boycotts. *Washington Examiner.* Retrieved from https://www.washingtonexaminer.com

News 4 JAX. (2013, Dec. 24). Gainesville police: Red cross worker stole $203K. *News 4 JAX.* Retrieved from https://www.news4jax.com

News 12 Westchester. (2008, Mar. 7). YMCA director in fraud probe takes leave of absence. *News 12 Westchester.* Retrieved from http://westchester.news12.com/story/34911887/ymca-director-in-fraud-probe-takes-leave-of-absence

Newsweek. (2009, Sept. 13). Left behind by Lehman. *Newsweek.* Retrieved from http://westchester.news12.com/story/34911887/ymca-director-in-fraud-probe-takes-leave-of-absence

Norris, F. (2014, Jan. 9). JP Morgan lost Madoff in a blizzard of paper. *The New York Times.* Retrieved from https://www.nytimes.com/2014/01/10/business/madoffs-trail-lost-in-a-blizzard-of-paper.html

NWC. International whistleblower protections. Retrieved from http://www.whistleblowers.org.

Observer-Reporter. (1990, Aug. 7). Red Cross hindered by bureaucracy. *Observer-Reporter.* Retrieved from https://observer-reporter.com

O'Brien, R. D. (2015). Former U.S. Rep. Michael Grimm sentenced to eight months in prison. *The Wall Street Journal.* Retrieved from https://www.wsj.com/articles/former-u-s-rep-michael-grimm-sentenced-to-8-months-in-prison-1437149636

Ochs, C. (2005, Oct.). Establishing a hotline: A way to detect fraud. *Peoria Magazines.* RSM McGladrey. Retrieved from http://www.peoriamagazines.com/ibi/2005/oct/establishing-hotline-way-detect-fraud

OECD. (2012). *Whistleblower protection: Encouraging reporting.* CleanGovBiz, Organisation for Economic Co-operation and Development.

O'Hara, P. (2005). *Why law enforcement organizations fail.* North Carolina: North Carolina Academic Press.

Office of the Comptroller of the Currency (OCC). (2010). Fraud and insider abuse. Exam handbook, Section 360. Retrieved from https://www.occ.gov/static/news-issuances/ots/exam-handbook/ots-exam-handbook-360.pdf

Office of the Comptroller of the Currency (OCC). (2013, Nov.). *Comptrollers handbook. Insider activities.* Retrieved from https://www.occ.gov/publications/publications-by-type/comptrollers-handbook/pub-ch-insider-activities.pdf

Oppel, R. A. (2001, Nov. 22). Employees' retirement plan is a victim as Enron tumbles. *The New York Times.* Retrieved from http://www.nytimes.com/2001/11/22/business/employees-retirement-plan-is-a-victim-as-enron-tumbles.html

Oppel, R. A. & Ross Sorkin, A. (2001, Nov. 9). Enron admits to outstanding profits by about $600 million. *The New York Times.* Retrieved from http://www.nytimes.com/2001/11/09/business/enron-admits-to-overstating-profits-by-about-600-million.html

Oppel, R. A., & Ross Sorkin, A. (2001, Nov. 29). Enron's collapse: The overview. *The New York Times.* Retrieved from http://www.nytimes.com/2001/11/29/business/enron-s-collapse-the-overview-enron-collapses-as-suitor-cancels-plans-for-merger.html

Oversight Systems. (2005). 2005 Oversight Systems financial executive report on Sarbanes Oxley. Retrieved from https://oversightsystems.com

Panetta, J. (2012, May 2). IRS focuses on nonprofit governance and significant diversion of assets. *Burr Pilger Mayer.* Retrieved from https://www.bpmcpa.com

Papst, C. (2016). Prince Georges hotline designed to protect tax dollars, wastes tax dollars. *WJLA 7 Washington D.C.* Retrieved from http://wjla.com/features/7-on-your-side/prince-georges-hotline-designed-to-protect-tax-dollars-wastes-tax-dollars

Patrick, P. A. (2010, Oct.). Be prepared before you blow the whistle. *Fraud Magazine* Association of Certified Fraud Examiners. Retrieved from http://www.fraud-magazine.com/article.aspx?id=4294968656

Pearlman, S., Mandelker, S., & Baddish, N. M. (2013, Sept. 24). SEC enforcement Official recommends that firms showcase their compliance programs. *Lexology.com.*

Peets Coffee and Tea. (2017). Peet's coffee and tea accounting fraud reporting hotline policy. Retrieved from https://www.peets.com/about-us/company-info/company-info-fraud-hotline

Penman, C. (2013). Analysis and benchmarking: Maximizing the benefits of hotline data. *NAVEX Global.* Retrieved from https://www.navexglobal.com

Penman, C. (2016). Top three findings from our EMEA & APAC benchmark report. *NAVEX Global*. Retrieved from https://www.navexglobal.com

Penman, C., & E. O'Mara. (2015). *2015 ethics & compliance hotline benchmark report. NAVEX Global*. Retrieved from https://www.navexglobal.com

Perez, D., & Barkhurst, M. (2012). *Paradoxes of leadership in police management*. Delmar: Cengage Learning.

Peterson, A. (2009). *Reporting of wrongdoing and using hotline data to improve the organization*. SAI Global. New York: Aspen Publishers.

Pictures, S. (Producer). (2010). *The inside job* [Motion Picture].

Ponemon Institute. (2013). 2013 cost of cyber crime study: United States. HP Enterprise Security. Retrieved from https://media.scmagazine.com/documents/54/2013_us_ccc_report_final_6-1_13455.pdf

Post Staff Report. (2017, Jan. 27). Wells Fargo whistleblower site vanishes. *New York Post*. Retrieved from http://nypost.com/2017/01/27/whistleblower-site-for-wells-fargo-workers-vanishes/

Post, W. (2013, Oct.). Millions missing, little explanation. *Washington Post*. Retrieved from http://www.washingtonpost.com/wp-srv/special/local/nonprofit-diversions-database/

Prince George's County Crime Solvers, Inc. (n.d.). Hotline Website. Retrieved from http://www.pgcrimesolvers.com/content/remain-anonymous

PricewaterhouseCoopers. (2007). Economic crime: People, culture and controls. The 4th Biennial Global Economic Crime Survey. Retrieved from https://www.pwc.com/gx/en/economic-crime-survey/pdf/gecs_engineering_and_construction_supplement.pdf

PricewaterhouseCoopers. (2011). Global economic crime survey: Middle east report. Retrieved from http://www.pwc.com/m1/en/publications/globalecnomiccrimesurvey.html

PricewaterhouseCoopers. (2014). Global economic crime survey: Economic crime: A threat to business globally. Retrieved from http://www.micci.com/downloads/digests/eberita/2014/15/pwc.pdf

PricewaterhouseCoopers. (2011, Nov.). Global economic crime survey: Cybercrime: protecting against the growing threat. Retrieved from https://www.pwc.com/ke/en/assets/pdf/gecs-2011-global-report.pdf

Pruthi, R. K. (2005). *Paradigms of public administration and civil services*. Grand Rapids: Discovery Publishing House.

PYMNTS. Wells CEO says the ethics hotline was mostly ethical. *PYMNTS.com*. Retrieved from http://www.pymnts.com/news/regulation/2016/wells-ceo-says-the-ethics-hotline-was-mostly-but-not-totally-ethical/

Rainey, H. (2009). *Understanding and managing public organizations*. Hoboken: John Wiley and Sons.

Ramshaw, E. (2012, July 20). In Medicaid fraud investigations, a controversial tool. *The Texas Tribune*. Retrieved from https://www.texastribune.org/2012/07/20/medicaid-fraud-investigations-controversial-tool/

Rajgopal, R. (2016, Mar. 30). Hotline-A tool for fraud detection. *KPMG*. Retrieved from https://home.kpmg.com/na/en/home/insights/2016/03/hotline-tool-for-fraud-detection.html

Rasor, D. (2011, Dec. 21). Would you blow the whistle? Many say yes, but perils abound. *TruthOut*. Retrieved from http://www.truth-out.org/news/item/5702:would-you-blow-the-whistle-many-say-yes-but-perils-abound

Rastogi, N. (2008, Aug. 7). Why do banks fail on Fridays? *Slate*. Retrieved from http://www.slate.com/articles/news_and_politics/explainer/2008/08/why_do_banks_fail_on_fridays.html

Ratliff, E. (2014, Dec. 31). The appalling career of Michael Grimm. *The New Yorker*. Retrieved from http://www.newyorker.com/news/news-desk/appalling-career-michael-grimm

Raval, A. (2014, Jan. 24). FBI warns retailers of more cyber attacks. *Financial Times*. Retrieved from https://www.ft.com/content/e52517f8-8480-11e3-b72e-00144feab7de

Reisinger, S. (2011, Nov. 1). When the whistle blows: Dodd-Frank's bounty provision has GCs staying up nights. *Corporate Counsel*. Retrieved from http://www.corp-counsel.com/id=1202473095226?id=1202473095226&hubType=Top%2520Story&When_The_Whistle_Blows_&slreturn=20170711145523

Reuters. (2011, Oct. 3). HK regulator fines Citi $770,000 for employees' ponzi scheme. *Reuters*. Retrieved from http://www.reuters.com/article/us-citigroup-fine-idUS-TRE7921C820111003

Reuters. (2011, May 7). Citi says former Indonesia employee committed fraud. *Reuters*. Retrieved from https://www.reuters.com/article/us-indonesia-citigroup-idUST-RE7460NK20110507

Reynolds, J. (2014, Feb. 11). Sheriff rolls out new cyber crime hotline. *The State Journal-Register*. Retrieved from http://www.sj-r.com/article/20140211/News/140219833

Rico, C. (2012, Feb. 23). Government bureaucracy impedes growth in the construction industry. *San Diego Source*. Retrieved from http://www.sddt.com/Construction/article.cfm?SourceCode=20120223cra&_t=Government+bureaucracy+impedes+growth+in+construction+industry#.WY3-scaZM0Q

Riddix, M. (2010, Apr. 26). Why does the FDIC wait until Friday to close banks? *Benzinga.com*. Retrieved from https://www.benzinga.com/242982/why-does-the-fdic-wait-until-friday-to-close-banks

Riley, D. D., & Brophy-Baermann, B. E. (2005). *Bureaucracy and the policy process: Keeping the promises*. New York: Roman and Littlefield.

Rogers, J. C. (2013, Oct. 23). Ethics rules stop most corporate lawyers from seeking federal whistle-blower bounty. *Bloomberg BNA*. Retrieved from https://www.bna.com/ethics-rules-stop-n17179878901/

Rosenberg, M. & Turner, R.H. (1981). *Social psychology: Sociological perspectives*. Livingston: Transaction Publishers.

Ross, B. (2011, Oct. 11). Ex-CEO used Tyco funds for personal expenses. *ABC News*. Retrieved from http://abcnews.go.com/Primetime/story?id=132070

Rubenfeld, S. (2015). Dodd-Frank rollback to spare SEC whistleblower program, experts say. *The Wall Street Journal*. Retrieved from https://blogs.wsj.com/riskandcompliance/2016/11/15/dodd-frank-rollback-to-spare-sec-whistleblower-program-experts-say/

San Diego Office of the City Auditor. (2008, Oct. 20). Fraud hotline administration plan. Retrieved from https://sandiego.gov

San Francisco Examiner. (1991, Jan. 2). Red Cross ready to apply first aid to itself. *Chicago Tribune News*. Retrieved from http://articles.chicagotribune.com/1991-01-02/news/9101010306_1_special-committee-disaster-relief-efforts-earthquake-and-hurricane-hugo

San Jose California. (n.d.). Office of the City Manager. Retrieved from https://www.sanjoseca.gov/index.aspx?NID=566

Schepp, D. (2002, Feb. 27). Enron employees campaign for pay. *BBC News*. Retrieved from http://news.bbc.co.uk/2/hi/business/1845643.stm

Schultze, S. (2012, June 26). Prosecutors say attorney for doe defendant leaked information. *Journal Sentinel*. Retrieved from http://archive.jsonline.com/news/milwaukee/prosecutors-says-attorney-for-doe-defendant-leaked-information-s35ti7m-160388765.html/

Schultze, S. (2012, July 20). County official gets out of jail. *Journal Sentinel*. Retrieved from http://archive.jsonline.com/newswatch/prosecutors-may-take-weeks-to-decide-on-whether-to-charge-webb-ac66kjo-163240826.html

Schultze, S. (2012, July 24). Milwaukee county official accused of taking kickbacks. *Journal Sentinel*. Retrieved from http://archive.jsonline.com/news/milwaukee/milwaukee-county-official-allegedly-took-kickbacks-in-billing-scheme-ou67ubc-163576626.html/

Schuman, I., & G. Keating. (2011, July 22). The whistleblower improvement act: New legislation takes aim at Dodd-Frank whistleblower bounty provisions. *Littler*. Retrieved from https://www.littler.com/publication-press/publication/whistleblower-improvement-act-new-legislation-takes-aim-dodd-frank

Scott, P. G. (2002). Examining red tape in public and private sector organizations: A further look at the role of individual perceptions and attributes. *The Social Science Journal, 39*, 477–482.

Security Executive Council. (2007) Hotline benchmarking report. Retrieved from https://www.securityexecutivecouncil.com/newsroom/details.html?pr=24775

SecurityWeek. (2001, Sept. 6). Former Citigroup VP pleads guilty to stealing more than $22 million. *SecurityWeek*. Retrieved from http://www.securityweek.com/former-citigroup-vp-pleads-guilty-stealing-more-22-million

Senate Commerce Science and Transportation Committee. (2002, Feb. 26). Transcript of senate commerce committee hearing on Enron. *The New York Times*. Retrieved from http://www.nytimes.com/2002/02/26/business/transcript-of-senate-commerce-committee-hearing-on-enron.html?mcubz=0

Seyfarth Shaw. (2010, July 21). Dodd-Frank act expands SOX's whistleblower provisions and creates whistleblower bounties and protections. Retrieved from http://www.seyfarth.com/index.cfm/fuseaction/publications.publications_detail/object_id/f6b0e9e8-a089-4e81-8324-a7d202bfe564/Dodd-FrankActExpandsSOXsWhistleblowerProvisionsandCreatesWhistleblowerBountiesandProtections.cfm

Seyfarth Shaw. (2010, Aug. 8). Companies wake up to stiff new whistleblower provisions from Dodd-Frank bill—Seyfarth Shaw offers recommendations for employers. Retrieved from https://www.hr.com/en/app/blog/2010/08/companies-wake-up-to-stiff-new-whistleblower-provi_gcmh2rrd.html?s=7y2HZAkia8Rr9CVtUCZ

Seyfarth Shaw LLP. (2013, Oct. 24). SEC's $14 million whistleblower reward likely to lure more tipsters. *Employment Law Lookout*. Retrieved from http://www.laborandemploymentlaw-counsel.com/2013/10/secs-14-million-whistleblower-reward-likely-to-lure-more-tipsters/

Shell, R. (2003). *Management of professionals, revised and expanded*. New York: Marcel Dekker Inc.

Shimabukuro, J. O., & Whitaker, L. P. (2012). Whistleblower protections under federal law: An overview. *Congressional Research Service*. Retrieved from https://fas.org/sgp/crs/misc/R42727.pdf

Shimabukuro, J. O., Whitaker, L. P., & Roberts, E. E. (2013). Survey of federal whistleblower and anti-retaliation laws. *Congressional Research Service*. Retrieved from https://fas.org/sgp/crs/misc/R43045.pdf

Sidel, R. (2011, Mar.). FDIC's tab for failed U.S. banks nears $9 billion. *The Wall Street Journal*. Retrieved from https://www.wsj.com/articles/SB10001424052748704396504576204752754667840

Sidel, R., Enrich, D., & Fitzpatrick, D. (2008, Sept. 26). WaMu is seized, sold off to J.P. Morgan, in largest failure in U.S. banking history. *Wall Street Journal*. Retrieved from https://www.forbes.com/sites/edwardsiedle/2011/05/12/sec-whistleblower-office-does-not-want-to-talk-to-you/#4efe38517186

Siedle, E. (2011, May 12). SEC whistleblower office does not want to talk to you. *Forbes*. Retrieved from https://www.forbes.com/sites/edwardsiedle/2011/05/12/sec-whistleblower-office-does-not-want-to-talk-to-you/#4efe38517186

Singer, B. (2013, Jan. 22). Securities and Exchange Commission revolving door spins for Mary Jo White. *Forbes*. Retrieved from https://www.forbes.com/sites/billsinger/2013/01/22/securities-and-exchange-commission-revolving-door-spins-for-mary-jo-white/

Singh, R. (2015). A whistleblowing hotline: Pitfalls and solutions. *Law 360*. Lexis Nexis, Retrieved from https://www.law360.com/articles/622789/a-whistleblowing-hotline-pitfalls-and-solutions.

Singhi, N.K. (1974). *Bureaucracy positions and persons: Role structures, interactions and value orientations of bureaucrats in Rajasthan.* India: Abhinav Publications.

Sinykin, J. H. (2004). At a loss, the State of Wisconsin after 8 years without the public intervernors office. *Marquette Law Review, 88* (3).

Slovin, D. (2006, June). Blowing the whistle. *Internal Auditor, 63* (3).

Smith, A. (1759) *The theory of moral sentiments.* London: A. Millar, 6th Ed.

Smith, R., Craig, S., & Lobb, A. (2008, Sept. 12). The Lehman stock slide hits home: employees face $10 billion in losses. *The Wall Street Journal*. Retrieved from https://www.wsj.com/articles/SB122117966831526067

Sol, M. (n.d.). The strategic importance of the 990 return. *American Bar Association Business Law Committee Newsletter*. Retrieved from https://www.wsj.com/articles/SB122117966831526067http://apps.americanbar.org/buslaw/committees/CL580000pub/newsletter/201107/sol.pdf

Solomon, M.R. (1983, Dec. 1). The role of products as social stimuli: A symbolic interactionism perspective. *The Journal of Consumer Research*, 319–329

Soren McAdam Christenson LLP. (2011). Sarbanes Oxley Act defined. Retrieved from http://www.smc-cpas.com/sarbanes-oxley-defined.htm

Sorkin, A. R., & Bajaj, V. (2008, Sept. 21). Shift for Goldman and Morgan marks the end of an era. *The New York Times*. Retrieved from http://www.nytimes.com/2008/09/22/business/22bank.html?mcubz=0

Soto, H. (2009, Apr. 28). Inzunza tapped as board chairman. *The San Diego Union-Tribune*. Retrieved from http://www.sandiegouniontribune.com/sdut-1b28chamber2192-inzunza-tapped-board-chairman-2009apr28-story.html

Space Coast Daily. (2015, Aug. 28). BCSO: Titusville woman arrested for making false report to DCF hotline. *Space Coast Daily*. Retrieved from http://www.brevardsheriff.com/home/nr-15-78-titusville-woman-arrested-for-making-false-report-to-dcf-hotline/

Spillane, R., & Martin, J. (2005). *Personality and performance: Foundations for managerial psychology.* Sydney: University of South Whales Press.

Stade, K. (2011, Mar. 2). EPA criminal investigators make for the exits. Public Employees for Environmental Responsibility (PEER). Retrieved from https://www.peer.org/news/news-releases/epa-criminal-investigators-make-for-the-exits.html

Stade, K. (2011, Apr. 4). Gulag EPA - Report finds discrimination meltdown. Public Employees for Environmental Responsibility (PEER). Retrieved from https://www.commondreams.org/newswire/2011/04/04/gulag-epa-report-finds-discrimination-meltdown

Stake, R. E. (1995). *The Art of Case Study Research.* Thousand Oaks, CA: Sage.

State of New York. (n.d.). Red flags for fraud. Office of the State Comptroller. Retrieved from http://www.osc.state.ny.us/localgov/pubs/red_flags_fraud.pdf

Steffensmeier, D. (1989). On the causes of "white collar" crime: An assessment of Hirschi and Gottfredson. *Criminology,* 27 (2), pp. 345–358.

Stein, J. (2012, Aug. 15). Ongoing john doe probe of Walker aides reaches state level. *Journal Sentinel.* Retrieved from http://archive.jsonline.com/news/statepolitics/ongoing-probe-of-walker-aides-reaches-state-level-h16ftb7-166327206.html/

Stemple, J., Gates V. (2013, July 21). Out of prison, former HealthSouth CEO Scrushy seeks redemption. *Reuters.* Retrieved from http://www.reuters.com/article/us-healthsouth-scrushy-idUSBRE96K04D20130721

Stendahl, M. (2013). $14M SEC whistleblower award is just the beginning. (LexisNexis, Producer) *Law 360.* Retrieved from https://www.law360.com/articles/477296

Stephens, J., & Flaherty, M.P. (2013, Nov. 1). Congress to review financial wrongdoing at charities. *The Washington Post.* Retrieved from https://www.washingtonpost.com/local/congress-to-review-financial-wrongdoing-at-charities/2013/11/01/9471f04c-430d-11e3-a751-f032898f2dbc_story.html?utm_term=.1916cea98282

Stephens, J. (2013, Oct. 26). Inside the hidden world of thefts, scams and phantom purchases at the nation's nonprofits. *Washington Post.* Retrieved from https://www.washingtonpost.com/investigations/inside-the-hidden-world-of-thefts-scams-and-phantom-purchases-at-the-nations-nonprofits/2013/10/26/825a82ca-0c26-11e3-9941-6711ed662e71_story.html?utm_term=.65bd599fba0b

Stevens, L. (2013, Apr. 15). Glassdoor breaks into global online job search. *North Bay Business Journal.* Retrieved from http://www.northbaybusinessjournal.com/csp/mediapool/sites/NBBJ/IndustryNews/story.csp?cid=4182929&sid=778&fid=181

Stock, H. J. (2010, Mar. 1). Surviving a bank failure. *Bank Investment Consultant.* Retrieved from http://www.bankinvestmentconsultant.com/bic_issues/2010_3/surviving-a-bank-failure-2665882-1.html?zkPrintable=true

Swensen, J. (2007, Aug. 6). John Rigas tells his side of the Adelphia story. *USA Today.* Retrieved from http://abcnews.go.com/Business/story?id=3450593

TeliaSonera. (2015, Mar. 27). TeliaSonera says whistleblowing scheme has exposed potential corruption. *Mobile World Live.* Retrieved from https://www.mobileworldlive.com/featured-content/home-banner/teliasonera-says-whistleblowing-scheme-helps-expose-corruption/

The American Institute of Certified Public Accountants (AICPA). (2003). Fraud hotlines: early warning systems. *The Practicing CPA.* Retrieved from https://AICPA.org

The Associated Press. (2003, May 21). Critics call WorldCom settlement insufficient. *The Gainsville Sun.* Retrieved from http://www.gainesville.com/article/LK/20030521/News/604157287/GS/

The Associated Press. (2006, May 26). Enron sentences will be tied to investor losses. *NBC News.* Retrieved from http://www.nbcnews.com/id/12993408/ns/business-corporate_scandals/t/enron-sentences-will-be-tied-investor-losses/#.WYCMUhPytxg

The Associated Press. (2010, Feb. 15). Citigroup to pay $158 million in mortgage fraud settlement. *The New York Times.* Retrieved from http://www.nytimes.com/2012/02/16/business/citigroup-to-pay-158-million-in-mortgage-fraud-settlement.html?mcubz=0

The Associated Press. (2012, Feb. 15). Citigroup to pay $158 million in mortgage fraud settlement. *The New York Times.* Retrieved from http://www.nytimes.com/2012/02/16/business/citigroup-to-pay-158-million-in-mortgage-fraud-settlement.html

The Associated Press. (2012, Aug. 16). Report: John Doe Probe Expands to Wisconsin Government. *The Chippewa Herald.* Retrieved from http://chippewa.com/news/state-and-regional/report-john-doe-probe-expands-to-wisconsin-government/article_00abc7a2-e7d8-11e1-abb3-001a4bcf887a.html

The Associated Press. (2014, Jan. 14). JP Morgan banker warns of more target-size cybercrime. *Newsday.* Retrieved from http://www.newsday.com/business/jpmorgan-banker-warns-of-more-target-size-cybercrime-1.6797721

The Economist. (2013, Sept. 7). The origins of the financial crisis: Crash course. *The Economist.* Retrieved from https://www.economist.com/news/schoolsbrief/21584534-effects-financial-crisis-are-still-being-felt-five-years-article

The Network. (n.d.). Best practices guide for global hotlines. Retrieved from http://documents.jdsupra.com/72c2cf54-29cd-441b-841c-1b3100049968.pdf

The Network. (2006–2013). Corporate governance and compliance hotline benchmarking report. New York: CSO Executive Council and the ACFE.

The Network. (2008). Best practices in ethics hotlines. Retrieved from http://la-acfe.org/images/downloads/Resources/bestpracticesinethics2005.pdf

The Network. (2012). Seven elements: Staying aligned with the federal sentencing guidelines. Retireved from http://documents.jdsupra.com/c44a29b1-bd15-4586-85a7-f011c5b941f6.pdf

The Network. (2013). 2013 Corporate governance and compliance hotline benchmarking report. Retrieved from http://documents.jdsupra.com/ef897ae1-aa7e-424a-9489-941a240e9cc6.pdf

The Network and BDO Consulting. (2015–2016). Corporate governance and compliance hotline benchmarking report. NAVEX Global. Retrieved from https://webcache.googleusercontent.com/search?q=cache:rC9N1ZjsEvAJ:https://www.bdo.co.za/getattachment/de0dddeb-7b1c-4e6c-b755-96891a3e1235/attachment.aspx%3Fdisposition%3Dattachment+&cd=2&hl=en&ct=clnk&gl=us

The Network and CSO Executive Council. (2006). Using benchmarking information to enhance and improve your hotline program. Retrieved from https://www.tnwinc.com

The Post Star. (2016, Sept. 26). Man charged for alleged false child abuse hotline report. Retrieved from http://poststar.com/news/local/crime-and-courts/man-charged-for-alleged-false-child-abuse-hotline-report/article_0cad71b1-2c00-5ac5-9751-a4ffa2f6dbac.html

The San Diego Union Tribune. (2011, March 3). Parks worker, saved from cuts, accused of theft. Retrieved from http://www.sandiegouniontribune.com/news/watchdog/sdut-parks-employee-accused-of-stealing-101000-2011mar03-htmlstory.html

The Wall Street Journal. (2010, July 14). The uncertainty principle. *The Wall Street Journal.*

The White House. (2012, Oct. 30). Remarks by the President at the American Red Cross. Washington, DC. Retrieved from https://obamawhitehouse.archives.gov/the-press-office/2012/10/30/remarks-president-american-red-cross

Thomas, J. (2016). Office of the whistleblower annual report: Remarkable success in principles & practices. *SEC Whistleblower Advocate.* New York: Labaton Sucharow.

Thomas, W.C. (2002, Apr.). The rise and fall of Enron. *Journal of Accountancy.* Retrieved from http://www.journalofaccountancy.com/issues/2002/apr/theriseandfallofenron.html

Thompson, V. A. (1961). *Modern Organization.* New York: Albert A. Knopf, Inc.

T-Mobile. (n.d.).Integrity line. *Ethicspoint.* Retrieved from https://secure.ethicspoint.com/domain/media/en/gui/27716/report.html

Tobe, C. (2013, Feb. 6). SEC whistleblower fund: 3,000 tips, little payout. *MarketWatch.* Retrieved from http://www.marketwatch.com/story/sec-whistleblower-fund-3000-tips-little-payout-2013-02-06

Tompkins, J. R. (2005). *Organization Theory and Public Management.*Belmont, California: Thomson Wadsworth.

Trimner, D. (2013). Washington post article reveals extensive nonprofit fraud and inadequate form 990 disclosures. CliftonLarsonAllen. Retrieved from https://www.cla-connect.com

Twardy, S. A., & D. Klein. (2011). The Dodd-Frank whistleblower program: Mutiny over the bounty. American Bar Association. *Criminal Litigation*, Vol. 11. no. 2.

Tyrell, S. A., & Benfield, B. N. (n.d.). Internal compliance solutions for mitigating SEC whistleblower litigation: The best defense in a good offense. *Bloomberg BNA.* Retrieved from https://www.bna.com/mitigating-sec-whistleblower-litigation

University of South Alabama. Whistleblower hotline. Retrieved from http://www.usouthal.edu/departments/financialaffairs/internalaudit/whistleblower/index.html.

United Nations Office on Drugs and Crime (UNODC). (2013, Feb.). Comprehensive study on cybercrime. Retrieved from https://www.unodc.org/documents/organized-crime/UNODC_CCPCJ_EG.4_2013/CYBERCRIME_STUDY_210213.pdf

U.S. Congress. H.R. (2011). 2483-112th Congress: Whistleblower Improvement Act of 2011. Retrieved from https://www.govtrack.us/congress/bills/112/hr2483

U.S. Congress. Congressional Record, V. 148, PT. 4, April 11, 2002 to April 24, 2002. P. 4333.

U.S. Environmental Protection Agency (EPA). (2005). Former EPA contractor sentenced for computer crime. Office of Investigations Report. Retrieved from https://www.epa.gov

U.S. Environmental Protection Agency (EPA). (2007). EPA Needs to respond more timely to reports of investigation. *EPA Office of Inspector General.* Retrieved from https://www.epa.gov/office-inspector-general/report-epa-needs-respond-more-timely-reports-investigation

U.S. Department of Health and Human Services. (2012, Jan. 13). Adverse determination letter to C. Hrouda. Retrieved from https://www.fda.gov/downloads/AboutFDA/CentersOffices/OfficeofGlobalRegulatoryOperationsandPolicy/ORA/ORAElectronicReadingRoom/UCM287834.pdf

U.S. Department of Homeland Security (DHS). (2010). Recommended practices for office of inspector general hotlines. Office of Inspector General. Retrieved from https://www.oig.dhs.gov/assets/Mgmt/ighotline1010.pdf

U.S. Department of Justice (DOJ). (2003, July). First year report to the president. *Corporate Fraud Task Force.* Retrieved from https://www.justice.gov/archive/dag/cftf/first_year_report.pdf

U.S. Department of Justice (DOJ). (2009). The nation's two crime measures. Retrieved from https://www.bjs.gov/content/pub/pdf/ntcm_2014.pdf

U.S. Department of Justice (DOJ). (2012, Apr. 25). Former Morgan Stanley managing director pleads guilty for role in evading internal controls required by FCPA. *DOJ Press Release.* Retrieved from https://www.justice.gov/opa/pr/former-morgan-stanley-managing-director-pleads-guilty-role-evading-internal-controls-required

U.S. Department of Treasury. (2010, May 18). Regulatory bulletin RB 37-54: Fraud and insider abuse. Office of Thrift Supervision. Retrieved from http://www.workingre.com/wp-content/uploads/2013/08/ots-appraiser-fraud.pdf

U.S. Food and Drug Administration (FDA). (2006, Sept. 8). FDA fines Red Cross $4.2 million for failure to meet established blood safety laws. Retrieved from https://www.fda.gov

U.S. Government Accountaibility Office (GAO). (1989). Fraud hotline operations. Briefing report to the chairman subcommittee on general services, federalism, and the district of Columbia, committee on governmental affairs, U.S. senate. U.S. General Accounting Office. Retrieved from https://babel.hathitrust.org/cgi/pt?id=uiug.30112033945368;view=1up;seq=8

U.S. Government Accountability Office (GAO). (1988). Fraud hotline 9-Year GAO fraud hotline summary. Retrieved from http://archive.gao.gov/d48t13/135590.pdf

U.S. Government Accountability Office (GAO). (2007). Cybercrime: Public and private entities face challenges in addressing cyber threats. Retrieved from http://www.gao.gov/new.items/d07705.pdf

U.S. Government Accountability Office (GAO). (1989). Inspectors general fraud hotline operations. GAO Report. Retrieved from http://www.gao.gov/assets/80/77551.pdf

U.S. Internal Revenue Service (IRS). (n.d.). Charity & nonprofit audits: Significant diversion of assets. Retrieved from http://www.irs.gov/Charities-&-Nonprofits/Exempt-Organizations-Examinations-Significant-Diversion-of-Assets

U.S. Internal Revenue Service (IRS). (2013). Instructions for Form 990 return of organization exempt from income tax. Retrieved from https://www.irs.gov/pub/irs-prior/i990ez--2013.pdf

U.S. Office of Personnel Management (OPM). (2017). Our inspector general: Whistleblower protection information. https://www.opm.gov/our-inspector-general/whistleblower-protection-information/

U.S. Pacific Fleet Inspector General. Hotline Complaint Procedure. Retrieved from http://www.cpf.navy.mil/inspector-general/complaint-procedure.pdf

U.S. Securities and Exchange Commission (SEC). (2002, Apr. 11). SEC v. Xerox Corporation. (02-272789) (DLC).

U.S. Securities and Exchange Commission (SEC). (2002, July 24). SEC charges Adelphia and Rigas family with massive financial fraud. Retrieved from https://www.sec.gov/news/press/2002-110.htm

U.S. Securities and Exchange Commission (SEC). (2003). Second amended complaint. New York: SEC v Samuel D. Waksal and Jack Waksal, Patti Waskal. Retrieved from https://www.sec.gov/litigation/complaints/comp18408.htm

U.S. Securities and Exchange Commission (SEC). (2003, Mar. 31). Report of investigation by the special investigative commission of the board of directors of WorldCom Inc. Retrieved from https://www.sec.gov/Archives/edgar/data/723527/000093176303001862/dex991.htm

U.S. Securities and Exchange Commission (SEC). (2003, June 4). SEC v. Martha Stewart and Peter Bacanovic. (03-CV-4070) (NRB).

U.S. Securities and Exchange Commission (SEC). (2003, June 5). Six former senior executives of Xerox settle SEC enforcement action charging them with fraud; Executives agree to pay over $22 million in penalties, disgorgement and interest. Retrieved from https://www.sec.gov/news/press/2003-70.htm

U.S. Securities and Exchange Commission (SEC). (2007, Sept. 20). SEC charges 38 defendants on multimillion dollar stock loan scams. Retrieved from https://www.sec.gov/news/press/2007/2007-192.htm

U.S. Securities and Exchange Commission (SEC). SEC charges five former San Diego officials with securities fraud. (2008, Apr. 7). Retrieved from https://www.sec.gov

U.S. Securities and Exchange Commission (SEC). (2010, Oct. 27). Former San Diego officials agree to pay financial penalties in municipal bond fraud case. Retrieved from https://www.sec.gov

U.S. Securities and Exchange Commission (SEC). (2011, May 25). 7 CFR Parts 240 and 249. Proposed rules for implementing the whistleblower provisions of section 21F of the Securities and Exchange Act of 1934. Retrieved from https://www.sec.gov/rules/final/2011/34-64545.pdf

U.S. Securities and Exchange Commission (SEC). (2012). Annual report to congress on the Dodd Frank whistleblower program. Retrieved from https://www.sec.gov/files/annual-report-2012.pdf

U.S. Securities & Exchange Commission (SEC). (2012, Nov. 15). SEC receives more than 3,000 whistleblower tips in FY 2012. Retrieved from https://www.sec.gov/news/press-release/2012-2012-229htm

U.S. Securities & Exchange Commission (SEC) (2012, Nov. 15). SEC whistleblower program received 3,001 tips in fiscal year 2012. *SEC Press Release.* Retrieved from https://www.sec.gov/news/press-release/2012-2012-229htm

U.S. Securities and Exchange Commission (SEC). (2013). Annual report to congress on the Dodd Frank whistleblower program. Retrieved from https://www.sec.gov/files/annual-report-2013.pdf

U.S. Securities and Exchange Commission (SEC). (2013, Oct. 1). SEC awards more than $14 million to whistleblower. Retrieved from https://www.sec.gov/news/press-release/2013-209

U.S. Securities and Exchange Commission (SEC). (2014). Annual report to congress on the Dodd Frank whistleblower program. Retrieved from https://www.sec.gov/about/offices/owb/annual-report-2014.pdf

U.S. Securities and Exchange Commission (SEC). (2015). Annual report to congress on the Dodd Frank whistleblower program. Retrieved from https://www.sec.gov/files/owb-annual-report-2015.pdf

U.S. Securities and Exchange Commission (SEC). (2016). Annual report to congress on the Dodd Frank whistleblower program. Retrieved from https://www.sec.gov/files/owb-annual-report-2016.pdf

U.S. Securities and Exchange Commission (SEC) SEC final rule: Standards relating to listed company audit committees. Retrieved from https://www.sec.gov/rules/final/33-8220.htm

U.S. Securities and Exchange Commission (SEC). (n.d.). SEC Office of the Whistleblower. Retrieved from www.sec.gov/whistleblower

U.S. Securities and Exchange Commission. Office of Inspector General. (2013). Evaluation of the SEC's whistleblower program. Retrieved from https://www.sec.gov/files/annual-report-2013.pdf

U.S. Security and Exchange Commission (SEC). Office of the Whistleblower. "Claim an Award." Retrieved from http://www.sec.gov/about/offices/owb/owb-awards.shtml

USA Today. (2003, Oct. 19). Sarbanes-oxley: Dragon or white knight. *USA Today.* Retrieved from https://usatoday30.usatoday.com/money/companies/regulation/2003-10-19-sarbanes_x.htm

USA Today. (2011, Mar. 3). Live ammo found outside Wisconsin capitol. Retrieved from https://usatoday30.usatoday.com/news/nation/2011-03-03-wisconsin-protests-ammunition_N.htm

Uy, N. (2010, Apr. 8). Insane...mindless bureaucracy. *San Diego Reader.* Retrieved from https://www.sandiegoreader.com/news/2010/apr/08/insanemindless-bureaucracy/

Vardi, N. (2014, Jan. 14). Bernard Madoff haunts JP Morgan's earnings. *Forbes.* Retrieved from https://www.forbes.com/sites/nathanvardi/2014/01/14/bernard-madoff-haunts-jpmorganss-earnings/

Vaughan, D. (1999). The dark side of organizations: mistake, misconduct and disaster. *Annual Review of Sociology,* 25, 271–305.

Wachtel, K. (2010, Dec. 29). Citigroup employee allegedly stole between $67 and $89 million from the bank's wealthy Indian clients. *Business Insider.* Retrieved from http://www.businessinsider.com

Waddell, M. (2011, May 12). Drawbacks of Dodd-Frank whistleblower rules debated at house hearing. *Thinkadvisor.* Retrieved from http://www.thinkadvisor.com/2011/05/12/drawbacks-of-doddfrank-whistleblower-rules-debated

Walker, S. (2014). How to set up a whistleblower hotline. *i-Sight.* Retrieved from https://www.slideshare.net/isightsoftware/how-to-set-up-a-whistleblower-hotline

Walsh, M. W. (2006, Nov. 15). San Diego agrees to settle SEC pension fraud case. *The New York Times.* Retrieved from http://nytimes.com

Ward, K. (2013, Dec. 11). Thousands of PSWs strike over wages, bureaucracy in the system. *CTV News Barrie.* Retrieved from http://barrie.ctvnews.ca/thousands-of-psws-strike-over-wages-bureaucracy-in-the-system-1.1585847

Washington Post. (2013, Oct. 26). Millions missing, little explanation. *Washington Post.* Retrieved from http://www.washingtonpost.com/wp-srv/special/local/nonprofit-diversions-database/

Wasik, J. (2012, Mar. 7). Stanford's ponzi scheme: The system is still broken. *Forbes.* Retrieved from https://www.forbes.com/forbes/welcome/?toURL=https://www.forbes.com/sites/johnwasik/2012/03/07/stanfords-ponzi-scam-the-system-is-still-broken/&refURL=https://www.google.com/&referrer=https://www.google.com/

Weinberg, N. (2016). *Trump's effort to gut Dodd-Frank law may spare whistle-blowers.* Bloomberg. Retrieved from https://www.bloomberg.com/news/articles/2016-11-15/trump-s-effort-to-gut-dodd-frank-law-may-spare-whistle-blowers

Wells, J.T. (2001, Feb.). Why employees commit fraud. *Journal of Accountancy.* Retrieved from http://www.journalofaccountancy.com/issues/2001/feb/whyemployeescommit-fraud.html

Weston, C. (2017). Central bank whistleblower hotline went unanswered. *Independent.ie.* Retrieved from http://www.independent.ie/business/personal-finance/central-bank-whistleblower-hotline-went-unanswered-35399044.html

WhiteHouse.gov. (n.d.). Foreign policy and cyber security. Retrieved from http://www.whitehouse.gov/issues/foreign-policy/cybersecurity

Willis, T.D. (2006, Jan./Feb.). Criminal liability in cyberspace. *GP Solo Magazine.* Retrieved from http://AmericanBar.org.

Wilson, H. (2010, Dec. 30). Citibank India employee arrested for alleged 57M fraud. *The Telegraph.* Retrieved from http://www.telegraph.co.uk/finance/newsbysector/banksandfinance/8232531/Citibank-India-employee-arrested-for-alleged-57m-fraud.html

Wisconsin Historical Society. (2006). *Scandals, Scandals, Scandals.* Retrieved from https://www.wisconsinhistory.org

Witt, E. (2015). Keys to a successful whistleblower hotline. The Compliance Report. *Convercent.* Retrieved from https://www.convercent.com/blog/keys-to-a-successful-whistleblower-hotline

WTMJ News. (2012, July 23). Milwaukee county business development leader investigated for fraud, embezzlement. *WTMJ News*. Retrieved from http://www.tmj4.com

Yormark, K. G. (2004). Preventing and detecting financial statement fraud: Sarbanes Oxley update. *Association of Certified Fraud Examiners*. Retrieved from http://www.acfe.com/fraud/view.asp?ArticleID=341

Young, S. (2002, Sept. 30). Getting laid off hurts worse when employer is bankrupt. *Wall Street Journal*. Retrieved from https://www.wsj.com/articles/SB1033335183303074553

Zaring, D. (2012, Apr. 29). Second thought about the SEC's whistleblower program. *New York Times*.

Index